always up to date

The law changes, but Nolo is always on top of it! We offer several ways to make sure you and your Nolo products are always up to date:

1 **Nolo's Legal Updater**

We'll send you an email whenever a new edition of your book is published! Sign up at **www.nolo.com/legalupdater**.

2 **Updates @ Nolo.com**

Check **www.nolo.com/update** to find recent changes in the law that affect the current edition of your book.

3 **Nolo Customer Service**

To make sure that this edition of the book is the most recent one, call us at **800-728-3555** and ask one of our friendly customer service representatives. Or find out at **www.nolo.com**.

please note

We believe accurate and current legal information should help you solve
many of your own legal problems on a cost-efficient basis. But this text
is not a substitute for personalized advice from a knowledgeable lawyer.
If you want the help of a trained professional, consult an attorney
licensed to practice in your state.

7th edition

Trademark

Legal Care for Your Business & Product Name

by Attorney Stephen Elias

SEVENTH EDITION	SEPTEMBER 2005
Editor	RICHARD STIM
Cover Design	TONI IHARA
Book Design	TERRI HEARSH
Illustrations for Examples	JOHN MILLER & HEATHER SNYDER
Indexer	THÉRÈSE SHERE
Proofreading	MARTIN ARONSON
Printing	DELTA PRINTING SILUTIONS, INC.

Elias, Stephen.
    Trademark : legal care for your business & product name / by Stephen Elias.--7th ed.
      p. cm.
    Includes index.
    ISBN 1-4133-0358-7 (alk. paper)
     1. Trademarks--Laws and legislation--United States--Popular works. 2. Business
names--Law and legislation--United States--Popular works. I. Title.

KF3180.Z9E43 2005
346.73044'88--dc22

2005047766

For information on bulk purchases or corporate premium sales, please contact the Special Sales
Department. For academic sales or textbook adoptions, ask for Academic Sales. Call 800-955-4775
or write to Nolo, 950 Parker Street, Berkeley, CA 94710.

Dedication

I dedicate this book to my mother, the late Edna Elias-Johnson, and to Stanley and Dorothy Pearson. They don't make 'em like they used to.

Steve Elias

Acknowledgments

The author extends his profound thanks and appreciation to:

Nolo publisher Jake Warner for the incisive intelligence that he brought to the book as its first editor, and Patricia Gima, Richard Stim, and Lisa Sedano for their fine editing work on subsequent editions;

Sarah Shena, the guiding light behind the chapter on registering trademarks with the PTO;

The fine Nolo production department for its dedication to excellence in designing the book's layout and graphics;

Andrew Bridges (of Wilson Sonsini Goodrich & Rosati in Palo Alto, California);

Jaleh Doane for her seemingly infinite patience;

Scott S. Havlick of Holland & Hart in Denver, who generously shared his time and expertise and gave encouragement at a time when the book seemed interminable;

R. Lee Hagelshaw of San Francisco, who was kind enough to read and comment on some drafts;

John Miller and Heather Snyder of SignDesign in Montepelier, Vermont, for creatively bringing to life many of the trademarks and service marks used to illustrate our remarks throughout the book;

The many small business owners in the Bay Area who shared their trademark stories, many of which appear in this book in one form or another;

Toni Ihara for her sterling cover artistry;

Ted Beatty, a California entrepreneur who graciously read and commented on the manuscript; and

The entire Nolo staff, a wonderfully uncompromising group that manages to be both perfectionistic and a nice bunch of people (some of whom are even recovering lawyers).

Table of Contents

3 How to Choose a Good Name for Your Business, Product, or Service

4 Trademark Searches—What They Are and Why You Should Do One

5 How to Do Your Own Trademark Search

14 Help Beyond this Book

Appendixes

A Class Descriptions

B Glossary of Terms

C Trademark Search Report

Index

20 Frequently Asked Trademark Questions

elow are brief answers to 20 of the most common questions about trademarks.

1. What does it mean to "trademark" a business or product name or logo?

When people say they plan to "trademark" a name or logo, they generally mean they intend to register the name or logo with the U.S. Patent and Trademark Office (PTO). Though federal registration provides important benefits, trademark ownership is actually determined by who uses the mark first in a commercial setting. So, by using a name, logo, or other symbol to identify goods or services in the marketplace, a trademark has been created and trademark ownership has been established.

2. What is the difference between a trademark and a service mark?

A trademark is any name, logo, symbol, or other device used to distinguish a product from competing products in the marketplace and to identify the product's source. A service mark is any name, logo, symbol, or other device used to distinguish a service from others in the marketplace and to identify the source of the service. Legally, there is no difference between the two terms, and the terms "trademark" and "mark" are often used for all types of marks, including service marks.

3. How long does it take to get a trademark registered?

The typical time it takes to federally register a trademark is between 12 and 18 months.

4. Suppose I register a trademark for a particular product. What happens when I want to use the same trademark for a different product?

Each product or service is categorized within a class. If you begin using your trademark on a product or service in a different class than the one for which you originally registered your mark—for example, you use your logo on a paint product when you originally registered it for painting services—you should file another application to register the new use of the mark (in the appropriate class). However, you must check that the mark is not being used by another business for a similar product. If it is, you may need the assistance of a trademark attorney before proceeding.

5. Can I apply to register a logo, name, and slogan all in one application? What happens if I want to use them separately?

If you want to use and protect each separately, you should register each separately. However, you can—if you wish—register them as one trademark and claim rights for the cumulative use.

6. What happens if I register my mark but later find out that someone else was already using the mark but never got around to registering it?

If the other mark was being used nationally, as is the case with most catalog and Internet sales, then your trademark registration may be subject to cancellation. In any event, the registration will not protect you from an infringement suit if the first user can establish that your use of the mark is creating the like-lihood of customer confusion. If the other mark was only being used locally, you will probably be entitled to use the name in any region of the country where the first user had not established a presence.

7. I've been told to do a trademark search before applying to register my mark. Why should I, if the PTO does one when it gets my application?

There are three good reasons:

(1) Filing an application for federal trade-mark registration costs $325 if filing electronically ($375 if filing a paper ap-plication). There is no point in filing an application for a name that the PTO will reject because it's already owned by someone else.

(2) It is up to you to decide whether the mark you eventually choose is both registrable and free from infringing an existing mark. The PTO may find a po-tentially confusing mark in the course of its search but still decide to register your mark on the basis of its internal guidelines. However, the PTO's decision to register your mark doesn't get you off the hook if the owner of the existing mark decides to take you to court.

(3) The PTO search only covers the fed-eral trademark register, not trademarks that are in use but not registered. Be-cause use, rather than registration, deter-mines ownership, the PTO search will not be as complete as your own search of both registered and unregistered marks.

8. What is a "common law" trademark, and what rights does it give me?

A common law trademark is any device (name, logo, slogan, etc.) that is being used to identify a business's goods or services in the marketplace and has not been registered with a state government or with the federal government. The owner of a common law trademark that is used in more than one state can use the federal courts to enforce its rights in the parts of the country where the mark is being used.

9. Why should I bother to register a trademark I'm already using on my business or products if I already have rights under the common law?

It's a lot easier to win a federal lawsuit against later users by establishing certain pre-sumptions—facts that you don't have to prove in court and the other side must rebut. Federal registration gives you two presump-tions: that you are the mark's owner, and that the later user deliberately copied the mark. These presumptions also make it easier to prove infringement and collect damages and attorneys' fees.

10. Can I do the application myself or should I hire an attorney?

Most people can handle their own trade-mark applications without an attorney. The PTO provides easy-to-use instructions and is willing to help you through the process. In addition, the PTO now lets you prepare and file your own trademark registration online using its Trademark Electronic

Application System (TEAS) at its website (www.uspto.gov).

If, however, you have questions that the PTO or online registration help files don't answer, you should consult with an attorney. Also, if the mark you are planning to register is unusual (a color, sound, or scent, for example), or for some reason the PTO doesn't want to accept your application, you will need to consult an attorney.

11. What if I find an exact match or near-exact match in a search? Can I still use my proposed trademark anyway? What's the worst that can happen?

Practically, if you are able to keep the dispute out of court by immediately stopping your use of the mark, you may escape with only having to pay all or part of the owner's attorneys' fees incurred up to that point. This is usually true if you are a small business, because the owner would have no reason to try to pick your pockets. However, the larger you are, or the more your business competes with the owner's, the more likely it is that any settlement will also involve some cash to make up for harm caused by your infringement, real or imagined.

If the owner decides to sue you for damages, you may be ordered to pay the owner:

- actual economic damages suffered by the owner as a result of your infringement or the amount of your profits earned while using the mark
- punitive damages in the amount of three times the amount of damages or profits awarded the owner, and

- attorneys' fees incurred by the owner in bringing the infringement suit.

In addition, of course, the court may order you to stop using the mark, which may result in additional expense as well as the need to rebuild goodwill around a new mark.

12. Can I register my domain name/Internet website address as a trademark?

Yes, you may apply to federally register your domain name as a trademark, provided that it is being used to market goods or services on the Internet. If, on the other hand, the domain name is not used to sell goods or services—for example, it is only being used for personal or family reasons—registration will be denied.

13. What's the difference between state and federal trademarks?

A state trademark is one that is used within the state and registered on the state's trademark list—unlike a federal trademark, which must be used in more than one state, or in any commerce regulated by Congress.

14. If my trademark search finds a mark identical or similar to mine and I find out that the owner is no longer in business (or that the mark is no longer being used by that business), am I free to use it? Can I register it with the PTO?

The answer to both questions is "not necessarily." Even if the original owner is no longer in business, the mark itself may have been assigned to another business, which is using it. Similarly, even if the original owner is still in business but no longer using the mark, it may be in use by someone else under an assignment. Finally, if the mark is a creative graphic such as a logo or trade dress, it may still be protected by copyright law (which protects creative works or expression).

15. If I combine my business or product name with a logo, does the combination distinguish the name from other names that are already registered or in use?

If the name accompanying your logo is the same as or very similar to a name that is federally registered or used, you will be precluded from using or registering the name/logo combination, even though the appearance of your name/logo combination and the other name is completely different.

16. What materials should I search in order to feel like I've been thorough enough?

At the very least, you should search the federal trademark register for names or other marks that possibly conflict with yours. In addition, you should search relevant trade publications, as well as the Internet.

17. What is the *Official Gazette,* published by the PTO, and who reads it?

The *Official Gazette* is read by anyone whose business involves keeping up with the latest PTO announcements and rules—mostly patent and trademark attorneys, patent agents, and others. One reason for its popularity is that all trademarks proposed for federal registration are published in the *Gazette,*

alerting the public in the event that there is an objection to registration. You can read the *Gazette* for free online at the PTO website. It is no longer published in paper format.

18. I've learned that I'll have to renew my trademark registration in a few years. Will the PTO notify me when the time comes, or do I have to keep track of this date myself?

The PTO will not notify you. You are responsible for keeping track of the required renewal dates. If you miss the deadline, your trademark registration will be cancelled. This does not affect your ownership of the mark, assuming you are still using it, but you will have to reregister the mark to maintain the benefits of registration.

19. How do I get the official PTO form to apply for a federal trademark registration?

The PTO discourages the use of paper applications and has changed its rate to reflect this preference (see below). (In fact, the PTO no longer provides a paper form for trademark applications.) However, you can get forms from trademark sources on the Internet and complete and mail them to the PTO. Currently, when applying for registration, you can:

- use the PTO's online TEAS program to fill in and file an application form online (currently $325 per class), or
- obtain, complete, and file a paper application (currently $375 per class).

20. How do I get an international trademark?

There is no such thing as an international trademark. It is possible to file one application for a group of countries using a procedure known as the Madrid Protocol. The Madrid Protocol includes 66 countries. In addition, you can file one application and obtain protection in 25 European countries (known as a Community Trademark). Otherwise, you must seek protection on a county-by-country basis. ■

Introduction

*U*ntil about ten years ago, a local business could reasonably expect its marketing activities to be limited to a neighborhood, town, city, county, or even one state. As long as its name (usually its only trademark) didn't conflict with any in use by other local businesses, there was little likelihood of customer confusion and therefore of any legal conflict. Though problems could arise from using a famous mark, there was no federal law on the subject, and state laws protecting famous marks were rarely enforced. So, as long as you checked the Yellow Pages and were able to get your proposed business name registered locally or with your secretary of state, there was not much else to worry about.

Today, the very concept of local is rapidly disappearing for many types of businesses. The most important force for this change is the Internet. For a very low price, any business can acquire a domain name and establish a website that not only allows the business to advertise its goods or services but also, in many cases, to demonstrate and sell them directly to its customer base instead of proceeding through wholesalers and other intermediaries.

Doing business on the Web may increase the scope of your business from local to national. You will then have to pay attention to how your name or other trademarks fit within the vast sea of trademarks that is the U.S. marketplace. (We discuss this and other Web-related trademark issues in Chapter 2, Trademarks, Domain Names, and the Internet.)

Even if you think that your business will be too local for you to worry about trademarks, it may succeed beyond your wildest dreams (many of today's most successful entrepreneurs started very small). If that happens, you will surely wish your name was really yours to market on a statewide or even national basis. In short, it makes sense to carefully choose and protect your name so that it is yours to use in any and all contexts.

A. What Parts of the Book Do You Absolutely Need to Read?

Every reader, whether you do business as a corporation, partnership, or sole proprietor, should at least read Chapter 1. Then, you can selectively choose which additional chapters to read based on your needs. For example, if you are choosing a new mark for your business, Chapters 2 through 7 take you step by step through the process of obtaining maximum protection for the mark and avoiding disputes over it. But not all readers will use every chapter.

Some readers will see no point to applying for federal registration because their proposed name is so ordinary (which cuts out Chapter 7). Others may decide to forego a trademark search. Those readers will not, therefore, need to read Chapters 4, 5, and 6.

If you are involved in a trademark dispute, you may only be interested in:

- Chapter 9, Evaluating Trademark Strength
- Chapter 10, Sorting Out Trademark Disputes
- Chapter 11, If Someone Infringes Your Mark, or

- Chapter 12, If Someone Claims That You Infringed Their Trademark.

Perhaps surprisingly, even here we strongly favor strategies that you can carry out yourself rather than sending you to a lawyer. The reason for this preference is simple: Very few small business trademarks are worth the expense of litigation, the one option that definitely requires a lawyer.

Some readers will have questions about specific trademark-related issues and wish to use this book as a reference text. For instance, you may own a federally registered mark and simply want information on how to renew it. (It's in Chapter 8, How to Use and Care for Your Trademark.) Or you may want to know what the effect of your corporate name registration is on an out-of-state corporation with the same name. (You'll find the information in Chapter 1, A Trademark Primer.) Directly preceding this Introduction we've included a list of 20 Frequently Asked Trademark Questions (and answers, with references to further discussions in the book). If your question isn't addressed there, consult the book's table of contents and index. For your convenience, a glossary of trademark terms is included in the Appendix.

B. What This Book Doesn't Cover

While this book addresses the range of trademark issues that may affect a small business owner, some issues are beyond the scope of the book. Thus, we do not tell you how to sue or defend a federal or state court lawsuit for trademark infringement. To do this we could easily fill three volumes. Nor, for this same reason, do we tell you how to:

- register your mark internationally, although we give you some background on the subject in Chapter 13
- handle a case brought in the U.S. Patent and Trademark Office to sort out conflicts between pending applications, oppose the registration of a trademark, or cancel a registration that has already occurred, or
- accomplish and record transfers or assignments of trademarks or business names.

We also do not provide detailed guidance for how to handle disputes with the Patent and Trademark Office that are related to federal trademark registrations. We do explain how to respond to the many minor issues that may arise in the course of navigating your trademark application through the PTO, but we recommend seeking help from a lawyer if your application is rejected for major substantive defects. See Section C3 below.

To help you get a handle on the issues that we don't cover, Chapter 14, Help Beyond This Book, describes several excellent additional resources that are available on the Internet or in a law library. The chapter also suggests some ways to find a good trademark lawyer if you want to pay for professional advice or need legal representation.

C. When a Trademark Lawyer May Be Helpful

This topic has no definitive answer. Certainly it is possible and customary to choose a business name, logo, or other identifier without a lawyer's guidance. Registering business and corporate names is also typically done without lawyers. And trademark searches are most frequently conducted by nonlawyer specialists. But in a number of other situations, a lawyer may be just the ticket, either as a consultant or as your representative. Certainly what you read in this book will help you better take advantage of a lawyer's assistance. Here are some situations where a lawyer's advice may well be worth the price:

1. Deciding Whether the Use of a Proposed Mark Will Get You in Trouble Because of an Existing Mark

Where trademark lawyers typically are brought into the name-selection process is when a trademark search discloses the existence of a mark that is the same as, or similar to, the mark proposed for use. The question, then, becomes whether use of the proposed mark will legally run afoul of the original owner's rights in the existing mark—possibly leading to an expensive lawsuit and loss of the right to use the proposed mark as well as money damages.

Evaluating whether one mark legally steps on (infringes) another mark is not a science; it is an informed guessing game, an educated stab at how consumers will react to somewhat similar names, and how a judge in the future will rule on the issue. Although this book offers some sound guidelines for dealing with this question, it offers no guarantees. This is because infringement is decided on a case-by-case basis, and clear-cut rules cannot be stated.

For this reason, you may be better off getting a more definite opinion about your situation from a trademark lawyer—who should be steeped in the many hundreds of trademark cases decided by our courts each year and who may be better able to fit the whole of trademark law to your precise situation. Still, in the end, the lawyer also will be unable to predict with certainty what would happen in court if a dispute arose.

2. Providing an Opinion Letter

There is another good reason to consult a lawyer when choosing a mark that might possibly infringe an existing mark. If the lawyer advises you to go ahead, you can later use that advice as a defense if you are accused of deliberately trying to copy the existing mark—which can produce a judgment for large money damages if proven. On the other hand, because the lawyer can't say for sure how a judge would rule in the case, lawyers tend to be conservative and may recommend against using a mark that in fact does not place you in much risk of an infringement suit. Since few people are comfortable in disregarding a lawyer's advice, the visit to the lawyer may do you more harm than good. The choice, such as it is, is yours to make.

3. Problematic Federal Trademark Registrations

Thousands of businesses handle their own trademark registrations every year—without incident. The personnel in the Trademark Division of the U.S. Patent and Trademark

Office (PTO) are usually quite friendly and willing to help you through the process. In routine cases there is no need for help from a lawyer.

However, not all cases are routine. There may be a dispute over whether your proposed mark qualifies for placement on the Principal Register, perhaps because the PTO believes your mark lacks adequate distinctiveness or is too close in meaning, sound, or appearance to another mark that is already registered or awaiting registration. Or the PTO may require you to limit your registration to certain categories, and you find the restriction un-acceptable. Or you may simply experience one of the glitches that can arise in any administrative system that you can't work out informally. If these kinds of issues arise, consider consulting a trademark lawyer. But beware. Often, pursuing the troublesome is more expensive than what is actually at stake.

If in the course of your registration the owner of another trademark challenges your right to register the mark, you will probably need a lawyer to meet that challenge in an administrative proceeding conducted by the PTO, assuming you want to fight rather than switch.

4. Disputes With Other Trademark Owners

If you are faced with a dispute over your proposed mark, or over a mark you are already using, you will probably want to consult a trademark lawyer to see what your options are. Although in Chapter 10, Sorting Out Trademark Disputes, we lay out the general principles used by the courts to resolve the major categories of disputes, there is nothing like getting an informed opinion from a knowledgeable human being about the issues involved in your particular dispute.

Icons Used in This Book

Look for these icons to alert you to certain kinds of information:

 Fast Track. This icon suggests that you pause and consider whether to skip or skim a section.

 Warning. The caution icon warns you of potential problems.

 Tip. This icon highlights helpful hints and considerations for specific situations.

 Expert. This icon lets you know when you need the advice of an attorney or other expert.

 Cross-Reference. When you see this icon, you will be referred to other sections of the book containing similar information.

Chapter 1

A Trademark Primer

*T*his chapter provides an introduction to the basics of trademark law. It will give you the background necessary to understand your rights and obligations in choosing and using a trademark to identify your business and products in the marketplace. If you already have a thorough grounding in trademark law, feel free to skip ahead. Otherwise, please read this chapter carefully.

A. Trademarks & Trademark Law

What's in a name? To Shakespeare, "A rose by any other name would smell as sweet." But what is true in love can be the opposite in business. *IBM* would not smell half so sweet by another name, nor would *Xerox, Apple Computer, McDonald's,* or *Levi-Strauss.* In the business world, the name of a successful product or service contributes greatly to its real worth. Every day, names such as *Allendale Auto Parts* or *Building Blocks Day Care* identify these businesses for their customers, help customers find them, and (assuming they provide a good product or service) keep the customers coming back again and again.

And it's not just a clever business or product name that pulls in the customers. Equally important in the vast U.S. consumer marketplace are the logos, packaging, innovative product shapes, cartoon characters, website address names (domain names), and unique product characteristics that businesses are using to hawk their wares. Even the look and feel of a business's site on the Internet—widely known as a Web page—are increasingly becoming important means for a business to identify itself and its products in the marketplace.

All of these devices—business and product names, logos, sounds, shapes, smells, colors, packaging—carry one simple message to potential customers: Buy me because I come from XYZ Company. To the extent that these devices are unusual enough to distinguish their underlying products and services from those offered by competitors, they all qualify as trademarks.

If a small business owner were to remember only one point in this book, it should be this: The instant a business or product name or any other identifying device is used in the marketplace—be it in advertising, on a label, on an Internet site, or in any other way intended to reach out to potential customers—it falls within the reach of trademark law. Trademark law will determine who wins a dispute over the use of the name. Few business owners can afford to disregard or run afoul of this body of law.

1. What Are Trademarks?

Trademarks fall into two general categories: marks that identify goods or products (known as trademarks) and marks that identify services (known as service marks). Though you may occasionally see this distinction in action, these terms are, in fact, legally interchangeable, and the even more general term—mark—commonly is used to refer to both. In this book, we tilt towards the terms "trademark" and "mark" and seldom use "service mark."

Technically speaking, a trademark is any word, design, slogan, sound, or symbol (including nonfunctional unique packaging) that serves to identify a specific product brand—for instance, *Xerox* (a name for a brand of photocopiers), *Just Do It* (a slogan for a brand of sport shoes and sportswear), *Apple's* rainbow apple with a bite missing (a symbol for a brand of computers), the name *Coca-Cola* in red cursive lettering (a logo for a brand of soft drink).

A service mark is any word, phrase, design, or symbol that operates to identify a specific brand of service—for instance, *McDonald's* (a name for a brand of fast food service), *Kinko's* (a name for a brand of photocopying service), *ACLU* (a name for a brand of legal organization), *Blockbuster* (a name for a brand of video rental service), the U.S. Postal Service's eagle in profile (a symbol for a brand of package-delivery service), *CBS's* stylized eye in a circle (a symbol for a brand of television network service), the Olympic Games' multi-colored interlocking circles (a symbol for a brand of international sporting event).

In addition to trademarks and service marks, federal trademark law protects two other types of marks—certification marks and collective marks.

Certification marks are only used to certify that products and services that are manufactured or provided by others have certain qualities associated with the mark. For example, *Good Housekeeping Seal of Approval* (a product approved by a homemaking magazine), *Roquefort* (a cheese from a specific region in France), and *Harris Tweeds* (a special weave from a specific area in Scotland) are all certification marks. Among the characteristics that this type of mark may represent are regional origin, method of manufacture, product quality, and service accuracy.

A collective mark is a symbol, label, word, phrase, or other distinguishing mark that signifies membership in an organization (a collective membership mark) or that identifies goods or services that originate from the member organization (a collective trademark). For example, the letters "ILGWU" on a shirt is a collective mark identifying the shirt as a product of members of the International Ladies Garment Workers Union. It distinguishes that shirt from those made by nonunion shops.

Another example of a collective membership mark is the familiar FTD found in many flower shops. This mark means that the flower shop is part of a group that participates in a national flower delivery system. To belong to that group—and thus obtain authorization to use the FTD mark—the shop must pay steep membership fees and conform its practices to the rules set out by the group.

Because a small business's need for collective or certification marks is relatively rare, we don't address them further in this book. If you need help in creating and protecting this type of mark, consult a trademark attorney. (See Chapter 14, Help Beyond This Book.)

Although most small businesses rely on their business name as their primary trademark, there are many other ways for a business to inform consumers about itself, its services, and its products.

a. Logos

Next to a name, the most popular commercial identifier is the logo, a pure graphic or a combination of a graphic and some aspect of

the business name. Examples abound. The block-lettered *Ford* set against a blue oval, the distinctive blue lettering used for *IBM*, the gold *McDonald's* arch, the universally recognized swirl used to denote Nike products, and the blue cross used to denote health care services all demonstrate how powerfully a logo can garner instant product or business recognition.

b. Slogans

Another popular form of trademark is the marketing slogan. "Obey your thirst" (*Sprite*); "It's everywhere you want to be" (*Visa*); "I love what you do for me" (*Toyota*); "Just Do It" (*Nike*); "Life is a sport, drink it up" (*Gatorade*), and "Life is a journey; enjoy the ride" (*Nissan*) are all devices designed to build customer recognition of the underlying businesses and their products, and therefore each qualifies as a trademark that deserves the same protection under trademark law as a business name.

c. Packaging, Decor, Product Shape, and Web Pages

In recent decades, a type of trademark known as trade dress has become more important to businesses trying to build customer recognition. Trade dress includes product packaging, external and internal store decor, product shapes, and perhaps the look and feel of a

business's Web page. As long as the appearance of the product or its packaging operates as a trademark, it will be treated and protected as a trademark, assuming it meets other trademark requirements such as distinctiveness. (See Section B below.)

d. Colors

Colors help to distinguish products and services. A box of film that is gold and black connotes a Kodak product. A yellow arch indicates McDonald's food services. When color is used with a name or graphic design of a trademark (such as the red lettering and blue star of Converse footwear or the yellow and black coloring of the Cliff's Notes book series) it is registered as an element of the trademark.

It was not until recently that the United States began to protect combinations of colors or single colors by themselves—that is, without any additional text or graphics. In the 1980s, Owens-Corning registered the color pink for its fiberglass insulation and, in 1995, the Supreme Court ruled that a manufacturer of dry-cleaning press pads could claim registration for a green-gold color. (*Qualitex v. Jacobson Products*, 514 U.S. 159 (1995).) Also, a federal appeals court has ruled that a color combination (signifying different tensions in an exercise band) could be protected. (*Fabrication Enters. v. Hygenic Corp.*, 64 F.3d 53 (2d Cir. 1995).)

Colors may not be protected on the grounds that they are inherently distinctive. Rather, to obtain protection, the owner of a potential mark for color must establish that, given its use in the marketplace, consumers have come to associate the color with the owner's products or services, as indeed was the case with the Owens-Corning pink fiberglass and the green-gold color for the dry-cleaning pads.

e. Internet Domain Names

Internet domain names are the names assigned to Internet sites for the purpose of uniquely identifying the site and providing an intuitive way for potential visitors to locate it. (We discuss domain names separately in Chapter 2, Trademarks, Domain Names, and the Internet.)

2. What Is Trademark Law, and Why Do You Need to Know About It?

If every business used a unique name or other mark to identify itself, its products, and its services in the marketplace, there would be precious little to write about in this book. In the real world, once customers come to associate a mark with a particular business or product, would-be competitors frequently copy some or all aspects of the mark—its sound, its appearance, its meaning—in an effort to lure customers away from the original business. Even well-intentioned business owners may violate trademark laws when they unwittingly pick a new business name, logo, or other type of trademark that conflicts in some way with a mark already in use somewhere in this large country of ours.

For these and other reasons, the U.S. marketplace is rife with trademark conflicts. It is the job of trademark law to sort out these conflicts in an equitable and consistent manner. It is this book's job to introduce you, the reader, to how trademark law works, so that you will know how to avoid legal trouble when deciding how to identify your business and products in the marketplace and what to do if, despite your best efforts, you end up in a trademark conflict anyway.

B. Basic Principles of Trademark Law

Trademark law is the body of principles that the courts use to decide disputes regarding names or other devices being used to identify goods and services in the marketplace.

Trademark law comes from many sources: federal and state trademark statutes, federal and state statutes defining and prohibiting "unfair competition" between businesses, and federal and state cases interpreting these laws. (Unfair competition refers to the legal rulings and statutes that protect against unethical business practices.) The federal law that governs trademark rights and registration is known as the Lanham Act. Although there are subtle differences in all these sources of law dealing with how businesses use commercial identifiers, federal trademark statutes and cases govern most trademark disputes. (In Section G we provide more information on these sources of trademark law.)

Here, briefly, are some basic concepts of federal trademark law that you will need to understand before we go any farther (we provide more details as we go along):

- The first business to use a trademark in the marketplace owns it as against later users.
- To qualify as a trademark, a name, logo, or other device used by a business in its

marketing activities must either be: (1) unique enough to earn customer recognition on its own (referred to in trademark law as inherent distinctiveness) or (2) have earned customer recognition through its continued use over time (known in the trade as "acquired distinctiveness" or "secondary meaning").

- A trademark owner can sue in federal court to stop another business from using the same or similar trademark if the owner's mark is famous or the use by the other business would cause potential customers to confuse one business or product with another.
- The more distinctive a trademark is, the easier it is for its owner to get the court to stop its use by others.
- The usual court remedy in trademark disputes is to order the loser to stop further use of the trademark in question. This can be painful, because business goodwill often is intimately connected with the business's mark, and expensive because all of the items that carry the mark will have to be pulled from use.
- If the court finds that one business deliberately used a famous or distinctive mark belonging to another business, the offending business can be ordered to pay substantial money damages to the trademark owner.
- The court will usually find that a mark was deliberately copied if the mark was listed on the federal trademark Principal Register at the time it was copied.

Ideally, just knowing basic trademark principles should be enough to answer all your questions and get you started on the road to choosing a clever name for your business or product. But not so fast. The phrases "customer confusion" and "distinctive mark" need some definition. Unfortunately, Congress has avoided hard definitions and instead opted to let judges decide, on a case-by-case basis, whether a particular mark is famous or risks confusion by customers with an existing mark. Although we provide some guidelines in this book for you to use when you are faced with interpreting these terms, the rock-bottom rules for dealing safely with the ambiguities in trademark law are these:

- Don't choose a business or product name that is the same as that used nationally by a large company. Even if you're in the right on some abstract level, the big company will most likely try to legally terrorize you into dropping the mark.
- Don't choose a trademark that is the same—in appearance, sound, or meaning —as a federally registered mark, unless the registered mark is used for a product or service that is definitely very different from the ones offered by your business.
- Don't try to piggyback your marketing efforts on a well-known trademark belonging to another business. For example, don't call your new Web design service "Jetscape."
- Don't choose a domain name for your business that is the same as the trademark of an existing business; if you do, you may be accused of infringement (if you have similar products or services), dilution (if the existing business has a famous trademark), or cybersquatting (if

you acquired the domain name in bad faith).

These rules are easy to understand. A fifth rule is not: Stay away from existing marks that resemble yours if there's a likelihood that customers would be confused by use of the two marks. Using the guidelines we lay out later in the book (see Chapter 3, How to Choose a Good Name for Your Business, Product, or Service), you should be able to select an appropriate name or to recognize when you need a professional opinion (see "When a Trademark Lawyer May Help," just below).

 When a Trademark Lawyer May Help. If any of these rules get in your way (you've got a hot name for your business and you want to run with it), a trademark lawyer can help you decide whether your situation is an exception to these rules and what you risk by going ahead with your proposed mark (see Chapter 14, Help Beyond This Book, for information on how to find a trademark lawyer).

1. Strong Marks v. Weak Marks: What Trademark Law Protects

Trademark protection is based on a "strength" classification system. Distinctive trademarks are strong and protectable. Trademarks that are not distinctive are considered weak and cannot be registered or protected unless the trademark owner creates consumer awareness.

Strong marks include coined words such as *Polaroid,* arbitrary terms, such as *Apple* for computer products, or terms that have a suggestive quality without describing the goods or services, for example *Roach Motel.* These marks are all born strong and are so memorable or clever that they are classified as "inherently distinctive."

Weak marks such as *Healthy Favorites, Beef & Brew,* or *Chap Stick* describe some quality, ingredient, or characteristic of the goods and services. Many businesses prefer to use weak trademarks because a descriptive mark provides information about the product to the consumer. For example, consumers know immediately that *Food Fair* is the name for a supermarket and *Raisin Bran* is the name for a cereal made with raisins and bran. A weak mark can acquire distinctiveness if, through extensive sales and advertising, the public becomes aware of the mark and associates it with a particular source.

Chapter 3, Section D, What Makes a Distinctive Trademark a Legally Strong Trademark?, revisits in more detail the subject of what makes an effective trademark. The question of what makes one mark strong and another mark weak often is the key to resolving trademark disputes and frequently must be understood to handle your own trademark issues.

2. Ownership of a Trademark: The First-to-Use Rule

In the United States, the first business to use a trademark owns it.

a. Two Types of First Use

There are two ways to qualify as a first user of a trademark:

- *actual use*—the first to use the trademark on a product that is distributed in the marketplace or, in the case of a service mark, the first to use the mark in connection with advertising or marketing of a service available to the public, or
- *intent to use*—the first to file an intent-to-use application with the U.S. Patent and Trademark Office provided that (1) the applicant files the application before the trademark is actually used by another party and (2) the applicant later puts the mark into actual use and completes the registration process by filing an additional form and paying an additional fee.

EXAMPLE: In 2003, Jonah begins publication of *Geezer Tennis*, a magazine for aging tennis players. In the year 2006, a business competitor sends Jonah a letter stating that Jonah is infringing its federally registered trademark *Geezer Games*. Jonah does a little investigating and learns that *Geezer Games* was first used as a mark in 2004, a full year after Jonah started using the mark. Jonah would be considered the owner of the *Geezer* mark and could in fact require *Geezer Games* to change its name, because the products of the two businesses compete and would therefore likely lead to customer confusion.

EXAMPLE: Assume now that in 2003 *Geezer Games* had applied for federal trademark registration on an intent-to-use basis, even though it hadn't actually put the mark in use commercially until 2004.

If Jonah started actual use of the *Geezer* mark in March 2003, and *Geezer Games* filed its application for registration in April 2003, Jonah would still be considered the owner. However, if the application filing date preceded Jonah's actual use, *Geezer Games* would be the ultimate owner, once it put the mark into actual use.

What constitutes actual use and intended use is discussed in detail in Chapter 7, Federal Trademark Registration.

b. Two Different Businesses Can Own the Same Mark

It is possible for a mark to be "owned" by two or more separate businesses as long as no customer confusion is likely to result. If the underlying products or services of two businesses are quite different and don't compete, then customer confusion is unlikely. Similarly, if the underlying products or services are distributed and marketed in different channels or parts of the country, then again there is little likelihood of customer confusion. For example, one U.S. district court ruled that the mark *Aisle Say* used for theater reviews could be owned by two different entities— one that published its reviews exclusively on the Internet and the other that published its reviews in print in the New York metropolitan area (*Albert v. Spencer,* 1998 U.S. Dist. LEXIS 12700 (S.D. N.Y. 1998)). But, as we pointed out earlier, the more famous or distinctive a mark is, the more likely it is that customer confusion will result (and the less likely it is there will be more than one owner).

c. When Dual Users Come Into Conflict

What happens if a mark is owned by more than one business because of different geographical markets, and one of the businesses decides to move into the other business's territory? Or suppose that dual ownership has been possible because one business used the mark on sportswear and another on lawn mowers, and both businesses decide to move into gardening clothes? In these situations, some rules kick in that help a court decide the respective rights of the owners. The rules revolve around such facts as:

- Did the second business to actually use the mark know of the first business's previous use?
- Is the first user's mark federally registered and, if so, did the second use begin before or after the registration?
- Is the second user's mark federally registered?
- How broad were the first user's marketing efforts when the second use began?

(Chapter 10, Sorting Out Trademark Disputes, deals with all these issues and tells you how the courts are likely to resolve them in specific fact situations.)

⚠️ **The Internet May Render Dual Ownership Obsolete.** As more and more businesses use the Internet to market their goods and services, it will be harder and harder for two marks to coexist, since they will be sharing the same marketing channel, which happens to be national and even international. The risk of confusing customers who are using the Web to shop will be high. (Customer confusion is discussed in more detail in Chapters 6 and 10.)

3. The Role of Customer Confusion in Trademark Law

As mentioned in the Introduction, virtually all trademark disputes that make it to court are resolved on the basis of the answer to this one simple question: Is simultaneous use of the marks likely to cause customer confusion? If there is no customer confusion, then the courts see no reason to intervene. (An exception to the customer-confusion rule is sometimes made for famous marks, which by law are entitled to be free from other uses that would dilute their strength or tarnish their reputation for quality. See Section B4 below for more on dilution.)

It's important to understand that two different marks can be confusingly similar for a number of reasons. Take, for example, the well-known mark *Microsoft*. Could a business avoid the likelihood of customer confusion by using a name that sounds the same as *Microsoft* but looks different, such as Mikkrowsought or Mike Crow Soft? Or that looks the same but sounds different, such as Macrosoft? Or that looks and sounds different but which means essentially the same thing, such as TinySoft? Or perhaps a fanciful arrangement of the words and letters, such as

MI

CRO

SOFT

The answer to all these questions is no. Why? A mark that is similar to another only in sound, appearance, or meaning is still similar and therefore likely to confuse potential customers. However, the weaker the original mark is, the less concerned the courts will be about possible customer confusion and the more acceptable changes in appearance, sound, or meaning will be as a way to distinguish one ordinary mark from another.

Even if two marks are exactly the same, customer confusion will not be likely and infringement won't occur if the goods or services identified by the marks aren't related in some way. For instance, Delta Faucet and Delta Airlines can both use the Delta mark because customers just aren't likely to confuse one with the other. But clothing and items that are both sold in sporting goods stores may be considered related products—because they are marketed in the same channel—and therefore customer confusion could be found to result.

(Chapter 6, How to Evaluate the Results of Your Trademark Search, provides an explanation of what standards are used to measure customer confusion.)

4. Special Treatment for Famous Marks: The Dilution Doctrine

In 1995, Congress passed the Federal Trademark Dilution Act (FTDA), a statute that gives the owners of certain famous marks protection against copycats even if there is no likelihood of customer confusion. This protection only applies if dilution of the famous mark's distinctive quality is shown. The Act defines dilution as "the lessening of the capacity of a famous mark to identify and distinguish goods or services." Courts have extended this definition to include two factors:

- blurring of the famous mark (which means detracting from the mark's uniqueness), and
- tarnishment (which means negatively affecting the famous mark's reputation for quality).

In addition to the FTDA, which has national application, about half of the states have their own dilution statutes that differ to a greater or lesser degree in how they define dilution. The main point you need to be aware of here is that famous marks may be protected against use by others even if consumers are not likely to be confused by the dual use. We explain dilution in more detail in Chapter 10, Section C.

5. How Trademark Law Protects Trademarks

The trademark system is self-policing. If you don't do anything about your business name or other mark getting ripped off by a competitor, no one else will. And so, even though the law provides "protections," you will have to step forward and use what tools the law provides.

As a general rule, these tools are very limited. In some situations it is possible to resolve a dispute by filing an administrative petition or complaint with the PTO (see Chapter 7, Federal Trademark Registration), but the vast majority of trademark disputes that can't be settled by negotiations are resolved by filing a federal court lawsuit claiming trademark infringement, or, in the case of a dispute between a mark and a domain name, by a federal lawsuit or an administrative arbitration.

Typically, an infringement lawsuit asks the court to immediately order a suspected infringer to stop using the mark in question, and to award the business bringing the suit monetary damages for harm caused by the infringer. Once the judge rules on the request for immediate relief, the case is then typically settled. If the court grants the immediate relief requested by the plaintiff, the case usually is settled on terms favorable to the plaintiff. If the judge denies the relief, the defendant usually fares better. Few trademark cases make it all the way to trial and, consequently, few cases result in damage awards, although large amounts of money may change hands as part of the settlement.

Litigation can get expensive in a hurry, easily running into tens of thousands of dollars in legal fees. The cost of litigation teaches one very important lesson when it comes to trademark disputes: Be flexible and don't get carried away by the right or wrong of the situation. Always treat the issue as a business decision— try to resolve it in the manner that will most benefit (and least harm) your business. Remember that negotiation is an option, and there are many ways to structure a settlement. Using a cease and desist letter if the law is on your side is a first step. (How to handle trademark disputes is covered in more detail in Chapters 11, If Someone Infringes Your Mark, and 12, If Someone Claims that You Infringed Their Trademark.)

C. The Role of Federal Registration in Protecting Trademarks

Trademarks can be registered with the PTO under a federal statute known as the Lanham Act. Trademarks are commonly registered with the PTO using one of two methods:

- The trademark owner files an application based upon use of the mark in commerce regulated by the federal government.
- The trademark owner files an application based on an intent to use the mark in commerce regulated by the federal government and subsequently uses it (known as an "intent-to-use" or ITU application).

In Chapter 7, Federal Trademark Registration, we tell you how to get the job done for registrations for business and product names.

Registration can increase a trademark owner's ability to win a lawsuit based on infringement of the registered mark and provide additional benefits as discussed in Section C1, below. Although registration increases protection, it's important to understand that in many cases it is possible for the owner of an unregistered trademark to stop someone from using a confusingly similar trademark. That's because, with the exception of ITU applications (discussed in Chapter 7, Federal Trademark Registration), trademark rights are held by the party who first uses the mark in commerce, not who first files an application for registration with the PTO. In federal court, a holder of a registered trademark is presumed to own the mark, but this can be rebutted with proof of earlier use of the mark. Thus, registration provides a trademark user with the presumption of ownership, but not actual ownership, of the mark.

1. The Principal Register

The PTO keeps two lists of all trademarks that it has decided to register—the Principal Register and the Supplemental Register. In addition to the trademarks themselves, these registers include the following information:

- the owners of the marks
- the dates the marks were registered
- the types of goods or services identified by the marks, and
- other potentially useful information such as how the marks were described by their owners in the application process.

Of the two lists, the Principal Register is by far the more important. Placement on this list provides a trademark with the protection that makes it worthwhile to register the mark in the first place.

a. Qualifying for Placement on the Principal Register

To be placed on the Principal Register:

- The mark must be in actual use in commerce involving two or more states or across territorial or international borders. Even if an application has been filed for registration based on intended use, the mark will not actually be registered until it is put into actual use.
- The mark must be sufficiently distinctive (inherently or acquired through use over

time) to reasonably operate as a product or service identifier in the marketplace.
- The mark may not be confusingly similar to an existing mark in a context where the confusion of customers would be likely.
- The mark may not fit within one of the categories that Congress has deemed to be off limits for trademarks (such as using "U.S." or the name of a living person without his or her consent).
- The mark may not consist primarily of a surname or a geographical name (unless the mark has become well known over time or the geographical term is clearly arbitrary but not deceptive).
- The mark may not consist of the title of a book, play, recording, or movie that is a single-issue artistic work (as opposed to a series or serial) unless the title has become well known over time.

b. Benefits of Registration on the Principal Register

Registration on the Principal Register provides these protective benefits:

- exclusive nationwide ownership of the mark (except where the mark is already being used by prior users who may not have registered the mark)
- official notice to all would-be later users that the mark is unavailable
- the right to put an ® after the mark, which also puts users on notice that the mark has been registered
- the right to immunize the mark from certain challenges if the mark is kept in continuous use for five years after the registration date

- a legal presumption that the registrant is the owner of the mark (which means the registrant won't have to prove ownership if a dispute over the mark ends up in court, although, as noted, the registrant may have to show prior use to rebut a contender's claim of ownership based on first use).

Taken together, these benefits make it easier to win an infringement lawsuit and make it more likely that large damages can be collected for the infringement (which means there will be money to pay the attorneys and make it worthwhile to bring the lawsuit in the first place). (See Chapters 10 through 12 for more on infringement lawsuits.)

2. The Supplemental Register

The Supplemental Register is an option for marks that aren't distinctive enough to qualify for placement on the Principal Register. (See Section B1, above, for a discussion on what makes a mark distinctive.) This lack of distinctiveness means that the courts are unlikely to give the mark much protection in the event of a lawsuit.

As a general rule, placement of a mark on the Supplemental Register does not help much if a dispute over the mark ends up in court. However, anyone doing a standard trademark search to find out whether the same or a similar mark is available for their use will discover the registration and most likely will decide to choose another mark, just to be safe. Also, placement on the Supplemental Register entitles the mark's owner to use the ® that, to the public, signifies a registered trademark. And finally, if the mark continues in use and remains on the Supplemental Register for five years, it is easier to apply to have the mark placed on the Principal Register (because it has acquired distinctiveness through continued use over time). The bottom line is that the Supplemental Register provides some practical benefits and therefore provides a sensible alternative if placement on the Principal Register is denied because of the mark's lack of distinctiveness.

3. State Trademark Registers

All states maintain separate trademark registers. The main function of these is to provide notice to would-be later users that the mark is already in use in that state. Unlike federal trademark registration, placement of a mark on most state registers confers few benefits other than an indication of when trademark rights in the mark were first claimed by the registrant. Because of the relative unimportance of state trademark registrations, we don't devote the space to explaining how to handle them. However, if you want more information on your state's trademark registration procedure and trademark laws, contact your state trademark registration office. You can also obtain more state trademark information at either Marksonline (www.marksonline.com) or the All About Trademarks website (www.ggmark.com).

D. Not All Business Names Are Trademarks

The most common method adopted by new businesses to identify themselves in the marketplace is their name. For the purposes of trademark law, there are two main types of business names:

- the formal name of the business, called its trade name, and
- the name the business uses to market its products or services, alternatively referred to as a "trademark," "service mark," or just plain "mark."

For most small businesses, this is a distinction without a difference. Almost all legal problems involving business names arise when a business name is used as a trademark—that is, used to build a customer base for the business—and not when the name is used as a trade name simply for billing, banking, and tax purposes.

The distinction between a trade name and a trademark can be a little confusing at first, because many businesses use at least a part of their trade name as the name they use to market their goods or services. For instance, every time a small business named something like *Pete's Graphic Designs*, *Elmwood Copymat*, or *Good Taste Organic Foods* puts its name on a store sign, window display, or brochure, it is using its trade name as a trademark. On the other hand, large businesses often use different names for each type of subsidiary activity. For instance, Ford Motor Company puts its name on its cars but also uses a subsidiary mark for each type of car (for instance, *Escort, Probe, Thunderbird*) and a different mark entirely for its auto parts division (*Motorcraft*).

Corporate and Fictitious Names

A corporate name is simply the name of a corporation as registered at the time of incorporation. It must generally be approved by a state official, such as the secretary of state or corporations commissioner (the names vary from state to state), and followed by a corporate identifier, such as Inc. or Corp., like *Time, Inc.*, or *Sony Corp.* A corporate name is a trade name in that it identifies the corporation and not necessarily any product or service the corporation offers.

Another form of trade name is the fictitious business name, which is any assumed business name or alias. When a person or partnership does business under a name not their own (and this also applies to corporations doing business under a name other than their corporate name), that person (or partnership) must usually file a fictitious business name statement with the county or state. For example, Laura Smiley uses a fictitious business name when she conducts her sole proprietorship business as *Le Petite Cafe* or *Laura's Bookkeeping*, but not if she operates under the name of *Laura Smiley Enterprises*. Similarly, if the partnership of Renauer, Randolph and Ihara operates the *Reader's Corner Bookshop*, they are using a fictitious business name.

E. Trade Name Formalities

Almost all businesses are required to register their business name with a local or state agency charged with keeping track of business names. What agency this is usually depends on whether the business is a corporate entity or a sole proprietorship. Here we provide an overview of the steps you'll likely have to take to get your particular business name registered with the appropriate agency.

1. Trade Name Registration Requirements

All names that identify business entities— corporate names; fictitious business names; assumed names; partnership names; the names of nonprofit, charitable, religious, and educational institutions; and the names of sole proprietorships—are trade names. With a few exceptions, every business is required by state law to take certain legal steps to list its trade name with a public agency. These vary somewhat depending on the form of the business—for instance, corporations must follow a different procedure than partnerships. Corporations usually must register with their state's secretary of state or corporation commissioner's office. Unincorporated businesses must usually register with an agency that keeps track of fictitious or assumed names.

In addition to providing a registry where members of the public can check on a business ownership, these name-registration procedures are designed to screen out the use of identical or very similar names within the state or county where the business is based. However, as we will see, they don't do a perfect job in accomplishing this. Rather than describe the specific requirements of all 50 states, we will explain generally the requirements for most of the states and give you enough information to easily find out the rest on your own.

a. Corporate Name Registration

Corporations are creatures of state law. By a legal fiction, they are considered persons— artificial persons. When they are created, we say they are incorporated (literally translated, given a body).

This process involves filing articles of incorporation, paying a fee (and possibly an advance on corporate taxes), picking a board of directors and, most important for our purposes, registering the corporate name with the secretary of state, state department of corporations, or corporations commissioner. Each state's laws on this are a little different. Registering a corporate name involves three steps.

Check Your Secretary of State's Website

Most corporate name registration agencies maintain a website on the Internet. As this edition goes to press, few states offer the opportunity to conduct your corporate name registration activities online. But this is expected to change, so make sure and check to see what services your state corporate name registration agency offers. This process may be easier than you think. To find the appropriate website, start at the Findlaw site, (www.findlaw.com), click "U.S. State Resources," choose your state, click "Government Resources," and follow links to the Executive Branch, which should lead you to your secretary of state and related corporate name registry information.

Step 1. Selecting a permissible name

All but three states (Maine, Nevada, and Wyoming) require you to include a word or its abbreviation indicating corporate status, like "corporation," "incorporated," "company," or "limited." Several states also require that the name be in English or Roman characters. In addition, most states forbid including in your corporate name words that imply a purpose different from the one stated in the articles of incorporation or that mislead or deceive the public. For example, if you are forming a corporation that will help people fill out their medical insurance forms, you probably shouldn't call it Oil Drillers, Inc.

Step 2. Clearing your name

Next, you will need to make sure that your corporate name is distinguishable from every corporate name already registered in your state. The reason is simple: Your state won't register a corporate name that too closely mimics a name already on file. To ease your task, the secretary of state or other corporate filing agency will do a search for you prior to authorizing the use of your name. In about half the states, you may phone to check on the availability of a name in advance. In the others, you must write to request a search. Often you may request a search of more than one name at a time. Those who are fairly confident that their name is unique may simply submit their articles of incorporation without a search and risk rejection if the name is already taken.

Generally, the state agency will compare your name with registered and reserved names of other corporations incorporated in your state and with those incorporated elsewhere that have registered to do business in your state. How thorough the search is varies from state to state; each state's rules vary on how different your name must be from an existing name. In every state, however, if your name is found to be confusingly or deceptively similar to another name, you will have to change it so that it is distinguishable from the existing name. This is true even if the two corporations are in very different fields—unless the owner of the registered name gives written permission to use the similar name proposed for registration.

Step 3. Reserving your corporate name

A corporation can usually reserve a name prior to actual incorporation if the name otherwise qualifies for registration. This freezes out other would-be registrants of that name (or one deceptively similar) during the period of reservation, usually 60–120 days. Most, but not all, states permit you to extend the reservation for one or more additional periods for additional fees. Also, some states allow corporations to register their names without doing business in the state and even to renew that name registration annually, which provides the equivalent of a long-term name reservation for out-of-state corporations. Check with the secretary of state to discover more about these options if you wish to use them.

Registering your corporate name with a state agency may give you far fewer legal rights than you think it does. As discussed in Section 2, below, it does not necessarily give you the legal right to use that name to identify your products or services, only to identify the corporation.

b. Fictitious Business Name or Assumed Name Registration

In all states, any person who uses a trade name other than his or her surname, and any organization that goes by a name other than the last names of the owners, must register the name with the state or county as a fictitious or assumed name.

This process, which is analogous to a corporate filing with the state, usually means paying a fee and filing a certificate with the county clerk that states who is doing business under that trade name. Many states also require business owners to publish these statements, often called DBAs (doing business as), several times in a local newspaper. Such a statement allows creditors to find the people behind the business.

Not every type of business must file a fictitious business name—it varies with the state. In almost all states, fictitious business name laws apply principally to individuals (sole proprietorships) and general partnerships. Because corporations have their own regulations, fictitious business name laws do not apply to corporations, except in the fairly rare situation in which a corporation does business under a name different from its corporate name. In most states, fictitious business name laws also do not apply to limited partnerships because other laws govern their registration. In some states, the law also covers nonprofit organizations and corporations, including churches, labor unions, and hospitals, etc.

Contrary to the effect of registering a corporate name, registration of an assumed or fictitious business name does not necessarily prevent others from registering the same name. Because many states do not maintain a central register of fictitious business names, few states "clear" a fictitious business name by checking it against any other lists before registering it. As a result, several businesses might use the same trade name in the same state.

This means that if your state has no central fictitious name register, the only way to be sure that no one else in your state is using the name as a trade name is to check any proposed fictitious business name against the records of every county, not just your own. But, as we discuss below, whether someone else is using the same trade name as yours is of less practical importance than if they were using the same trademark or using the same trade name as a trademark as well. For this reason, we aren't suggesting you check every county list if all you are concerned about is use of a trade name.

2. The Legal Relationship Between Trade Names and Trademarks

As mentioned, people often think that once they have complied with all the registration requirements for their trade name, they have the right to use it for all purposes. Because this point is so important, let us again emphasize that this isn't so. As we have seen, there are two very different contexts in which a business's name may be used:

- the formal name of the business for purposes of bank accounts, creditors, and potential lawsuits (trade name)
- the name that the business uses to market its goods or services (trademark or service mark).

The registration requirements address the first context only. They don't address the second. That is, Backyard Fantasies, Inc., may be properly registered as a corporate or fictitious business name (trade name) but, because of the previous use of that name by someone else as a trademark, be legally unusable as the name the business puts on its signs, displays, advertising, and products (trademarks, service marks).

A trade name acts like a trademark when it is used in such a way that it creates a separate commercial impression or, put more directly, when it acts to identify a product or service. This can sometimes be a tricky determination, especially comparing trade names and service marks, because they often both appear in similar places—on letterheads, advertising copy, signs, and displays. But some general principles apply:

- If the trade name is used with its full name, address, and phone number, it's probably a trade name. For instance, consider "The Goodnight Meat Company." It appears with an address, and the eye scans it, registering it as information only. This impression is intensified if an obvious trademark that also belongs to the company ("Sunrise Sausage") is used alongside it. *Sunrise Sausage* serves as the identifier of goods, while the Goodnight Meat Company only identifies the company.
- If a shortened version of the trade name is used (for instance, "Goodnight Meats"), especially with a design or logo beside or incorporating it, the trade name becomes a mark. Large companies, such as Consolidated Agriculture, often use a shortened version of their trade name (for instance, *ConAgra),* alongside marks for specific goods that they produce, including *Swift Meats, Hunt-Wesson Oils, Peter Pan Peanut Butter,* and *Banquet Frozen Dinners.* Used this way, the name *ConAgra* acts like a mark because it has a design surrounding it, and it is sufficiently different from the full corporate name, which is Consolidated Agriculture.

Simply put, if the name you have registered as a corporate or fictitious business name was already in use or federally registered as a trademark or service mark, you will have to limit your use of the corporate name to your checkbook and bank account. The minute you try to use the name in connection with marketing your goods or services, you risk infringing the existing trademark or service mark. (See Chapter 10 for more on infringement.) If your corporate name figures in your future marketing plans, you must search for use of the name as a trademark in addition to complying with the corporate name registration requirements. If you plan to market your goods or services on the Internet, then you'll also want to check to see whether someone else has already taken your proposed name as their domain name, which would mean, at the least, that you'd have to use a slightly modified name (because every domain name is unique). (See Chapter 2, Trademarks, Domain Names, and the Internet, for more about domain names.)

F. Trade Dress and Product Designs

Trade dress refers to the total image of a product or service created with a combination of such features as size, shape, color or color combinations, texture, graphics, or even particular sales techniques. Product design, a subcategory of trade dress, refers to the shape and appearance of a product, for example, the appearance of a line of clothing or furniture.

To the extent that the decor of a business, the packaging of a product, or the shape of a product are both distinctive and intended to operate as marks, they will be treated as marks and can even be registered as marks with the PTO. Visitors to a Hard Rock Cafe can identify various features that distinguish this chain of restaurants from competitors. In a liquor store, you can distinguish the bottles of Absolut vodka from those of its competitors. Most everyone can tell the difference between Kodak (yellow) and Fuji (green) film containers. Because each of these devices signals to customers that the product or service originates from a particular source, they are all examples of trade dress that qualify for trademark protection.

A complete discussion of trade dress is beyond the scope of this book, but basic legal principles that apply to trade dress are presented below and may be helpful, particularly in relation to the use of product and service names with trade dress elements.

1. Distinctiveness

Whether or not a particular trade dress qualifies for protection as a trademark depends on several basic factors. First is the trade dress distinctive?

a. Inherent Distinctiveness

Some types of trade dress may be considered distinctive simply on the basis of the trade dress itself (inherent distinctiveness). For example, the U.S. Supreme Court found that a Mexican restaurant chain's decor could be considered inherently distinctive because, in addition to murals and brightly colored pottery, the chain also used a specific indoor and outdoor decor based upon neon-colored border stripes (primarily pink), distinctive outdoor umbrellas, and a novel buffet style of service. (*Two Pesos, Inc. v. Taco Cabana, Inc.,* 505 U.S. 763 (1992).) However, product designs such as the appearance of a line of children's clothing are not considered to be inherently distinctive and can only be protected if they acquire distinctiveness through sales or advertising. (*Wal-Mart Stores, Inc. v. Samara Brothers, Inc.,* 120 S.Ct. 1339 (2000). See sidebar below, *"Wal-Mart v. Samara:* The Supreme Court Makes It Harder to Protect Product Designs.")

b. Acquired Distinctiveness (Secondary Meaning Rule)

Secondary meaning is a demonstration that the consuming public associates a mark with a single source, usually proved by advertising, promotion, and sales. If the trade dress is not inherently distinctive, distinctiveness can,

with exceptions, still be acquired through extensive sales and advertising. A red star may not be inherently distinctive, but when it is used extensively in advertising for gasoline sales and automotive services ("Look For the Big Red Star") then it may have acquired secondary meaning.

Some types of trade dress—such as a single color or a product design—may never be considered inherently distinctive because customers would have no way of associating the trade dress with the underlying products or services, or their source, without becoming familiar with them over time. For example, the use of a single color could not be inherently distinctive because consumers would not immediately associate a color with one product or company. In that case, the color sought to be protected must have acquired distinctiveness under the secondary meaning rule.

2. Trade Dress Can Be Registered With the PTO

As a general matter, distinctive trade dress can be registered with the PTO and will receive extra protection as a result. However, as with trademarks generally, distinctive trade dress also qualifies for protection against copying even if it's not registered.

3. Likelihood of Confusion Is Required

As with other types of trademarks, infringement of trade dress occurs only when there is a likelihood of customer confusion between the underlying goods or services, or their origins. Even when two different trade dress packages are similar in appearance, if customers have an easy way to tell one product or service from another, the courts have been reluctant to find that infringement has occurred. For example, a federal court found that there was no trade dress infringement in the case of two skin-care products with similar lettering, colors, and graphic design. The court determined that the prominent use of each company's name on its own product would prevent consumers from being confused by the similar trade dress.

4. Functional Trade Dress Is Not Protected as a Trademark

The trade dress feature for which you seek protection cannot have a functional purpose other than to distinguish the product or service in the marketplace. This may seem confusing, because all trade dress features have at least some utilitarian function. For instance, packaging protects products against wear and tear, and a uniquely shaped bottle holds the bottle's contents. But if the design elements are not essential for the underlying product's purpose (for instance the curved shape of an Absolut or Coca-Cola bottle isn't a necessary part of the product), then the trade dress is considered nonfunctional in a legal sense. On the other hand, the blue dot on Sylvania flashcubes was considered too functional to qualify for separate trademark status, because it served the utilitarian purpose of indicating when a bulb was used (when the blue dot turns black). Some examples of products that may have nonfunctional design features are

furniture, automobiles, sweaters, and notebooks. If the design features of any of these items become well established as a means of identifying their source, and are nonfunctional, they may qualify as protectible trade dress.

Wal-Mart v. Samara: The Supreme Court Makes It Harder to Protect Product Designs

In *Wal-Mart Stores, Inc. v. Samara Brothers, Inc.*, 120 S.Ct. 1339, 146 L.Ed. 2d 182 (2000), the Supreme Court ruled that product designs, like colors, are not inherently distinctive. Samara created a line of children's clothing that featured one-piece seersucker outfits decorated with appliques of hearts, flowers, and fruits. Wal-Mart asked another clothing company to copy Samara's designs and then sold the knock-offs at a lower price. Samara brought a federal lawsuit against Wal-Mart. The trial court ordered Wal-Mart to pay Samara $1.6 million in damages, and the ruling was upheld on appeal. The Supreme Court overruled the appellate decision, stating that the Samara designs were not protected under trademark law because product designs were not inherently distinctive and Samara had not demonstrated secondary meaning. The result is that no matter how creative a designer makes a product's appearance or shape, it will only be protected under trademark law if the owner can demonstrate that the public associates that product design with a single source.

5. If Your Product Design Is Both Functional and Novel

If your design is functional and novel you should research whether it can be protected as a utility patent. For example, let's say you have created a unique method of packaging compact disk recordings. If it is functional and protected under trademark law, it may still be protectible under patent laws. For more information, review *Nolo's Patents for Beginners* (Nolo).

G. Sources of Trademark Law

Three basic sources of law govern the use of trademarks:

- the federal Lanham Act
- state statutes governing trademarks, and
- the common law (based on court decisions, not statutes) of trademark and unfair competition.

The coverage of these laws overlaps frequently—in fact, an infringer may violate all of these at once. Below we explain how to apply these sources of law for purposes of trademark registration and trademark-related disputes.

1. The Federal Lanham Act

As discussed in Section C, the federal statute known as the Lanham Act (17 USC §§ 1051 et seq.) provides for a system of registering trademarks. If your mark meets the requirements (see Chapter 7, Federal Trademark Registration), your application will be allowed and your trademark will be placed on the Principal Register.

In addition to providing for the registration of marks used "in commerce," the Lanham Act includes a provision—Section 17 USC § 1125(a), also known as 43(a)—that prohibits false advertising, trade libel, and trademark infringement for unregistered marks.

In 1996, Congress amended the Lanham Act to prohibit dilution of famous marks, an activity previously only prohibited by state laws. Dilution is the use of a famous mark in a way that would diminish the mark's strength or tarnish its reputation for quality. (For more information on dilution see Chapter 10, Section C.)

In 1999, Congress amended the Lanham Act to prevent cybersquatting, which it defined as registering, trafficking in, or using a domain name with the intent to profit—in bad faith—from the goodwill of a trademark belonging to someone else. Lawmakers were stepping in to end the practice of buying up domain names that were the exact name, or similar to the name, of an existing business with the intent of selling the names back to the business. (For more information on cybersquatting, see Chapter 10, Section D.)

2. State Trademark and Unfair Competition Laws

States have four types of laws that deal with trademarks:

- A number of states have antidilution laws. Like the federal antidilution statute, these laws allow the owner of a well-known mark to stop the use of a similar mark without having to establish the likelihood of customer confusion.

- All states have statutes providing for a trademark registration system.
- All states have statutes that govern trademark disputes.
- All states have statutes or a body of court-developed common law that prohibits unfair competition.

State trademark statutes and the state rules against unfair competition usually dictate that the first to use a distinctive mark will have trademark precedence over a second user when the potential for customer confusion exists. State trademark rights apply on a statewide basis only.

State trademark registers are most useful when your mark is only used within your state. However, even if you plan to acquire a federal registration, it won't hurt to also register in your state. The fees are usually quite modest, and you never know when someone local who wants to use your mark will only search your state's trademark register. You can obtain state trademark registration application forms and other information about your state's trademark agency through the links provided at All About Trademarks (www.ggmark.com).

3. Common Law of Trademarks

Both state and federal courts have developed a body of "common law" that covers trademarks. This law originated in judge-made decisions, but over the years much of it has been placed in statutes (codified). In general, this court-made law applies to all trademarks, registered or not, and reflects the principles we set out in this chapter—that to be protected, a mark must be distinctive or must have developed secondary meaning. And for a legal conflict to exist, there must be a likelihood of customer confusion.

The common law is usually listed in the litany of claims when one trademark owner sues another. However, common law claims, by themselves, rarely provide the basis for modern trademark decisions—judges now make such decisions usually based on state or federal laws.

H. The Difference Between Trademark and Copyright

The terms "trademark" and "copyright" are often used interchangeably by the general public. However, trademark and copyright protect different aspects of creative expression. Trademark protects expression that is used to identify and distinguish a product or service in the marketplace. Copyright protects all creative expression except for slogans, names, titles, and short phrases, the very things that are protected by trademark. Let's take a closer look at what copyright does protect, because when it comes to logos, trade dress, and graphics used on Web pages, trademark and copyright may both apply.

Copyright provides writers, artists, photographers, musicians, software programmers, and other creators of expressive works the exclusive right to control how their works are used. But it is important to understand that only the expression itself is protected—not the ideas being expressed. For example, assume that Lloyd Sagal, a self-identified but unknown philosopher, writes a book exploring the religious implications of life on other planets. Under copyright law, other philosophers are free to use any or all of Lloyd's ideas in their own books (and don't even have to give him credit, although most would because of professional scruples). However, each of these other authors will have to do their own writing. They can't just copy verbatim how Lloyd has expressed the ideas. (For a good explanation of the dichotomy between expression and ideas, see *The Copyright Handbook*, by Stephen Fishman (Nolo).)

A copyright attaches to a work of expression the instant the work takes a tangible form—for instance, on paper, tape, disk, CD, film, or canvas. It is common to give notice of the copyright by placing, next to the author's name, a © and the year the work is published. The creator can optionally register the work with the U.S. Copyright Office to gain some additional protections. Whether registered or not, the copyright lasts for the life of the creator plus 70 years, with some exceptions.

Copyright covers the many types of creative expression, including: advertising copy, catalogs, directories, compilations of information, fiction, interviews, lectures, speeches, leaflets, letters, magazines, newspapers, newsletters, periodicals, journals and other serial publications, nonfiction, plays, poetry, reference books and technical writings, screenplays, song lyrics, textbooks, music, art, graphic designs, motion pictures, sculptures, videos, websites, software of all types, architectural designs and blueprints, choreographic works, pantomimes, photographs, and slides.

Copyright law and trademark law commonly intersect in trademark logos, packaging, websites, and advertising copy. Trademark law protects the name of the product or service, any distinctive slogans used in the advertising or website, and distinctive features associated with the name or logo, such as its color or lettering style. Copyright law protects any additional literal expression that the ad or website contains, such as the text, artwork, music, or software. (For more information on the protection of trademarks in websites, see Chapter 2, Trademarks, Domain Names, and the Internet.)

I. The Difference Between Trademark and Patent

By filing for and obtaining a patent from the PTO, an inventor is granted a monopoly on the use and commercial exploitation of the invention described in the patent for a limited time. There are several types of patents. The most common is what's called a utility patent, which lasts for 20 years from the date the application is filed or at least 17 years from the date the patent issues. A utility patent protects the functional features of a machine, process, manufactured item, composition of matter, or new use for any such items. To qualify for a utility patent, an invention must be novel and surprising (nonobvious) to somebody who is familiar with the field of technology into which the invention falls. There is almost no intersection between this type of patent and trademark.

It is also possible to obtain a design patent on an innovative design of a manufactured item if the design serves an ornamental rather than functional purpose. A design patent lasts for 14 years from the date it is issued. Because trademark protects a product shape that is intended to operate as a trademark rather than a functional part of the product, it is sometimes possible that a product design or shape can be protected under both patent and trademark law. For more information on patents and how to apply for them, see *Patent It Yourself*, by David Pressman (Nolo).

Book and Movie Names Can't Be Trademarked

Can the name "Braveheart" be used by anyone, given its wide recognition as the title of a blockbuster Mel Gibson movie? As a general rule, the titles of books and movies, as used only on the book or movie, are not considered trademarks, because each title is unique to that particular item and not an indicator of the product's source or a means to distinguish it from competitors. If a movie or book title is used as part of a series—for example, *The Matrix*—or if the title develops secondary meaning because of ancillary product sales—for example, *The Lion King*—then the title will be protected under trademark law.

Chapter 2

Trademarks, Domain Names, and the Internet

*I*n this chapter we discuss the use of business and product names on the Internet. If you are not planning on doing business on the Net, you can proceed directly to Chapter 3, How to Choose a Good Name for Your Business, Product, or Service. If you are planning to sell goods or services on the Web, you should review some preliminary issues regarding domain names—those dot.com monikers such as macys.com or walmart.com that indicate a business's location in cyberspace.

Domain names have various functions. They can serve as an address (whitehouse.gov), as a trademark (amazon.com), or as an expression of free speech (governmentsucks.com). Unlike a trademark, a domain name is awarded to the first person to pay for it. That's why, for many businesses on the Web, acquiring the right domain name is more important than whether the name qualifies as a trademark. In this chapter we'll explain how to acquire a domain name, and we'll discuss the relationship between your business, domain names, trademarks, and the Internet.

Domain Name Disputes. Disputes occasionally arise between domain name owners and trademark owners on the Internet. For information on these cyber disputes and how they are resolved, review Chapter 10, Sorting Out Trademark Disputes.

Registering a Domain Name as a Trademark. For information on registering a domain name as a trademark, see Chapter 7, Federal Trademark Registration.

A. How to Clear and Register Domain Names

A domain name is the unique Internet "address" that directs your computer to a website on the Internet. For example, typing in www.nolo .com takes you to the website for the publisher of this book. Most companies want a domain name that is the same as or similar to the company's business or product name, for example, fedex.com, pbs.org, or staples.com.

Since domain names, unlike trademarks, are granted on a first-pay, first-serve basis, many businesses have been surprised to find that the domain names they want have already been purchased, either by someone with a legitimate intention to use the domain name, or by a speculator who hopes to make money selling it. How crowded is the world of domain names? One survey found that of 25,500 Standard English words found in a dictionary, 90% had already been purchased as domain names. Because of the land rush for domain names—over two million have already been registered—it's generally a good idea to acquire a name if it is available.

1. Check Domain Name Availability

How do you find out if the domain name you want is already taken? The easiest way is to check availability at one of the dozens of online companies that have been approved to register domain names. You can access a listing of these registrars at either the InterNIC site (www.internic.net) or at the ICANN site (www.icann.org). ICANN is the organization that oversees the process of approving domain name registrars. Every registrar provides a searching system to determine if a domain name is available. Type in your domain name choice, and the registrar will tell you if it is available.

> **EXAMPLE:** We accessed www.internic.net, clicked on "The Accredited Registrar Directory," and selected Register.com from the list. We typed in our choice for domain name, "goodgrammar.com," and were informed that the domain name had been taken and was not available for registration.

2. Check Domain Name Ownership

In addition to determining whether a domain name is available, you may want to locate information about the owner of the domain name. For example, if a domain name is taken, you may want to locate the owner to discuss acquiring, sharing, or disputing ownership of the name. You can check ownership at www.whois.net. Type in the domain name, and the website provides the contact information supplied by the domain name registrant.

> **EXAMPLE:** We accessed whois.net (www.whois.net) and typed in the domain name "goodgrammar.com." The site reported that the domain name was owned by an entity in Oakland, California, and provided a telephone number for the registrant.

Beware that some registrants, especially those acting in bad faith, may supply false information about domain name ownership and, in these cases, there's not much you can do to track down the domain name holder. Don't let this stop you if you believe you are dealing with someone who is holding a domain name for ransom. As we explain in Chapter 10, Sorting Out Trademark Disputes, there are ways to wrestle a domain name from a bad faith registrant even if you don't know the identity of the registrant or where the registrant is located.

Keep in mind that if you have a federally registered trademark, someone else may still have the right to own the domain name. Many different companies can own the same trademark for different services and products, but only one company can obtain the domain name. For example, you may be one of many different companies who have federally registered the trademark *Executive* for goods or services. Each of these companies may want www.executive.com, but the first one to purchase it—in this case, Executive Software—is the one that acquires the domain name.

3. Register the Domain Name

If the domain name you have chosen is available, you should consider acquiring it. But before you do so, you need to be sure that nobody else is using it as a trademark for similar goods and services. If another business is selling similar goods or services with a similar name, your use of the domain name can be terminated.

EXAMPLE: Bob registers the domain name ahab.com to sell artwork depicting whales. Jim has a catalog company, Ahab, that has been selling ocean-themed artwork and merchandise since 1980. Jim has registered the Ahab trademark with the PTO and can stop Bob's use of the domain name ahab.com.

If Bob had registered the domain name with the intention of selling fishing gear, his use of ahab.com would not infringe Bob's trademark, and he could proceed as shown by the *Executive* example above.

To check whether your choice of a domain name is being used as a trademark, review Chapter 5, How to Do Your Own Trademark Search. Keep in mind you only need to be concerned about using someone else's trademark if the trademark is famous (such as *Wal-Mart* or *McDonald's)* or if your company is selling or likely to sell similar goods or services.

Once you are confident that the domain name won't conflict with another's trademark for similar goods or services, you should register the domain name. Access any of the domain name registrars approved at either InterNIC or ICANN (www.icann.org) and complete the online form indicating basic contact information (name, telephone number, address). The fee is usually $35 (or less) per year, and you can pay online by credit card. The whole procedure takes a matter of minutes, and you are notified by email of your domain name ownership, which is effective immediately.

4. Now That You Own a Domain Name …

When you pay the annual fee for a domain name, all you acquire is an address on the Internet. To use it with your business, you must establish a Web hosting arrangement with an ISP (Internet service provider) usually for a fee of approximately $20 or less per month. You must also construct and upload a website and coordinate the reassignment of the domain name from the domain name registrar (the company that sold you the domain name) to the ISP.

Domain name registration grants you exclusive title, and no one else can stop you from using it, with the following exceptions:

- **You fail to pay annual domain name fees.** Domain name ownership, unlike trademark ownership, must be renewed annually (or, in some cases, every two years). If you fail to pay the renewal fees, your domain name will be terminated and could be sold to another buyer.

- **You are a cybersquatter.** If you registered a domain name in bad faith—for example, for the purpose of selling it back to a company with a similar name, your domain name can be taken away from you under federal law or under international arbitration rules for domain name owners. (The standards and procedures for these domain name disputes are discussed in Chapter 10, Sorting Out Trademark Disputes.)

- **You are an infringer.** If your domain name is likely to confuse customers because it is similar to another trademark, you may have to stop such use. For example, if you registered adoobie.com for the purposes of selling software, it's likely that the Adobe company, makers of graphics software, could sue successfully to stop your use.

- **You are a diluter.** If your domain name dilutes the power of a famous trademark, the owner of the famous mark can sue you under federal laws to stop your continued use. Dilution refers to the fact that your domain name is being used for commercial purposes, and it blurs or tarnishes the reputation of a famous trademark. For example, if you registered guccigoo.com for the purpose of selling baby clothes, the owners of the *Gucci* trademark could probably stop you from using the domain name. (The standards and procedures for these dilution disputes are discussed in Chapter 10, Sorting Out Trademark Disputes.)

B. What to Do If the Domain Name You Want Is Already Registered

There are two reasons someone registers a domain name: The registrant may be using or have a good faith intention to use the domain name; or the registrant may have invested in the registration in the hopes of selling it.

Usually, it's easy to determine whether the domain name is for use or sale. Type the domain name into your Web browser. If a

functioning website appears that bears some relationship to the domain name, the registrant is probably using the domain name in good faith. If a site comes up that says "This domain name is for sale" or something similar, then the name is for sale by the registrant. If a Web page appears that states, "Site is Currently Under Construction" or something similar, then the registrant's intentions are unclear, since many cybersquatters use this designation, as well as legitimate domain name owners who have not yet constructed a website. In these "under construction" cases, you should contact the person listed as the registrant by using the method described in Section A.

1. Choose a New Name

If the domain name you want is already registered, the easiest solution is to choose another domain name that's available. Many domain name companies will suggest alternatives if your domain name is taken. For example, a registrar informed us that "goodgrammar.com" was taken and suggested available alternatives such as:

- goodgrammar.net
- goodgrammar.org
- findgoodgrammar.com, and
- goodgrammaronline.com.

2. Buy or Share the Domain Name

If you have sufficient funds, you can try to buy the domain name rights from someone who acquired the domain name in good faith. For example, altavista.com was being used in good faith by a company with trademark rights to the term "alta vista." Compaq, the computer company, wanted to use the domain name for its Alta Vista search engine and was willing to pay $3.3 million for the domain name.

In rare cases, a company may agree to share the domain name. For example, if two companies in different states operate under the name First Washington Bank, they can share the domain name firstwashingtonbank.com. An opening page at the website would allow a viewer to click on either bank to access their services.

3. Fight for the Name

A registrant who has taken a domain name based upon your trademark primarily for the purposes of selling it to you is a cybersquatter

---

Should You Use .Net or .Org?

As you are probably aware, every domain name consists of two parts. The ".com" portion is termed a top-level domain name (TLD) while the section with the business name is termed a second-level domain name (SLD). The reason the .com part is called a top-level domain is that the Internet is organized into several broad categories including:

- com (for commercial groups)
- edu (for educational institutions)
- gov (for governmental institutions)
- org (for nonprofit organizations)
- net (for interactive discussion groups)
- biz (for use by businesses)
- info (for sites that offer information)
- name (for those maintaining personal name websites)
- aero (for the air-transport industry)
- coop (for cooperative organizations)
- museum (for museum websites), and
- pro (for accountants, lawyers, physicians, and other professionals).

In addition, the .mil domain is reserved exclusively for the United States military, and the .int domain is used only for registering organizations established by international treaties between governments. Also, two new TLDs have been proposed but not yet adopted—.jobs and .travel.

The .com extension is by far the most popular, primarily because it is the default extension when you are guessing at a company's domain name. For instance, if you wish to visit the Best Buy website, you would most likely enter www.bestbuy.com into your search engine. If Best Buy used a .net or a .org after its name (which it could, even though it's not a network or an "organization"), most people would not think to use those extensions. Of course, if you are using a search engine such as Google (www.google.com) and just enter "Best Buy," the domain name extension won't make any difference.

Some 30 additional top-level domain names known as national top levels, are available for countries and some states. For example, sony.be is the Web address for the Sony Company in Belgium. For a list of all of the foreign TLDs and their registrars, access the database at www.iana.org.

and is violating the Lanham Act's anticyber-squatting provisions. You can pursue the cybersquatter in federal court or you can arbitrate against the cybersquatter (a less-expensive alternative) using procedures created by ICANN (www.icann.org). (For an explanation of anticybersquatting rules, see Chapter 10, Section D.) You are also free to buy the domain name from a cybersquatter if you choose, although the cost will probably be several thousand dollars.

Brokering Domain Names

Not everyone selling a domain name is a cybersquatter. Many people buy domain names that are not being used as trademarks, such as drugs.com, loans.com, or cinema.com. Because these domain names do not infringe anyone's trademark rights, it's not cyber-squatting to sell them through brokering services such as Great Domains.com (www .greatdomains.com). One reason many do-main names have not been used as trade-marks is that they may have difficulty achieving protection under trademark law because they are highly descriptive of the services, and this generic quality can prevent a term from acquiring trademark protection. However, many Internet companies are pre-pared to sacrifice some trademark rights for an easy-to-remember domain name such as forsalebyowner.com.

C. Domain Names and Trademarks

The legal relationship between trademarks and domain names has not been completely sorted out. A few more years of lawsuits and new laws will probably make it clearer. Two things are certain:

- Registration of a domain name does not automatically grant trademark rights, and
- You can be sued by a trademark owner if your domain name is likely to dilute a famous trademark or to confuse customers.

1. Domain Name Registration Does Not Guarantee Trademark Rights

Domain name registration, by itself, does not permit you to stop another business from using the name for its business or product. For example, if you acquire the domain name greatgrammar.com, that does not mean you can stop others from using Great Grammar for services or products online or off. It only means that you have the right to use that specific Internet address. Your domain name will function as a trademark only if you use the domain name in connection with the sale of goods or services, and customers associate the name with your business. When that happens, you can stop others from using a similar name so long as those others weren't using the term in the marketplace before you.

Consider Amazon.com, a domain name that functions as a trademark because customers associate the name with a certain company and its services. Amazon.com achieved trademark status because the company was the first to use this distinctive name for online retail sales, and the name has been promoted to customers through advertising and sales. If another company sold books online or offline under the name Amazon, the owners of Amazon.com could sue under trademark law to stop the use.

In short, to be protectible as a trademark, your domain name must meet the standards described in Chapter 1: The name must be distinctive or must achieve distinction through customer awareness, and you must be the first to use the name in connection with your type of services or products.

2. Trademark Owners Can Sue Over Your Domain Name Use

You could run into a problem if your domain name legally conflicts with an existing trademark. For example, if you launched a website with the domain name Xon.com to sell automobile accessories, you might be asked to stop using the name by the owners of the Exxon trademark because Exxon has the right to stop look-alike and sound-alike business names that are likely to confuse customers of a wide range of auto products.

Whether your domain name would legally conflict with an existing trademark depends on (1) which was first put into actual use, (2) whether use of the domain name would confuse customers regarding the existing

mark, or (3) whether the existing mark is famous. The legal standards used in these conflicts are no different than in other trademark disputes. (In Chapter 10, Sorting Out Trademark Disputes, we provide more detail on how these disputes are resolved.)

D. Other Trademark Issues in Cyberspace

If you are establishing a website for your business, there are other trademark concerns besides domain names. Be careful about misusing other company's trademarks within your links, programming code, or content. Deceptive and misleading uses can open the door to angry letters, lawyers, and lawsuits. The law on many of these issues has not been resolved. For current information on trademarks and websites, we recommend you consult the Internet Law section of the Nolo encyclopedia (www.nolo.com). Below we provide a summary of common website issues.

As a general rule, word links—where text such as the word *Nike* is used to link to another site—are not likely to create trademark problems. Graphic links—where a graphic trademark logo such as the *Nike* swoosh is used—may raise trademark issues. To minimize liability for any trademark activities that occur when a visitor is taken to a linked website, you may want to include a prominent linking disclaimer.

Sample Linking Disclaimer

By providing links to other sites, [name of your website] does not guarantee, approve, or endorse the information or products available at those sites, nor does a link indicate any association with or endorsement by the linked site to [name of your website].

In addition, we recommend that you do not use another company's trademark to misdirect customers to your website. This is commonly done by means of a meta tag— programming code used in the creation of a website. Even though an Internet user never sees this code, meta tags have been the subject of trademark lawsuits because companies have used them to divert or confuse customers. We recommend avoiding any other company's trademarks in your meta tags because they can be easily uncovered, and many well-known trademark owners regularly troll the Net searching for such violations.

You *are* permitted to use another company's trademark in your website if you are commenting upon or criticizing the other company. For example, if you have an Internet newsletter and write an article critical of Microsoft, you can use the Microsoft logo. Keep in mind that your right of free speech doesn't prevent a trademark owner from hassling you with a lawsuit. The economics of litigation often silence critics despite their free speech rights. Two factors may convert such commentary and criticism into a lawsuit based on trademark infringement or dilution: Your website is offering goods and services as part of its criticism, or your website is likely to confuse users as to the sponsorship of the site.

The Controversy Over Keywords

Most people find their Web destinations via search engines, which have two types of listings: relevant and sponsored. Relevant listings are the primary search results that appear on the search page. Relevance (the order in which they are listed) is determined by the search engine algorithm, a mathematical formula that uses factors such as the content in a site, its domain name, material in its header (the headline that appears in the bar on top of your browser), information in its metatags (information buried in the website code), and the number of sites that are linked to it.

Sponsored links usually appear at the top and in the right margin of the Web page. You can become a sponsored link by purchasing (or bidding on) keywords at a search company. For example, at Google.com you can click on the "Advertising Programs" link and buy keywords (Google calls them "Adwords") for a small setup fee (approximately $5). Keywords are the terms that people type into the search engine. For example, if you had purchased the words "crochet" and "baby," then your ad would pop up when a user searched for crocheted baby hats.

An issue has arisen when a company buys a keyword that is a competitor's trademark. For example, several companies have purchased the keyword "Nolo" (the trademark for the publisher of this book). When a person types "Nolo" into their search engine, the competing business appears as a sponsored link. Does that use infringe Nolo's trademark rights?

Probably not. In December 2004 a Virginia federal court, in a case involving the Geico Insurance trademark, ruled that selling the Geico trademark as a keyword search term doesn't qualify as trademark infringement under current law. As of publication of this book (August 2005), a case involving the American Blind and Wallpaper Company is before the Ninth Circuit.

In that case, Google argues that the trademarks at issue—*American Wallpaper* and *American Blind*—are merely descriptive, and on that basis the sales of keywords cannot infringe. For example, consumers may be looking for window blinds made in America (or the American Foundation for the Blind).

The rules are unclear outside the United States. A French court, in a case involving the *Louis Vuitton* trademark, has ruled that the practice of purchasing another company's trademark as a keyword is illegal.

■

Chapter 3

How to Choose a Good Name for Your Business, Product, or Service

*N*ow that you have absorbed some trademark basics in Chapter 1, and learned about the relationship between trademarks and domain names in Chapter 2, it's time to set about choosing a trademark for your business or its services and products. Because most developed trademark principles apply to names rather than other types of business and product identifiers, we focus on names in this chapter.

The goal of this chapter is to help you choose a name that will:

- do a good job of identifying your products and services in the marketplace, and
- have enough legal strength to give you the exclusive right to use it.

Not all readers will care about these goals. For instance, the name *Rob's Pastry Center* may be just the ticket for the bakery Rob Johnson plans to open, but the name certainly won't leap out and grab the average consumer's attention. Nor would the law give such a name much protection, because of its ordinary and descriptive nature. Nevertheless, Rob likes the name, and so he should use it despite what the lawyers say (yes, the author is a lawyer).

What follows, then, is the type of information you'll need if you do agree with our goals or at least want more information before you decide whether to pursue them.

Much of the information in this chapter is taken to greater depths in Chapter 9, Evaluating Trademark Strength. Chapter 9 is intended for people who need to evaluate the legal strength of their mark in the context of a conflict between marks that a trademark search turns up or when a real-world trademark dispute arises. This chapter, on the other hand, is intended as a brief introduction to the difference between strong and weak trademarks in the context of choosing a mark for a business or product. If you want to read everything this book has to offer on what separates legally strong marks (the ones the courts will fully protect) from legally weak ones, read both chapters.

A. Anatomy of a Product or Service Name Trademark

It's always important to distinguish between the name you choose for your products or services and the name of the underlying class of goods or services. You can protect the former but not the latter. Here are some basic principles.

1. A Name Is Not a Trademark if It's the Generic Term for the Underlying Products or Services Offered by the Business

As we have mentioned, for a name or other symbol to qualify as a mark, it must be unique enough to distinguish the underlying product or service from others in the marketplace. Sometimes, however, a mark chosen for a product or service is very close or identical to the generic name for the underlying type of product or service. For example, assume that a business names its new soft drink product *"Diet Cola."* As it turns out, "diet cola" describes a group of carbonated soft drinks with cola flavoring and some form of sugar substitute. That fact makes the would-be *"Diet Cola"* mark generic and not a trademark at all, because it could refer to any of several brands of the underlying diet cola product. *"Shasta,"* however, qualifies as a trademark for diet cola because it specifies one particular brand of the several diet colas available on the market. Other examples of generic terms are lite beer, super glue, softsoap, matchbox cars, and supermarket.

In summary, the PTO will not register, and courts will not provide, protection for a mark that is essentially the generic name for the underlying product or service.

2. A Trademark Can Include Generic Terms

Sometimes, a trademark includes a generic identifier of the goods or services. For example, *Wildside Pet Shop* has two elements: the term *"Wildside"* that distinguishes this from other competing businesses, and the generic term "Pet Shop" that describes the class of services. Although the full name of the business can be protected as a trademark, the term describing the class of services (pet shop) will never be separately protectible. The applicant for registration must disclaim the separate use of the generic term. That way anyone is free to use the words "pet shop" as long as it is in combination with terms other than the term "wildside."

B. Distinctive Names Make Legally Strong Trademarks

As we stress throughout the book, the more unique a business, product, or service name is, the easier it is to protect the name from use by others. Because distinctive names make legally strong trademarks, it behooves you to choose a unique name. A product or service name can be unique for a number of reasons, including:

- The name may be coined (made up), as in *Exxon* petroleum products.
- The combination of words and letters in the name may be so creative that no one else has come up with it, as in *Trader Joe's* food market chain.
- The name may carry a clever double meaning, as in *Pea in a Pod* maternity stores.
- The name may have a clever appearance, as in *Toys Я Us* (with a backward facing "R").

- Certain words in the name may be completely arbitrary in the context and therefore highly original, as in *Diesel, a Bookstore*.

Whatever the reason, a unique name is by nature considered to be a distinctive name, and a distinctive name is by law entitled to protection as a trademark. We explain how to make your mark distinctive in Section D below.

C. How Trademark Law Treats Marks With Common Terms

If unique trademarks are deserving of the most protection, then common or ordinary trademarks are entitled to little or no protection. But when deciding whether a trademark is legally strong or legally weak, you have to look to the whole mark. For example, many marks that the law will protect are completely made up of ordinary words. Consider the example of *"Pea in a Pod"* as a name for a maternity store. There is nothing terribly unusual about any of the words, but the phrase is clever—because of its double meaning suggestiveness of a uterus (the pod) and an embryo (the pea) and would definitely qualify as a distinctive mark.

Though this subject is taken up in detail in Chapter 9, the basic rules that apply to marks containing ordinary terms are these:

- If the overall mark is distinctive, it will be protected no matter how many ordinary terms are used.
- The owner of a trademark using ordinary terms cannot claim ownership to the terms themselves, but only to the overall mark.
- If the ordinary terms in a mark do not create a distinctive or clever whole, the mark will not be given protection unless (a) the terms are distinctive in the context of the product or service (for instance the ordinary word "apple" becomes distinctive in the context of computers) or (b) over time consumers come to associate the mark with the underlying

product or service, as in *Best Buy* (retail electronic products).

Let's examine these rules in a little more detail.

1. Most Ordinary Words Are Not Protected

So far, you should know that on a protection scale of 1 to 10, generic terms rate a zero while distinctive marks are near the 10 end. Now let's lump all the rest of the terms that businesses frequently like to use as names of services or products into a category we will call "ordinary names."

Into this category are consigned all the sorts of words that aren't usually distinctive by themselves but that aren't generic either:

- place names (*Downtown Barber*)
- personal names (*Harris Sales, Rubin's Assembly Service*)
- words that describe the product or service (*Slim-Fast Diet Food*), and
- laudatory words or words of praise (*Tip-Top Pet Shop*).

Misspellings or alternative spellings (like "lite") cannot make an ordinary term (like light) distinctive. Nor do common foreign language equivalents, like *"le"* for "the" and *"casa"* for "house."

Because marks that use ordinary terms in ordinary ways are, by definition, not distinctive—that is, the terms aren't unusual or surprising in the context—they receive little legal protection at the outset of their use. That means that under the principles of trademark law, it's more difficult to keep others from using them or something similar.

For example, the mark "Dependable Dry Cleaners" merely describes the business, without distinguishing it from its rivals. In fact, some of the rivals might also need to advertise their services as reliable or efficient. If trademark law prevented such ordinary uses of common terms, our language would be seriously depleted. As a result, *Dependable Dry Cleaners* gets little protection as a mark from the courts. Does this mean you can't protect the trademark of a dry cleaner? Of course not. A fanciful name like *Cinderella Dry Cleaners* (if it's not already used by someone else) is a distinctive and therefore fully protectible trademark.

2. Even Undistinctive Marks May Be Entitled to Protection Once They Become Widely Recognized as Marks

As mentioned in earlier chapters, there is an important exception to the general rule that weak marks are difficult to protect. It's this: Consumer familiarity with an ordinary mark can make the mark distinctive and therefore legally protectible. This is called the "secondary meaning" rule. Many of the most famous and effective marks, like *McDonald's* or *American Airlines*, originally consisted of ordinary terms that over time became widely recognized as product and service identifiers and thus were transformed into strong marks (*McDonald's* is probably one of the strongest marks in the world).

Even *Dependable Dry Cleaners* might make it into the ranks of secondary meaning marks if a "Dependable" franchise became a household name through extensive marketing activities.

Using a mark that can't be protected until it has acquired secondary meaning can be a serious drawback to the small business owner. Either the business owner must accept the fact that the mark will be weak—and therefore subject to use by others—until the mark's reputation has been built up over time, or the owner must be prepared to spend a lot of money to promote the mark when it is first used, so that the public recognizes it sooner. Unless money is no object, it may be better to start out with an unusual word, phrase, or design that is protectible from the outset as a mark.

As with other topics touched on in this chapter, we discuss secondary meaning in detail in Chapter 9, Evaluating Trademark Strength.

Real Ray's Best Famous Original Pizza

Here's a Big Apple anecdote that illustrates the problem with trying to protect a name that's not distinctive. In New York City, which many view as pizza heaven (along with Chicago), there has been a proliferation of *Ray's Pizzas*, some of which are known for great pizza. There now are more than two dozen in the city, most of them under separate ownership. They call themselves *Ray's Original Pizza, Real Ray's, Famous and Original Ray's*, and variations on that theme. From a pizza lover's point of view, when two people set a date to meet at *Ray's*, no one knows which pizzeria anyone means. (*Ray's* on 7th Ave.? *Ray's* on Christopher St.? Which *Ray's* on 2nd Ave.? Or is it *Ray's* on Houston?) Consumers never know what quality to expect because they don't know which *Ray's* are related. The pizza parlors get each others' mail and complaints, and none of the owners can sort it out. Resort to the courts has failed because, with so many *Ray's*, no owner can prove that consumers associate the name *Ray's* with any one pizzeria. So none is distinctive enough to be protected as a trademark.

D. What Makes a Distinctive Trademark a Legally Strong Trademark?

Let's take our earlier discussion of distinctive-ness a little farther to explore why distinctive marks make legally stronger marks. A distinctive mark has a greater ability to ward off copiers than does a common name, for three reasons.

1. The more distinctive a mark is, like *Kodak*, the greater an impression it makes on the customer's memory, and the more likely it is that a similar mark, say *Kodec*, will remind the customer of the original mark. That can lead to con-fusion. The customer may think *Kodak* and *Kodec* are the same brand, or that they are related. They may buy one instead of the other, or they may be misled into thinking the reputation of one applies to the other. In either case the customer is confused, and the right-ful owner of the *Kodak* mark will have probably lost profits.

2. The more distinctive a mark is, the more likely it is that potential customers will assume that all products and services carrying the mark originate from one source. This is the opposite of what consumers are likely to think when confronted with ordinary marks that are similar to each other. For instance, it's reasonable to assume that *Double Rainbow Ice Cream* is manufactured by one company, whereas you wouldn't make that same assumption for several ice cream outlets that use some combination of *Tastee* in their marks. The greater the likelihood that customers will associate a product or service carrying a particular mark with a particular source, the greater the need to protect them against the confusion that would likely result if the same or similar mark was adopted and used by another business.

3. The more time, money, and creativity that goes into making a mark distinctive, the more sense it makes to provide the mark with adequate protection. And if the distinctiveness comes from widespread customer recognition over time (the secondary meaning rule), it also makes sense to protect the business goodwill that has been built up under the mark. Although the main reason for the trademark laws is to prevent customer confusion, the dilution principle (mentioned in Chapter 1, Section B4, and discussed in detail in Chapter 10, Section C) recognizes that the value of a well-known mark should be protected in its own right, whether or not customers are confused.

State and Federal Unfair Competition Laws Can Provide Limited Protection to Weak Trademarks

There's one more important point to understand about descriptive and ordinary words or phrases used as trademarks. Though they are not effective as trademarks without secondary meaning, ordinary names can receive certain kinds of limited protection from confusing use by other businesses under state statutes or cases barring activities that amount to "unfair competition."

Protection from unfair competition is most useful when the second user of your trade name or mark is trying to create the impression that their business is affiliated with your business. In other words, unfair competition laws can help you if someone isn't making it clear through a variety of ways that they are not connected to your business.

We discuss unfair competition more fully in Chapter 10, Sorting Out Trademark Disputes.

E. Guidelines for Making a Mark Distinctive

Short of words that have been coined for the precise purpose of operating as trademarks, such as *Exxon*, the quality of distinctiveness in a mark is most likely to arise from downright cleverness. For a name mark to be clever and therefore distinctive, it need not use words that are unusual or even weird. For example,

detail on this in Chapter 9, Evaluating Trademark Strength.) These, therefore, are the kinds of marks we advise you to use, taking into account the marketing considerations outlined in Section F below.

1. Marks Using Coined Terms—Such as *Kodak, Exxon,* and *Rackafrax* —and Terms Made Up of Parts of Different Words, Such as *Unisys*

These are wholly new, made-up words with no meaning and probably not even any connotation other than the one you will create for it with your advertising and other marketing activities. The key to a coined mark is making it pronounceable and appealing to both eye and ear, or at least suitable to the image you want to project for your product or service. To avoid coined terms that evoke unintended images, run your choices by a variety of people and note their responses to the sound and appearance of the mark. (Sample surveys of customers should be saved for marks that have passed the legal availability test.) As mentioned in Chapter 1, the best way to make a mark distinctive is to make it up.

Despite their legal strength, most coined words require extensive marketing efforts—and the attendant costs—to get established as product or service identifiers in the first place. More than any other kind of mark, coined words require lots of initial advertising, because coined words don't mean anything to the general public without it. That's a major drawback for a small business with limited start-up capital.

distinctive trademarks often consist of ordinary words used creatively in an unusual context (example: *Camel* for cigarettes, *Apple* for computers), or several ordinary words combined in an interesting way (*Thistle Dew Inn*) or with an innovative design (*Sc[i]3*), and words that evoke fanciful associations (*Double Rainbow Ice Cream*).

Also commonly used for distinctive marks are ordinary words that indirectly suggest what the underlying product or service is all about without describing it outright. Examples of these suggestive marks are: *Verbatim* (for computer disks), *Banana Republic* (for a store that originally specialized in stylish rugged-wear clothes), or *Bloomers* (for a flower shop).

Clearly, whether a trademark is distinctive will depend on both its components and the context in which these components are used. Here we describe the sorts of marks that are routinely considered by the courts to be inherently distinctive and therefore legally strong. (Again, we go into much greater

Opting for a coined term as your trademark has a second drawback. With over 200,000 new trademarks being federally registered each year, the well of coinable words is fast being drained. Despite our rich Celtic, Anglo-Saxon, Norman, and Latin linguistic heritage, new combinations that sound good and look appropriate—that is, ones that are marketable and not already in use—are becoming harder to develop.

2. Marks That Suggest but Don't Outright Describe the Product or Service, or Some Aspect of It (Such as *Obsession* Perfume, *Sharp's* Nonalcoholic Beer, *Intuit* Software)

A mark is usually considered suggestive when you need to take at least one more mental step to figure out what is being suggested. Suggestive marks are favored by marketing folks because they operate to evoke an image or idea they want customers to associate with the product or service being marketed. "*Obsession*," for example, creates the aura of irresistibility, certainly a desirable attribute for a perfume. This kind of mark is especially effective for the sorts of services or products that sell by affecting one's self-image, like beauty services, clothing, jewelry, sports businesses, or even cars. Again, test your ideas out on a number of people to see if they perceive the suggestion you hope to send.

Though suggestive marks may also require marketing to become broadly identified with a product, they are usually easier to promote than coined ones, because they connote some-thing about the product or service. Some name consultants argue that suggestive names are the most useful, because of their comparative legal strength (customers remember them), and because the images they evoke make them very effective marketing tools. On the other hand, it takes lots of thought to come up with one that's appropriately evocative, suits your customer base, and hasn't been taken.

3. Marks That Use Fanciful Terms in the Context of Their Use (Such as *Bugle Boy* Clothes, *Double Rainbow* Ice Cream, *Yahoo!* Internet Services, and *Penguin* Books)

These types of marks are fun to invent, because you can use any term or combination of terms that does not in fact describe your service or product in any way. The trick is to think up a term that is interesting, memorable, and somehow appropriate without literally describing some aspect of your service or product. For example, *Guess?* works for youthful sportswear—it carries the idea of a company/products that are innovative, unusual, and related to adventure. Of course, clothes by themselves have none of these attributes, but that doesn't matter. Also, being the first to use such an original mark (a verb with a question mark) makes the company seem innovative. A company that comes along later and names its products *Why?* would only seem imitative.

Clearly consumer responses to these types of marks are subjective and intuitive, and the creator of a fanciful or arbitrary mark must therefore try to consider all the possible evocations that a mark may have and make the most of them.

4. Marks That Use Arbitrary Terms in the Context of Their Use

Words that are descriptive or ordinary when associated with one product or service (and thus, unprotectible altogether) can be very strong for another. For example, the trademark *Apple* Computer is distinctive and therefore strong because apples have nothing to do with computers, whereas the trademark *Green Apple* Applesauce is weak because it literally describes the product. Similarly, the word *Cherokee* works well as a trademark on a 4-wheel drive utility vehicle and on women's apparel, because in each case the word is arbitrary in the context—that is, it doesn't describe any aspect of the underlying products. But *Cherokee* wouldn't work well as a trademark on Native American crafts, because in that context it simply describes the expected origin of the goods. Finally, *Jellibeans* is a distinctive name for a skating rink, but is mundane (and probably generic) as the name of a line of oval, colored, chewy candies.

5. Common Terms in Uncommon Arrangements

As mentioned earlier, the individual terms that make up strong marks need not themselves be inherently distinctive. So far we have focused primarily on what are essentially one-word trademarks—such as *Yahoo!*, *Exxon,* and *Apple*. However, the distinctiveness of a trademark can also reside in a phrase, or in

several words put together in an unusual way. Their common characteristic is that taken together they are somehow different from everyday words and names. For example, *Taco John's* has weak components—taco is a common food item, and there are millions of Johns in the world—but the way the two words combine make the whole trademark distinctive and therefore protectible.

When evaluating a phrase to see if it's a strong or weak trademark, it is the overall impression that counts. If the phrase as a whole has an original ring to it, the fact that some of its elements are ordinary won't matter. For example, *Speedy Turtle Delivery Service* is memorable for the contrast of speed and turtle. This makes it distinctive, despite the fact that *Speedy Delivery Service* without the "Turtle" would be purely descriptive and therefore weak.

6. Ordinary Terms Combined With Novel Designs

Distinctive design elements can add distinctiveness to an otherwise trite name. *Toys Us* (with a backwards "R") is one example of a trademark where the words themselves incorporate a design that lends the name originality. More often, the words have a conventional design, but they are portrayed as part of a distinct design or type style that accompanies them. One example is the bell inside a circle that indicates one of the *"Baby Bell"* telephone companies. Others are the profiled eagle with red and blue bands signifying the *U.S. Postal Service*, the script letters "G" & "E" inside a circle indicating *General*

Electric, the red *Texaco* star, or the face of an Eskimo on the tail of *Alaska Airlines* planes.

Again, remember that what counts in evaluating a trademark's strength is the overall impression that the trademark creates in the mind of the consumer, rather than the impact of any single word or design element.

Sources of Marks That You Might Not Think Of

Though it may seem that all the good marks have been taken, there is in fact a virtually inexhaustible supply. But like diamonds, they usually aren't just lying on the ground for the taking; a little mining must take place, and like the diamond in the rough, some cutting and polishing may be required to make them shine. Some of the sources for finding a distinctive name for a trademark are:

- new combinations of existing words (*Palmolive, Diehard*)
- combinations of word roots (*Navistar, Soloflex*)
- distinctive foreign words (*Sirocco* car, *Soleil* watches)
- abandoned marks that are no longer in use but that were once famous can make strong marks. They may bring a certain cachet to your product or service, if their former image corresponds to the one you now want to project.

If you do discover a mark you know has been in use at one time, you should find out if it is now available for your use by doing the sort of searches we describe in Chapter 4.

---

7. Names to Avoid

Now that we've suggested what types of words make distinctive marks, it will help to describe the types of words that cut against distinctiveness (unless they obtain secondary meaning through use over time).

a. Personal Names, Including Nicknames, First Names, Surnames, and Initials

Probably the most common type of name trademark used for a business is one that carries the owner's first or last name. *Mary's Pizza* (yes, it is owned by Mary), *Thurlow's Web Designs*, and *Brian Loman Electronics* are examples. For the most part these personal name trademarks are legally weak and not much good for customer recognition outside the business's locale. But combined with a non-name term, such as *Taco John's* or *Trader Joe's*, a mark built around a personal name can be quite distinctive. And if you have a name like *Orville Redenbacher*, you have no distinctiveness worries at all.

When Can You Use Your Own Name as a Trademark?

One of the reasons that personal names are not protectible is the idea that no one should have a monopoly on a personal name. Unless the name has already come to mean a particular service or product through the secondary meaning rule, it isn't fair for one Jones to prevent all the other Joneses from using their family name. For this reason, the courts used to say that anyone had an absolute right to use his or her own name to identify a product or service.

That's been qualified over the years. Now individuals still have the right to use their own names, but not if it will confuse consumers or smack of an unfair attempt to ride on the coattails of their famous namesakes. Generally, that means you can use your own name but not in the same line of work as a trademark owner of the same name. So, for example, Prosper Champion (unrelated to the original sparkplug Champion) was not allowed to make and market spark plugs under his name. Nor would anyone named Marriott be permitted to open a hotel under that name. For the same reasons, a person who sells his name as the mark for a business can't later go into the same field using his own name again. Finally, you won't be able to use your own name as an Internet domain name if somebody else has beat you to it (unless you have been using your name as a trademark and can establish bad faith on the part of the domain name registrant). For information about domain names and trademark law, see Chapter 2, Trademarks, Domain Names, and the Internet.

b. Practical Pointers on the Use of Personal Names as Trademarks

Now that you have a general idea of how personal names fit into the general rules regarding strong and weak marks, here are some pointers on using specific types of personal names.

Surnames. Using your surname (last name) as a trademark has a few drawbacks you might want to consider. You may want to sell the business someday, and it will be necessary, as a practical matter, to sell the name with it. This means a stranger will be operating under your name. And perhaps worst of all, the sale of your business may prevent your children or other relatives from capitalizing on the family expertise by opening their own similar business under their own name. Finally, as we saw, marks that are "primarily surnames" do not qualify for federal registration, absent a showing of secondary meaning or perhaps an association with another term that makes the combination inherently distinctive as a whole, such as *Warner's Wasteland* for a line of stores specializing in recycled products.

First Names and Nicknames. First names are generally even weaker as trademarks than surnames, because most are so much more common. But, for the same reasons, they have fewer of the disadvantages that go with selling the business. And, as we have seen, they can also become unusual simply with the addition of an unusual modifier, like *Trader Vic's* or *Aca Joe*.

As with surnames, anyone can use their first name or nickname on a business unless it's too close to a famous one. For example,

"Sony" Florendo can't call her restaurant Sony's, and Mayo Priebe can't call her drugstore Mayo's Drugs. Sony Corp. and the Mayo Clinic objected to these uses and won, even though there was little likelihood of confusion between the local businesses and their more famous namesakes. Perhaps the judge felt that these were really attempts to capitalize on the more famous trademarks or that the second uses diluted the original marks. (See Chapter 1, Section B4.) But one is tempted to conclude that the size and wealth of the complaining parties was a significant factor.

Initials. Use of initials won't change the strength or weakness of the trademark if they are part of what is essentially a first or last name. For example, the owners of *P.T. Dann's* (as a trademark for a national clothing chain) won't infringe on the rights of others using the Dann name. On the other hand, until the company develops a lot of public awareness of the name as a mark (that is, it acquires a secondary meaning), they probably can't stop anyone else from using the same or similar trademark, except in the retail apparel business. But if another Dann opened up competing clothing stores, even without secondary meaning, P.T. Dann could probably stop them under unfair competition laws, as well as under trademark laws, once secondary meaning is shown.

A trademark consisting completely of letters that aren't a person's initials is not inherently weak. Rather, its trademark strength depends on the strength of the words the initials represent. If the initials do not stand for anything and are an uncommon arrangement of letters, the mark can be distinctive from the outset.

For instance, ABC is not considered distinctive because this combination of letters is in such common use as a mark (except, of course, in the media world, where the network initials have secondary meaning). However, a mark consisting of *XQE* may be.

c. Marks That Describe Attributes of the Service or Product or Its Geographic Location

The main reason to avoid these marks is that they are legally weak and therefore not extensively protectible until they have been in use long enough that they have become easily recognized by your customers. However, many business owners believe that if they use some words in their trademark that either describe the type of business or some positive characteristic of the business, they will benefit far more by the marketing payoff than they risk from would-be copiers. (See Chapter 9, Evaluating Trademark Strength, for more on why these marks have such limited legal protectibility.)

d. Names With Bad Translations, or Unfortunate Homonyms (Sound-Alikes) or Unintended Connotations

These you should avoid because they can easily backfire as advertising tools. A famous example is the French soft drink called *Pschitt*, which had to be renamed for sale in this country. Also the Chevy *Nova* is an unwise trademark for a car in Spanish-speaking countries (including perhaps our own because of the high proportion of Spanish speakers) because the mark means "it does not run" in Spanish.

Be Careful About Deception When Using Geographic Marks

Earlier we warned about using deceptive or misleading marks. This warning is especially appropriate for geographic terms that are used fancifully. There are really two types of possible deception in the use of geographic marks:

- actual deception in which the customer is induced to buy a product in the belief that the item comes from the region on the label
- deceptive misdescription in which the public might make a false geographic connection but wouldn't particularly rely on the geographic factor in buying the service or product.

For instance, a deceptive trademark would be the mark *Limoges* for china that was neither made in France nor of French clay; or *American System*, for clothing made in Italy. A deceptive trademark is not protectible and can never become so even if it acquires secondary meaning. Further, using a deceptive mark may subject you to legal liability for false advertising.

On the other hand, using a mark like *Neapolitan* (especially with an Italian flag on the label) for Italian sausages made in Florida is seen as merely "deceptively misdescriptive."

That is, some people might be confused into thinking the sausages come from Naples, but that's either unlikely or not the main reason they would buy the sausages. Another example is calling a chewing tobacco *Durango* even though it is not from the noted tobacco growing region of Durango, Mexico. Such marks are not protectible until they have developed secondary meaning. Once the mark has secondary meaning, the potential for confusing the public is lessened, because presumably the public knows the product for what it is, and doesn't care where it comes from.

Obviously, the trademark implications of geographic terms can get a little muddy. We suggest this general rule: Don't use a geographical term, even if the place named has nothing to do with the origin of the product, as long as a reasonable consumer might think it does. If you decide that you absolutely have to use a geographic trademark, either make sure your mark has only a vague suggestive connection to your product or service (like *Sedona*, for a Portland, Maine, restaurant) or try combining it with other more inherently distinctive terms that make the trademark protectible from the outset, like *The Abilene Albatross* for a bar.

e. Names That Closely Resemble Well-Known Marks

If you definitely want to avoid being sued for trademark infringement, avoid using famous marks or obvious variations of them. Whether they succeed or not, claims of trademark infringement and dilution (a type of protection for well-known marks) are commonly brought by owners of famous marks in order to clear the field. McDonald's regularly sues companies that use the "Mc" prefix or yellow arches. Often they succeed—preventing the use of "*McSleep*" for motels and yellow arches for a computer company. (See Chapter 11, If Someone Infringes Your Mark.)

F. Marketing Considerations When Choosing a Name Mark

Now that we have dissected what makes a mark distinctive, here are a few practical pointers that combine the legal information just discussed with some marketing savvy that is part of picking the "right" name for your business, service, or product.

1. General Advice

George Eastman, founder of Kodak, and a man with an eye for a good trademark, suggested that trademarks should

- be short
- be vigorous
- be easily spelled, and
- mean nothing.

Though this advice certainly worked for him, it may not apply to your situation. If not,

heed the advice of other trademark experts who recommend that name marks be:

- pronounceable
- memorable
- graphically attractive (for instance, no hyphens), and
- legally available.

Chapters 4 and 5 explain how to find out whether your mark is legally available. Whether your mark meets the other criteria discussed in this section is a more subjective decision that you will have to make yourself. However, these lists of desirable trademark characteristics omit an important poin: Your mark must also be tailored to meet the needs of your business and your customers.

2. How to Come Up With a Good Name

Like most business decisions, your choice of how to select a good name mark will reflect your own personal style of decision making. Here are some alternative methods:

- Delegate the job to a committee.
- Throw a naming-brainstorming party and invite all your friends.
- Make lists yourself.
- Devise a contest to generate a name.
- Use all of the above methods.
- Hire a professional name consultant. (See Section 4, below, for more on this method.)

Whatever method you use, you will probably want to develop a long list and a short list. The long list would consist of likely possibilities that meet the criteria we discuss in Section 3, below, for tailoring your mark to your needs. Then you can use any of the above methods again to narrow the list to five or ten of the most likely.

When you have your short list, you must find out how to tell which of your trademark possibilities can also be used as an Internet domain name (Chapter 2), and then turn to Chapters 4 through 6 to discover which possibilities meet the all-important criterion of legal availability. Only when you have searched and cleared each name for possible conflicts with existing marks and Internet domain names (if you plan to use the Internet for marketing purposes) can you make a final decision based on aesthetics or marketability or whatever you decide is your ultimate criterion.

3. Useful Concepts in Creating a Name Mark for Your Product or Service

The most useful concepts in creating a name mark are the same ones you or your advertising consultant would think about in devising a marketing scheme. Your mark is, after all, the most important aspect of your advertising plan. What will help you invent your mark are basic commonsense conclusions about what kinds of advertising will work best with your product or service, based on what you know about your customers.

Use the following questions to develop criteria that are specific to your needs and that you can then use, along with the suggestions in Section 2, above, to develop a list of potential marks. If you already have developed these criteria, this section tells you how to

apply them to trademarks. And if you haven't, you might as well figure this stuff out now.

- What is your (projected) customer base? Is it a broad economic group, within a small region? Or is it a select group of professionals scattered nationwide? This is the most important factor, as it affects all of the other criteria below.

- What are your customers' demographics and income/educational level? This will tell you the tone and style of your advertising, as well as what sort of words to use in your mark—for example, whether to use words that are young and hip or older and more traditional, funny or serious, or highly literate or simple.

- What are your customers' buying habits? Are they typically made in a hurry or more carefully considered? If they tend to buy in a rushed manner, then your trademark needs to be simple with a high visual impact. If your customers tend to buy in a more considered manner, then your mark can be more subtle and complex.

- What aspect of your service/product will appeal to your potential customer base? This affects the image you want to project —if the main appeal of your service is convenience, then the trademark should somehow evoke that idea.

- Can you distill the essence of your product or service into a word or phrase? If there is a dominant idea connected with your service or product, then a mark that incorporates or reflects that idea will be easier for you to promote and for your customers to remember.

- What image do you want to associate with your service or product? If the image you have is not exactly the one you want, you can try to develop a mark that reflects better your vision of your service or product. A mark incorporating symbols popular with teenagers may not help you if you seek to appeal to stable young families.

- How is your service or product different from the competition's? Perhaps the main thing about your service or product is that it is unique—the mark should help identify that characteristic—or that it's cheaper, or fancier, or whatever sets you apart in the marketplace.

- How will the mark be advertised—in what media and with what level of visibility? This affects whether you need both a logo and a name, whether a short word is essential or a longer phrase will do, or whether you want to focus on trade dress (creative packaging, etc.). Also, how broadly and where you will advertise your mark—on business cards, letterhead, pamphlets, a storefront, signs, packaging, radio ads—affects what sort of mark to use. That's because a complicated logo may translate well to business cards, but you may not be able to see it clearly on a storefront.

The answers to some of these questions will also help you figure out what sources to use to create your mark, and what attributes the mark should have. For example, if your customer base is gourmet coffee drinkers, you could consider using foreign words, mythological names, or literary references in creating a mark that evokes sophistication/good taste. But if your customers comprise a broad section of the population whose main concerns are value and convenience, you might want a more straightforward simple name using American roots or references.

4. Using a Professional Name Consultant

Most name consulting firms cater to large corporations and are not likely to meet the needs or the budgets of small businesses. To find one that will help you on a smaller scale, take the advice of Ira Bachrach of Namelab, a corporate name consulting firm in San Francisco. He recommends calling a small- to medium-sized ad agency and asking them to help you create a name as a discrete, time-limited project for a fixed fee.

He advises you to specify what they are expected to produce for that fee, and to propose paying when you get the result, or paying half in advance, half at the end. Often, at ad agencies, creative people will have little gaps of free time in which they could work on your project. If you explain that you are not a potential client, they will treat you as a one-time project. Bachrach also says that he is often surprised at how many established agencies will sometimes help small businesses in naming their product or service.

A few well-established naming firms do routinely consult for smaller companies. One such is Name-It Creative Naming Company (www.nameit.com).

Where to Find More on Trademark Strength

Now that we have taken a closer look at what makes an effective trademark, you may want to go on to Chapter 9, Evaluating Trademark Strength. That chapter teaches you how to classify your (or another's) mark in terms of its legal strength. It discusses in much greater detail the varieties of distinctive and ordinary trademarks, including coined, fanciful, and suggestive categories of distinctive marks, and descriptive, geographic, personal name, and initial types of ordinary marks.

■

Chapter 4

Trademark Searches—What They Are and Why You Should Do One

*I*n this chapter we introduce you to the process of finding out whether your choice for a mark is already being used by someone else—a task commonly referred to as a trademark search. Then, in Chapter 5, we tell you how to do it. If your search turns up an existing mark that is the same or similar to your proposed mark, you will then want to proceed to Chapter 6, How to Evaluate the Results of Your Trademark Search, which helps you decide whether the existing mark legally conflicts with yours.

A. What Is a Trademark Search?

A trademark search is a systematic hunt for the existence of any registered or unregistered trademark or service mark that:

- is the same or similar to a mark proposed for use by the searcher
- is being used anywhere in the country (or world if the proposed mark is to be used internationally), and
- is being used in a context that would likely result in customer confusion if the proposed mark is put into use.

B. Why Do a Trademark Search?

There are two good reasons to search for potentially conflicting marks. If you are not the first user of the mark for the goods or services in the marketplace, you may have to change your mark and, in some cases, possibly pay damages to the first user if a judge concludes

that your use creates a likelihood of customer confusion. In addition, if you are planning to apply for federal registration of the mark, you will save time and money by discovering whether your proposed mark is already registered for similar goods and services.

C. What Resources Are Used in a Trademark Search?

A trademark search may involve some or all of these resources, depending on the scope of the search:

- **The federal trademark register:** a list of all trademarks and service marks that have been authorized for federal trademark registration
- **Pending trademark applications:** a list of all trademarks and service marks for which a federal registration application has been filed
- **State trademark registrations:** a list of all trademarks and service marks that have been registered at the state level (usually with a state's secretary of state)
- **Publications containing relevant product and service names:** trade magazines, print directories of commercial names, Yellow Pages, and electronic databases containing product and service names that are in use in the United States generally, or in respect to specific fields, for example, computers, biotechnology, or bicycles
- **The Internet:** domain names, Internet sites, and goods and services being offered on the Internet

D. Where Are Trademark Search Resources Located?

Many of the resources used in a typical trademark search are available online for free. Others are only available through proprietary databases that can be accessed directly or over the Internet by any member of the public who is willing to pay for the privilege. It is possible to do a free, reasonably competent trademark search by using workstations and print collections found in special public libraries known as Patent and Trademark Depository Libraries, or PTDLs. (See Section H, below, for more on doing a trademark search in a PTDL.)

1. Trademarks on the Federal Trademark Register and in Pending Applications

Perhaps, the most important resource for a trademark search is the list of federally registered trademarks called the federal trademark register. It is also important to search the list of trademarks awaiting registration. Applications typically take a year to make it into the Federal Register. Although the federal trademark register obviously doesn't include nonfederally registered trademarks—which may cause trouble down the road if you don't know about them in advance—a search of the federal trademark register and pending applications is a necessary first step.

There are a number of different ways that the public can search the federal trademark register and its accompanying list of pending applications. Most important, the United States Patent and Trademark Office has put its own

trademark database (called TESS, for Trademark Electronic Search Service) on its website (www.uspto.gov), which can be searched for free. Another Internet resource, SAEGIS by Thomson & Thomson (www.saegis.com), involves some fees and a considerable learning curve. However, its search engine is better suited to what we later refer to as an analytical search. Our recommendation is that you first use TESS to search the federal trademark register for marks that are the same as or very similar to yours. Later, you may want to spend the money and time to run your proposed mark through the SAEGIS search engine.

2. Trademarks Registered With State Agencies

Many trademark owners who use their trademark solely within a particular state register the mark with that state's trademark agency. Because such a registration might block the use of a later proposed mark within that state, the owner of the proposed mark will often search for instances of state registration. You can do this yourself by using the TrademarkScan State Database, available through SAEGIS, or by calling the secretary of state's offices for the states you are interested in. (For a list of state trademark agencies and statutes, access the state trademark links at www.ggmark.com.)

3. Unregistered Trademarks and Service Marks

Because trademark ownership is based on who uses the mark first, it is important to search for marks in actual use if you wish to avoid a conflict somewhere down the line. To do this, you must hunt for the use of your proposed mark (or something very similar) on products and services that are similar to the products or services you plan to use the mark with. While this hunt will undoubtedly produce many marks that appear on the federal trademark register, it will also turn up marks that don't.

There are several approaches to performing this type of search (called a "common law search" because the importance of unregistered marks stems from court decisions, which are called the common law):

- Use an Internet search engine such as Google (www.google.com) to search for use of your proposed mark on the Internet and as a domain name.
- Use SAEGIS at (www.saegis.com) to search its common law database on the Internet and all domain name registries for a modest fee.
- Use SuperPages at (www.SuperPages.com) or the Thomas Register of Products and Services at (www.thomasregister.com) to search for trade and corporate names for free on the Internet.
- Use print resources in a PTDL or a large public library that contain listings of product and service names.
- Use DIALOG (www.dialog.com) to access a number of databases listing product and service names in use around the country (this service can be costly, and a learning curve is involved).

E. Different Levels of Trademark Searches—What They Are; When They're Appropriate

In Section A we defined a trademark search in its broadest sense. In fact, there are three different levels of trademark searching:

- direct hit searching
- analytical searching, and
- comprehensive searching.

1. Direct Hit Searches

This type of search looks for marks on the federal trademark register that are the same as or very similar to the mark you propose to use. It is, in essence, the starting place for any trademark search. Its essential purpose is to get a quick fix on the marks that are most likely to cause your proposed mark trouble in the future. If you adopt and use a mark that clearly conflicts with one already on the Federal Register, whether or not you actually know of it, you will be considered a willful infringer of that mark and may be sued for substantial money damages. The obviousness of your infringement will greatly reduce your ability to negotiate an acceptable settlement with the existing mark's owner. A direct hit search prevents this sort of difficulty.

In addition, a direct hit search tells you whether it's worthwhile applying for a federal trademark registration. Your trademark won't qualify for placement on the Federal Register if the PTO thinks customers are likely to confuse it with a mark already on the register. (See Chapter 7, Federal Trademark Registration.) This means that a direct hit search can potentially expose marks that may conflict with yours and tell you whether or not an examiner is likely to approve your application.

A direct hit search will tell you if your proposed mark has been registered for so many goods or services within the same class or classes as your mark that it would receive little protection under the federal trademark laws. You may want to use the mark anyway, but at least you'll have a better idea of its relative strength. (See Chapter 9, Evaluating Trademark Strength, for what makes a mark legally weak.)

Practically speaking, a direct hit search is especially helpful when you have several choices of potential trademarks and you wish to narrow the field by eliminating obviously unavailable marks.

Direct hit searches are quick and easy to do. All it takes is to enter your mark into the search box in the PTO's TESS database and see what comes up. In addition, you can browse the registered marks that alphabetically come before and after your proposed name. (We tell you how to do all this in Chapter 5, How to Do Your Own Trademark Search.) By using TESS you will save approximately $30–$50 per mark searched, the amount it typically costs to get a direct hit search from a professional search service.

2. Analytical Searches—Going Beyond a Direct Hit Search

For most businesses, especially those that plan to operate regionally or nationally, direct hit searching is only the first step to clearing a name. Especially if the proposed name is distinctive, a more thorough search will be in order. However, if you already know that your proposed name is legally weak, or your business is small and local and you can tolerate some risk that an undiscovered prior user will pop up at a later time, the direct hit search is really all the searching for registered marks that you'll need to do.

Depending on the type and complexity of your mark, the analytical search compares your mark with all federally registered and pending marks that sound or look like your mark, plus all marks that mean the same or in some other way might lead to customer confusion between them and your mark. It frequently involves searching for homonyms, synonyms, phonetic equivalents, alternative spellings, anagrams (words with the same letters rearranged), marks with similar components, and marks that start or end the same, or that have any other similarity. This type of search is more thorough, or "deeper," than a direct hit search, and consequently more expensive and time-consuming. However, it permits you to uncover more potential conflicts.

For example, an analytical search for the mark *Bioscan* might reasonably include a look at all the marks that immediately surround *Bioscan* alphabetically, and then look up all Bio marks, then all -scan marks, then all marks with the sounds -io or -osc in the middle. Next you would search for all synonyms you could think of. Then you might want to check for anagrams (scaniob), and alternative spellings (bayou-, -skan). This degree of complexity might not be called for in the case of a more straightforward mark, such as *Fish Head Graphics*.

An analytical search is essential for any business that wants to make sure its proposed mark isn't likely to be challenged on the grounds it is confusingly similar to, or evocative of, an existing federally registered mark. For instance, assume the manufacturer of certain gas barbecue components wants to use the mark *Flamethrower*. Because the components will all be stamped with this mark, the manufacturer wants to make sure that no existing mark has priority. To do this, an analytical search would look for all marks with the word "flame," all marks with the word "thrower," and all marks with words that sound like or mean the same thing as either of these.

It is especially wise to do this level of search if your prospective mark is distinctive. Because a distinctive mark can be protected to a much greater degree than a mark that lacks distinctiveness, it's worth making sure the distinctive mark is clear of all conflicts. For instance, the maker of *Raintree* Shampoos would want to do an analytical search before marketing their product regionally, as would the operator of an 800-number information service that had a distinctive name. For companies that expect to expand their use of a particular mark in the future, an analytical search reduces the likelihood of eventual problems due to customer confusion caused by marks that are not identical but are reminiscent of each other.

The PTO's TESS database is ideal for doing analytical searches. However, doing a competent analytical search involves a moderate learning curve. (We give you the basics in Chapter 5, How to Do Your Own Trademark Search.) TESS provides good online help, but you should plan on spending at least half an hour familiarizing yourself with the system before launching a search. By using TESS you will save approximately $100 per mark searched, the amount it typically costs to get an analytical search from a professional search service.

In some ways the SAEGIS search engine (which uses the proprietary TrademarkScan database) is even better than TESS in that it automatically provides an analytical search. However, it takes some time to learn how to use SAEGIS and may end up costing you as much as a professional search service. Of course, the better you get at doing a SAEGIS search, the more efficient your search will be and the less it will cost you. (We provide some tips on using SAEGIS in Chapter 5, How to Do Your Own Trademark Search.)

3. Comprehensive Trademark Searches

A comprehensive trademark search includes both direct hit and analytical searches of the federal trademark register and examines other resources where unregistered marks and state registered marks might be found, such as proprietary online databases, hardcopy and electronic telephone directories (Yellow Pages), trade directories, the Internet, product catalogues, business ratings services, and so on. The goal is to discover any actual use of your proposed mark, whether or not it is officially registered. As mentioned, the reason for this is that most disputes between marks are resolved in favor of the first user.

For local businesses, a comprehensive search should, at a minimum, consist of checking the relevant Yellow Pages, newspapers, trade and product journals, and any other resource that might show a possibly conflicting locally used mark. For businesses that have broader horizons in mind, including Internet start-ups and e-commerce enterprises, this type of search can involve many different hard copy and online resources and can therefore become costly.

So far we have suggested that you can do direct hit and analytical searches yourself. The same is true with comprehensive searching. The Internet, print resources in the major libraries, and collections in many PTDLs all provide ways to systematically search for unregistered marks that are in actual use in commerce. However, there is no current way of searching state registered trademark databases on the Internet unless you are willing to pay a fee to use TrademarkScan, available through SAEGIS. If you are planning on sinking a lot of money into your new business or website that will carry your proposed mark, and your mark is inherently distinctive, you might do well to hire a professional search service to cover all the bases for you. Comprehensive searches run between $200 and $500 per mark searched.

Because of this price tag, you can save yourself a lot of money by using the direct hit and analytical search techniques as a screening mechanism. That is, once you decide to spring for a comprehensive search, you should first assure yourself that your proposed mark does not legally conflict with registered or pending marks on the federal or state trademark registers. This will prevent you from paying for a comprehensive search for a mark that you most likely would decide not to use.

F. Planning Your Trademark Search

Now that you have a good idea of what is involved in a trademark search, you need to decide on the appropriate search for you and your particular situation.

1. The Trademark Uncertainty Principle

Let us start by saying that if time and money are no problem, you will be well advised to do a comprehensive trademark search for every mark you plan to use. You can only gain from being as careful and conscientious about clearing your mark as possible. But two warnings apply here:

a. Your Results Will Be Incomplete No Matter How Thorough Your Search

No search is going to uncover every possible conflict in the United States and certainly not internationally. It's just too difficult to know if there's a prior unregistered user of a similar mark in North Noluk when you are in South Sunstroke. The best you can do is to make sure that your proposed mark doesn't obviously conflict either with registered marks or with any unregistered marks you can find by systematically examining pertinent sources of trademarks, service marks, or trade names.

This means no matter how thoroughly you search, you will have to live with a small degree of uncertainty that someone else began using your mark first. What does it mean, legally, if they did? Nothing, if the other user doesn't object. Even if they do object, and sue you in court to force you to stop using the mark, you probably would be allowed to continue to use the mark in your present marketing territory (unless both marks are used to market related or competing goods or services on the Internet). However, you may be prevented from acquiring the nationwide exclusive rights to your mark that otherwise would be available to you by being the first to register it. (See Chapter 10, Sorting Out Trademark Disputes, for a discussion of priorities among trademark users.)

b. Your Search Results Will Be Legally Uncertain

As you are undoubtedly tired of hearing by now, there are no absolute answers in trademark law. Even the most extensive search will probably not end your uncertainty, because it will likely uncover at least some somewhat similar marks used on products that are at least vaguely related to yours. Whether such a trademark definitively infringes on another is a decision that only a judge or jury can make when the dispute is brought before them. In other words, it's only after you have been sued and a ruling has been made that you will know with some certainty (every case can be appealed) whether your mark infringes. In many real-world situations, you can be

sure that the other user is unlikely to sue. But a thorough search will give you as much assurance as possible under the circumstances.

2. Planning the Scope of Your Search

Since the best you can do is weigh factors and estimate probabilities, it's important for you to decide what level of risk is acceptable to you now. That way you can tailor your search to minimize the risk in line with your decision. Below we set out some general rules to follow when planning the scope of your trademark search.

There are six basic rules that apply to all trademark searches:

Rule 1: Always check the Federal Register for a direct hit

All searches should check the federal trademark register first for the same or very similar mark as the one you propose to use. As mentioned, it is relatively easy to do, it's free, and it is the best way to uncover conflicts that necessarily require you to pick another mark.

Rule 2: A big advertising budget warrants a more extensive search

Because comprehensive searches—full analytical and common law searches—can cost time and money, it may not make sense for a small business to check for every possible conflict. Whether or not you should depends on the size of your business, your future goals, your mark, and how you plan to use it. A good general rule is that if you plan to spend a fair proportion of your budget on promoting your mark, you should first spend whatever it takes (perhaps hundreds of dollars) making sure the name is safe for you to use. Otherwise you risk wasting your advertising dollars if you have to change the mark later. On the other hand, if your advertising budget is small, it may make more sense to accept a more limited search as sufficient.

Rule 3: A strong mark requires a thorough search

How extensive a search is appropriate for you will depend on how much protection you need or can get for your mark. With a strong mark, there is more to protect, and a thorough search process is a better investment than in the case of a weak mark, where the extent of your rights is likely to be more limited anyway. The more distinctive, and therefore the stronger, the mark, the greater degree of assurance you need that no one else is using a similar mark elsewhere. If you have a strong mark and your goal is to be able to use your mark exclusively regionally, nationwide, or even worldwide, that will entail thorough direct hit, analytical, and common law searches.

One important reason you need a comprehensive search to protect a proposed strong mark is that the existence of similar marks may prove that your chosen mark is not as strong as you originally thought. Remember that marks are distinctive either because they are inherently memorable (fanciful, suggestive, or coined), or because they become well known to the public through widespread use over time. If existing marks sound or mean the same thing as your proposed mark, or look like it while sounding different, or have elements in common with it, your proposed

mark may not be as legally strong as you had hoped.

You want to be sure not to evoke unintended connotations because of a likeness to another mark in an unrelated field. For example, a sports fishing manufacturer would want to avoid the mark *National Harpoon*, because it evokes *National Lampoon*, the mark of a business specializing in satire. You can't avoid such unintended effects unless you uncover them through a deep search.

Rule 4: Think long term

In determining your trademark search goals, consider the future. For example, if your local engineering consulting service is limited to one city now, but there is a possibility you'll want to expand later—perhaps through the Internet or franchising—you'll want to conduct a more extensive search than might otherwise be appropriate for a firm of your current size. Rather than facing the possibility of having to change your mark later, you should conduct your trademark searches with those long-term goals in mind. This involves doing both direct hit and analytical trademark searches, as well as thorough common law searches. By contrast, if you run a local hobby or kitchenware shop and plan to stay small, a direct hit search coupled with a local or statewide common law search should prove sufficient (unless, again, you plan to market on the Web).

Rule 5: Geographic scope of the use affects the size of the search

As we said before, where you will use your mark will determine what kind of a search you need to perform. This makes each case a fact-specific determination. Nevertheless, the following general guides are reliable:

- **For a mark used only in one region of one state, and for which there is no expectation of expansion:** Generally speaking, the smaller the geographic area in which you market your goods or services, the less extensive the search needs to be. If you check federal and state registered trademarks for direct hits and then do a thorough common law search for your area and type of business, you should be relatively well protected. That's because if another similar mark is not registered federally or with the state, and is not in use in your geographic area or line of business, you will not likely cause customer confusion. The only potential concern you may have is dilution, and if the other mark is not famous enough for you to run across it through these searches, then it is not famous enough to get relief under the theory of dilution.

- **For a mark in use in two or more states:** Suppose you are clearing a mark for your new computer program, gardening supply catalog, or 800-number phone service. You can only clear such a mark with a comprehensive search. That ideally should include federal and state analytical searches and a thorough common law search. This more extensive search is necessary because other businesses may have rights through registration in marks that are not yet being used in your particular region. In addition, because

such marks are marketed nationally, they will face a greater array of potentially conflicting marks and thus the greater potential for infringement claims. Thus, a more thorough search is necessary to clear them.

Remember that the Internet is rapidly eliminating the very concept of local marketing territories, and if you expect to do business on the Web some day, you'll want to do your search just as if you planned to do business on a national level.

Rule 6: Marketing channels affect the size of the search

- **For a mark used in a narrow niche of the market:** It may be cleared with a search that is limited to direct hits on similar names used on related and competing goods. That's because with a narrow circle of competitors and limited marketing avenues, you can minimize the chances of a confusingly similar mark hurting your sales by looking only at similar marks in the same market. For example, a mark used only on industrial ball bearings probably need only clear conflicts within industries related to machinery and steel, along with the recommended direct hit search of the federal trademark register.

- **For a mark used by one owner on a wide variety of goods or services:** If you plan to use one mark on several different services or products, then you must be careful to find all other marks that are even vaguely similar. That's because your investment in such a mark will be high, and because you will need to be sure it evokes no other connection other than to your business. For example, if you intended to develop a mark for use on clothes, shoes, luggage, jewelry, and cosmetics, you would conduct the most thorough search possible.

G. Using a Professional Search Service

Before you decide whether to do your searching or farm it out, let us suggest that a combination of approaches may give you the best legal protection for your time and money. For example, using your computer to access the TESS database on the trademark section of the PTO's Internet site (www.uspto.gov) can be quick, easy, and provide good preliminary information. And if you are willing to pay the fees and spend the time learning the system, SAEGIS gives you access to the state trademark databases and a good search of the Internet and domain name registries. But unless you have the opportunity to practice, you probably should not attempt a comprehensive search on your own. For that you should pay someone who knows what they're doing. In Appendix C, we provide portions of a comprehensive search that Nolo commissioned from a professional search service in 2003. Feel free to take a look, but don't get stuck there. The example assumes that you are familiar with the material in this chapter and Chapter 5.

1. Why Use a Search Service?

Next to hiring a trademark attorney, paying a trademark search firm is the most expensive means of clearing your mark. However, except for a direct hit search—which you can reliably do yourself—a search service is likely to provide more reliable results than you will produce on your own. There are several reasons for this. Most important, analytical and comprehensive searches come with a considerable learning curve, regardless of which database or resources are being used. Searching for possible conflicts is a kind of art form that involves a lot more than typing in a word or phrase and asking whether it appears on the source being searched. An additional benefit is that search services have access to databases that are not yet available to the public for free, such as proprietary databases used in doing common law searching.

2. What Trademark Search Services Cost

The services provided by various trademark search firms, and the fees they charge for different types of searches, vary considerably. Often the cost of the service will depend on how much massaging of the information is done before it is delivered to you. Generally, the more raw the data you receive, the cheaper it will be. Only attorneys are allowed to offer opinions about potential trademark conflicts, and as a result, trademark search services offered by attorneys tend to cost the most because they come with legal advice.

The Role of Attorneys in Trademark Searches

If you decide to hire a trademark attorney to advise you on the choice and registration of a trademark or service mark, the attorney will be able to arrange for the trademark search. Some attorneys do it themselves, but most farm the search out to a search firm, the same as they've always done. Once the report comes back from the search firm, the attorney will interpret it for you and advise you on whether to go ahead with your proposed mark. Although you are getting considerably more in this attorney package than you'll get from a search service, it will cost you.

What do search services charge? Firms that search (but do not give legal advice) generally charge as follows:

- direct hit search (for identical marks)—from $30 to $100 per mark searched
- analytical federally registered trademark search (for similar or related marks)—from $85 to $300 per mark searched
- common law search only—from $100 to $200 per mark searched
- comprehensive search (combining analytical federal, state, common law, and domain names)—between $185 and $500 per mark searched.

The difference in rates may reflect variations in the coverage of the search, the sort of report you get, the experience of the searchers, or simply economies of scale. On the other hand, some firms may advertise an unusually low price to draw in customers, but then add on charges that end up exceeding another firm's total price (a professional version of bait-and-switch). For example, does one fee cover the whole cost, or is there also a per-page charge for the report? Obviously, to sensibly shop you need to know the total cost of each service.

3. How to Find and Use a Trademark Search Service

There are many trademark search services in the country. Because trademark searching is a purely information-based business, you don't have to worry about where a particular service is located. Telephone, fax, and email make it possible for a customer in Bangor, Maine, to comfortably deal with a service in California, Texas, or Virginia. With this in mind, we have decided to feature only three trademark search services in this section:

- The Sunnyvale Center on Innovation, Invention and Ideas (Sc[i]3)
- Trademark Express, and
- Thomson Compumark.

Trademark search firms will not interpret their search results; that task is left to you. In Chapter 6, How to Evaluate the Results of Your Trademark Search, we take you step by step through a sample search report.

By featuring these search services, we don't guarantee their results or vouch for the quality of their services. Rather, we intend them as examples of what search services cost and the types of services they provide. And all are completely accessible by fax, phone, and email.

If you don't like doing business at a distance, you can find trademark search services in your area by looking in the Yellow Pages of the nearest good-sized city under trademark consultants or information brokers. If that yields nothing, consult a legal journal or magazine for your area. You'll find the ads of a number of trademark search firms. Though these are aimed at lawyers, many of these companies will also do searches for individuals and businesses. Finally, if you are connected to the Internet, you can find a good list of trademark search firms at www.ggmark.com.

Beware of Aggressive Marketing Techniques

Some trademark search services will try to convince you that you are stupid if you don't search every corner of the globe for possible conflicts. Before taking the bait, review our remarks in Section E, above, about the different levels of searching, and make an independent decision about what scope of search is appropriate for you. Also, some search services provide additional services—such as the preparation of applications for federal and state trademark registrations. As with trademark lawyers, these businesses have a vested interest in convincing you that you will be better served by paying them to handle the tasks in question than by doing them yourself. If you feel that this point of view—which may in some cases be perfectly reasonable—is being too aggressively pushed in your situation, get a firm hold on your wallet and consider finding another service.

a. Using Sc[i]3 to Do Your Trademark Search

The Sunnyvale Center on Innovation, Invention and Ideas ((Sc[i]3) pronounced Sigh-Cubed) (www.sci3.com) is one of two Patent and Trademark Depository Libraries—the other being in Detroit—that have formed partnerships with the U.S. Patent and Trademark Office. Under this partnership, Sc[i]3 is encouraged to offer a variety of information services—including trademark searches—for very reasonable fees.

For example, as of May 2005, a comprehensive trademark search (including federal, state, and common law sources) was $199. The library will perform partial searches for less money at hourly rates. Check the Sc[i]3 website for current pricing or call 408-730-7300.

Also, the library can do partial searches for less money than the $199 comprehensive search (for example, just state or just common law).

b. Trademark Express

Trademark Express (www.tmexpress.com) is a private company that, in addition to other trademark-related services, offers a full choice of trademark searches. Trademark Express pricing is reasonable, though slightly higher than Sc[i]3—for example, as of May 2005, a Trademark Express search of federal and state marks (not common law) was $250. The company can also do international and domain name searching. For more information on rates, check the Trademark Express website.

⚠️ **We Make No Guarantees.** We are listing Trademark Express only for the purpose of using its trademark search service as an example of what you can find. We do not intend to guarantee the results of any particular search or make any representation as to the quality of its services. Further, as we are only concerned with trademark searching in this chapter, we make no representations—and provide no information—about any additional services offered by Trademark Express.

c. Thomson Compumark

Thomson Compumark (www.thomson-thomson.com) is the trademark search service of choice for the legal professional. As with the other services they vary their rates depending on the type of search and how soon you need the results. Pricing is hard to locate at the Thomson Compumark website, so for current rates, you may find it easier to telephone the company at 800-692-8833 or email them at support@t-t.com.

H. Using a Patent and Trademark Depository Library to Do Your Own Search

Using a Patent and Trademark Depository Library (PTDL) to do your federal trademark search involves less cash outlay than hiring a search service, but it will cost you in time and transportation expenses unless you live or work close to one. Most PTDLs offer free access to the CASSIS CD-ROM. The CASSIS trademark list is a good way to search for a

direct hit. It is possible to use CASSIS to do an analytical trademark search, but the results are not likely to be as reliable as would be the case if the TESS database were used.

If you are computer-challenged, or the wait to use the PTDL CASSIS workstation is too long for comfort, every PTDL has print materials that let you search the federal registered trademark database.

Whether or not the use of a PTDL is cost-effective for you will depend on such factors as:

- how many potential marks you wish to search for
- how far you are from the nearest PTDL
- whether you can free up the time to visit a PTDL during regular working hours, and
- the time it takes you to learn the CASSIS system (library staff will provide help).

For those of you who opt to visit a PTDL, see Chapter 5, How to Do Your Own Trademark Search, which explains how to conduct a PTDL trademark search.

A list of the PTDLs can be found at the PTO website.

By now you should have a good idea of what is involved in a trademark search, and have made some decisions about what sort of search you want to undertake, what source of information you want to use, and whether you want to do the search yourself or have someone do it for you. If so, you are ready to go on to Chapter 5, How to Do Your Own Trademark Search.

I. Does Your Failure to Search Mean You Acted in Bad Faith?

In 1998, designer Tommy Hilfiger was found to have acted in bad faith when adopting the mark "Star Class" for nautical sportswear. (*SCYRA v. Tommy Hilfiger, U.S.A., Inc.*, 80 F.3d 749 (2d Cir. 1996).) Mr. Hilfiger's attorney performed a search of federally registered marks and found no conflicts, but Mr. Hilfiger disregarded his attorney's advice to obtain a complete trademark search for state and common law trademarks, which would have revealed an unregistered trademark for "Star Class" owned by an international yachting organization. The court ruled Mr. Hilfiger should have been aware of the need for a full search since "Star Class" was a common term in yachting. As a result, Mr. Hilfiger was assessed special damages for acting in bad faith. In other words, Mr. Hilfiger had to pay more than usual for infringing a trademark because of his failure to search.

In a subsequent case, a map company adopted the mark *Streetsmart*, without conducting a formal trademark search. A court of appeals ruled this was not bad faith because the company had not disregarded its attorney's advice, had previously used similar marks with the prefix "smart," and was aware of the conflicting mark, *Streetwise*, but believed the two terms were not confusing. (*Streetwise Maps, Inc. v. Vandam, Inc.* 159 F.3d 739; 1998 (2d Cir. 1998).)

In another case, a court summarized the standard by stating that a failure to search equals bad faith only if:

- the trademark owner had reason to believe it was infringing another mark or
- its attorney advised it to perform a more complete search. ∎

Chapter 5

How to Do Your Own Trademark Search

Searching for registered or pending trademarks on your own by using the PTO's online search system is easy. A typical direct hit search takes only about 15 minutes. An analytical search using TESS takes longer but still can be accomplished in well under an hour once you have learned the basics. And if you learn to use SAEGIS, an analytical search will be even faster but will involve costs that depend on the number of search results you wish to review (usually, $2.50 per mark displayed). For either system, you can make best use of your time by downloading the PTO's help file and studying it before starting your search.

Both the PTO and SAEGIS searches allow you to compare your proposed mark with registered trademarks and trademarks that are pending registration with the PTO. The results you come up with will include a list of the trademarks that meet your search parameters, and the names, addresses, and contact information for the owners of those trademarks. You'll also learn how the trademark is being used (on what products or for what services) and what international class (category of goods or services) the mark has been assigned to by the trademark owner or applicant. This information is key in deciding whether you can go ahead and use the name without creating the likelihood of customer confusion. (See Chapter 6 for more on evaluating the results of your trademark search and Chapter 4 for a basic understanding of available trademark search resources and trademark searching in general.)

A. Meet TESS—The Trademark Electronic Search System

TESS is an acronym for Trademark Electronic Search System, the search system that the PTO has made available to the public for free on the PTO's website. It is about as good a system as you can find anywhere and is roughly equivalent to the PTO's internal trademark search system known as X-Search. It's updated every day, has enormous flexibility in terms of the type of search that may be performed, and all in all is a most valuable gift from the federal government. TESS comes with its own comprehensive help file, and if you are doing your own trademark search, you will be wise to study it before beginning your search.

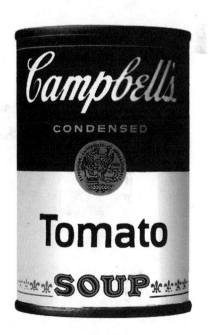

The PTO's Four Ts: TESS, TEAS, TARR, & TDR

THE PTO provides four powerful databases at its PTO site, TESS, TEAS, TARR, and TDR. These databases are distinguished as follows:

TESS (Trademark Electronic Search System). Use TESS when searching through federal trademark registrations and prior-filed applications.

TEAS (Trademark Electronic Application System). Use TEAS when applying for a trademark, collective mark, certification mark, filing a Statement of Use/Amendment to Allege Use, or other application and post-registration forms.

TARR (Trademark Application and Registration Retrieval). Use TARR when you want to retrieve information about the status of your application (or other applications) or the status of registered marks.

TDR (Trademark Document Retrieval) is the newest addition to the USPTO online services. Debuting in 2005, TDR offers the public an advanced electronic portal to PDF viewing, downloading, and printing of an array of information and documents for more than 460,000 trademark applications totaling more than eight million document pages. For example, copies of applications, assignments, and oppositions will all be available. As new applications are filed, they will be added to the database. It is expected that more than 300,000 application files will be added annually. Over the next five years, the remaining paper files of approximately 1.2 million active trademark registrations will be converted into digital format for TDR access.

B. Getting Started With TESS

The first step is to go to the PTO's website (www.uspto.gov). Click Search Trademarks on the bottom right of the screen. You'll encounter the page set out below.

1. Choose the Type of Search

TESS offers four basic approaches to searching:
- New User Form Search (Basic)
- Structured Form Search (Boolean)
- Free Form Search (Advanced Search), and
- Browse Dictionary (View Indexes).

The New User Form Search and Structured Form Search are similar. The main difference is that the Structured Search allows for a more flexible search. In this chapter we take you through the Structured Search, but by all means use the New User search if you want less of a learning curve. As you become more skilled at using TESS, you may want the greater flexibility offered with the Free Form Search. (For more on the Free Form Search, see Section F below.) Regardless of which of the first three approaches you take, you'll also want to do a quick browse through the dictionary.

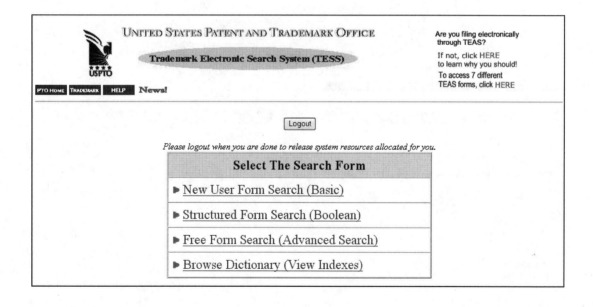

2. Browse the Dictionary

The dictionary is an alphabetical listing of all the marks that appear in the TESS database. Assume that you wish to search for the mark "Domain Name King." Simply click the "Browse Dictionary" link and enter the name "domainnameking" as one word in the search box. Click the browse button, and you'll see the page set out below.

By obtaining a listing of marks that alphabetically precede and follow the name you're searching, you can get a quick overview of marks that are alphabetically close to yours.

Sometimes you will encounter a list of marks in the dictionary that starts with the full word and then shows the same word several times with a decreasing number of letters at the end. For example, browsing for the word "domain" also shows domainalyzer, domainalyzer*, domainalyze*, Domainalyz*, and domainaly*. The terms with the asterisk in this example are not registered marks but rather are roots of the term "domainalyzer" and show up in the index for search purposes only. Terms with asterisks that follow a term without an asterisk may safely be ignored.

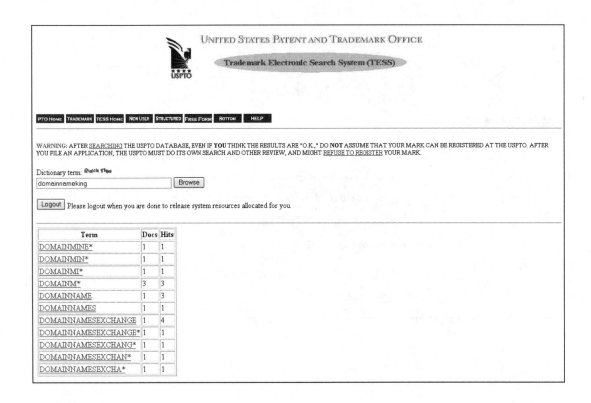

C. Understanding the TESS Structured Form Search

First let's look at the Structured Form Search page (below).

1. Search History

The first active link is titled View Search History and is designed to keep track of your searches so you can easily go back over ground that you covered before. Each previous query is identified with a number, as in s1, s2, and so on. You can reproduce the search by simply entering the search number into the first

Search Term box. But beware. The system will kick you off after 15 minutes of inaction, and when you are kicked off, your Search History goes away. Unfortunately, you cannot save your Search History from one session to another.

2. Records Returned

This drop-down menu gives you the option of returning 50, 100, or 200 records as a result of your search. The default is 100, and there is little reason to change it unless your search results indicated a larger number of records meet your search specifications.

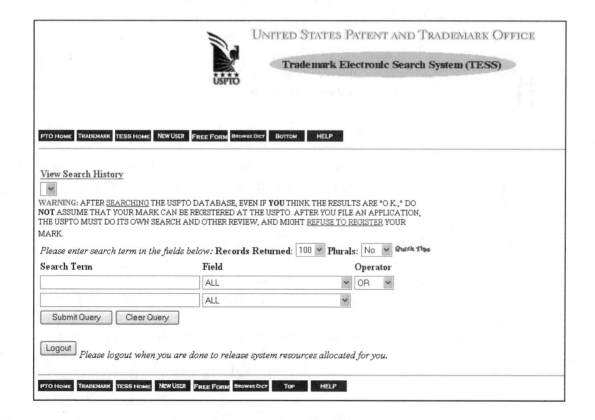

3. Plural

This drop-down menu allows you to automatically retrieve the plural as well as singular forms of words that you enter into the Search Terms boxes. The default choice is no, but most searchers will want to change this to yes unless using the truncation feature. (See Section D5 below for more on truncations.)

4. Search Terms

The Structured Form Search lets you search for one or two terms. The terms can be individual words, or they can be phrases. You may only need to search for one term. For instance, if your proposed mark is *Mandalay*, initially to be used with your famous lemon pies, you might want to search only for the word "Mandalay," the distinctive element of your name. If so, you would enter that word in the top search box and then click "Submit Query." Or, if you want to see if there are any marks containing the phrase "lemon pie" in connection with Mandalay, you could enter "lemon pie" surrounded by quotation marks in the top search box and Mandalay in the bottom box. (See Section C6 below for how to use the Operator feature.)

Incidentally, because you might want to expand the use of *Mandalay* to other types of pies or baked goods, the most appropriate search in this context would be *Mandalay* in class 30 (baked goods). (See Chapter 6, How to Evaluate the Results of Your Trademark Search, for more on the trademark classification system.)

5. Field

This drop-down menu lets you specify which specific fields of the TESS database records you want to search. Every trademark record has a number of fields, including the trademark's owner, its registration date, its registration number, the description of goods or services that the mark is used to market, and the classification assigned to the mark by the PTO. If you want to focus on records that show your search terms in the marks themselves, then you should choose the Basic Index field. However, if you wish to produce every record that contains your search terms regardless of which field they occur in, select the "all" fields option.

If you are searching for two terms, you can choose separate fields for each term. For instance, you might want to use the Description of Mark field for the term in the top box and the Basic Index field for the term in the lower box.

6. Logical Operators

If you enter terms in both the top and bottom Search Term boxes, you'll need to pick what's called an "operator" to connect them. You can use the drop-down menu to choose among the available operators.

a. The AND Operator

If you select AND from the pull-down menu of operators, you are telling TESS to pull up all trademark records that contain both of the search terms entered in the search term boxes. For example, the search query "mandalay AND lemon pie" will produce every record that contains both "mandalay" and "lemon pie." It will not produce a record that doesn't have both. The advantage of using AND is that you can narrow your search to only those marks that have both terms. The disadvantage to AND is that you won't get any marks that don't have both terms as you have entered them in the Search Term box, which means you might miss marks that you should know about. For example, if you require the search results to contain both "mandalay" and "lemon pie," you would miss all marks that contain "mandalay" but not "lemon pie" and likewise all marks that contain "lemon pie," but not "mandalay."

b. The OR Operator

If you enter these same search terms but select the OR operator—making your query "mandalay OR lemon pie"—your search will produce a list of all trademarks with the term "lemon pie," all trademarks with the term "mandalay," and all trademarks with both terms. Needless to say, that list would be very long, because so many trademarks are likely to have either term in them.

However, this approach can be very useful if your proposed mark contains two distinctive words and you want to review every trademark that has either word. For instance, suppose you're considering the mark *AnalogAstromaps* for a website featuring a series of star charts. You would most likely want to use the OR operator to search for any trademarks containing either "analog" or "astromaps." Any trademark with either term might knock out your proposed mark if the context showed a likelihood of customer confusion.

Although the OR operator has the advantage of inclusiveness—that is, you are less likely to miss a relevant mark than when you are using the AND operator—it can have the disadvantage of producing much too long a list of marks to intelligently assess. The more common the terms being searched, the greater the risk of an unwieldy list of results. Probably the best approach is to initially use the OR operator and see what turns up. If the resulting list is too long, you can retreat to the more restrictive AND operator.

c. The NOT Operator

A third operator—NOT—can be used to exclude from the search results any term you enter in the lower Search Term box. For instance, you may decide that you want to see every trademark with the term "astromap" but no trademark with the term "starchart." This search query would look like this: astromap NOT starchart.

d. The XOR Operator

A fourth operator—XOR—lets you search for any trademark that has either the first Search Term or the second Search Term, but not both. For example, if you searched for "analog XOR astromap," your search would turn up trademarks with either "analog" or "astromap," but not trademarks that contain both terms. There is seldom a reason to exclude a combination of two terms.

e. Additional Operators

TESS also provides additional operators that are most appropriate for searching fields in the trademark records that contain whole sentences or paragraphs. For instance, you can specify that the two terms you enter in the boxes be in the same sentence (WITH) or paragraph (SAME), or within a certain proximity of each other (for instance, within two words of each other in any order (NEAR), or in the order specified (ADJ). You will find these operators most helpful if you want to search the "Goods and Services" or "Description of Mark" fields. For most trademark searching purposes, however, the AND, OR, and NOT operators should be sufficient.

D. Tips on Using the TESS Structured Form Search

As mentioned, TESS provides help for each aspect of the Structured Form Search. However, there is always room for improvement. The tips we outline here are specifically intended for basic trademark searching. As you get more familiar with TESS, you should feel free to experiment with the many options it offers.

1. Focus on the Most Distinctive Part of the Mark You're Searching

You should focus on the part of your mark that is most distinctive because it is that part of your mark that would most likely cause customers to confuse your name with an existing trademark using that same term. For instance, if your proposed mark is *Zoroaster Designs*, the word to use in your search is "Zoroaster," because it is by far the more distinctive of the two words. "Designs" is a generic word that can be used in a lot of different trademarks

without creating customer confusion. So although you may wish to search for any mark that contains either "designs" or "Zoroaster"— just to see what's out there—you are primarily interested in "Zoroaster."

2. Search for Distinctive Syllables

It is wise to go a step farther and search for marks that contain one or more of the distinctive syllables in your name. For example, if your proposed mark is *Bioscan*, you should search for trademarks that contain either "bio" or "scan," because you might turn up something similar like "biosearch" or "cellscan." But it wouldn't make much sense to search for marks containing syllables that wouldn't likely be used. For example, the syllables "ga," "zoon," and "tite" (as in the website gazoontite.com) are not nearly as likely to be used in existing marks as are "bio" or "scan."

3. Don't Use the .com in Your Search

There are two reasons you may be searching for conflicts for your proposed domain name. You may be seeking to federally register your domain name, or you may be seeking to determine if your proposed domain name (regardless of whether you will federally register it) will conflict with a registered trademark. In either case, when checking for trademark conflicts with domain names, the best approach is to separate the domain name into its various components and search only for the distinctive components.

For instance, if your domain name were zoroasterdesigns.com, you should start your search with "Zoroaster." That search would turn up all federally registered *Zoroaster* marks (including those with the .com or any other top-level domain name suffix such as .org or .net). This is especially important when choosing a domain name because the owner of a federally registered mark can stop you from using a similar mark as your domain name if you are offering similar products or services. For example, the owner of the federally registered mark *Zoroaster Furniture* might be able to stop your use of zoroasterdesigns.com if your website offered furniture or similar goods.

Keep in mind that even though a large number of domain names are being registered as marks, for example, priceline.com, it is the portion of the name to the left of the dot that will create the trademark conflict. The PTO requires that the registrant disclaim the ".com" portion of the mark because it is a generic term. This is true for all top-level domains such as .org, .net, and the new top-level domains, such as .biz, .info, and .name. (For more information on registering domain names as trademarks, see Chapter 7, Federal Trademark Registration.)

4. Searching for Phrases

As we saw with the lemon pie example, you can use two or more words as a single search term by enclosing them in quotation marks. For example, a sensible search for "Big Daddy's Sweet Tooth Donuts" would include a search for the phrase "Big Daddy's" and the phrase "Sweet Tooth." You would do this by entering:

- "Big Daddy" in quotation marks in the upper Search Term box and

- "Sweet Tooth" in quotation marks in the lower Search Term box.

If you only want to search for a single phrase, as in "Sweet Tooth Munchies," simply enter the phrase in quotation marks in the top Search Term box and run the search. Note that you cannot use the truncation feature described in Section 5, below, when enclosing a phrase in quotation marks.

5. Use the Truncation Feature Where Appropriate

When you search for a particular term, it's useful to also search for slight variations of the term—for instance, if you are searching for the word "saber," you'll want to know about trademarks using the British spelling, "sabre." The computer won't find these variants for you without special instructions. Fortunately, it's easy to locate slight variations using TESS by using the truncation feature.

a. Right Truncation

One of the options offered by TESS is what's called word truncation. There is "right truncation" and "left truncation." Right truncation allows you to chop off as much of the right-hand portion of a word as you wish and have the computer search for all words that start with what's left. For instance, instead of wondering whether to search for "sabre" or "saber," you could search for all trademarks that contain the root segment "sab." This would pull up both variations of "saber" but would also produce unrelated terms, such as "sabbath." To create this truncation effect, simply put an asterisk at the end of the string of letters that you want to search, as in "sab*."

If you are using "right truncation," turn off the plural function. You can do this by choosing "No" from the drop-down menu above the Operator Box. Otherwise, the search engine will become confused. In addition, you cannot use the truncation feature when enclosing a phrase in quotation marks. For example, the TESS system will not retrieve truncations for the phrase "Big Daddy*" when it is enclosed in quotation marks.

b. Left Truncation

If you use left truncation, for example "*time," the search results will produce all marks that have words to the left of "time," for example Drive Time, Doubletime, Bed Time Stories, and Comfy Time. Unlike right truncation, the plural function works fine with left truncation.

c. Using Both Left and Right Truncation

TESS allows you to search for words that have both left truncations and right truncations. For instance, if you want to use the word "Geezer" in your mark, you might want to do a search for all marks that contain the "eez" portion of the word, because all marks with those three letters will resemble each other at least a little bit. You would get this result by truncating "eez" with an asterisk on both sides, as in *eez*. Again, remember to turn off the plural function.

d. Wildcards

TESS also allows you to substitute "wildcard" characters for specific letters in a word. For instance, if you want to search for all occur-

rences of women or woman, you should enter the search term wom?n, which would retrieve both words because the question mark stands for any character in that particular position.

TESS comes with an entire set of wildcards, such as characters that stand for vowels, consonants, and the like. As you become more familiar with trademark searching in the TESS system, you'll pick these up as you go along.

6. Search for Sound-Alikes

In addition to searching for names that are similar to yours in appearance, it is also important to search for words that sound alike. For example, gazoontite.com and gesundheit.com don't look that much alike, but they sound identical and might well confuse customers. The best approach to searching for sound-alikes is to focus on the most distinctive syllables in the proposed mark and search for these by themselves. You might pull up a longer list of marks than you want to deal with, but if you do find a mark that sounds like yours and is in use with goods or services that are commercially related to yours, you would do well to choose another mark.

If you are using the TrademarkScan Autoquery search that is available through SAEGIS, you will find that the search automatically searches for sound-alikes. See Section H1 below for more on SAEGIS and Autoquery.

7. Search for Foreign Translations

If your mark has exactly the same meaning as another mark in a different language, the owner of the other mark can challenge your mark if it can be shown that customers would likely be confused. For instance, if you wanted to name your restaurant The *Milkhouse* and somebody already had a mark for *Casa de Leche*, you have the potential for a trademark infringement charge. The bad news is that there is no do-it-yourself trademark search system that pulls up translations. The good news is that these types of conflicts are relatively rare. If you are using distinctive terms in your mark that have an independent meaning (which would be the case with arbitrary or suggestive marks), consider using a foreign language dictionary to find translations and then search for those as well as your proposed mark.

E. Trademark Searching With TESS: An Example

Here we provide an example of a typical search using TESS. In this case we are searching for the term "Hooky Wooky" for use as a trademark for crafts products, specifically crocheted clothing and accessories.

We start by using the Structured Form Search and enter "Hooky" in the top Search Term box and "Wooky" in the lower Search Term box. We choose "Yes" for plurals and choose "AND" from the pull-down menu of operators and change the drop-down menu for fields to "Basic Index."

The search results show no registered trademarks using the combination of terms. Next, we search for each term separately. We perform a search just for "wooky" and get no results.

We perform another search, this time using "hooky" in the top Search Term box and leaving the lower Search Term box blank. This time, the search turns up 10 items that use the word "hooky."

Of the ten entries (at the time we did the search), five are listed as "live" and five are listed as "dead." Live means that the mark is either registered or pending registration, whereas dead means that the mark used to be in the system as a registered or pending mark but has since been canceled or abandoned.

The five live trademarks are for use as follows: for board games, wall hooks, spiral

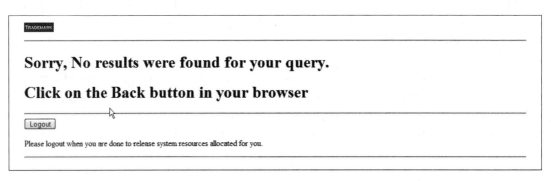

Sorry, No results were found for your query.

Click on the Back button in your browser

[Logout]

Please logout when you are done to release system resources allocated for you.

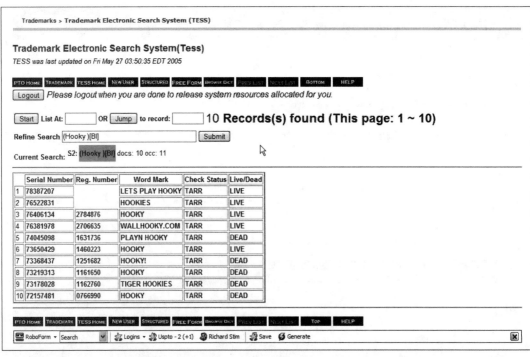

Trademarks > Trademark Electronic Search System (TESS)

Trademark Electronic Search System(Tess)

TESS was last updated on Fri May 27 03:50:35 EDT 2005

| PTO HOME | TRADEMARK | TESS HOME | NEW USER | STRUCTURED | FREE FORM | BROWSE DICT | PREV LIST | NEXT LIST | BOTTOM | HELP |

[Logout] *Please logout when you are done to release system resources allocated for you.*

[Start] List At: [   ] OR [Jump] to record: [   ] 10 **Records(s) found (This page: 1 ~ 10)**

Refine Search [(Hooky)[BI]   ] [Submit]

Current Search: S2: [(Hooky)[BI]] docs: 10 occ: 11

	Serial Number	Reg. Number	Word Mark	Check Status	Live/Dead
1	78387207		LETS PLAY HOOKY	TARR	LIVE
2	76522831		HOOKIES	TARR	LIVE
3	76406134	2784876	HOOKY	TARR	LIVE
4	76381978	2706635	WALLHOOKY.COM	TARR	LIVE
5	74045098	1631736	PLAYN HOOKY	TARR	DEAD
6	73650429	1460223	HOOKY	TARR	LIVE
7	73368437	1251682	HOOKY!	TARR	DEAD
8	73219313	1161650	HOOKY	TARR	DEAD
9	73178028	1162760	TIGER HOOKIES	TARR	DEAD
10	72157481	0766990	HOOKY	TARR	DEAD

| PTO HOME | TRADEMARK | TESS HOME | NEW USER | STRUCTURED | FREE FORM | BROWSE DICT | PREV LIST | NEXT LIST | TOP | HELP |

RoboForm ▾ Search ▾   Logins ▾ Uspto - 2 (+1)   Richard Stim   Save   Generate binding machinery, indoor and outdoor action games, and golf clubs. None of these would conflict with our intended use for crocheted clothing and accessories. Further, even though they use the term "hooky," they seem suitably distinguishable from the term "hooky wooky." Therefore, we conclude that the term appears to be available for our intended use.

Finally, although it doesn't necessarily reflect on federal registration, we check with Register.com (www.register.com) and find that the domain name hookwooky.com is unavailable for domain name registration. A company in Japan owns the domain name and is using the site to broadcast a radio station. However, alternates such as hookywooky.net and hookywooky.org are available.

Timed Out by TESS

To maintain its system resources, the TESS program will terminate your searching session after 15 minutes of inactivity. All searches and results will be lost, and you will receive a message: "This search session has expired. Please start a search session again by clicking on the TRADEMARK icon, if you wish to continue." You must exit and re-enter TESS to continue searching. If you wish to save searches, you can use the "save" feature of your browser and save the results in an html file.

F. Understanding the TESS Free Form Search

The TESS Free Form Search lacks the ease of the Structured Form search but adds a substantial degree of flexibility. Let's first take a look at the Free Form Search (see below).

The Free Form Search page resembles the Structured Form Search page described in Section D, with two major differences:

- Instead of separate Search Term boxes, the page provides one box that permits the construction of complex search queries, and
- The bottom of the page sets out the various fields that are available for searching and provides hypertext links to descriptions of these fields.

1. Using the Free Form Search Box

Probably the most important feature of the Free Form search option is that you can combine Boolean operators (unlike the Structured Search Form that only gives you one Boolean operator for your entire query). For example, suppose your proposed domain name is MiracleMediations.com. You may have started out with the Structured Search Form entering "mirac*" in the top Search Term box and the term "mediat*" in the bottom box. You choose the AND operator to search for trademarks that contain both terms.

This search is a good start, but as you review your search results you realize that you want to search for trademarks that contain

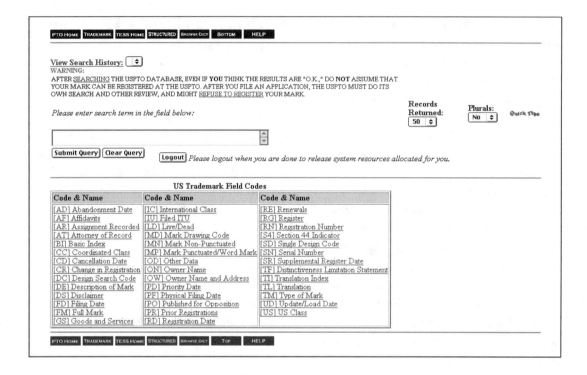

the word "arbitration" as well. To do this, you use the Free Form Search to create a new search query that looks like this:

"mirac* [bi]" AND "mediat* [bi]" OR "arbitrat* [bi]"

This search expression tells the computer that you want all trademarks that appear in the Basic Index and that contain a variant of the truncated term "mirac*" and either the term "mediat*" or the term "arbitrat*."

2. How to Use the Field Codes

The [bi] that follows the truncated terms is what's known as a field code. The Free Form Search requires the use of these field codes if you want anything other than an "all fields"

search. For instance, if you want to search for all marks owned by a particular company, you can use the field code "[on]" in connection with the company's name. Similarly, use of the field code "[gs]" lets you search for all marks that are used on goods or services containing the terms you use in your search query.

You aren't limited to one field code. You may search in as many fields as you wish. For instance, you will get a deeper search by combining the [bi] and [ti] fields. (The "ti" field contains English equivalents to foreign words or characters used in a trademark.) You combine fields for each term by separating the fields with a comma, as in geezer [bi,ti]. In fact, in the help it provides for TESS, the PTO seems to suggest that when you are using the Free Form Search to find occurrences of a term in a trademark (as opposed to one of the other types of fields in a trademark record), you search both the "bi" and "ti" fields.

For more on field codes, use the table that appears on the Free Form Search page and click whatever field code you wish to know more about.

G. Understanding the Results of Your Search

It's one thing to search for marks using TESS; it's another to understand what is reported back to you. The screen shot below indicates one of the reported items from our Hooky Wooky search.

PTO HOME | TRADEMARK | TESS HOME | NEW USER | STRUCTURED | FREE FORM | BROWSE DICT | BOTTOM | HELP | PREV LIST | CURR LIST | NEXT LIST | FIRST DOC | PREV DOC | NEXT DOC | LAST DOC

Logout | Please logout when you are done to release system resources allocated for you.

Start | List At: [   ] OR Jump | to record: [   ] **Record 3 out of 10**

Check Status *(TARR contains current status, correspondence address and attorney of record for this mark. Use the "Back" button of the Internet Browser to return to TESS)*

Typed Drawing

Word Mark	HOOKY
Goods and Services	IC 007. US 013 019 021 023 031 034 035. G & S: Machines for spiral, double-loop and plastic comb binding. FIRST USE: 19821031. FIRST USE
Mark Drawing Code	(1) TYPED DRAWING
Serial Number	76406134
Filing Date	May 3, 2002
Current Filing Basis	1A
Original Filing Basis	1B
Published for Opposition	November 12, 2002
Registration Number	2784876
Registration Date	November 18, 2003
Owner	(REGISTRANT) Boyadjian, Hratch INDIVIDUAL SWITZERLAND OBSTGARTENSTR. 8 CH-8703 ERLENBACH SWITZERLAND
Attorney of Record	Brian J. McNamara
Type of Mark	TRADEMARK
Register	PRINCIPAL
Live/Dead Indicator	LIVE

PTO HOME | TRADEMARK | TESS HOME | NEW USER | STRUCTURED | FREE FORM | BROWSE DICT | TOP | HELP | PREV LIST | CURR LIST | NEXT LIST | FIRST DOC | PREV DOC | NEXT DOC | LAST DOC

1. Understanding the Report Returned by a TESS Search

Let's take a few moments to interpret the various lines of information on the screen shot above.

Word Mark: This shows the mark as registered (or as shown in the trademark application if the mark is pending).

Goods and Services: This line identifies the international classifications (the IC class) under which the mark is registered and provides brief descriptions of the underlying goods and/or services. In this case the mark is registered under international classification 007. The U.S. classifications following the international classification are artifacts of an earlier time when the United States had its own classification system. (See Chapter 6, How to Evaluate the Results of Your Trademark Search, where we explain the importance of classes in deciding whether there is a likelihood of customer confusion.)

Mark Drawing Code: If the mark consists of words only (even if they are imaginatively arranged or come with stylistic fonts), this line says "Typed Drawing." However, if your mark consists of a logo with graphical elements, this line will show a set of six numeric characters that reflect how the PTO has classified the logo.

Serial Number: This is the number that is assigned to the trademark application by the PTO.

Filing Date: This is the date that the application for registration was filed.

Current Filing Basis and Original Filing Basis: If, as here, the application was originally filed on an intent-to-use basis (1B), that fact will be indicated here. If the application was filed on an actual use basis (1A), that will be indicated as it is here for the "Current Filing Basis."

Published for Opposition: This line indicates the date the PTO published the trademark application to give the public a chance to oppose the mark (usually on grounds that they think the proposed registration legally conflicts with their trademark).

Registration Number: This line will only appear if the mark has, in fact, been registered. Pending marks, for instance, do not have a registration number.

Registration Date: This line will only appear if the mark has been registered.

Owner: This line identifies the person or entity that was named as owner of the trademark in the application, and also provides the owner's address.

Attorney of Record: This line indicates the name of the attorney, if any, managing the application.

Type of Mark: This line identifies the label given the mark by the PTO. For most purposes, this label makes little difference. However, if two potentially conflicting marks are very similar, but one is a service mark while the other is a trademark, the type of mark may make a difference in terms of whether a legal conflict exists.

Register: This line designates whether the mark has been registered on the Principal Register or the Supplemental Register. Marks on the Principal Register get more protection, and marks on the Supplemental Register are deemed by the PTO to be too descriptive to be placed on the Principal Register—which means that the likelihood of a successful infringement action being brought on behalf of that mark is small.

Live/Dead Indicator: This line indicates whether the mark is registered or pending, or whether it has been canceled (because of the owner's failure to renew or file statements of continued use) or abandoned in the course of the application.

⚠️ Even though a mark is labeled as dead, it may in fact be very much alive in the world of commerce and can spell trouble for you if you adopt a legally conflicting mark. The dead/live label only refers to the mark's status in the PTO, not to whether it is or isn't in actual use in the economy.

2. Determining a Mark's Status

Each item page has a link to the PTO's Trademark Application Registration Retrieval database (known as TARR). This database shows the status of the mark (registered, pending, canceled, published for opposition, etc.). When we clicked the Status link to the Hooky item page, we got the status report shown at right.

The status report has some of the same information as the item page and also provides a chronological history of the mark's journey through the PTO. This status report is most helpful when you discover a pending mark and want to know where it is in the process.

Thank you for your request. Here are the latest results from the TARR web server.

This page was generated by the TARR system on 2005-05-28 19:46:36 ET

Serial Number: 76406134

Registration Number: 2784876

Mark (words only): HOOKY

Standard Character claim: No

Current Status: Registered.

Date of Status: 2003-11-18

Filing Date: 2002-05-03

Transformed into a National Application: No

Registration Date: 2003-11-18

Register: Principal

Law Office Assigned: LAW OFFICE 114

If you are the applicant or applicant's attorney and have questions about this file, please contact the Trademark Assistance Center at TrademarkAssistanceCenter@uspto.gov

Current Location: 900 -File Repository (Franconia)

Date In Location: 2004-01-21

GOODS AND/OR SERVICES

International Class: 007
Machines for spiral, double-loop and plastic comb binding
First Use Date: 1982-10-31
First Use in Commerce Date: 2001-09-30
Basis: 1(a)

PROSECUTION HISTORY

2003-11-18 - Registered - Principal Register
2003-09-25 - Allowed for Registration - Principal Register (SOU accepted)
2003-09-25 - Case file assigned to examining attorney
2003-09-24 - Case File in TICRS
2003-08-04 - Statement of use processing complete
2003-08-04 - Amendment to Use filed
2003-08-04 - PAPER RECEIVED
2003-02-04 - Notice of allowance - mailed
2002-11-12 - Published for opposition
2002-10-23 - Notice of publication
2002-09-10 - Approved for Pub - Principal Register (Initial exam)
2002-08-26 - Case file assigned to examining attorney

H. An Introduction to SAEGIS— A Great Fee-Based Search System

SAEGIS is a Web-based trademark search interface that provides access to a number of useful databases for a fee. In addition to the federal trademark database, which TESS also uses, SAEGIS lets you search state trademark databases and trademark databases of selected foreign countries. In addition, SAEGIS offers a search of Web pages and all domain name registries. The fees at SAEGIS depend on the type of search you do and the number of trademarks called up by your search that you decide to review.

Before you can use SAEGIS, you'll need to register online. Registration is free, but they will promptly ask you by phone for a credit card number in case there is a problem with the billing. You will then be sent a user name and password by email. Once you have those, you can get into the system, read the help and, short of actually finding trademarks, explore how the system works without charge. We recommend that you download the help and study it before you get on the system for real. Also, a few days after you register, SAEGIS sends you a Subscriber's Guide that will prove very helpful in understanding how to use this powerful tool.

There are two basic approaches to using SAEGIS for searching the U.S. and state trademark databases:

- TrademarkScan Autoquery, and
- TrademarkScan Custom Search.

1. TrademarkScan Autoquery

TrademarkScan Autoquery will produce a competent analytical search for less than any of the professional search services we are familiar with. For example, as of May 2005, an Autoquery of U.S. federal, state, and Canadian records was $80.

To use TrademarkScan Autoquery, you:

- select the database you want to search (federal, federal and state, state, or one or more foreign databases)
- enter your trademark
- enter one or more international classes (see Chapter 6, Section D), and
- provide a description of your goods or services.

You can then preview what your entries will pull up. As you will see from this preview, TrademarkScan Autoquery will not only search for an exact match but also rotates prefixes and suffixes and breaks down your proposed mark in other ways that might produce registered marks of interest. You can use this preview to pare down the search to 75 marks or even modify the information you entered in the boxes to obtain a more precise search. For instance, if you were searching for Nolo, you could eliminate the search query that reports all instances of when Nolo occurs in the middle of the mark, as in "technology," or at least limit the number of marks reported in that particular query by restricting your search to the most appropriate classes (see Chapter 6, Section D).

Though TrademarkScan Autoquery is thorough, this very thoroughness may end up costing you a bundle, because you will be charged per extra mark reviewed. Fortunately, at any time during the search, you can check your online account to review the charges associated with your current search session, so you can keep track of the costs and modify your search strategy accordingly.

2. TrademarkScan Custom Search

The TrademarkScan Custom Search provides more flexibility per mark searched but requires more skill from you in crafting your search query. You will be charged per mark that your search produces for your review. To save money and use the TrademarkScan Custom Search efficiently, we recommend that you wait until you receive your Subscriber's Guide and then use that resource to learn the ropes.

3. Browsing the Index

Like TESS, you can browse the database alphabetically for free and see what comes before and after your proposed mark. While this can be useful, remember that you are only viewing marks where your term comes at the beginning. For instance, if you search for Rabbit, you will see a list of marks that start with Rabbit, but you won't see marks such as *Hip Rabbit* or *Run Rabbit Run*.

! TrademarkScan Custom Search Can Empty Your Pockets Fast. Make sure you spend adequate time learning how to use this tool and pay close attention to your search queries so that you don't pull up any extraneous marks. Each time you are about to take an action,

TrademarkScan will alert you to the potential cost and give you the opportunity to pare your search back to an affordable level. As a general rule, we recommend that you use great caution when using this search engine.

I. Searching for Designs

So far we have focused on how to search the U.S. trademark database for marks made up of words. However, many trademarks consist of or contain graphic elements that word searches don't accommodate. Design marks, as these types of trademarks are referred to, must be searched by using a set of codes assigned to them by the PTO upon registration. The codes describe various types of graphical elements and are publicly available in a publication known as the *Design Search Code Manual*, available on the PTO's site.

To search for other possible instances of a design mark that you wish to use, you must first figure out the code for the design elements that your mark incorporates, and then enter this code in the search box (for either the Structure or Free Form search) and select the Design Search Code field (DC).

J. Searching State Registered Trademarks and Trade Names

To search for trademarks on state trademark registers, you must check the registers for each state. (For information about determining how many state registers to search, see Chapter 4, Section F2.) Usually you will only search in your own state. But if you plan to operate in several states, you would want to check each. If you decide to search in more than a few states, you would be smarter to have your trademark search done by a professional, or to search state trademark databases by computer.

The method for doing a search for state registered trademarks varies from state to state. Many states will do a preapplication search for you by phone, either for free or for a small charge. In other states, request a search by mail. In still others, the PTO will not search for you but will let you peruse the microfiche or loose-leaf lists of registered trademarks in person. The state agency in charge of trademarks is generally within the department of state, the department of corporations, or the department of revenue.

Regardless of who does it or how the search is performed, state trademark agencies provide limited types of search services—most commonly marks can only be searched in alphabetical order. Sometimes they are broken down by class of goods or services. (In Chapter 6, How to Evaluate the Results of Your Trademark Search, we explain that all trademarks are assigned a class when registered.) If so, you will need to specify which class to search.

The main drawback to state searches is that state laws vary somewhat about what constitutes a conflict with a registered trademark. This means the criteria the state uses to conduct its search may not be the same as federal or common law criteria. As a result, while obtaining a state clearance probably means there are no directly identical marks in

your class, it may not give you any assurance that your trademark does not legally conflict with other marks in that state. When searching state trademarks, the same principles apply as for searching the federal trademark register— look for synonyms, homonyms, phonetic equivalents, etc., both in your class and in as many other classes as might be relevant.

K. Searching for Trade Names and Unregistered Marks

The goal here is to make sure your mark won't conflict with a trade name or corporate name in use in your state. Although trade names, used solely to identify businesses, do not have all the same kinds of rights attached to trademarks (for instance, unlike trademarks, they cannot be registered), they can be protected by unfair competition law. For example, someone can sue you if you use their trade name as a mark in a way that causes the public (or suppliers) to confuse you with them. Also, if the trade name is being used as a mark but is not registered as such, a search of one of the trade name indexes we describe below may result in discovering a mark that no other search method would have brought to your attention. In short, you will need to make sure your mark is not going to conflict with a registered corporate name or unregistered trade name by searching all sources of trade names that you can reasonably find.

One good way to search for a trade name conflict is to make sure no corporation registered in your state already uses the name. You can do this via a phone call or letter to the agency in charge of corporations, usually the department of corporations or the secretary of state. (See Chapter 1, Section D, for more about corporate names.)

The fact that you have already incorporated and wish to use your corporate name as your mark does not mean you should skip a trade name search. When you incorporated, your proposed corporate name was checked against other corporate names, not against trademarks or any other trade names. So you still need to check how it compares to marks, other trade names, and perhaps even corporate names in other states if your mark will have a presence in those states. If you need to search for corporate names in more than one state, it may be easier to use Dun & Bradstreet's Electronic Business Directory (www.dnb.com) that includes noncorporate business names as well.

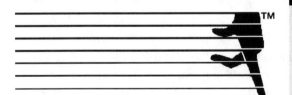

1. Searching Telephone Directories

The purpose of this search is to find unregistered service marks and trade names acting as service marks that are currently in use. Telephone directories are excellent sources for

these. Most of the major Internet search engines provide access to a database known as the national Yellow Pages, for instance, SuperPages (www.SuperPages.com) (see sidebar, "SuperPages Search Techniques," below) or Google (www.google.com). Most large city public libraries also have a complete selection of white and Yellow Pages for all the major cities in the country and for all the areas in your state. If yours doesn't, enlist the aid of the librarian in finding a library that does. (In that case, you will also need his or her help in locating the other books you'll need for a trademark search.) At a minimum, you should consult all the phone books for your marketing area. This is a big task, recommended mostly for those who want the greatest degree of certainty possible that no conflicts exist, so decide if you really need to do it before starting, or hire a helper.

SuperPages Search Techniques

SuperPages (www.SuperPages.com) is one of the most useful sites for searching trade corporate names because it offers a variety of search options. In addition to its Simple Search listing businesses by trade name or category, there are more detailed search possibilities, including the Distance Search that lets you find businesses that are located within a set distance from a particular location that you specify. SuperPages also provides searching of Canadian businesses.

2. Trade Associations/Directories

Trade associations are usually limited to a particular field. Find the association for the field you plan to use your mark in (your library's reference section will have a guide to associations), and examine its directory. This should provide you with a good idea of whether the mark is already in use. You may already be familiar with relevant trade associations or directories in your fields, or you may have to go to the library card catalog or computer index and look under several relevant subject headings to find them. Most types of businesses, from anchovy fishermen to zoo suppliers, will have them, but a few small or new endeavors won't. Contact the chamber of commerce or your librarian for further help in tracking them down. For example, the trade journals *Candy Industry* or *Candy Marketer* would help you find trademarks and names in use among candy manufacturers.

3. Business Directories

Several publishers compile business directories that cover all businesses. They contain lists of as many business names and marks as the authors can find. One example is *Brands and Their Companies* (formerly the *Trade Name Dictionary*), published by Gale Research Co., a guide to over 220,000 consumer-oriented trade names, brands, and marks with the names and addresses of the companies to which they belong, compiled from trade journals and direct contact research. Another is the *Trade Name Index/Standard Directory of Advertisers*, published by the National Register Publishing Company, which contains over 62,000 of the better-known trade names and trademarks currently in use by national advertisers. A third is the *Thomas Register of American Manufacturers*, which has names and brands listed by business category, also available online at www.thomasregister.com

You will want to examine these in your class or field, for direct conflicts as well as similar-sounding or looking names, applying the same criteria we discussed for online federal trademark searching. Because here you are working in alphabetical order, you will have to remember to make separate checks on synonyms, variations in spelling, and punctuation and other differences. (See Chapter 14, Help Beyond This Book, for other resources.)

4. Google Searching

Google (www.google.com) is an invaluable tool when searching for common law marks. Google offers two modes of search: Basic and Advanced. If you're using the Google Toolbar—a feature that provides a searching window on your Internet browser—you can access the Advanced Search mode by clicking the word "Google" and choosing Google Links, Advanced Search from the drop-down menu. If you're on the Google search page, click Advanced Search.

The Advanced Search mode relies on the same Boolean approach to keyword searches described in this chapter. As a general rule, you'll do a better search if you use the Advanced Mode than the basic mode. However, because we want to give you a search methodology that doesn't require much of a learning curve, we'll use the Google Basic Search mode for most of this section.

When performing searches with Google, here are some tips and tricks to keep in mind:

- **Google ignores many common words and characters.** Google disregards words such as "where," "the," "how," "why," and some single digits and letters. (Google believes these slow down your search without improving the results.) You can see which words are ignored on the search results page—for example, if you type this search: "Who is the owner of the Shasta trademark?" Google will tell you that the words "who is the" were not included in your search: So if the mark you are searching for contains a common word such as "the," "what," etc. put a "+" sign in front of it. For example, if you were searching for *Lover of Salsa,* type "Lover +of Salsa." (Be sure to include a space before the "+" sign.)
- **You can make Google search for synonyms.** If you want to search not only for your search term but also for its synonyms, place the tilde sign ("~") immediately in front of the search term. For example, if searching for *Lover of Salsa* and you wanted to find similar or related products, you might type, "Lover +of ~Salsa"

- **You can search for a range of numbers.** If you want to obtain results within a numerical range—for example, you want to use *10 Decibels* as the name of your record company, but you want to check any other uses of numbers with the word "decibel," just include the range of numbers, separated by two periods, with no spaces, into the search box along with your search terms. For example, type, "decibels 1..1000."
- **Use quotation marks for phrases.** Often you'll want results that include an exact phrase, such as *Independence starts with I.* In this case, put quotation marks around your search terms—for example, "Independence starts with I."
- **Get rid of multimeaning terminology.** If your search term has more than one meaning, you can focus your search by putting a minus sign ("-") in front of words related to the meaning you want to avoid. (Be sure to include a space before the minus sign.) For example, let's say you're searching for "Pot Luck" but want to avoid common results such as cooking pot, coffee pots, or melting pot. You would type "pot luck -cooking -coffee -melting" and it would eliminate many unnecessary common results. ■

Chapter 6

How to Evaluate the Results of Your Trademark Search

*T*his chapter explains how to evaluate the results of your trademark search. It's one thing to search for marks that are the same as or similar to the mark you propose to use for your own business, goods, or services. It's quite another to decide how to proceed once you have the results of the search in your hands.

A. What's Involved in Evaluating Trademark Search Results?

If you are choosing a mark, evaluating your trademark search results is essentially a preventive study. You are trying to make sure that your proposed mark qualifies for registration (if you choose to register it) and will be secure against attacks by other trademark owners. If the PTO decides that your mark is confusingly similar to an already-registered mark, registration will be denied your mark. And even if your mark is registered, a trademark owner can successfully sue you in the future if it discovers your mark and convinces a judge that the use of your mark creates a likelihood of customer confusion.

If you already have a mark but are involved in an infringement dispute, you will want to use the material in this chapter to help you sort out whether there is a likelihood of customer confusion caused by the use of the

TIFFANY & CO.

two marks. If not, and the other mark isn't famous, then you are in better legal shape than if the opposite were true.

1. The Importance of Customer Confusion in Trademark Law

As you probably gathered from previous chapters, the core decision you'll need to make here is whether the simultaneous commercial use of your mark and any marks that your search turns up would likely create customer confusion as to the underlying goods or services, or their source. If you conclude that customer confusion would be likely, you'll want to pick another mark. If no customer confusion is likely, then you can feel reasonably confident about using the mark—unless it happens to be identical or very similar to a mark that the courts would consider famous.

2. Likelihood of Customer Confusion Is a Slippery Concept

Being able to assess whether customer confusion is likely in a particular situation is a skill that depends as much on experience and intuition as it does on any hard-and-fast principles. Though we can and do explain how the courts generally go about assessing the likelihood of confusion, each case is inevitably unique in some particular. Predicting the future outcome of any given case is definitely an art rather than a science. As we suggest in the book's Introduction, if you are uncertain about the correct course of action after applying our guidelines to your situation, you will be wise to consult with an experienced trademark lawyer. (See Chapter 14, Help Beyond This Book.)

3. Even a Lawyer's Opinion Can't Give You Certainty

Even if you consult with a lawyer, remember that trademark lawyers are subject to the same limitation as is the author of this book—that is, there is no firm way to predict the outcome of a trademark dispute should one erupt over your choice of a mark. All a trademark lawyer can do is give his or her professional opinion. But if that opinion turns out to be wrong, it is you and not the lawyer who will face the consequences, with one important exception. A lawyer's opinion that your mark doesn't conflict with a mark on the federal trademark register may save you from a stiff damage award if you go ahead and use the mark and are later sued for infringement.

Knowing that they aren't likely to get in trouble if they act conservatively, most lawyers won't give you the go-ahead if there is much of a chance of a trademark dispute in the future. In short, the lawyer's advice may be both a disservice in that it may be overly cautious and an important service in that you will feel more confident about your choice if it passes the lawyer test.

⚠ The discussion in this chapter assumes that any mark you come across in a trademark search is currently being used and was either (1) put into use or (2) was the subject of an "intent-to-use" application before you started using your mark. In these instances, a conclusion that customer confusion is likely will also portend the results of any trademark infringement suit that is brought against you for going ahead with your proposed mark. If, however, you started using the mark first, or the would-be registrant fails to follow up on an intent-to-use application, the results may be quite different. In this chapter we primarily explore how likelihood of confusion is determined. (In Chapter 10, Sorting Out Trademark Disputes, we help you assess the legalities of any trademark disputes that might arise.)

B. What Is the Likelihood of Customer Confusion?

You will most likely first encounter the issue of customer confusion if and when you do a trademark search and the results indicate that the same or similar mark is already being used by another business. Whether or not you should go ahead with your mark depends on whether your use would create a likelihood of customer confusion.

1. Understanding the Likelihood-of-Confusion Test

First let's look at the term "likelihood." In the trademark context, "likelihood" means that confusion is probable—not necessarily that it has happened, or that it will happen, but that it is more likely than not that a reasonable customer will be confused by the simultaneous use of two separate marks.

Confusion in this context can mean two different things. Most commonly, it means that the goods or services a customer buys are different than what the customer intended to buy. For instance, if a consumer wants to purchase the services of ABC Emergency Care on the basis of a friend's recommendation, but he ends up going to ABD Emergency Room by mistake because of the similarity of the two names, you have an example of customer confusion between the two services.

The other situation that creates customer confusion is where a misleading mark causes the customer to believe—wrongly—that a product or service is sponsored by, approved by, or somehow connected with a business that the customer already frequents or knows about. In other words, the customer is confused about the source of the product or service. This would be the case, for example, if a customer took a TV to a repair shop called IBM Electronics because they thought that IBM somehow sponsored the business.

Just to see how judges apply this likelihood-of-confusion standard, let's examine a hypothetical conflict between two uses of very similar trademarks.

EXAMPLE 1: Ethereal Fragrance Company produces a line of products, including perfume, carrying the distinctive and therefore strong registered trademark *Ekbara Scents*. These products are marketed in boutiques throughout California and several other western states primarily to women in the middle- and upper-income brackets. The *Ekbara* mark has been used in this manner by Ethereal for two years when Rubin Santiago of Oakland, California, opens a small printing company specializing in business cards, which he calls

Ekbara Cards. The cards are marketed to small businesses in the San Francisco Bay Area. Ethereal claims infringement and demands that Rubin stop using the *Ekbara* mark on his cards. When Rubin refuses, Ethereal files a trademark infringement lawsuit and seeks a preliminary injunction (an order to bar Rubin from further using the *Ekbara* mark). There is no question in this case that Ethereal was first to use the *Ekbara* mark. There is also no question that if use of *Ekbara* on the cards creates a likelihood of customer confusion, Ethereal is entitled to a court order stopping use of the *Ekbara* mark in that context. The key point for the judge to decide in this example is, simply, whether Rubin's use of the *Ekbara* mark creates a likelihood of customer confusion.

In deciding this question, a knowledgeable judge would probably engage in something like the following analysis:

"It is not likely that purchasers of business cards will think a fragrance company is involved in the printing business. Neither business is likely to go into competition with the other. The purchasers of the two products as well as the distribution channels are likely to be quite different. There is no similarity between the two goods in terms of what they accomplish. Ethereal's customers are unlikely to care who manufactures or distributes business cards. There is no indication Rubin Santiago intended to get a free marketing ride on Ethereal's mark. By contrast, the only factor supporting Ethereal's claim of infringement is the strength of the word *Ekbara* as a mark (it

suggests the Middle East, which itself is suggestive of fragrances). This is simply not enough to overcome all the other factors that lean against the likelihood of customer confusion."

EXAMPLE 2: Rubin Santiago creates a line of enamel earrings, calls them *Ekbara Designs*, and franchises them for sale in shopping malls that also feature boutiques that carry Ethereal's products. In this case the judge's decision would be different because the likelihood of confusion is much higher due to the fact that the two marks are used on goods distributed in the same channels, the same consumers are exposed to both marks, and the underlying goods might actually compete with each other in the sense that customers searching for impulse gifts might buy the earrings instead of the fragrance, and vice versa.

(See Section C, below, for more on the factors courts use to determine whether two marks create the likelihood of customer confusion.)

2. Do the Hypothetically Confused Customers Have to Be Reasonable Customers?

Before we go on to discuss all the factors that can help you assess a likelihood of confusion, let's take a moment to examine who these hypothetically confused customers really are. The law imagines a "reasonable" customer who exercises ordinary care to distinguish among the products or services being purchased. This reasonable customer is neither someone who confuses two products as a result of bizarre reasoning, nor someone who obsessively checks all references before buying a product or service, but rather someone in between.

Courts recognize that a reasonable consumer will often make a snap judgment. If, after only a hurried glance, Mrs. Serrano is confused between *Heartbeat* and *Heartlite* cooking oils, then the marks are too similar. However, the law would surely not find it reasonable if a customer confused *Heartbeat* cooking oil with *Esther's Cooking Oil* because her Aunt Esther had recently died of a heart attack. Nor would a customer be reasonable in confusing *Heartbeat* with *Esther's* because of similar packaging, so long as the very different names are prominently displayed on the packaging.

The law says that in cases of conflicting trademarks, the challenger must show that a reasonable customer might be confused. How is this done? Typically, the challenger must somehow prove that a significant percentage of customers would likely be confused—anywhere between 5% and 50%, depending on the situation. A more exact number can't be given, because the number varies from one court decision to the next.

C. An Overview of How Marks Are Evaluated for Their Potential to Cause Customer Confusion

Court decisions have produced a number of criteria to determine when there's a likelihood of confusion between two marks. As would a judge, you will want to ask the following questions:

Factor 1: Are the goods and services represented by the marks related—that is, are they sold in the same marketing channels to the same general group of customers?

Factor 2: Do the goods or services compete—that is, will the decision by customers to buy one business's product or service be made at the expense of the other business?

Factor 3: How similar are the marks in sound, appearance, and meaning?

Factor 4: How strong is each mark? (Is the mark in question very distinctive when compared to a competing mark?)

Factor 5: How much do the underlying goods or services cost? (How carefully does the public usually decide whether to buy the goods or services offered by the two businesses?)

Factor 6: Do the two marks share the same customer base?

Factor 7: Does one owner use the mark on several different products or services, or is he likely to do so in the future?

Whether use of a trademark is likely to cause customer confusion depends on the exact facts of the case, how the criteria listed above are weighed in light of the facts, and the subjective perceptions of the judge, based on the evidence.

The three most important factors to examine in deciding how likely it is that the use of a mark will cause customer confusion are the first three on our list.

Factor 1: How closely related are the goods/services?

Two similar services or products with the same or similar names that are distributed in the same markets are far more likely to confuse the public than if very similar names were to grace dissimilar products. In this latter case the confusion is more likely to come from confusion about the source of the products than from confusing one product with another. (See Section D below for more on what makes goods and services related.)

Factor 2: Do the goods or services compete?

If the underlying goods or services directly compete with each other, then the use of the same or similar marks on both is likely to cause the type of confusion that will lead to the customer purchasing the wrong product.

Factor 3: How similar are the marks in terms of their appearance, meaning, or sound?

The more similarities two marks share, the more likely it is that they will confuse someone. This is known as the "sight, sound, and meaning" test for customer confusion.

You should apply these three factors first to your situation. In a borderline case, you will want to consider the four additional factors that we discuss in Section G below. Or you can pick which of these seven factors seem most relevant to your situation and use them selectively to determine if your mark may cause a likelihood of confusion with another.

Before you conclude that you are safe in going ahead with your chosen mark, look at the final three factors in Section H, below. They do not predict a likelihood of confusion so much as a likelihood of success in a lawsuit, which may be a more practical determination anyway.

D. How Closely Related Are the Goods/Services?

A good place to start when deciding whether one mark conflicts with another is to ask if the goods and services that the two marks promote are related—in a commercial sense. That's because when products or services are considered to be totally unrelated, the courts will generally find that there is no likelihood of customer confusion and thus no infringe-ment—unless the existing mark qualifies for special protection under the dilution doctrine (see Chapter 1, Section B4).

If, on the other hand, a court finds the products or services to be related, it is also likely to find that a likelihood of customer confusion exists and to issue judgment for the owner of the existing mark should an infringe-ment lawsuit be brought. This is because when similar marks are used on related marks, the risk of consumer confusion is high. You can determine whether the potentially conflicting marks are used on related goods or services by asking either of two questions:

- Do the goods or services belong to the same international "classes" of goods or services?
- Are the goods or services distributed through the same marketing channels?

We discuss these two questions in further detail below.

1. An Overview of the International Trademark Classification System

"International Classes" are descriptive categories of goods or services used by the U.S. Patent and Trademark Office to help keep track of the many thousands of new marks that they register every year. There are 42 classes in all, 34 for products and eight for services. The Appendix contains a complete list of all 42 classes.

The purpose of the International Schedule of Classes of Goods and Services is to group together in the same class goods or services that are offered through the same channels of trade and to the same general types of consumers. The International Schedule helps the PTO determine whether or not the specific goods or services associated with conflicting marks are so closely related to each other, for example, they are likely to be marketed in the same channels and sold to the same consumers).

EXAMPLE: Mark is a jeweler with a line of handmade jewelry (necklaces, bracelets, and earrings) that feature small, black, rubber parts with an industrial look. He calls this special line of jewelry *The Rub*. Jackie's Tool Shop, Inc., has designed and manufactured a line of hand tools with rubber handles for three years and has a registered trademark for the name of the line, *The Rub*, under Class 8, for hand tools. Mark would like to register the mark, *The Rub*, for his line of jewelry. Can he still do so, even though Jackie's has already registered it?

Mark will likely succeed in registering his mark if Jackie's mark is the only obstacle to registration. Mark's line of jewelry would be registered under Class 14, for jewelry. The fact that Jackie's mark is registered under Class 8 and Mark's mark for the jewelry line would be registered under Class 14 indicates that these goods are not marketed in the same channels and to the same consumers. Jackie's hand tools are marketed to hardware stores, home improvement stores, and the hardware section of department stores. Mark's jewelry is marketed to jewelry and clothing boutiques. The fact that the marketing contexts do not overlap indicates that

consumers would not likely be confused by the use of the same mark on both goods.

⚠ Even if your proposed mark falls into a different class than another mark, we recommend that you not use your mark if it is very similar to the other mark and would appear in the same marketing channels. Keep in mind that the prohibitive cost of litigation usually makes all borderline decisions too risky.

If and when you search the list of registered trademarks (see Chapters 4 and 5) to see whether someone else got to your mark ahead of you, the search results will indicate the class for each similar mark that the search turns up. If your mark belongs in the same class as one or more of the existing marks, this is a good indication that the underlying products or services will be considered related. And if your search comes up with unregistered marks, you will want to try to assign a class to them, and then compare those classes with the probable class that your mark fits under.

Here are some examples to help familiarize you with how this classification system works.

Class 001 Chemicals, including those used in industry, science, and agriculture (such as neon), but not those used in medical science (see Class 005)

Class 003 Cosmetics and cleaning preparations, including soaps, substances used for laundry and cosmetics, but not degreasing preparations used in manufacturing (see Class 001)

Class 005 Pharmaceuticals (and other substances used for medical purposes), but not deodorants for personal use (see Class 003)

Class 014 Jewelry, including precious metals and their alloys, clocks, and watches, but not gold used by dentists (see Class 005) or gold writing pens (see Class 016)

Class 016 Paper goods and printed matter, including writing instruments and other office tools, but not artists' tools

Class 035 Advertising and business, including, for example, advertising agency services, but not commercial enterprise services primarily involving the sale of merchandise

Class 038 Communication, including distribution of television and radio programs, but not radio advertising services (see Class 035)

2. Fitting Your Goods and Services Into the Appropriate Class

It may take a little study to determine the class to which a product or service fits best. For instance, does a belt made of woven cord belong under Class 022, which includes cordage and fibers? As it turns out, the answer is "no," because the cord is made into clothing, which belongs in Class 025. Similarly, if a mark represents a new type of service or product, it may be difficult to decide how to

categorize it. For example, if you are running an Internet-based store-to-home grocery ordering and delivery service, you may wish to register in a variety of classes, including international classes 029 (meats and processed foods), 035 (advertising and business), 009 (electrical and scientific apparatus), and 039 (transportation and storage).

Because goods or services in the same class are usually considered related or competing, the use of the same or similar marks within the same class has a high potential for customer confusion. For example, the owner of *Titan* brand cigarettes was able to stop a cigar maker from using the *Titan* mark. Cigars and cigarettes are in the same PTO class, Class 034, which also encompasses "tobacco, raw or manufactured, smoker's articles, and matches."

On the other hand, the owner of *Titan* cigarettes probably couldn't stop a maker of biodegradable soap, which is in Class 003, from using the same mark. That is because cigarettes and soap do not compete in any way; they are not considered related goods; and the *Titan* mark could be used on both without creating the likelihood of customer confusion.

It's important to understand that by itself the fact that two products or services are in the same or different classes does not conclusively establish whether two marks are legally in conflict. Because the international classification system has packed all goods and services into only 42 classes, combining, for example, abrasive cleansers and cosmetics, products within the same class may be marketed in totally different ways so as to avoid customer confusion. So, in evaluating a conflict, you may at least argue that a trademark for a scouring powder that is similar to a trademark for lipstick won't confuse customers. As we've pointed out, even if two goods or services are in separate classes, the actual means used to market them may create a likelihood of customer confusion. Simply put, the classification system should be used as an indicator of possible confusion rather than as a means to definitely determine its likelihood.

Coordinated Classes

The PTO has grouped the various international classifications into what it calls "coordinated classes." If you search for a mark and designate a particular class for it, the search will return marks in the coordinated class group. For instance, if you designate the International Class for software when you are performing your search, your results will also include marks in classes 010, 016, 028, 035, 038, and 042. Although the PTO considers these classes "related" for the purpose of trademark searching, the goods and services described by the related classes are not necessarily related for the purpose of determining the likelihood of customer confusion.

To place a product or service within its appropriate class, follow these steps:

Step 1: Study the list of classes in the Appendix. See whether the goods or services for which the mark will be (or is being) used naturally fits into one of the groupings.

Step 2: If you are unsure, study the list in the Appendix that provides examples of goods and services for each class. Does that help?

Step 3: If you are still not sure, use the *Acceptable Identification of Goods and Services Manual.*

a. The *Acceptable Identification of Goods and Services Manual*

Probably the best source for finding the right class or classes for your goods or services is the list of approved descriptions the PTO has prepared for its examiners to use when reviewing applications. This list is found in the PTO's *Acceptable Identification of Goods and Services Manual.* This manual contains an alphabetical listing of goods and services; their descriptions; the proper class for each; a designation of "A," "D," or "M" indicating that the listing was either added, deleted, or modified; and the date of the change. The "added" designation means that the class is a new class on the list. The "deleted" designation means that the class is no longer available (so you can't use it). The "modified" designation means that the class was somehow changed recently. Perhaps it was broadened to include more types of goods or services, or perhaps its scope was pared down to include fewer goods or services.

The manual is available for browsing and searching on the PTO's website. Searching is recommended, because browsing can be cumbersome with such a large document. To search the manual at the PTO's website:

Step 1: Go to the PTO website (www.uspto.gov). Click the Trademark button on the left side. On the "Trademarks" page, under "Manuals," click "Acceptable Identification of Goods and Services Manual."

Step 2: On the page titled "Acceptable Identification of Goods and Services Manual," click the "Search" button at the bottom of the page.

Step 3: Enter a word or words in the "Search For" box that you would use to identify your good or service—for example, "wrench," "accounting," or "telephone"
—using the appropriate logical operator (see Chapter 5, Section C6).

To remind you, by using the "and" between words, you search for listings in the manual that contain all of the words you type in. By using the "or" between words, you search for listings that contain any one of the words you type in, but not necessarily all of them. After you click on the Search button on the left of the screen, the search engine will return a list of class information for the product or service you entered. (Samples appear below.)

For example, if you wanted to find the correct classification for your website design and hosting service, you could use the search words, "computer and network." Using the general terms "computer" and "network" provides you with a broad base of possible results, making your search more fruitful. The results you would find are shown below.

The tenth listing from the top (with an arrow pointing to it) shows the correct information for your website design service. The appropriate class is Class 42. The sixteenth listing from the top (also pointed to with an arrow) demonstrates the correct information for your website hosting service. The appropriate class is, again, Class 42.

Suppose, as another example, that you have created a line of paper coffee filters for use in automatic drip coffee makers. Your filter paper is printed with retro, playful, and unique designs to make your coffee filters more interesting to look at and fun to use. You want to register the mark for your line of paper coffee filters, *Zoo Filters*. To find out what class the PTO deems correct for this product (goods) and what description to use for your application, you could simply do a search using the word "coffee."

Your search would produce the results shown below. Close to the bottom of this list, indicated by an arrow, is the item you would be looking for. It states, "G 016 Filters for coffee makers (Paper) A 1991-04-02." From this line item, you can see that the PTO considers Class 16 as the appropriate class for paper coffee filters. Note that a simple search using "coffee and filters" would have produced only the line item highlighted.

**Trademark Acceptable Identification
of Goods and Services Manual**
Search Results

The S field indicates the status of the record: A=added, M=modified, D=deleted. The Date field indicates the date of that status. Minor corrections to an entry, e.g., typos, are not considered changes in status.

T IC S DATE GOODS

Result of search for "computer and network":

G 009 A 4/12/99 Communications software for connecting [specify, e.g., computer network users, global computer networks]

G 009 A 4/12/99 Computer e-commerce software to allow users to perform electronic business transactions via a global computer network

G 009 A 6/1/01 Computer network hubs, switches and routers

G 009 A 4/12/99 Computer software [specify the function of the programs, e.g., for use in database management, for use as a spreadsheet, for word processing, etc. and, if software is content- or field-specific, the field of use] that may be downloaded from a global computer network

G 009 A 6/1/01 Computer software for accessing information directories that may be downloaded from the global computer network

G 009 A 10/1/01 Consumer coupons downloaded from a global computer network

G 009 A 7/1/01 Global positioning system (GPS) consisting of computers, computer software, transmitters, receivers, and network interface devices

S 038 A 1/2/97 Broadcasting programs via a global computer network

S 042 A 6/1/01 Computer network design for others

➡ S 042 A 1/2/97 Computer services, namely, designing and implementing network web pages for others

S 042 A 1/2/97 Computer services, namely, providing search engines for obtaining data on a global computer network

S 038 A 6/1/01 Electronic delivery of images and photographs via a global computer network

S 041 A 4/12/99 Entertainment services, namely, providing a radio program in the field of [indicate subject matter or field] via a global computer network

S 041 A 4/12/99 Entertainment services, namely, providing a television program in the field of [indicate subject matter or field] via a global computer network

S 041 A 9/4/01 Entertainment services, namely, providing prerecorded music, information in the field of music, and commentary and articles about music, all on-line via a global computer network

➡ S 042 A 1/2/97 Hosting the web sites of others on a computer server for a global computer network

S 035 A 9/4/01 Integrated tracking and management of commercial transactions on a global computer network

S 038 A 8/6/01 Online document delivery via a global computer network

**Trademark Acceptable Identification
of Goods and Services Manual**
Search Results

The S field indicates the status of the record: A=added, M=modified, D=deleted. The Date field indicates the date of that status. Minor corrections to an entry, e.g., typos, are not considered changes in status.

TIC S DATE GOODS

Result of search for "coffee":

G 033 A 4/12/99 Alcoholic coffee-based beverage

G 030 A 4/2/91 Chicory based coffee substitute

G 030 A 4/2/91 Coffee

G 030 A 2/20/96 Coffee beans

G 021 A 4/2/91 Coffee cups

G 021 A 4/2/91 Coffee measures [domestic]

G 021 A 4/2/91 Coffee pots not of precious metal

G 014 A 4/2/91 Coffee pots of precious metal

G 011 A 4/2/91 Coffee roasting ovens

G 021 A 4/2/91 Coffee services not of precious metal

G 014 A 4/2/91 Coffee services of precious metal

G 021 A 4/2/91 Coffee stirrers

G 030 A 4/2/91 Coffee substitutes [grain or chicory based]

G 030 A 4/12/99 Coffee-based beverage containing milk

G 032 A 4/12/99 Coffee-flavored ale

G 032 A 4/12/99 Coffee-flavored beer

G 032 A 4/12/99 Coffee-flavored soft drink

G 007 A 4/2/91 Electric coffee grinders

G 011 A 4/2/91 Electric coffee makers

G 011 A 4/2/91 Electric coffee percolators

G 011 A 4/2/91 Electric coffee pots

G 021 A 4/2/91 Hand-operated coffee grinders

G 029 A 4/12/99 Milk-based beverage containing coffee

G 014 A 4/2/91 Non-electric coffee servers of precious metal

G 021 A 4/12/99 Non-electric coffee makers

G 021 A 4/2/91 Non-electric coffee percolators

G 021 A 4/2/91 Non-electric coffee pots not of precious metal

G 021 A 4/2/91 Non-electric coffee servers not of precious metal

 G 016 A 4/2/91 Paper filters for coffee makers

G 007 A 4/2/91 Power-operated coffee grinders

S 040 A 4/2/91 Coffee roasting and processing

S 043 M 1/1/02 Coffee supply services for offices

S 043 M 1/1/02 Office coffee supply services

**Trademark Acceptable Identification
of Goods and Services Manual**
Search Results

The S field indicates the status of the record: A=added, M=modified, D=deleted. The Date field indicates the date of that status. Minor corrections to an entry, e.g., typos, are not considered changes in status.

T IC S DATE GOODS

Result of search for "coffee and filters":

G 016 A 4/2/91 Paper filters for coffee makers

---

b. Search for Classes Used by Competitors

If the U.S. Patent and Trademark Office *Acceptable Identification of Goods and Services Manual* doesn't do the trick for you, you might consider examining the database of marks registered with the PTO to find out what classes have been assigned to the marks registered by your competitors. Also, once you conduct a trademark search in the course of adopting your mark, the report generated by that search may provide some good tips as to what class you should use.

As you know from Chapters 4 and 5, if you have access to the Internet, you also have access to a free database of marks (called TESS) that have already been registered with the PTO. (Go back to Chapter 5, Section B, where we explain how to access and use TESS.) For this type of search use the Free Search Form. Enter some terms that best describe the goods or services you and your competitors are offering the public, and put "gs" in brackets after each of the terms. For instance, if you want to start a delivery system that operates

from an Internet website, enter delivery [gs] and Internet [gs] and click submit. This will produce a long list of marks that are used on goods or services that have been described with the terms "delivery" and "Internet."

Another approach is to enter one or more terms that a competitor is using in its trademark and then examine the registrations to see what classes have been assigned to that mark.

EXAMPLE: You have created a new kind of coloring crayon that makes the colors brighter when applied to any type of paper or poster board. You know that Crayola has been making crayons for decades. You type in the word "Crayola" in the Search box and click on the Search button. You will get a long list of all the registered trademarks containing the term "Crayola." If you look at registration number 1279429—Crayola, you will learn that crayons have been assigned to International Class 016.

Related Goods and Product Expansion

Each trademark has a net of protection defined by the channels of commerce and class of goods. In some cases, this net may be very broad if a court determines that the owner of the mark is likely to expand into new markets. For example, in the case of a famous mark, the net is very wide because the owner of a famous mark is likely to expand into many product areas. In other cases, the net is not too wide because a smaller company is not likely to move into other areas. For example, it is possible that the owners of the *Gallo* trademark will expand into the sale of cheese because the trademark is associated with wine, and the consuming public identifies wine with cheese. However, the net of protection may not extend to cheese for a lesser-known wine trademark. There is no simple method of predicting how either the PTO or the courts will measure the net of related goods. Sometimes product expansion can be determined by the actions of the company (for example, evidence that the company is considering new products) and sometimes it is determined by marketplace factors (for example, record companies often expand into producing films). In either case, attorneys and judges weigh the relevant case law when making decisions regarding registration and litigation.

c. Trademark Assistance Center

If after reading this section you are still in doubt about the proper class or classes for your product or service, you can call the Trademark Assistance Center of the PTO (703-308-9000), describe the product or service, and ask them which class or classes may be involved. The trademark information specialist will answer your question and normally give you sound advice. Unfortunately, you don't have the legal right to rely on this opinion. For instance, if you later decide to register your mark, and you apply for registration in the class recommended by the Trademark Assistance Center, the person who eventually examines your application may disagree with the answer you were given. No big deal. You'll just have to assign a different class to the product or service—one that's acceptable to the examiner.

3. Marketing Channels

In addition to using the classification system for determining whether two marks are related and thus might confuse customers in the marketplace, it is also useful to look at the marketing channels through which the goods or services reach the public.

Goods and services are considered related when they are sold in similar outlets, marketed in similar media, placed near each other in stores, and generally considered alike by the consumer. If they are marketed quite differently, then no likelihood of confusion can exist, regardless of what class they are in for registration purposes.

For example, you should determine if the same sorts of information sources (billboards, websites, television, newspapers, magazines, radio) carry ads bearing both marks. Would both marks appear in ads in the same trade journals? Might the products or services be displayed or sold in the same store/catalog, or under the same heading in a trade directory? Will they both target the same customer base? Do both marks appear in advertising on the same types of websites? In any of these cases, it's fair to say that the marks are being used in the same marketing channels, which increases the likelihood of customer confusion.

⚠️ To some extent the Internet is one large marketing channel, and all goods and services moving through it are related to a degree. This is partially because of the way people search out information by using a search engine to locate sites containing a set of words chosen by the user. Unfortunately, cases dealing with the issue have not yet made their way up to the appellate level where law is made, so we can't be more specific about marketing channels on the Internet. In coming years we will learn whether the courts view the Internet as one large channel (that is, the equivalent of a Wal-Mart on the Net) or a series of smaller channels (like specialty shops at a mall).

E. Do the Goods or Services Compete?

Goods and services directly compete if the purchase of one negatively affects the purchase of the other. Two brands of bacon sitting side by side in a grocery display compete. So do airlines, fast food restaurants, personal computers, mobile telephones, and computer game stations.

F. How Similar Are the Marks?

The third factor in determining whether using similar marks will cause a likelihood of confusion is how similar the marks are. Do they sound or look alike, and if so, how much? Do they convey the same meaning? The closer two marks are in sight, sound, and meaning, the more likely it is that a legal problem will arise.

In comparing marks, remember that variations in spelling or punctuation do not make marks different if they sound the same. Thus, *Phansee-pants* is the same as *Fancy Pants*, and *Duncan Doughnuts* duplicates *Dunkin Donuts*. Even using foreign language equivalents can't make a mark different enough, if most of the public could tell they mean the same. So *La Petite Boulangerie* would infringe on *The Little Bakery*, and *El Sombrero Blanco* probably infringes on *The White Hat*.

Even marks with more definitive differences may be confusingly similar, in the same market. So courts have found *Quirst* is too close to *Squirt*, *Sarnoff* too much like *Smirnoff*, and *Lorraine* too reminiscent of *La Touraine*. Each of these pairs of marks were used on nearly identical goods. Probably the use of such duplicate marks would have passed legal muster if they had been on very different kinds of products. Again, that's because the more competitive marks are in a class or market channels, the less similar the marks have to be to cause confusion.

Are Two Marks Confusing? Use the Golden Rule and Get Some Feedback!

Telling whether the simultaneous use of two marks risks customer confusion can be a very subjective exercise, heavily influenced by the experience and mind-set of the person doing the analyzing. Nevertheless, there are two ways to get a handle on the question of potential confusion. First, ask yourself how you would feel if you were out there using your proposed mark and the other business came along with theirs. If you think you'd become energized to take some action, you have your answer. Second, if you are able to arrange for several objective friends or relatives to eyeball the two marks and give their honest impression of how they would react as customers, you'll probably have a good idea of how a judge would react. If even one of your friends or relatives thinks they might be confused by the marks, then chances are a judge would reach the same conclusion as to hypothetical customers and rule that the simultaneous use of the two marks would create the likelihood of customer confusion. Because this is a risk you don't want to take, chances are you'll want to pick another name.

G. Additional Factors

The next four factors from our list also affect whether likelihood of customer confusion exists between any given pair of marks.

1. How Strong Is Each Mark?

A strong mark is generally given a wider range of protection than a weak one. Remember from Chapter 2 that a mark is considered strong either because:

- the words, phrases, or symbols it consists of are distinctive (arbitrary, coined, or suggestive), or
- long and continuous use has made the public recognize it as the symbol of a particular product or service (the secondary meaning rule).

The point is, the stronger the original mark, the more likely it is that the second mark will be found to be confusingly similar if it has any similarities to the original mark at all. Conversely, the weaker a mark is, the less legal protection it is given and the more likely it is that a second mark will be found to not be confusingly similar, even if it has many similarities. This means you are safer in using a mark that is similar to an existing weak mark than a mark that is similar to an existing strong mark.

2. How Much Do the Goods or Services Cost?

Cost will also affect the likelihood of customer confusion. Because customers tend to take their time and consider carefully when buying an expensive item, the more expensive the item, the less chance of confusing customers. Conversely, an item that is cheap or subject to impulse buying is more likely to result in customer confusion if sold with a mark that is similar to another on goods that are even slightly related.

3. Are the Two Marks Directed Toward the Same Customers?

Two businesses that use similar marks to sell to the same customers are highly likely to cause customer confusion. Conversely, if businesses have separate customer bases, then the use of similar marks is unlikely to confuse anyone. For example, the market for replacement wood windows is likely to be limited to contractors and homeowners. As a result, a window manufacturer who uses the mark *Walls of Light* in its advertising probably won't confuse the customers of a magician who calls his show the *Wall of Lights*, because the two groups of customers won't often overlap.

It's useful to look at how large a sector of the market uses your product or service. If a small sector of the market knows and purchases a service, a similar mark used by a different small group is unlikely to confuse the two sets of consumers. But if a large segment of the public knows one mark, use of a similar mark is more likely to cause customer confusion, even if aimed at a slightly different market, because of the greater potential for overlap between the two groups.

4. Does One Owner Use the Mark on Several Different Products or Services?

A red flag should go up when you see a potentially conflicting mark that has already been used on a variety of products or services by the same mark owner, even if you wish to use it on a product that is unrelated to any of these uses. The problem is that because the first mark owner has already begun to use their mark on several products or services, it has asserted what is called in legal lingo the "right of expansion." Some examples of businesses that do this are *Calvin Klein* or *Pierre Cardin* (although the "dilution" rule would also keep anyone from using an identical mark or marks—see Chapter 1, Section B4).

Once this right of expansion is asserted (by using the mark on a number of different products), the courts will assume that the first user may wish to expand its use further and protect this right of expansion by permitting very few other uses of the same mark. So a second user seeking to use such a mark even on greatly dissimilar products will have less luck than if the mark were being used in a more limited fashion. By the same token, the public, having seen the mark on a variety of goods by the same owner, is more likely to assume that any new uses also belong to that owner, and thus are likely to be confused. Thus, the public would expect the mark *Yamaha*, which already appears on motorcycles, lawnmowers, and guitars, to represent the same company if it also appeared on computers or musical recordings.

H. Final Factors

After you have determined whether there is a likelihood of customer confusion between the marks you are evaluating, look at the following additional factors. They will help you determine the likelihood of getting into a lawsuit or of prevailing if you are mired in one. Then you will have a very clear idea of whether it's wise to use a particular mark.

1. History of Trademark Infringement Lawsuits

This is the most practical factor in predicting the likelihood of a lawsuit. It makes great sense to be wary of using a mark if the owner of a similar mark has a history of bringing trademark infringement suits. This generally means that the other mark owner will vigorously challenge any uses that are potentially confusing, and perhaps even some that are clearly not. Even if you eventually win such a suit, the cost, averaging $100,000, is rarely worth it in the long run. For example, anyone who follows these matters knows that *McDonald's* vigorously protects its golden

arch and the prefix "Mc" when it comes to any type of fast, efficient, and low-cost service business. For this reason, you should stay away from using anything that might get McDonald's ire up.

One way to discover a company's litigation history is to look up some of the secondary sources of trademark law listed in Chapter 14, Section A. Those books have tables in the back that list cases by the names of the litigants (parties to a lawsuit). If you don't find the name of the business with which you may have a conflict there, the records of the county and federal courthouses nearest their corporate headquarters will probably list cases in which they have been litigants (not all of which will be trademark cases). Or, you can consult an attorney, who will search for the company name on one of several comprehensive legal databases that list all cases in a given field. Consulting an attorney is likely to be the most expensive, but also the most effective, method.

2. How Long Has the Allegedly Infringing Business Used the Mark?

If an alleged infringer has used a mark for a long time without complaint from the owner, that may establish two things:

- It makes it look as though the alleged infringement has not harmed the true owner very much. This is known in legalese as "sleeping on your rights," and a court is less likely to give the owner any relief if it has not taken action to protect its rights despite another's use of the same mark for a long time.

- The alleged infringer has established some rights in the mark that may be superior to the true owner's rights, if only in the geographic area in which it has been used. (See Chapter 10, Sorting Out Trademark Disputes, for more on legal priorities in such situations.)

3. What Did the Alleged Infringer Intend in Adopting and Using the Mark in Question?

The intent of the alleged infringer also affects the question of whether one mark infringes on another. If it appears probable to the court that a business could only have chosen its mark in order to take advantage of its similarity to another mark, then the court is very likely to find an infringement to exist. If, for example, a successful and well-known marketer of French bread uses *Staff of Life* as a trademark, and a new rival calls its product *Stuff of Life*, the court will be very suspicious about the intent of the rival—and it may be hard to persuade the judge or jury that the owner of the *Stuff of Life* mark did not intentionally copy the first mark.

I. How to Read a Trademark Search Report

In previous sections we advised you what to look for when evaluating a trademark search. In this section, we'll walk you through a typical search report, and we'll answer some common questions. In Appendix C to this book, we have included relevant sections from a search report generated by Sc[i]3. We requested the Sc[i]3 search for the name *Incorporator Pro*, which Nolo (the publisher of this book) intends to use as the name for a software program that assists users forming a corporation.

The Sc[i]3 search is the broadest type of search report in which a searcher trolls through three groups of trademarks—those that are federally registered, those registered with state governments, and those that are not registered (common law). All of the major search report companies generate similar comprehensive searches.

⚠️ **No Guarantees.** Trademark searchers and database inputters make mistakes. But don't be deterred from getting a report just because search companies won't guarantee their results. These reports are still the established legal standard for prejudging a trademark choice.

1. Jump Right In

Before starting any search, you must know what you're seeking. In our case, we're looking for marks that are:

- identical to *Incorporator Pro* on similar or related goods or services
- similar to *Incorporator Pro* on similar or related goods or services, or
- famous and similar to *Incorporator Pro*.

The easiest way to start is to pick up the report and start reading. This task might seem overwhelming considering the bewildering number of entries. Don't worry. For now, you can disregard the information about search strategies, databases, or other explanatory text and just look at the actual entries. You'll notice that each section usually starts with a list of possible matches, followed by individual analysis of each relevant entry.

Page through the report and make a cursory review. We did this with the report in Appendix C. (Note, not all of the report is reproduced in the Appendix, just those portions relevant to our discussion.) Initially we noted that there are no marks—federal, state, or common law—that are identical to our proposed mark, *Incorporator Pro*. There were also no marks that included both the words "Pro" and "Incorporator," such as "Legal Pro Incorporator." We also didn't recognize any of the marks in the report as being famous. We made a table as shown below.

Standard	Mark
identical to Incorporator Pro (on similar or related goods or services)	None
similar to Incorporator Pro (on similar or related goods or services)	*Corpro* *Incorporation Primer* *Internet Incorporators* *Procorp* *Incorporate* *California Incorporators* *The Professional Solution*
famous and similar to Incorporator Pro	None

After completing this first pass, we took a second tour of the search report, examining more of the search details.

2. Federal Trademark Search

Search reports are usually divided into tabbed sections for federal, state, and common law. As noted, each section usually starts with a list of entries, followed by details relevant to each entry. These individual entries provide the most helpful decision-making data, for example, whether the mark is live or dead, the type of goods, the class of goods, the owners, and the length of registration. The federal trademark search portion is always first.

Below we provide some questions and answers describing how this data affects your trademark decisions.

- **Am I free to use dead (cancelled or abandoned) marks?** Trademark search reports always indicate whether a mark is live (active and currently registered) or dead (abandoned by the owner or canceled by the PTO). For example, the search report provides information about the mark *Incorporation Primer*. This mark was registered in 1977 but was canceled in 1983. The cancellation after six years was probably the result of the failure to file a Section 8 affidavit. However, the cancellation doesn't mean the trademark is available for use. If a mark shows up as dead on the report, it's quite possible that the mark is still being used, albeit in an unregistered status. As long as the mark is still in use, no one else can use it (in a way that would create the likelihood of customer confusion) without infringing it. There are many ways to determine if a trademark is no longer being used. The simplest method is to call the company and ask if the product can be purchased. If the response is something like, "No, we haven't sold that product in years," then there is a chance that the trademark is truly abandoned. A presumption of abandonment arises after three years. If you can afford additional expenses, professional investigators can help you determine the extent of the company's use. If you believe that a mark has been abandoned, even if it is showing up as live on the search report, you may file a Petition for Cancellation based upon abandonment with the Patent and Trademark Office.

- **What importance should I place on trademarks on the Supplemental Register?** That depends on the similarity of the marks and how long the mark has been on the Supplemental Register. As you may remember from Chapter 1, Section C2, the Supplemental Register is used to register weak or descriptive marks. These marks get very limited rights. After five years on the Supplemental Register, however, the mark becomes eligible for the Principal Register. Consider the trademark "Incorporate": The goods are identical to those for *Incorporator Pro.* The names are similar. The mark is registered on the Supplemental Register, not the Principal Register, and the five-year period has recently passed. We need to perform more research, if possible, to find out if the product is still

available, and if possible, whether the trademark will move to the Principal Register. We also learn that the term "Incorporate" is considered weak when used on these goods. That standard may affect what happens when we attempt to register.

- **What if the report indicates that the trademark owner has disclaimed some portion of the trademark? Does that mean I'm free to use it?** Yes and no. You're free to use the disclaimed terms without infringing, but if you attempt to register your mark, you'll probably have to disclaim the same terms. In other words, you won't be able to stop anyone else from using those terms either. As explained in Chapter 7, a disclaimer is a statement that a trademark owner asserts no exclusive right in a specific portion of a mark, apart from its use within the mark. Disclaimers are required by PTO examiners as a condition of registration. For example, in the *Incorporator Pro* search in Appendix C, you will note Disclaimer Statements for terms such as "Nationwide Incorporators," "Incorporators Ltd," and "Internet Incorporators." You may wonder, how can the owner of the "Internet Incorporators" trademark claim any trademark rights, if its whole name has been disclaimed? In the case of this and many other marks, the owner claims limited rights to the stylized appearance of the mark and the accompanying graphics. By reading disclaimers, you will learn what will have to be

```
***  User: suns1  ***  Serial Number: 73033102  ***  9/13/02 4:28:00 PM  ***
                           [Typed Drawing]
Mark
      INCORPORATION PRIMER

Goods and Services
      (CANCELLED) IC  016.  US 038.  G & S: BOOKLETS PUBLISHED FROM TIME TO
      TIME, RELATING TO THE INCORPORATION, QUALIFICATION, AND STATUTORY
      REPRESENTATION OF CORPORATIONS.  FIRST USE: 19560000.  FIRST USE IN
      COMMERCE: 19560000

Mark Drawing Code
      (1) TYPED DRAWING

Serial Number
      73033102

Filing Date
      September 26, 1974

Registration Number
      1065261

Registration Date
      May 10, 1977

Owner Name and Address
      (REGISTRANT) CT Corporation System UNKNOWN New York NEW YORK

      (LAST LISTED OWNER) CT CORPORATION SYSTEM CORPORATION DELAWARE 277 PARK
      AVE. NEW YORK, N.Y. 10017 NEW YORK NEW YORK 10017

Assignment Recorded
      ASSIGNMENT RECORDED

Type of Mark
      TRADEMARK

Register
      PRINCIPAL

Live Dead Indicator
      DEAD

Cancellation Date
      October 4, 1983




*** Search: 2 *** Document Number: 46 ***
```

```
*** User: suns1  *** Serial Number: 75128694  *** 9/13/02 4:22:26 PM ***
                          [Typed Drawing]
Mark
     INCORPORATE

Goods and Services
     IC 009.  US 021 023 026 036 038.  G & S: software for creating the
     legal documents to form a corporation and installation and instruction
     manuals sold as a unit therewith.  FIRST USE: 19950323.  FIRST USE IN
     COMMERCE: 19950413

Mark Drawing Code
     (1) TYPED DRAWING

Serial Number
     75128694

Filing Date
     June 10, 1996

Supplemental Register Date
     February 17, 1997

Registration Number
     2085108

Registration Date
     July 29, 1997

Owner Name and Address
     (REGISTRANT) UNABRIDGED SOFTWARE, INC. CORPORATION TEXAS 5959 West Loop
     South, Suite 300 Bellaire TEXAS 77401

Type of Mark
     TRADEMARK

Register
     SUPPLEMENTAL

Live Dead Indicator
     LIVE

Attorney of Record
     Rita M. Irani




*** Search: 1 *** Document Number: 104 ***
```

disclaimed when applying for your trademark.

- **What if a mark is pending but has not yet been registered?** The trademark search report always informs you as to the status of the mark, whether it's presently registered, or if it's a pending application. As explained in Chapter 7, pending applications, including intent-to-use applications (assuming they issue as registrations), will have priority over owners who commence use after the earlier application filing date. So, if there's a pending mark that's similar and will be used on similar goods, that's an important strike against your proposed use.

- **What if the search report indicates that a company has assigned the mark to another business. Should that affect my determination?** No, the assignee (the company that has purchased the mark) acquires all of the rights of the original owner and can enforce those rights and stop you from using a similar mark.

- **Which matters more, whether the mark is used on similar goods or in the same class?** Generally, your first concern should be whether the goods and services are similar. This is especially true in crowded classes like Class 9, in which the *Incorporator Pro* trademark will be registered. That's because Class 9 is the class for most scientific, technical, computer, and Internet marks, and it's the class in which 20% of all trademark applications are filed. In Class 9, for example, it's possible for similar marks to be registered for different goods, say, video games or nautical equipment. For our purposes, therefore, we're much more concerned with companies that offer similar goods (whether books or software) or similar services. (Note, this distinction between goods and classes may not be as dramatic in less-crowded classes.)

```
*** User: suns1  *** Serial Number: 75404152  *** 9/13/02 2:39:57 PM ***
```

Mark
  INTERNET INCORPORATORS

Goods and Services
  IC 042. US 100 101. G & S: Legal services, namely, formation of
  corporations, resident agent services and office headquarters services
  for others. FIRST USE: 19980411. FIRST USE IN COMMERCE: 19980411

Mark Drawing Code
  (5) WORDS, LETTERS, AND/OR NUMBERS IN STYLIZED FORM

Serial Number
  75404152

Filing Date
  December 11, 1997

Filed ITU
  FILED AS ITU

Supplemental Register Date
  September 13, 1999

Registration Number
  2458702

Registration Date
  June 5, 2001

Owner Name and Address
  (REGISTRANT) Sierra Holdings Limited CORPORATION NEVADA PO BOX 1490 VERDI
  NEVADA 89438

Assignment Recorded
  ASSIGNMENT RECORDED

Disclaimer Statement
  NO CLAIM IS MADE TO THE EXCLUSIVE RIGHT TO USE "INTERNET INCORPORATORS"
  APART FROM THE MARK AS SHOWN

```
*** Search: 8 *** Document Number: 5 ***                (cont)
```

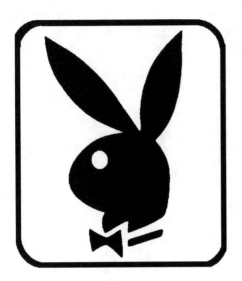

3. State Registration Search

If you are having a trademark search done for you, it's always a good idea to have the search firm include a search of the state trademark registration database. The state search report section, like the federal search section, starts with a list of state registered marks that is followed by details on each relevant listing. Almost all such reports, regardless of the searching company, are performed using the TrademarkScan database owned by Thomson & Thomson.

How do you quantify the effect of a state trademark registration versus a federal registration? A federal registration creates a presumption of national priority. Not so with a state registration or a common law mark. The impact of these types of marks is quite often local. Nonetheless, a local user can obstruct you if you attempt to sell goods or services in their geographic area. For that reason you

need to determine the extent of the use. Are the products distributed or services offered over a wide geographic area? Does the company's trademark have an Internet presence? Obviously, the less of a presence and the more localized the use, the less of a threat there is to your proposed use.

Also, it's important to keep in mind that claiming state and common law rights does not require the same standardized scrutiny as federal registration. Consider the data provided for the state registration for "California Incorporators The Professional Solution" in the *Incorporator Pro* search. The "Goods/Services" are vaguely described as "new business in California," so it's not even clear whether the trademark is used for goods or services. Because many state trademark offices simply rubber stamp applications without a thorough analysis, these marks are sometimes more susceptible to challenges on the basis of descriptiveness or genericness.

4. Common Law Report

The common law trademarks section includes trademarks that aren't registered anywhere, as well as company names and other names that may not actually be used as trademarks. The search companies wade through many sources, including public databases, product announcements, business products databases, and proprietary database records. The rules for state registrations apply for common law marks: If you are concerned about an identical or similar mark, do more research to determine whether the name is actually (and currently) used as a trademark.

5. Our Conclusions

We made two conclusions after reviewing the *Incorporator Pro* search. First, we did not find any marks so similar in appearance or phonetics to merit serious concern of infringement. In other words, the coast was clear. The reason that the coast was clear, however, led to our second conclusion that terms such as "Incorporator" or "Incorporate" and "Pro" may be considered descriptive and may have to be disclaimed or may require registration on the Supplemental Register. In short, even though Nolo is free to use the term, it may run into problems if the company attempts to register it on the Principal Register.

Your trademark search results, obviously, will differ. If in doubt about your conclusions or the search report data, your best course of action would be to consult with a trademark attorney for help. ■

Chapter 7

Federal Trademark Registration

7his chapter helps you register your trademark with the U.S. Patent and Trademark Office (PTO). Registration is optional, but it provides a number of significant advantages to the trademark owner. Registration on the Principal Register provides you with exclusive nationwide ownership of the mark (except where the mark is already being used by prior users who haven't registered the mark) and official notice to all would-be later users that the mark is unavailable. In addition, registration provides a legal presumption that you are the owner of the mark, which means it's easier for you to prove ownership if a dispute over the mark ends up in court.

Taken together, these benefits make it easier to win an infringement lawsuit and make it more likely that damages can be collected for the infringement. That may mean more money to pay the attorneys, which often makes it worthwhile to bring the lawsuit in the first place.

To use this chapter, you should first have a basic understanding of:

- how trademark law works on and off the Internet (Chapter 1)
- how to choose a legally strong trademark (Chapter 3)
- how to find out whether other marks exist that might conflict with yours (Chapters 4 and 5), and
- how to tell whether your mark is confusingly similar to another (Chapter 6).

New Fees: Use Paper, Pay More!

As of 2004, the USPTO has adopted a two-tiered fee system—applicants filing electronically using TEAS pay $325 per class while applicants filing with paper applications pay $375 per class. Check the USPTO website for current fees.

A. Brief Overview of Federal Registration

If you are already using the mark, here are the four steps required for federal registration:

- gather the necessary information, such as the date you first starting using the mark anywhere, the date you first used it in commerce that Congress may regulate (for example, interstate commerce), and a specimen showing how the mark is actually being used
- complete an application—either online or on hard copy
- file the application with the PTO—either online or by mail—accompanied by a specimen of how your mark is being used and a fee of $325 per class of good (if filing electronically) or $375 per class of good (if filing by mail), and
- if required, modify the application in response to the trademark examiner's comments.

If you are not using the mark but wish to reserve it for future use, apply on an intent-to-use basis. You will not have to supply a specimen, but once you start using the mark you'll have to:

- file an additional form notifying the PTO that you are now using the mark
- provide a specimen of the use, and
- pay an additional $100.

More fees and forms are required if you delay getting the mark into use within six months after the PTO approves the mark for registration.

B. What Marks Qualify for Federal Registration

Now that you have an overview of the trademark registration process, let's start by examining the basic qualifications for placement of a mark on the federal trademark register. There are, in fact, two trademark registers— the Principal Register and the Supplemental Register. Your goal is to get your mark placed on the Principal Register, because it provides most of the benefits of federal registration. However, if your mark doesn't qualify for the Principal Register, you may have it placed on the Supplemental Register—which does provide a few benefits. (See Chapter 1, Section C2, for more on the Supplemental Register.)

From this point on, when we speak of federal registration, we are referring to registration on the Principal Register.

In Chapter 1 we spoke about qualifications for federal trademark registration. To review, a mark qualifies for placement on the Principal Register if:

- the PTO considers the mark distinctive, either inherently so or because it has

obtained a secondary meaning through use over time

- the mark does not legally conflict with an existing registered mark
- the mark is in actual use
- use is in commerce that Congress may regulate (that is, it moves across state, territorial, or international borders, or affects commerce across these borders), and
- the mark is not scandalous, immoral, or deceptive.

The first two qualifications—distinctiveness and nonconflicting marks—have been explained in Chapters 3 and 6, respectively. Now we will cover the last three.

1. Is the Mark in Actual Use?

A mark must be in actual use before it can be placed on the Federal Register. This doesn't mean that you have to be using the mark when you apply for registration (see Section C, below, on intent-to-use applications) but only that the mark will not be registered until you notify the PTO that the mark has been put into actual use, provide a sample, and pay an extra fee.

What constitutes actual use? As a general rule, "in use" means that the mark is being utilized in the marketplace to identify your goods or services. This doesn't mean that you need to have actually sold the product or service, just that the product or service associated with the mark is available for sale in the marketplace. The criteria used to determine whether a trademark is in use are different, depending on whether the trademark is being used for a product or a service.

For products (tangible goods), your mark is in use if the mark appears on the goods or on labels or tags attached to them, and the goods have either been shipped to a store for resale or use as a sample, or are available for sale by mail or over the Internet. However, a token sale made only for the purpose of getting your mark "in use" doesn't count. The use has to be a true attempt (sometimes called a "bona fide" attempt) to identify and distinguish your goods or services in the marketplace. The following examples show legitimate uses of the marks for purposes of registration.

> **EXAMPLE 1:** Ben sent a sample of his *No-Knees* pants to a department store interested in selling them.

> **EXAMPLE 2:** Emily's earrings were shipped in a box carrying the label *All Ears*, for the legitimate purpose of resale by a local street vendor.

> **EXAMPLE 3:** Peter developed a system for taking orders and processing credit-card payments over the Internet, and he launched the sale of his *Bearware* software online. He used the mark *Bearware* prominently on his website.

For services, your mark is in use if the services are actually being marketed under the mark and you can legitimately deliver the services to customers.

> **EXAMPLE 1:** Toby purchased a 900 number phone line for providing sports trivia

under the name *Sportorific*. As soon as his lines were up and running and he had advertised his services under the name *Sportorific*, his mark was in use.

EXAMPLE 2: Helen decided to call her housecleaning service *Mistress Tidy*. When she first advertised her services under that name on a bulletin board at a local market, she put her mark into use.

EXAMPLE 3: Alice started her own Internet service provider business under the mark *CosmoNet*. She set up her system and prepared all of the equipment she would need to offer her services. The day she first started advertising her services under her mark and with all of her systems in place and ready to go, she put her mark into use.

2. Are You Using the Mark in Commerce That Congress May Regulate?

Even if the mark is in actual use, it won't qualify for federal registration unless it is in use "in commerce that Congress may regulate." To satisfy this requirement, you must do one or more of the following:

- ship a product to which the mark is attached across a state line (most manufacturers, wholesalers, and mail-order businesses do this regularly)
- ship a product to which the mark is attached between a state and a territory or between a territory and another territory (for instance, between New York and Puerto Rico, or between Puerto Rico and the Virgin Islands)

- ship a product to which the mark is attached between a state or territory and another country (for instance, between California and Hong Kong, or between Puerto Rico and Cuba)
- use the mark in advertising in which your business offers services outside the state (many businesses that have sites on the Internet and other businesses, such as Disneyland, do this regularly)
- use the mark in the course of conducting a service business across a state line (such as most trucking operations, many 900 numbers, and, increasingly, businesses that offer e-commerce over the Internet)
- use the mark to identify a service business in more than one state (such as *McDonald's, Holiday Inn, Hilton Hotels*) or across international or territorial borders
- use the mark in the course of operating a business that caters to interstate or international travelers (such as a hotel, restaurant, tour guide service, or ski resort) or
- use the mark in a business that is regulated by the federal government.

The basic reason for this commerce requirement is that the federal government has no constitutional authority to regulate marks that are used only within one state's borders.

Here are examples of marks used in commerce that Congress may regulate:

Goods

Alan's mousetrap is sold in three states under the mark *MiceNoMore*, and the mark appears on the packaging.

Rosebud, Inc., distributes a computer program called *Rosecare* to nurseries throughout the country. The mark appears on the packaging and opening screen of the software.

Ruth lives in White River Junction, Vermont, a town just across the river from Hanover, New Hampshire, where Dartmouth University is located. She sells a brand of baked goods in both towns—under the label *Ruth's Bakery Delights*.

Travelers come to Berkeley, California, from around the world to buy *Peet's Coffee*. Peet's doesn't advertise, but it draws a national and international trade under the service mark *Peet's* and the trademark *Peet's Coffee*. Peet's also operates a brisk international mail-order business and has a great website.

Services

Etta's computer consulting services are marketed by telephone and direct mail to potential customers in Canada, California, and Nevada under the mark *Quick-Bytes*.

Toby Drysdale's 900 phone number for sports trivia, *Sportorific*, is marketed through ads on national radio and television networks and is also available to purchasers in Puerto Rico and Mexico.

Rose's newspaper advice column is syndicated in three Northeastern states under the name *Rosie to the Rescue*.

Doug's mail-order shoe-repair service is marketed under the name *Sole Security* via ads in national magazines and newspapers.

Ninth Wave Surfing provides lessons in Hawaii to vacationers from all over the world.

This last example shows an "effect" that a business can have on interstate commerce. Though the "effect" may also qualify a mark for federal registration, it is not as clear-cut a case as when the mark actually appears in more than one state—for instance, in advertising or mail-order catalogs.

As a general rule, the PTO trademark examiners do not investigate whether the mark for which registration is being sought is being used in "commerce that Congress may regulate." Nor is there any place in the application to describe exactly where, geographically, the mark is being used. So, applications are seldom, if ever, rejected because the commerce requirement hasn't been satisfied. However, if you ever have to defend your registration—in court or before the PTO—you may be required to prove that the mark was in fact being used in commerce at the time of its registration.

3. Is Your Mark Immoral, Deceptive, or Scandalous?

You may not register a mark if the mark:

- contains "immoral," "deceptive," or "scandalous" matter. For example, a mark resembling a sex organ would be considered immoral; a mark suggesting miracle properties in a product that are not substantiated would be deceptive; and a mark showing a mutilated corpse would be scandalous.

- disparages or falsely suggests a connection with persons (living or dead), institutions, beliefs, or national symbols (see examples, below)

- includes the flag or coat of arms or other insignia of the United States, any state or municipality, or any foreign nation, or includes any simulation of such flag or insignia

- consists of or contains a name, portrait, or signature of a particular living individual (except with his or her written consent) or the name, signature, or portrait of a deceased president of the United States during the life of his widow, if any (except with the written consent of the widow)

- is already taken by an organization that has been granted the exclusive right by statute to use the marks or symbol (such organizations include the Boy Scouts and the U.S. Olympic Committee, and the Department of the Interior for the character name *Smokey the Bear*)

- is misleading or just plain false (such as a trademark that suggests chocolate in a product that contains no chocolate)
- is primarily a geographic name or a surname (see Chapter 3 for a discussion of these types of names and when they are and are not considered distinctive).

Examples of Disparaging or Unauthorized Marks

- a mark showing a picture of the United States president standing on the American flag
- a baseball-related mark suggesting a connection with Babe Ruth (unless authorization was given by Babe Ruth's heirs), or
- a silhouette of a defecating dog (*Greyhound Corp. v. Both Worlds Inc.*, 6 U.S.P.Q.2d 1635 (TTAB 1988)).

C. If You Haven't Started Using Your Mark, Should You File an Intent-to-Use Application?

If you are not yet using your mark, you can wait until you put it into use before filing a trademark application, or, you can file an application on the grounds that you intend to use it within six months of the date the mark is approved for registration by the PTO. If you are unable to put the mark into use within that period, you can purchase additional six-month extensions, one at a time until three years have passed, if you are able to convince the PTO that the reasons for the delays are legitimate.

The advantage of filing an intent-to-use application is that your filing date will serve as the date of your first use of the mark—assuming you go on to put the mark in actual use and take the other steps necessary to get the mark placed on the federal trademark register. This first-use date can be very important in the event a conflict develops with another mark—in the PTO or in the marketplace. (See Chapter 1, Section B, for the importance of the date of first use.) Once you decide to file on this basis, you should do so as quickly as possible, to obtain the earliest possible date of first use.

As mentioned, the intent-to-use approach is more expensive than filing an actual use application—at least $100 more expensive, plus $150 for each additional six-month extension that is needed. Therefore, it is most appropriate to use the intent-to-use application when you have come up with a truly distinctive mark (see Chapter 3, How to Choose a Good Name for Your Business, Product, or Service) or you plan to spend big bucks "tooling up" to use the mark and you don't want to lay out the cash until you know that the mark will be yours.

If your mark is legally weak—for instance, it uses common words in a common way or is descriptive of the products or services—you will have little choice but to wait until you have put the mark into use and can demonstrate that the public associates the mark with your product or service. Keep in mind that the PTO will only issue a Notice of Allowance for marks that are distinctive, either inherently or under the secondary meaning rule.

D. What Examples of Your Mark Will You Submit With Your Application?

➡ If you are filing an intent-to-use application, you will not yet have specimens and need not deal with this information at this time; you should skip ahead to Section E. However, if and when you put the mark into use and file the proper documents necessary to complete the registration process, you will need the information in this section.

When applying for federal registration on an actual-use basis, you must submit an example of how your mark is being used in commerce, known as a specimen. If you plan to apply for registration under more than one trademark class, you will need to submit a separate specimen showing use for each class.

Most likely you will be filing online using TEAS. In that case you will need to submit the specimen as a JPEG file that can be "attached" to your online application (more on this in Section G). You should prepare this photographic or graphic file before beginning the application process. It must be under two megabytes file size and should be scanned at 300 DPI or higher.

If you are using the printed forms, you will need to include a physical specimen in your mailing to the PTO. The specimen may not exceed 8½ inches (21.6 cm) wide and 13 inches (33 cm) long, and it must be flat. There is no minimum size. As we emphasize later, the specimen must portray the exact same mark as appears in the drawing you will be submitting with the application.

1. Specimens for Marks on Goods (Trademarks)

Specimens of how the mark is used with goods must show a very close association between the mark and the goods. Acceptable specimens usually include labels, tags, or containers showing the mark.

a. Displays As Specimens for Goods

Displays, such as banners and window displays, may also be used, but with caution. The display must be meant to catch the buyer's attention where the sale is made (for instance, at the store), and the mark must be prominent and clearly connected to the goods. For example, a window sign in a drugstore that reads "See our All Ears earrings special!" would probably qualify as an appropriate specimen. However, the line between displays and advertising can be fuzzy, and advertising is not sufficient for specimens of marks used for goods. If you have a choice, use another type of specimen.

b. Marks on Goods As Specimens

If you place your mark on your goods by using a rubber stamp or stencil, you may submit a specimen of an impression of the stamp or stencil on a piece of paper.

c. Photographing Your Specimens

If your *Solve-it Solvent* mark is used in connection with 55-gallon drums of solvent and printed only on the drums, you would submit a photograph (in JPEG format, when filing electronically) of a drum or drums clearly showing the whole mark. The photograph must show the whole item, or enough of it so the examiner can clearly see what is shown in the picture, and all writing on the item must be visible. If a photograph of the whole item does not show the mark in enough detail, send one photo of the whole item and another close-up photo of the writing including the mark (the two photos together would constitute one specimen). If there is writing on more than one side, either send more than one photo or place several items in one photo so they show all sides of the item on which writing appears.

> **EXAMPLE:** Suppose your mark *Solve-it Solvent* appears on the front and back of the drum in large type, surrounded by other writing describing the contents. Your first photo should portray three or four drums, each showing a different part of all the writing (*Solve-it Solvent* and the description). You would then want a few more photos, from a closer range, so that by looking at them the examiner could see all the writing that appears on a typical drum. (Again, all the photos together would constitute one specimen.) If the writing could not be made legible for some reason (maybe too small to photograph well), a separate piece of paper including all text on the drum should also be submitted.

The reason all the writing has to be visible is that the PTO wants to see the context in which your mark is used to be sure it is con-sistent with the class under which you are registering the mark.

d. Domain Name Specimens

If you are registering your entire domain name, the specimen should be a JPEG of your Web page showing your domain name. This can be done using the screen capture feature in Windows (try hitting the Control and Print Screen simultaneously and then pasting that into a graphics program file) or by using a software program such as Snag-It. If you are just registering the unique part of your domain name (without the .com), your specimen may be an advertisement of your services. Either way, make sure your speci-men shows your name exactly as you portray it in the "mark drawing" box in the applica-tion.

Your domain name specimen must show two things:

1. You are using your domain name as a trademark. A specimen that shows your website and the domain name typed into the address line of your browser is not sufficient. Your domain name should be a prominent part of the design of your home page. Ideally, it should be at the very top of the page, easy to spot and easy to read, and it should dominate the quadrant of the page in which it is located.

2. The services being offered on your website match the description of the services in your application. If you are providing financial information as your service, for example, make sure your specimen shows that you are doing so.

If I Registered My Trademark, Do I Need to Register My Trademark.com?

Let's say you have been using the name *Loudness* as a trademark for a line of menswear. You registered Loudness with the PTO. Now you're going online and selling the same menswear on your website with the domain name Loudness.com. Do you need to register Loudness.com with the PTO?

In this case, there's little to be gained from registering Loudness.com with the PTO because you already have the ability to stop anyone from using Loudness for menswear whether they are selling it online or off. Another reason not to bother is that you cannot claim any separate trademark rights in ".com," because the PTO considers top-level domain terms such as ".com," ".org," and ".edu" as unprotectible.

You should consider registering Loudness .com if you will be establishing some services or products unique to your Internet business. For example, if you are establishing an online store that will offer a fashion newsletter as well as your menswear, then you should consider registering Loudness.com.

e. Unacceptable Specimens for Marks on Goods

The following are *unacceptable* specimens for marks on goods:

- advertising material, including anything that is produced for the sole purpose of telling potential buyers about your product, even if you package it with the goods (such as cards packaged with a new pen telling how wonderful it is and what it's made of)
- price lists, catalogs, trade directories, and publicity releases
- instruction sheets
- internal company documents, including invoices and memos sent within an applicant company
- specimens showing the mark with the ® symbol—it is illegal to use the ® symbol until after your mark is officially registered with the PTO (see Chapter 8, How to Use and Care for Your Trademark). Specimens with a TM next to the mark are okay.
- any use of the mark merely to identify your business (not in direct connection with particular goods or services), including letterhead stationery, labels carrying only a company name and return address, and bags and boxes used at store cash registers to carry sold merchandise.

2. Specimens for Marks Used for Services (Service Marks)

When you are offering a service, you have no product to which you can affix a label. Acceptable specimens for services include a variety of materials that can't be used for product marks. This includes scanned copies of advertising and marketing materials such as newspaper and magazine ads, brochures, billboards, direct mail pieces, and menus (for restaurants).

Letterhead stationery and business cards showing the mark may be used if the services are plainly reflected on them, because the name or symbol being claimed as a mark would, in that context, be used to identify the services provided—that is, as a mark rather than as a trade name (remember, trade names as such may not be registered—see the sidebar, "Trade Names," below).

> **EXAMPLE 1:** Etta's business cards for her personal computer consulting services include her mark *Quick-Bytes* and the text, "consulting services for the PC user."

> **EXAMPLE 2:** Toby's sports trivia 900 line grew and he had stationery printed, including the line, "*Sportorific* Gives You The Latest Sports Trivia 24 Hours A Day." The stationery would be accepted as a specimen.

A letter on stationery will even be accepted as a specimen for a service mark if the mark appears and the services are described in the letter. Assume Toby's letterhead only said

"Gen-X Sports" and gave the address and phone number. He could submit a copy of a letter sent to a national sports magazine asking that his 900 number be listed in their directory, as long as the letter described the services.

Gen-X Sports
555 First Street, West
Sonoma, CA 95476

Dear Sirs:

As you may know, our sports trivia line, *Sportorific,* 900-555-7777, has been providing customers with sports trivia 24 hours a day for the past year. We would be honored if you would consider listing our line in your directory.

---

a. Audiotapes

Most marks appear in writing somewhere. If your mark represents a service, and it appears only on radio ads or in some other audio form, you may submit a sound file of the audio. This can be done through the TEAS application. The sound mark specimen, consisting of a WAV file or MP3 file, can be sent as an email attachment directly to the TEAS Support Team, at teas@uspto.gov. However, because the TEAS form will require a JPEG attachment for the specimen, the applicant must still create a JPEG file for this purpose, but it will merely consist of a statement that "A WAV file (or MP3 file) has been sent directly to the TEAS Support Team for pro-cessing." For easier association of the WAV (or MP3) file with the proper application, the applicant should submit the actual appli-cation first and then reference in the email to the TEAS Support Team the assigned se-rial number and an indication that this is a "new application." All other filings (e.g., an Allegation of Use, a Section 8, etc.) should be done in the same manner, with the serial number or registration number referenced in the email, and a clear indication of the type of filing.

b. Internet Pages

A screen shot of the full Web page should be fine. As noted, this can be done using the screen capture feature in Windows (hitting the Control and Print Screen simultaneously and then pasting that into a graphics program file) or by using a software program such as Snag-It. If the mark is being prominently displayed on the home page, so much the better.

c. Unacceptable Specimens for Services

The following are unacceptable specimens for marks for services:

- news releases or articles based on news releases
- documents showing trademark rather than service mark usage (use of the mark in connection with goods rather than services)
- invoices and similar documents such as packing slips
- specimens showing trade name usage only (use of the mark to identify a com-pany, such as on letterhead). As discussed

earlier, one exception to this is if the let-terhead or the text of the letter identifies the services represented by the mark.

Trade Names

Remember from Chapter 1, A Trademark Primer, a trade name is the name of a com-pany and is not registrable as a trademark or service mark unless it is used for more than identification purposes. To be registrable, the trade name must also be used to identify goods the company sells (trademark) or to market or promote services (service mark). However, it is very common for a company's trade name and the trademark used in providing the company's services to be the same, which makes the trade name regis-trable in its capacity as a mark.

E. What International Class Is the Best Fit for Your Product or Service?

Part of the trademark registration process involves assigning your product or service to one or more international classes. A list of these classes is in the Appendix. We explain the classification system in Chapter 6, Section D.

If after reading the material in Chapter 6 you are in doubt about the proper class or classes for your product or service, you can always call the Applications section of the PTO and ask which class or classes may be appropriate for you. The clerk will answer your question and normally give you sound advice. Unfortunately, you don't have the legal right to rely on this opinion. If the person who eventually examines your application in the PTO disagrees with the answer you were given, you will have to assign a different class to the product or service.

It's possible to apply for registration of a mark under more than one class. The reason you would do this is that the class you register under can be an important determinant of the scope of protection you receive.

> **EXAMPLE:** Etta, who both sells computer software and offers consulting services under the mark *Quick-Bytes*, registers the mark under Class 9 (electrical and scientific apparatus). This registration should go far to protect Etta against the same or similar marks used on computer software and other related products. But it may not protect her against uses of the mark in connection with computer services. Only if she also registers the *Quick-Bytes* mark under the appropriate service class (Class 35 or Class 41) will she obtain the maximum possible protection of her mark.

⚠️ The classification system is designed more for the convenience of the PTO when making registration decisions than as a means for the courts to determine whether infringement exists. Quite simply, courts may find a likelihood of customer confusion (and thus infringement) where two marks are in different classes, and find no likelihood of customer confusion where two marks are within the same class. Still, the more classes a mark is registered in, the wider the protection the courts are likely to give its owner.

The number of classes you should include in your initial application depends on your circumstances. The down side of registering under more than one class is that an additional application fee (currently $325, if filing electronically) must be paid for each additional class. For this reason, applicants sometimes apply under one class and then wait to see if the mark (and their business) is successful enough to warrant applying under other classes as well.

Some applicants who can afford the fees register under several classes in their initial application with the idea that this will preserve future rights in those classes and broaden the scope of protection by the courts. But the classes you can register under are restricted to those which encompass the goods or services you are already offering (as shown by the specimens you submit) or that you plan to offer (if you are registering on an intent-to-use basis). (See Chapter 6, Section D, for how to assign your product or service to the appropriate class.)

F. Deciding How Many Marks You Want to Register

So far we have assumed that you have one mark to register—typically a business or product name. However, what may seem like only one mark may in fact be viewed as several different marks. The most common examples of this are marks that combine graphic designs or distinctive typefaces with a business or product name, and marks that combine a business or product name with a slogan. In these situations, the name can be considered as one mark while the combination of a graphic design or a slogan with the name may be viewed as a separate and distinct mark. On the front, back cover, and spine of this book you may find several manifestations of the word "Nolo," for instance, *Nolo* with the scales of justice, or *Nolo* in connection with the website nolo.com. Each of these manifestations using the word *Nolo* is really a separate mark.

The fact that you may be technically dealing with more than one mark doesn't mean that you have to register more than one mark. After all, the registration fee for each mark is $325 if filing electronically, and funds may be too scarce to accomplish all possible registrations. Also, if you want to register a mark in more than one class, the combination of multiple marks and multiple classes can make it prohibitively expensive to cover all bases. Below we suggest some ways to think about this issue for the most common multiple mark situations.

1. Name Marks Combined With Unusual Typefaces

If your name mark uses an unusual typeface (the *Nolo* example described above), your mark has two important aspects—the words that constitute the name, and the look and feel of the typeface. If money is no object, register both separately. But if funds are short—as they usually are—you probably will want to choose one or the other. As a general rule, you will be better off registering the unadorned name. This gives you the flexibility of using the name in many different configurations in the future without having to effect new registrations.

2. Name Marks Combined With Graphic Designs

If you use your name with a graphic image—for example, the word *Nolo* with an image of the scales of justice—you will have several choices when it is time to register:

- register the name alone
- register the combined name and graphic image, or
- register both the name and the combination of the name and graphic image.

Again, if money is no object, the last option is the best. But if every dollar counts, you should probably start with the combination name/graphic image, assuming the graphic image is distinctive. If the graphics are not particularly distinctive, however, register the name by itself. The idea is to get the most mileage for your initial registration, and if you are limited to one mark, it is wise to register the mark that has the most distinctive elements.

G. Applying for Registration Online

Filling out and filing a trademark application for your mark with the PTO is a snap. The PTO website offers TEAS, an acronym for Trademark Electronic Application System. The TEAS program lets you complete and file the application online. According to the PTO, it shouldn't take more than 20 minutes to complete the application (whichever program you use), assuming you have the necessary information at your fingertips. At the end of this chapter, we provide two examples of completed trademark applications—one based on an intent to use and the other based on actual use.

Although it's easy and quick to apply for trademark registration, the processing of your application by the PTO can take a year or

more due to the fact that the PTO is swamped and understaffed. In the meantime, your actual or intended mark will appear (a few months after the filing date) in the PTO's trademark database as pending registration. This means that anyone doing a trademark search will likely find your mark and know that you are claiming it as yours. This in itself gives you a lot of protection because it will scare off potential copiers.

Once you decide to register your mark with the PTO, get it done quickly. If the PTO receives two or more applications for the same mark, the one filed first will be examined (reviewed by the PTO) and published for opposition first. All conflicting applications will wait in line until the outcome of the first application is known. Also, if you are filing an intent-to-use application (and you follow up by putting the mark into actual use and getting it placed on the federal trademark register), your date of filing will be the date of first use of your mark, which may prove very important in the event of a later conflict. Though it's impossible to say whether a particular filing date will make a difference in your particular situation, yours might be the one case in a thousand where a day's difference in filing date will mean that your rights are senior to another filer's.

But Wait ... There's More

Created in 1997, TEAS really only provided one service during the first four years of its existence—the ability to automate the preparation of a trademark application for the Principal Register. But gradually the PTO rolled out more online services and now offers a wide range of automated forms, including a Preliminary Amendment, Allegation of Use, Request for an Extension of Time, Request to Divide, Certification Mark applications, Collective Trademark/Servicemark applications, Collective Membership Mark applications, and application for filing on the Supplemental Register.

The PTO Disfavors Hard Copy

For a variety of reasons, some people will prefer to work strictly with print copies of the trademark application and file them by mail. That is, instead of filling out an application on your computer, you may wish to complete the application by hand or by typing in the details. Unfortunately, the PTO has discontinued providing blank downloadable application forms. The PTO's reluctance to supply blank forms is part of its attempt to make the TEAS program the standardized format for filing.

1. How to Use TEAS to Register Online

Using TEAS can be fun. Just follow along with our step-by-step instructions below. If you need additional help, the PTO provides its own help system.

Your first step is to go to the PTO's website (www.uspto.gov). On the home page, on the left, click "File" under the word "Trademark." This will take you to the Trademark Electronic Application System (TEAS) home page. (See screen shot below.)

Trademark Electronic Application System

file online

The United States Patent and Trademark Office (USPTO) is pleased to present TEAS - the Trademark Electronic Application System. TEAS allows you to fill out a form, check it for completeness, and then submit the form directly to the USPTO over the internet, making an official filing on-line.

Scheduled Outage Notice

The USPTO Data Center is moving to Alexandria, Virginia. For weekends beginning April 29, 2005 and ending May 30, 2005, outages will occur between **5:00 p.m. Friday evenings** and **6:00 a.m. Monday mornings.** During this scheduled outage period, we cannot guarantee site resources or completion of online activities. We apologize for any inconvenience this may cause.

NOTE: New Filers are encouraged to review **Where Do I Start** information before beginning the application process.

Up-Coming Enhancements

- Response to office Action form and Suspensions. *New 05/20/2005*

- Sound Marks and electronic filing. *New 05/20/2005*

- Date Problem Resolved for Allegation of Use form. *New 04/26/2005*

- Expanded Image File Types. *Updated 01/05/2005*

Important Notices

- Paper Filings. *Updated 11/02/2004*

- Form Session Time Limit.

- Ensuring Receipt of All Information.

- Keeping Data When "Backing Up" in Forms.

- Eastern Time Controls Filing Date.

- Three Payment Options Available.

- Image Files for TEAS Must Be in JPG Format.

- Avoiding Formatting Problems.

- Filing Fee and Refund Policy.

- Ensuring delivery of emails sent from the USPTO. *New 12/21/2004*

- Contact Us.

Forms

Click here for **TEAS TECHNICAL INFORMATION**, **TEAS TUTORIAL** (step-by-step instructions for filing your application directly over the Internet), and **ELECTRONIC FILING TIPS** *New.*
Click below to access the correct form:
Trademarks

- Apply for a NEW mark

- File a PRE-registration Form
  - File Preliminary Amendment
  - File Extension of time or Allegation of Use/Statement of Use
  - File form after receiving your Notice of Allowance (NOA)
  - File Request to Delete Section 1(b) basis, Intent to Use *New*

- File a POST-registration form or Renew an Existing Registered Mark

- Response to Office Action Form

- Change of Address Forms *New*

- Express Abandonment Form *New*

- Petition Forms *New*
  For Petition Information Sheet for a paper filing, please click here.

- Withdrawal of Attorney & Revocation/Appointment of Attorney/Domestic Representative Forms *New*

Madrid Protocol Forms *New 11/01/2004*

Assignments

Trademark Trial and Appeal Board Forms

FAQ About Trademarks

Help Desk & Bug Report

Trademark Home

USPTO Home

Click on the "Apply for a NEW Mark" link in the TEAS box. This will take you to the screen on the next page. (See screen shot below.) This gives you a choice of forms to fill in.

Here we are talking about the "Trademark/Servicemark Application, Principal Register." When you click the link, you'll get the next screen (see screen shot below). This is the

---

Trademark Electronic Application System *file online*

Please click on the following to access a form for:

■ **Trademark/Servicemark Application, Principal Register**
Use this form to file an initial application for either a trademark (used or intended to be used for goods) OR a Servicemark (used or intended to be used in providing a service). If you use this application to file based on a "bona fide intent to use" the mark some time in the future, i.e., the applicant has not actually used the mark yet in commerce, but can claim in good faith that it plans to do so later, you must also file a second form (the Statement of Use/ Amendment to Allege Use) before we can register the mark (even though otherwise approved based on the information in the original Trademark/Servicemark application).

NOTE: The electronic filing fee is $325.00 per class of goods and/or services (*i.e.* if an application is for one mark, but the mark is used on goods and/or services in two different classes, *e.g.* computer software in Class 9 and t-shirts in Class 25, then the overall electronic filing fee is $650.00— $325.00 x 2 classes). Only one mark is permissible per application, although a mark may consist of several elements that are joined to form a composite whole (*e.g.* words plus a design). Also, the electronic filing fee is a processing fee for the application. This fee is NOT returned even if ultimately the USPTO does not issue a registration. You should take all necessary steps to ensure the mark is registrable before filing the application.

■ **Trademark/Servicemark BLANK Application, Principal Register**
(A downloadable blank form, for use by experienced parties who file multiple applications, to create standard templates containing repetitive information)
Use this version of the Trademark/Servicemark Application, Principal Register, only if you plan to do multiple filings; otherwise, please use the regular form, above. Before creating and using the blank form, please note the following: 1) each slight variation of an application will require creation of its own unique blank form; i.e., a blank form for filing under Section 1(b) in one class will require one form; 1(b) in two classes a different form; 1(b) and 44(d) in one class a third form; etc. You cannot create one "master" form to handle all types of applications; and 2) any time that the USPTO must change the version of TEAS currently posted on the site (e.g., due to improvements to the forms themselves, etc.), all portable forms previously created using any prior version of TEAS will be obsolete, requiring creation of new forms using the later edition of TEAS.

NOTE: The Trademark/Servicemark Application, Principal Register, is the only form for which the downloadable blank form option currently exists.

■ **Trademark/Servicemark Application, Supplemental Register**
Use this form to file an initial application for a trademark/servicemark on the Supplemental Register, rather than the Principal Register. Almost all marks are filed directly on the Principal Register. However, certain marks that are not eligible for registration on the Principal Register, but which are *capable* of distinguishing an applicant's goods or services, may be registered on the Supplemental Register. If you file on the Principal Register, but are only eligible for the Supplemental Register, you will be permitted to amend the application to change registers during the prosecution of the application.

NOTE: The electronic filing fee is $325.00 per class of goods and/or services (i.e., if an application is for one mark, but the mark is used on goods and/or services in two different classes, e.g. computer software in Class 9 and t-shirts in Class 25, then the overall electronic filing fee is $650.00— $325.00 x 2 classes). Only one mark is permissible per application, although a mark may consist of several elements that are joined to form a composite whole (e.g. words plus a design). Also, the electronic filing fee is a processing fee for the application. This fee is NOT returned even if ultimately the USPTO does not issue a registration. You should take all necessary steps to ensure the mark is registrable before filing the application.

NOTE:
1. If you have installed Anti-Spam filters or software on your email service, please ensure that legitimate emails from TEAS@uspto.gov or TEAS@uspto.gov are not falsely identified as spam or junk.
2. This form uses pop-up windows to display critical information. To use this site properly, you must disable any existing pop-up filters (through either anti-virus software or a pop-up killer program).
3. Before filing an application requesting registration on the Supplemental Register, or amending to the Supplemental Register, you must be lawfully using the mark in commerce, on or in connection with the goods and services (unlike an application on the Principal Register, which may be based on an intent to use the mark in the future, under §(b) of the Trademark Act). The only exception from the use requirement in seeking registration on the Supplemental Register is for applications based solely on §4 of the Trademark Act (*i.e.*, based on a foreign application and/or registration).

■ **Certification Mark Application, Principal Register**
Use this form to file an initial application for a Certification mark (used or intended to be used by authorized persons on designated goods and/or services to certify something; e.g., a particular regional origin of the goods; a characteristic of the goods or services; or that labor was performed by a particular group). A copy of standards that the applicant uses or will use to determine whether the goods and/or services will be certified must be submitted.

NOTE:

1. If you have installed Anti-Spam filters or software on your email service, please ensure that legitimate emails from TEAS@uspto.gov or TEAS@uspto.gov are not falsely identified as spam or junk.
2. This form uses pop-up windows to display critical information. To use this site properly, you must disable any existing pop-up filters (through either anti-virus software or a pop-up killer program).

■ **Collective Membership Mark Application, Principal Register**
Use this form to file an initial application for a collective membership mark (used to indicate membership in a specific organization; e.g., a social club or labor union). The applicant must control, or will intend to control, use of the mark by its members by a specified method of control.

NOTE:

1. If you have installed Anti-Spam filters or software on your email service, please ensure that legitimate emails from TEAS@uspto.gov or TEAS@uspto.gov are not falsely identified as spam or junk.
2. This form uses pop-up windows to display critical information. To use this site properly, you must disable any existing pop-up filters (through either anti-virus software or a pop-up killer program).

■ **Collective Trademark/Servicemark Application, Principal Register**
Use this form to file an initial application for a collective trademark/servicemark. The applicant must control, or will intend to control, use of the mark by its members by a specified method of control.

NOTE:

1. If you have installed Anti-Spam filters or software on your email service, please ensure that legitimate emails from TEAS@uspto.gov or TEAS@uspto.gov are not falsely identified as spam or junk.
2. This form uses pop-up windows to display critical information. To use this site properly, you must disable any existing pop-up filters (through either anti-virus software or a pop-up killer program).

■ **Transformation into a National Application** (under development)
The holder of an international registration may use this form to request transformation of its extension of protection to the United States into an application for registration under Section 1 and/or Section 44 of the Trademark Act, if the international registration was cancelled (in whole or in part) by the International Bureau of the World Intellectual Property Organization under Article 6(4) of the Madrid Protocol, due to the cancellation of the basic application or registration. The request for transformation must be filed within three months of the date of cancellation of the international registration.

NOTE: The holder must pay an application electronic filing fee of $325.00 for each class of goods/services identified in the request for transformation.

FAQ About Trademarks

Trademark Home

Help Desk & Bug Report

USPTO Home

PTO Form 1478 (Rev 9/98)
OMB No. 0651-0009 (Exp. 09/30/2005)

TRADEMARK/SERVICE MARK APPLICATION FORM WIZARD
TEAS
Version 2.50 : 01/31/2005

To file the application electronically, please complete the following steps:

1. Answer each question below to create an application form showing only sections relevant to your specific filing. Although we strongly recommend that you use this FORM WIZARD, you can skip by clicking on Standard Form.
2. For more information regarding any of the questions, go to HELP or click on the underlined word. While the different sections of the form may appear straightforward and easy to fill out, we strongly suggest that you read the HELP instructions very carefully for each section prior to completing it. Failure to follow this advice may cause you to fill out sections of the form incorrectly, jeopardizing your legal rights.
3. After answering all wizard questions, click on NEXT button at bottom of wizard.
4. Once in the actual form, complete all fields for which information is known. Fields with a red * symbol are mandatory fields for filing purposes and must be completed.
5. Validate the form, using the "button" at the end of the form. If there are errors, return to the form to enter correction. A "warning" may be corrected or by-passed.
6. Double-check all entries through the links displayed on the Validation page.
7. You may save your work for submission at a later time by clicking on the Download Portable form button at the bottom of the Validation page.
8. When ready to file, use the Pay/Submit button at the bottom of the Validation page. This will allow you to choose from three (3) different payment methods: credit card, automated deposit account, or electronic funds transfer.
9. After accessing the proper screen for payment, and making the appropriate entries, you will receive a confirmation screen if your transmission is successful. This screen will say SUCCESS! and will provide your assigned serial number.
10. You will receive an e-mail acknowledgement of your submission, which will repeat the assigned serial number and provide a summary of your submission.

Once you submit an application, either electronically or through the mail, we will not cancel the filing or refund your fee, unless the application fails to satisfy minimum filing requirements. The fee is a processing fee, which we do not refund even if we cannot issue a registration after our substantive review.

NOTE: This form has a session time limit of 60 minutes. A session begins once you create and enter the form via the Form Wizard. If you exceed the 60 minute time limit, the form will not validate and you must begin the entire process again. Therefore, you should have all information required to complete the form available prior to starting your session.

1. What is your filing basis?

NOTE: More than one basis may be selected, but do NOT claim both §§1(a) and 1(b) for the identical goods or services in one application. If claiming a Section 1(a) basis, it is NOT necessary or appropriate also to claim a Section 1(b) basis for the same goods or services, simply to indicate an intent to *continue* using the mark for those goods or services - the Section 1(a) basis covers this.

Intent to Use (Section 1(b))

○ Yes ◉ No

Use in Commerce (Section 1(a))

◉ Yes ○ No

Right of Priority based on Foreign Application (Section 44(d))

○ Yes ◉ No

Foreign Registration (Section 44(e))

○ Yes ◉ No

2. Are your Goods and/or Services in more than one class?

○ Yes ◉ No
If the answer is Yes, enter the number of classes [1 ▾]

3. Do joint applicants own the mark?

○ Yes ◉ No
If the answer is Yes, enter the number of owners [1 ▾]

4. Is there one applicant but more than one signatory?

○ Yes ⊙ No
If the answer is Yes, enter the number of signatories 1 ▾

5. Is an attorney filing this application?

⊙ Yes ○ No

6. Do you want to appoint a Domestic Representative ?

○ Yes ⊙ No

7. Do you need to enter an additional statement, e.g., a disc laimer, translation, or claim of ownership?

○ Yes ⊙ No

8. What signature approach do you want to use? Choose one from below.

⊙ Sign electronically directly on this application
○ E-mail Text Form to second party for electronic signature
○ Handwritten pen-and-ink signature
○ Submit application unsigned (a signature *must* be supplied later)

[NEXT]   [CLEAR]

Privacy Policy Statement

The information collected on this form allows the PTO to determine whether a mark may be registered on the Principal or Supplemental register, and provides notice of an applicant's claim of ownership of the mark. Responses to the request for information are required to obtain the benefit of a registration on the Principal or Supplemental register. 15 U.S.C. §1051 et seq. and 37 C.F.R. Part 2. All information collected will be made public. Gathering and providing the information will require an estimated 12 or 18 minutes (depending if the application is based on an intent to use the mark in commerce, use of the mark in commerce, or a foreign application or registration). Please direct comments on the time needed to complete this form, and/or suggestions for reducing this burden to the Chief Information Officer, U.S. Patent and Trademark Office, U.S. Department of Commerce, Washington D.C. 20231. Please note that the PTO may not conduct or sponsor a collection of information using a form that does not display a valid OMB control number.

Form Wizard page, which asks some questions. Here is how to answer.

Question 1: What is your filing basis? If you are already using the mark on goods or services, select the Yes button for "Use in Commerce" and the No button for "Intent to Use." If you are not yet up and running with your mark, do the opposite.

The procedures for each filing basis are somewhat different, and the intent-to-use basis will cost an additional $100 when you do put the trademark into actual use.

Previous Foreign Registration. If you are filing in the United States on the basis of a previous foreign registration, see a lawyer before continuing. This book doesn't cover U.S. registrations based on foreign registrations.

Question 2: Are your Goods and/or Services in more than one class? As we explain in Chapter 6, the PTO categorizes trademarks in 42 different classes based on the goods and services the business offers. Before answering this question, click the link that says "in more than one class" for information about the classification system and links to PTO sources that will help you choose one or more classes for your mark. (Also, review the information in Chapter 6, Section D.)

Question 3: Do joint applicants own the mark? The applicant is the person or business that will own the trademark. If at all possible, only one person or business entity should own the domain name. This can be an individual, a partnership, a corporation, a limited liability company, or a joint venture. If your situation dictates that there be two or more owners, click "more than one owner" and read the instructions.

Question 4: Is there one applicant but more than one signatory? If there is a single applicant, only one person is needed to sign the application. If the applicant is a corporation, and corporate policy dictates that two or more officers sign the application, then enter the appropriate number here. If there will be more than one owner, then each potential owner (or their designated signatory) must sign the application.

Question 5: Is an attorney filing this application? If you plan to be represented by an attorney in your dealings with the PTO, click "attorney." The PTO will not communicate directly with you if an attorney is representing you.

Question 6: Do you want to appoint a domestic representative? If you live outside the United States, you'll need to appoint a U.S. resident to receive any legal papers that might be coming your way in your capacity of owner of a U.S. registered trademark.

Question 7: Do you need to enter an additional statement? You can safely click the No button for this question. If you click Yes, you will be given a choice of additional qualifying statements to be added to your application. These statements may be required at some point to process your application, but you do not have to enter them now. Your application will be accepted for filing without additional statements, and the PTO will alert you if you should make one in the course of pushing the application through the registration process. If you want to make an additional statement now, you can choose one or more specific and preworded statements that will appear in the application. The statement that is most relevant is what's called the disclaimer (see "Disclaimers—Do It Now or Later?" below).

Question 8: What signature aproacah do you want to use? Here you have four choices: sign electronically directly on this application (the easiest choice), email Text Form to second party for electronic signature, provide a handwritten pen-and-ink signature, or submit your application unsigned (a signature must be supplied later).

Review the TEAS help for more information on the Text Form. After you've answered this question, click "Next." This takes you to the Trademark/Service Mark Application, Principal Register (see screen shot below), which is divided into five parts below.

Carefully read the information at the top of the screen shown on the next page. The first block explains the help system and lets you turn off the help text that automatically appears at the bottom of the page. It also explains that only the blanks marked with an asterisk are mandatory. We recommend that you leave the help on and read the help for each step. We also recommend that you be as complete as possible in your responses; even if the information isn't mandatory, it may save you time and trouble down the line. Some of the

PTO Form 1478 (Rev 9/98)
OMB No. 0651-0009 (Exp. 09/30/2005)

Trademark/Service Mark Application, Principal Register

Version 2.50: 01/31/2005

Each field name links to the relevant section of the "HELP" instructions that will appear at the bottom of the screen. Fields containing the symbol " * " **must** be completed; all other relevant fields should be completed if the information is known.
Note: ☐ check here if you do not want the scrolling help to be automatically shown at the bottom of the screen.

Important: ONCE AN APPLICATION IS SUBMITTED ELECTRONICALLY, THE OFFICE WILL IMMEDIATELY PROVIDE THE SENDER WITH AN ELECTRONIC ACKNOWLEDGMENT OF RECEIPT OF THE APPLICATION. Please contact TEAS@uspto.gov within 24 hours of transmission (or by the next business day) if you do not receive this acknowledgment.

Contact Points:
For **general** trademark information, please e-mail TrademarkAssistanceCenter@uspto.gov, or telephone 1-800-786-9199. If you need help in resolving **technical** glitches, please e-mail TEAS@uspto.gov. Please include your telephone number in your e-mail, so we can talk to you directly, if necessary. For **status** information on an application that has an assigned serial number, use http://tarr.uspto.gov.

NOTE: Do NOT attempt to check status until at least 45 days after submission of a filing, to allow sufficient time for our databases to be updated.

Applicant Information

Note: This identifies who **owns** the mark, **not** necessarily who is **filing** the application.

* Name	Richard Stim
	[If an individual, use the following format: Last Name, First Name Middle Initial./Name]

Entity Type: Click on the **one** appropriate circle to indicate the applicant's entity type and enter the corresponding information.

⦿ Individual	Country of Citizenship	United States ▾
○ Corporation	State or Country of Incorporation	Select State if U.S. Corporation ▾ OR Select Country if non-U.S. Corporation ▾
○ Partnership ○ Limited Partnership ○ Joint Venture	State or Country Where Organized	Select State if U.S. Entity ▾ OR Select Country if non-U.S. Entity ▾
○ Sole Proprietorship ○ Trust ○ Estate	Name and Citizenship of all General Partners, Active Members, Individual, Trustees, or Executors	
	Specify Entity Type	Select Domestic Entity ▾ Select Foreign Entity ▾ If not listed above, please select 'OTHER' and specify here:
○ Other	State or Country Where Organized	Select State if U.S. Entity ▾ OR Select Country if non-U.S. Entity ▾
	Name and Citizenship of all General Partners, Active Members, Individual, Trustees, or Executors	CA
	* Street Address	950 Parker Street
	Internal Address	
	* City	Berkeley
* Address	State	California ▾ If not listed above, please select 'OTHER' and specify here:
	* Country	Other ▾ If not listed above, please select 'OTHER' and specify here: USA
	Zip/Postal Code	94710

Phone Number	
Fax Number	
Internet E-Mail Address	richstim@nolo.com While the application may list an e-mail address for the applicant, applicant's attorney, and/or applicant's domestic representative, **only one** e-mail address may be used for correspondence, in accordance with Office policy. The applicant must keep this address current in the Office's records. ☑ Check here to authorize the USPTO to communicate with the applicant or its representative via e-mail. NOTE: By checking this box, the applicant acknowledges that it is solely responsible for receipt of USPTO documents sent via e-mail. The applicant should check the status of its application through the Trademark Applications and Registrations Retrieval (TARR) database at least every six (6) months from the filing date of the application, to see if the assigned examining attorney has e-mailed an Office Action. If an action has been sent to the provided e-mail address, the USPTO is not responsible for any e-mail not received due to the applicant's security or anti-spam software, or any problems within the applicant's e-mail system.

Mark Information

Before the USPTO can register your mark, we must know exactly what it is. You can present a mark in one of two ways: (1) standard characters; or (2) stylized and/or design. When you click on one of the two circles below, and follow the specific instructions, the system will automatically create a separate page that displays your mark. Only **one** mark may be submitted per application. Also, you may **not** be able to correct your mark after filing this application. While minor changes in the mark are *sometimes* permitted, any material alteration will **not** be permitted and will result in a refusal being issued on that ground.

WARNING: AFTER SEARCHING THE USPTO DATABASE, EVEN IF YOU THINK THE RESULTS ARE "O.K.," DO NOT ASSUME THAT YOUR MARK CAN BE REGISTERED AT THE USPTO. AFTER YOU FILE AN APPLICATION, THE USPTO MUST DO ITS OWN SEARCH AND OTHER REVIEW, AND MIGHT REFUSE TO REGISTER YOUR MARK.

⦿ Standard Characters	Click on this circle to register a word(s), letter(s), and/or number(s), or any combination thereof, with **no** design element **and** without claim to any particular font, style, size or color. Enter the mark here: (Note: The entry can be in capital letters, lower case letters, or a combination thereof.) hooky wooky

	OR

* Mark	○ Stylized and/or Design	Click on this circle to register a stylized word(s); letter(s); number(s); or a design, either by itself or combined with stylized word(s), letter(s), and/or number(s). Click on the 'Browse' button to select a properly-sized JPG image file (the **only** accepted format) from your local drive that shows the complete, overall mark (*e.g.* the stylized representation of the words; or, for a mark consisting of a design and words, the image of the complete "composite" mark, **not** just the design element alone). If claiming color, you **must** submit a color image; otherwise, the image must be clear black-and-white. **NOTE**: The image files for the mark and the specimen (if filing under Section 1(a), use in commerce, and showing actual use in commerce of the mark at the time of this filing) should **NOT** be the same files. The mark file should **ONLY** show the mark by itself, and *not* a representation of how the mark is used, e.g., on the overall packaging for the goods or within an advertisement for services. The file that shows the complete package for the goods or a full advertisement for the services, with the mark clearly displayed thereon or within, would be, e.g., the appropriate attachment in the specimen section of this form (which only appears where a Section 1(a) filing basis has been claimed). [_____] [Browse...] For any image that also includes a word(s), letter(s), and/or number(s), enter the LITERAL ELEMENT only of the mark here: [_____] **NOTE**: Do **not** enter any word(s), letter(s), or number(s) that do not appear in the attached image; the image file **must** reflect the overall mark, consisting of the design **and** the word(s), letter(s), and or number(s). ☐ Check here if you are claiming that the mark consists of standard characters without claim to any particular font, style, size or color. NOTE: Do **not** check this box if you have already made an entry in the standard character section, *above* ☐ Check here if claiming color as a feature of the mark, and identify the colors (*e.g.* enter red and blue): [_____] ☐ If other than a mark in standard characters, describe the mark, and if appropriate, list the portions of the mark that are in color and the corresponding color for each. **NOTE**: Enter a description of the mark **ONLY** if what the mark represents is not immediately clear, or to identify the portions of the mark that are in color. I.e., if the mark is black-and-white, and is not abstract or overly stylized, no description is necessary; the description is appropriate only where the degree of stylization is so great that the intended mark is not necessarily apparent (e.g., a stylized C that is also intended to form the body of a cat). The mark consists of: [_____]

Basis for Filing and Goods and/or Services Information

☑ **Section 1(a), Use in Commerce**: The applicant is using the mark in commerce, or the applicant's related company or licensee is using the mark in commerce, or the applicant's predecessor in interest used the mark in commerce, on or in connection with the identified goods and/or services. 15 U.S.C. § 1051(a), as amended. Applicant attaches or will later submit one specimen for *each class* showing the mark as used in commerce on or in connection with any item in the class of listed goods or services. If filing a specimen electronically, applicant must attach a JPG specimen image file for each international class, regardless of whether the mark itself is in a typed drawing format or is in a stylized format or a design. A specimen image file may be in color, and the image must be in color if color is being claimed as a feature of the mark.

Specimen Image File

> **NOTE**: For attachment, JPEG image file(s) showing specimen(s) must be on your local drive. This image file should NOT be the same file as was used in the mark section. The mark file should ONLY show the mark itself, *not* a representation of how the mark is used, e.g., on the overall packaging for the goods or within an advertisement for services. The file to be used here for the specimen should show, e.g., the complete package for the goods or a full advertisement for the services, with the mark clearly displayed thereon or within.

> [Click here to Attach/Remove Image(s)]
> **Note: a separate window will be launched for the attachment(s). MULTIPLE specimens CAN be attached.**
> WARNING: The image size cannot exceed 2 megabytes per attachment.

Describe what the specimen submitted consists of:

a label as applied to the goods

International Class	025 ▼ If known, enter class number 001 - 045
* **Listing of Goods and/or Services** **USPTO Goods/Services Manual**	NOTE: Do **not** enter a Class Number or any other code in the field below. You must enter **only** the common commercial name for the specific goods and/or services associated with the mark. Also, do **not** include any html or other programming code or language that may create links in the listing of goods and/or recitation of services. crocheted hats and clothing
Date of First Use of Mark Anywhere	at least as early as: 11/01/2001 MM/DD/YYYY
Date of First Use of the Mark in Commerce	at least as early as: 11/01/2001 MM/DD/YYYY

☑ Check here if an attorney is filing this application on behalf of applicant(s).

---

nonmandatory information may be useful to the examiner in evaluating your application and expeditiously communicating with you if a problem arises. For example, your phone number isn't mandatory, but how will the examiner call you if you don't include it?

The name, entity, address, email address, fax number, phone number, and email blanks all come with excellent help should you need it.

As you fill in the rest of this form, make sure that your specimen, mark information,

and description of goods and services are all consistent with each other. That is, if your specimen shows a different mark than what you enter in the Mark Information box (or submit in JPEG file), you'll have some explaining to do. Similarly, if your specimen shows a different product or service than you describe in the application, you'll have to submit another specimen or change your product/service description. If you are filing an intent-to-use application, you won't be worried about the specimen requirement at this stage in the process, but you will ultimately

Attorney Information

Correspondent Attorney Name	
Individual Attorney Docket/Reference Number	
Other Appointed Attorney[s]	

Attorney Address

Street Address		
Internal Address		
City		
State	Select State	If not listed above, please select 'OTHER' and specify here:
Country	Select Country	If not listed above, please select 'OTHER' and specify here:
Zip/Postal Code	94121-2550	

Firm Name	
Phone Number	
FAX Number	

Internet E-Mail Address

While the application may list an e-mail address for the applicant, applicant's attorney, and/or applicant's domestic representative, **only one** e-mail address may be used for correspondence, in accordance with Office policy. The applicant must keep this address current in the Office's records.

☐ Check here to authorize the USPTO to communicate with the applicant or its representative via e-mail. NOTE: By checking this box, the applicant acknowledges that it is solely responsible for receipt of USPTO documents sent via e-mail. The applicant should check the status of its application through the Trademark Applications and Registrations Retrieval (TARR) database at least every six (6) months from the filing date of the application, to see if the assigned examining attorney has e-mailed an Office Action. If an action has been sent to the provided e-mail address, the USPTO is not responsible for any e-mail not received due to the applicant's security or anti-spam software, or any problems within the applicant's e-mail system.

Fee Information

Number of Classes Paid   1

Note: The total fee is computed based on the Number of Classes in which the goods and/or services associated with the mark are classified. $ 325   = Number of Classes Paid x $325 (per class)

* **Amount** $ 325

NOTE: Three payment options (credit card, automated deposit account, and Electronic Funds Transfer) will appear after clicking on the PAY/SUBMIT button, which is available on the bottom of the Validation Page after completing and validating this form.

---

have to submit a specimen (once you begin using the mark) to complete your registration.

Mark Information: Here you have a choice. If your mark consists of unstylized words or numbers (or both), click the circle above the words "Standard Characters." In the box just below the words "Enter the mark here," en-

ter your mark. If your mark is a domain name, you can enter the complete domain name, including the .com, or just the unique part of your name. For instance, Nolo might choose to register its domain name as Nolo.com or just Nolo. Because domain names are such a new species of trademark, there are no firm rules. If your mark is stylized

Declaration

The undersigned, being hereby warned that willful false statements and the like so made are punishable by fine or imprisonment, or both, under 18 U.S.C. §1001, and that such willful false statements may jeopardize the validity of the application or any resulting registration, declares that he/she is properly authorized to execute this application on behalf of the applicant; he/she believes the applicant to be the owner of the trademark/service mark sought to be registered, or, if the application is being filed under 15 U.S.C. §1051(b), he/she believes applicant to be entitled to use such mark in commerce; to the best of his/her knowledge and belief no other person, firm, corporation, or association has the right to use the mark in commerce, either in the identical form thereof or in such near resemblance thereto as to be likely, when used on or in connection with the goods/services of such other person, to cause confusion, or to cause mistake, or to deceive; and that all statements made of his/her own knowledge are true; and that all statements made on information and belief are believed to be true.

Electronic Signature

The application will not be "signed" in the sense of a traditional paper document. To verify the contents of the application, the signatory must enter any alpha/numeric character(s) or combination thereof **of his or her choosing**, preceded and followed by the forward slash (/) symbol. The USPTO does **not** determine or pre-approve what the entry should be, but simply presumes that this specific entry has been adopted to serve the function of the signature. Most signatories simply enter their names between the two forward slashes, although acceptable "signatures" could include /john doe/; /jd/; or /123-4567/. The application may still be validated to check for missing information or errors even if the signature and date signed fields are left blank.

Signature	Richard Stim	Date Signed	
		MM/DD/YYYY	
Signatory's Name			
Signatory's Position			

Click on the desired action:

The "Validate Form" function allows you to run an automated check to ensure that all mandatory fields have been completed. You will receive an "error" message if you have not filled in one of the five (5) fields that are considered "minimum filing requirements" under the Trademark Law Treaty Implementation Act of 1998. For other fields that the USPTO believes are important, but not mandatory, you will receive a "warning" message if the field is left blank. This warning is a courtesy, if non-completion was merely an oversight. If you so choose, you may by-pass that "warning" message and validate the form (however, you cannot by-pass an "error" message).

Validate Form	Reset Form

Note: To either print the completed application, in whole or in part, download and save the validated application, or electronically submit the application to the USPTO, click on the Validate Form button.

Privacy Policy Statement

The information collected on this form allows the PTO to determine whether a mark may be registered on the Principal or Supplemental register, and provides notice of an applicant's claim of ownership of the mark. Responses to the request for information are required to obtain the benefit of a registration on the Principal or Supplemental register. 15 U.S.C. §1051 et seq. and 37 C.F.R. Part 2. All information collected will be made public. Gathering and providing the information will require an estimated 12 or 18 minutes (depending if the application is based on an intent to use the mark in commerce, use of the mark in commerce, or a foreign application or registration). Please direct comments on the time needed to complete this form, and/or suggestions for reducing this burden to the Chief Information Officer, U.S. Patent and Trademark Office, U.S. Department of Commerce, Washington D.C. 20231. Please note that the PTO may not conduct or sponsor a collection of information using a form that does not display a valid OMB control number.

---

or in design format (such as a logo or trade dress), read the help and attach a JPEG file showing the mark. Keep in mind that there is a two-megabyte limitation on each graphic file submitted to the USPTO.

 If you are filing for a stylized mark (you want the word to appear in a specific graphic manner) or design mark, you must submit two types of image files: One is the graphic file showing the mark, the other is the specimen—the mark as used in commerce (see below). Be careful not to confuse the images, and attach an image meant to be a specimen as the mark image because in most instances this is often difficult to correct.

Disclaimers—Do It Now or Later?

If, as part of your mark, you are using a word or phrase that cannot be protected under trademark law, the PTO will want you to disclaim (give up) trademark rights in those specific words, even though you have a trademark in the name as a whole. For example, suppose you manufacture a highly successful line of perfume called *Candor*, and you wish to register the trademark *Candor Perfume*. The PTO will likely ask you to disclaim the word "perfume" because it is generic. Similarly, if you had a gossip website called candor.com, the PTO would require that you disclaim the ".com." In both cases, the word "candor" is still registrable as a trademark respectively for a line of perfume and for Internet services. That's okay, because these generic terms "perfume" and ".com" can't be registered or protected anyway. Disclaiming a term doesn't mean that you lose part of your trademark, it only means that you cannot stop a competitor from using a similar generic term as part of their mark. For example, in the case of *Candor Perfume*, you have the exclusive right to use "perfume" with the mark "Candor," but you cannot stop others from using "perfume" with their marks, as well.

If you are positive you will have to disclaim part of your mark—for example you know that all of your competitors have had to disclaim the word "sauce" or "shuttle"—then you may as well make the disclaimer now. Check "Yes" in Question 7 and enter the term you are disclaiming. If you are not absolutely positive, we recommend that you check "No" in Question 7 and not disclaim anything until required to do so during the examination process. If this should be necessary, the trademark examiner will tell you what you should disclaim.

If scanning any image that is to be a black-and-white image, the scanner must be set specifically for black and white, not color. If the improper setting is used, the produced image may appear to be black and white, but will actually consist of thousands of colors, and it will result in an image of unacceptable quality when received at the USPTO. In addition, images with thousands of colors may exceed the two-megabyte limitation.

Basis for Filing and Goods or Services Information: The information required in this part of the application will vary, depending on whether you are already using your mark in commerce (Section 1(a) Use in Commerce), or are filing on an intent-to-use basis (Section 1(b) Intent to Use).

Specimen Image File: If you're filing under Section 1(a), you'll need to provide a specimen image file in JPEG format as well as a description of the specimen in the next box. The file should be scanned at least at 300 DPI and should be under two meabytes. If you're an intent-to-use applicant, you will not have a specimen information section on your application and should go to the International Class step.

Description of Specimen: The next part of the specimen box asks you to describe the specimen. See the help topic for what is required.

International Class: Enter the number of the class you selected for the goods or services associated with your mark. (See Section E, above.) Or, if you prefer, you can send in your application without specifying a class and let the trademark examiner help you.

⚠️ In the previous page you were asked whether you will be registering under more than one class. If you said no but now find that you want to register in two or more classes, use your browser's back button, change your answer, and then come back to this page. You will be asked to fill in a separate specimen/ goods or services description for each class.

Listing of Goods or Services: Here is where you describe the goods or services to which your mark is (or will be) attached. The good news is that you are only expected to make your best guess. A trademark examiner who doesn't approve of your description, or is confused by it, will let you know and work with you to come up with an appropriate description. If you don't feel like guessing, click the help link (Listing of Goods and/or Services), view the help topic on the bottom of

the screen, and click the link to the *USPTO Goods and Services Manual*—a long list of goods and services that will help you come up with a proper description of the ones you plan to offer on your website. These descriptions are written by the PTO, so you can copy them directly. You can also determine appropriate goods and services by reviewing your competitor's registered marks at the PTO trademark database.

Try to make your description as precise as possible. If your description is too broad, it may describe services in more than one class. And remember, each extra class added to your application will cost another $325. The examiner will probably contact you before adding more classes, so it won't be a surprise. But it may delay the processing of your application.

➡️ If you are filing an intent-to-use application, the following two items about use will not appear. Skip to "Final Instructions for All Applicants."

Date of First Use of Mark Anywhere: Here you are asked to provide the date you first started using the mark in connection with your product or service in the marketplace. (See Section B1 above.)

Date of First Use of the Mark in Commerce: Enter the date when you first used the mark in commerce across state, territorial, or international borders. If you have an existing business, this date may be different than the date of first use that you just entered. For example, you may have first used the name to market your local business and later gone national or international. The first date would be your use anywhere, and the second date would be the date the scope of your business expanded. (See Section B2 above for more on this "commerce" requirement.)

If you've been using a mark for years and don't remember the exact date of its first use anywhere or across state lines, make your best estimate. Use dated documents that you have gathered over the years, such as old advertisements or business licenses, to help jog your memory. If necessary, use imprecise dates, such as "before March 25, 1998," "on or about January 16, 1975," "in 1966," or "in February 1984." Use the earliest possible date that you can reasonably assert as correct.

2. Final Instructions for All Applicants

These final instructions apply for all applications:

Amount: If you are registering in just one class, as most people do, enter $325. The fee will be $325 more for each additional class.

Declaration: The Declaration is a statement that the facts in the trademark application are true. Read it carefully. If there are statements in the declaration that raise serious doubts or questions in your mind, do not file the application until you see a trademark lawyer. (For information on finding a lawyer, see Chapter 14, Help Beyond This Book.)

Signature: The information box right above the signature section provides the surprising information that your electronic "signature" can be any combination of letters, numbers,

or other characters. Each signature must begin and end with a forward slash (/). For example, /pat smith/; /ps/; and /268-3421/ are all acceptable signatures. There's no trick here. Unless you've developed some special internal system for tracking electronic signatures in your office, entering your own name is the simplest option. Click the signature link just below the information box for the PTO's own words on this subject.

Validate: The screen shot below shows the Validation page. This page alerts you if you forgot to include any information that is mandatory. You will then have a chance to go back and fill in the missing information. A warning message will also appear for non-mandatory missing information, but you are not required to go back and include that information. Once the validation is done, click "Pay/Submit" at the bottom of the Validation screen. Because you are using a credit card for payment, you will next be asked to enter payment information (see screen shot below). If your transaction is successful, you will receive a confirmation screen.

Later, you will receive email acknowledging the submission of your application. Hold on to that email, because it is the only proof you'll have that the PTO has your application. It is also proof of your filing date and contains the serial number assigned to your application.

Payment: There are three ways to pay the fees for your trademark application: Credit card, "Deposit Account Payment," and Electronic Funds Transfer. Read the descriptions of these options by clicking the appropriate links.

Trademark/Service Mark Application, Principal Register

Validation Page

Sun May 29 14:43:00 EDT 2005. You completed all mandatory fields (but we have not yet determined whether the information is correct). Please continue below either to print the application, download and save it, or actually electronically pay the filing fee by credit card and submit the validated application to the USPTO for filing.

■ **STEP 1**: Review the application data in various formats, by clicking on the phrases under Application Data. Use the print function within your browser to print these pages for your own records. If the Mark and Specimens appear huge, click here.
Note: It is important that you review this information for accuracy and completeness now. Corrections after submission may not be permissible, thereby possibly affecting your legal rights.

Application Data				
■ Input	■ Mark	■ Correspondence	■ XML File	■ Text Form

■ **STEP 2**: If any of the information is incorrect, click on the Go Back to Modify button (bottom of this page) to make changes; then re-validate the application by clicking on the Validate Form button (bottom of the application form).

> **Note**: If you originally selected standard character format, but are not satisfied with USPTO-created image of mark (accessed above):
> 1. Return to the Mark Information Section;
> 2. Select the Stylized/Design format;
> 3. Affix your own JPG file;
> 4. Check the box to claim that the mark is presented in standard character format; and
> 5. Enter the literal element of the mark in the appropriate field.
> If you do not have a JPG image file ready at this time, you should
> 1. Save this application, using the Download Portable form button at the bottom of this page;
> 2. Create your own JPG image file of the mark;
> 3. Retrieve the saved form; and
> 4. Continue as per steps 1-5, above.

■ **STEP 3**: If there are no errors and you are ready to file this application electronically, confirm the email address for acknowledgment. Once you submit an application electronically, we will send an electronic acknowledgment of receipt to the email address entered below. If no email address appears, you must enter one. If we should send the acknowledgment to a different email address, or to an additional address(es), please enter the proper address or additional address(es). **For multiple addresses/receipts, please separate email addresses by either a semicolon or a comma.**

Email for acknowledgment: richstim@nolo.com

To ensure we can deliver your email confirmation successfully, please re-enter your email address here:
Email for acknowledgment: richstim@nolo.com

■ **STEP 4**: Read and check the following:

Important Notice:
Once you submit an application, either electronically or through the mail, we will not cancel the filing or refund your fee, unless the application fails to satisfy minimum filing requirements. The fee is a processing fee, which we do not refund even if we cannot issue a registration after our substantive review.
☑ If you have read and understand the above notice, please check the box before you click on the **Pay/Submit** button.

■ **STEP 5**: To download and save the application, click on the Download Portable Form button at the bottom of this page.

■ **STEP 6**: If you are ready to file electronically:
Click on the Pay/Submit button at the bottom of this page. NOTE: If a fee payment is required, screens for entering payment information will come up after you have clicked on the Pay/Submit button. After successful entry of payment information, you can complete the submission to the USPTO. A complete transaction will result in a screen that says **SUCCESS!** Within 24 hours, the email acknowledgment will also be sent. NOTE: After clicking on the Pay/Submit button, you **must** complete the transaction within 24 hours; otherwise, the link to the form will totally expire.

Go Back to Modify	Download Portable Form	Pay/Submit

**United States
Patent and
Trademark Office**

The U.S. Patent and Trademark Office supports Secure Sockets Layer (SSL) for the security of all transactions. If you would like to read more about the security of your transaction click here.

Credit Card Payment

The USPTO accepts the following credit cards for payment:
Visa, Master Card, Discover and American Express.

[Pay by Credit Card]

Deposit Account Payment

The Deposit Account payment method authorizes USPTO to deduct your payment from your USPTO Deposit Account. If you do not have a USPTO Deposit Account please choose another payment method.

[Pay by Deposit Account]

EFT Payment

If you maintain a checking or savings account in a US or affiliated bank then you may be able to make your payment by EFT (Electronic Funds Transfer). The EFT payment method will allow the cost of your payment to be withdrawn directly from the checking or savings account that you designate. If you would like to read more about the EFT payment method click here. If you do not have an account with a US or affiliated bank, you must first establish such an account, or you will not be able to pay by EFT.
NOTE: Some banks do not allow EFT payments from a savings account; please check with your financial institution to verify whether they allow this type of funds transfer.

[Pay by EFT]

[Click here to cancel this transaction]

H. If You Are Filing by Mail

If filing your application by mail, you must pay a filing fee of $375 per class (versus $325 per class when filing electronically). Mail your application to Commissioner of Trademarks, P.O. Box 1451, Alexandria, VA 22313-1451. The PTO keeps track of all applications by assigning them serial numbers. Once your application is filed, all your communication with the PTO must include this serial number. The fastest way to be sure your application reached the PTO and to get your serial number is to include with your application a self-addressed, postage-paid postcard with your mark printed clearly on it. The PTO will stamp the card with your serial number and the date your application was received and return it to you. You should receive it within two weeks after you mailed the application. Keep the card in a safe place, as you may need to refer to your serial number frequently during the process.

We recommend using the mailing method that will get your application to the PTO in the shortest amount of time so that you may obtain the earliest possible filing date. Express Mail sent "Post Office to Post Office," is your best option.

About six to eight weeks after mailing your application, you should receive the PTO's filing receipt. The current form is an 8½" x 11" white form titled "Filing Receipt for Trademark Application." The filing receipt includes your application serial number, the date of filing, the mark, the applicant's name and address, and other information. The information

on the receipt should be checked carefully. If there is a mistake, you should send a correcting letter to the PTO immediately. (See Section J below on corresponding with the PTO.)

The PTO filing receipt will explain that you should not expect to hear anything about your application for approximately three months. If you have not heard anything in three and a half months, it is wise to call and inquire as to the status of your application. There are three ways to do this:

- Check TARR: The online Trademark Applications and Registrations Retrieval system page (http://tarr.uspto.gov) allows you to access information about pending trademarks obtained from the PTO's internal database by entering a valid trademark serial number.

- TRAM automated system: TRAM stands for trademark reporting and monitoring. From any touch-tone phone, Monday through Friday, from 6:30 a.m. to midnight, Eastern time, dial 703-305-8747. After the welcome message and tone, enter your mark's eight-digit serial number and the pound symbol. You should immediately hear the computer give you the current status of your mark along with the effective date of the status.

- If you want additional information or would prefer talking with a human, call the Trademark Assistance Center at 703-308-9400 and request a status check.

I. What Happens Next?

You will likely receive some communication from the PTO within three to six months. If there is a problem with your application, you will receive what's called an "action letter." This is a letter from your examiner explaining what the problems are. Most problems can be resolved with a phone call to the examiner.

When the examiner approves your application for publication, you will receive a Notice of Publication in the mail. Your mark will then be published in the *Official Gazette*. For 30 days following publication, anyone may oppose your registration. Only 3% of all published marks are opposed, so it is very unlikely you will run into trouble.

Once your mark has made it through the 30-day publication period, and you are filing on an actual-use basis, you will receive a Certificate of Registration. The PTO sometimes has a difficult time moving applications through this long process. As a result, it may take a year or more to process your application.

⚠ Once you accomplish your registration, you'll still have some paperwork to do five years down the line. See Chapter 8 for more on what awaits you.

If you filed on an intent-to-use basis, your mark will not be placed on the trademark register until you file an additional document with the PTO when you put it into actual use. This form is called "Statement of Use/Amendment to Allege Use for Intent-to-Use Application." It tells the PTO the date you started using the mark and completes the registration process. You must also provide a specimen at that time, showing how you are using the mark. (See Section D above for more on specimens and Section L below for more on following up an "intent-to-use" application.)

J. Communicating With the PTO

The chances are great that you will be communicating with the PTO after you have filed your application. Few applications sail through completely unscathed.

You are required to be diligent in pursuing your application. If you are expecting some action from the PTO (the ball is in their court) and more than six months have elapsed without your hearing from them, immediately check the TARR system or call the PTO Status Line (the TRAM automated system, described in Section H above). If you discover a problem, bring it to the PTO's attention. If you fail to respond in a timely manner to a request from a PTO examining attorney, your application may be considered abandoned. If that happens, you may petition the commissioner for trademarks within 60 days to reactivate your application.

If the examiner wants you to change your application, such as claiming a different description of services or goods, there is usually some room for negotiation.

> **EXAMPLE:** Frieda claimed her mark was used in connection with buying services for nonprofit institutions and organizations, and submitted a specimen showing an advertisement of food products aimed at schools. That description was found to be too indefinite, and the examiner suggested "buying services for nonprofit organizations and institutions in the field of food products." If Frieda's services extended beyond food products to include items such as medical and automotive supplies, she probably wouldn't want to agree to the examiner's suggestion. However, after talking with the examiner she should be able to arrive at a description inclusive enough for her, yet definite enough for the examiner. In this instance, perhaps, this would be "buying services for nonprofit institutions and organizations in the fields of food products, medical supplies and automotive parts."

An examiner with a brief question might call you and then issue and mail you an Examiner's Amendment. This is a form on which the examiner records in handwriting a phone conversation or meeting with the applicant. Read the amendment carefully to make sure it matches your understanding of the conversation. If you disagree, or don't understand the amendment, first call the examiner, and then, if necessary, write the examiner a letter with your concerns, explaining your point of view on the communication.

One common example of an examiner's amendment is when you use words as part of your mark that, by themselves, don't qualify for registration. The examiner will ask you to formally disclaim those words (see sidebar, "Disclaimers—Do It Now or Later?" in Section 2, above). After making the disclaimer, your mark will be registered in its entirety, but you cannot prevent your competitors from using the disclaimed terms as part of their trademark.

> **EXAMPLE:** The Exotic Perfume Company manufactures a line of fragrances fancifully named after various wildflowers that themselves don't carry any particular fragrance. One of these is called *Violet Snapdragon Parfum*. If Exotic wants to register this mark, it will have to disclaim "Parfum"—a foreign-language term for perfume—because it is a descriptive term and thus not registrable. If Exotic refuses to disclaim "Parfum," the PTO will probably refuse registration. If a disclaimer is made, however, the entire mark can be registered and the company will be able to stop others from using the combination of terms "violet," "snapdragon," and "parfum." However, the company will not be able to stop someone that is only using "Parfum." For example, if a competing fragrance company comes out with *Wild Rose Parfum*, there will be no infringement. On the other hand, if a competitor produces *Purple Snapdragon Fragrance* or *Dragon Snap Parfum*, it is likely that a court will find infringement.

K. If the Examiner Issues a Rejection Letter

An examiner may write three kinds of action letters that constitute trademark application rejections:

- **Technical rejections.** These usually involve minor or procedural matters that can be corrected by amendment as described earlier.
- **Substantive rejections.** These usually involve issues such as potential confusion with another mark. Responding to these takes more effort and may well require the help of a trademark lawyer, or
- **Final rejections.** These usually are written only after you have been given at least one chance to respond to a technical or substantive rejection.

The examining attorney may notify the applicant of the basis for the rejection by telephone or mail. Often smaller issues are resolved over the phone while more substantive issues require mail notification. PTO correspondence usually includes an adhesive-label "caption" with a mailing date. This caption can be peeled off and placed on the applicant's reply response.

Rejections always specify how much time you have to respond (usually six months). If your response is not received within the time specified, you risk having your application deemed abandoned (which means you have to start over if you wish to pursue registration of the mark), so always send the response as early as possible.

If you receive a rejection, you have three choices:

- respond to it yourself,
- hire a trademark attorney to prepare the response, or
- abandon your application.

1. Responding to an Objection Yourself

Whether you should respond to a rejection yourself depends on the nature of the problem and your comfort level in dealing with a trademark examiner. You'll have to weigh both and make your decision.

In the event of an objection by the examining attorney, it may be necessary to amend the application or provide response to a rejection. An "amendment" is a correction usually made in response to a request by the PTO. A "response" is a legal argument advanced by the applicant to overcome an objection. The reply should include the "caption" (an adhesive label peeled off the examining attorney's letter). A response *must* be provided to the PTO within six months of the date of mailing of the office action. If not, the application will be deemed abandoned.

a. Common Rejections That Are Easy to Correct

Below are some common correctable errors that most applicants can rectify easily:

- **Name of Applicant.** The application lists the wrong trademark owner. For example, the founder of a company may mistakenly believe that he owns the mark, not the company.
- **Authority for Applicant.** The authority and position of the person signing the application is ambiguous. Officers of a

corporation, for example, should be specifically identified by their title.

- **Using the Class Heading as Listing of Goods.** Instead of identifying and describing the specific goods or services in the application, an applicant describes the goods by the International Class heading.

- **Scattered Listing of Goods.** You filed for a trademark in several classes but did not clearly group the goods in appropriate classes. The PTO prefers that goods be grouped according to class in the description of goods and in the drawing.

- **Incorrect or Inadequate Description of Goods.** The application does not accurately describe or reflect the goods or services. For example, the applicant describes the goods as "computer programs" instead of "computer programs and accompanying manual intended for use in instructional applications."

b. Substantive Rejections Are More Challenging to Correct

The errors in the previous section were fairly easily to correct. However, certain objections by a trademark examining attorney require substantial effort to overcome. These objections are usually based on the statutory bars to registration established in Section 2 of the Lanham Act (known as "statutory bars") and described in detail in Section B, above. These bars include:

- **Likelihood of Confusion.** The trademark examining attorney determines that the mark when used on the identified goods is likely to be confused with a registered

mark. For example, a shoe manufacturer attempts to register *KNIKE* for shoes.

- **Generic or Other Disclaimed Material.** The trademark examining attorney determines that a portion of the mark is generic and must be disclaimed. For example, the owner of the trademark *Nebraska Opry* may have to disclaim the word *Opry,* as it is a generic term for country and western music entertainment.

- **Descriptive Mark.** The trademark examining attorney determines that the mark when used on the identified goods is merely descriptive of the goods. For example, the mark *Nasal No-Hair* for a nose-hair clipper.

Sometimes extensive legal and factual arguments must be prepared to overcome objections. Since these arguments are often similar to the arguments made in infringement lawsuits (for example, likelihood of confusion or descriptiveness), the basis for such responses is discussed in various chapters throughout this book (for example, Chapter 6, Section B, discusses Likelihood of Confusion). The procedure for preparing such responses is also documented in treatises such as *Trademark Registration Practice,* by James E. Hawes (West), and *McCarthy on Trademarks* (West).

2. Hire a Trademark Attorney to Prepare a Response

It is almost never necessary to use an attorney to successfully respond to a technical rejection. Because this type of rejection usually is based on a clerical deficiency in your

Responding to the PTO Just Got Easier

The PTO provides an automated method of responding to office actions. You may find it easier to use this automated response system, rather than the traditional "snail mail" response, when replying to a PTO rejection or other office action. To access this automated response system, click "File " under the word "Trademark" at the PTO website (www.uspto.gov). On the next page choose "Response to an Office Action." Clicking on this link presents the applicant with 11 questions:

1. Do you want to pay an additional fee?
2. Do you want to present arguments related to a substantive refusal(s)?
3. Do you need to add a new classification(s) and/or listing of goods and/or services?
4. Do you need to change the listing of goods and/or services?
5. Do you want to correct any other procedural matter(s) / informalities / applicant information?
6. Do you want to modify your mark?
7. Do you want to make any additional statement(s) of record to address a requirement, e.g., a disclaimer or claim of a prior registration?
8. Does more than one applicant own the mark?
9. Do you need to change the correspondence address?
10. Do you need to submit a signed declaration?
11. What signature approach do you want to use for the response itself?

   Answer the questions as appropriate to your PTO response and follow the rules described in this section. There is also plenty of online help for these questions provided by the TEAS program.

application, it does not take a legal education to figure out the correct response. Substantive rejections are another matter. This type of rejection is based on the examiner's assessment that the mark itself doesn't qualify for registration. Changing the examiner's mind on this point requires advocacy skills and a good working knowledge of trademark law—both attributes of competent trademark attorneys. (See Chapter 14, Help Beyond This Book, for information on how to find a good trademark attorney.)

As desirable as it may be to use an attorney to help push your application through the PTO, this is almost always an expensive option. If you have a significant amount of money or business goodwill already tied up in your mark, then the expense may be justified. However, if you don't have a lot invested in your mark, it may be the wiser course to handle the matter yourself, even though an attorney might get better results. Why? Pure economics. Keep in mind that you are only out $325 if you don't succeed in your first application and need to file a new one.

This amount is roughly the same as the normal hourly fee charged by trademark attorneys—and fighting with the PTO can easily end up costing you $4,000 to $5,000 worth of an attorney's time. Though you may not be able to register your chosen mark, there are plenty of other potential marks in the world. Let your answer to this question be your guide: Would you be willing to sell your mark for an estimated minimum attorney's fee of $3,000–$5,000 and use the money to develop a different mark?

3. Abandon Your Application

If your application is based on actual use of your mark, your ownership of the mark will depend on the first date of that use. Registration itself does not confer ownership except when the application is based on an intent to use (in which case the filing date becomes the date of first use). If you already own your trademark, all registration accomplishes is giving the world notice of your mark and giving you a leg up (in terms of what you have to prove) if you end up in court in an ownership or infringement dispute.

Rather than pay an attorney or spend dozens of hours of your own time haggling with the PTO, you may be better off dropping your application and continuing to use your mark as you have before. This is especially true in the case of a descriptiveness rejection. If your mark is, in truth, descriptive, getting it registered will not offer much in the way of additional protection. If, however, the rejection is based on "confusion" grounds, then you should take a stern eye to the reasons for the rejection and decide whether you might be sued for infringement if you continue to use your chosen mark.

You can expressly abandon your application by filing a Request For Express Abandonment (Withdrawal) of Application using TEAS. Click "File" under Trademarks on the PTO home page.

All Abandonments Are Not Equal. Here we are talking about abandoning an application, which will only result in the loss of whatever rights you would have obtained by completing the application. If, however, you stop using a mark over a period of time, or fail to maintain quality control over how the mark is used, you may be considered to have abandoned the mark itself, and therefore lose the exclusive right to use it. (See Chapter 8, How to Use and Care for Your Trademark, for more on how to avoid abandoning the mark itself.)

Also, if you filed an intent-to-use application, abandonment of the application may affect your ownership of the mark. For example, assume a business starts using the same or similar mark after you file your intent-to-use application but before you put your mark into actual use. If you follow through with your registration, then you can claim the original filing date as the date of first use and be considered the owner of the mark. If, on the other hand, you abandon the application, the other user will be considered the owner—because you will no longer be entitled to the filing date as your date of first use.

4. Final Rejection: An Objection Cannot Be Overcome

If the PTO determines that the mark is not registrable, a final rejection will be mailed to the applicant. In the event of a final rejection, the applicant can:

- **Appeal to the Trademark Trial and Appeal Board (TTAB).** An appeal to the TTAB is made when the basis for the final rejection is *substantive*, for example, a statutory bar to registration such as descriptiveness or likelihood of confusion.

- **File a Petition to the Commissioner.** A Petition to the Commissioner is used when the basis for the rejection is that the applicant or the PTO failed to adhere to procedural rules. For example, a final rejection that is based upon an improper time limit for response would be a procedural basis for a Petition to the Commissioner.

- **Request further reconsideration.** The applicant can request that the examining attorney make another examination of the mark.

- **Abandon or suspend the application.** Abandonment of the application terminates the application process. Suspension of the application permits more time to prepare a response.

- **Amend the application to seek registration on the Supplemental Register** (37 C.F.R. § 2.75). If the basis for rejection is that the mark is descriptive, the mark may still qualify for registration on the Supplemental Register.

L. Follow-Up Activity Required for Intent-to-Use Applications

➡ If you are filing an actual-use application, skip this section. An intent-to-use application involves more steps than an actual-use application. This is because to complete your registration and own the mark, you must actually get it into use in commerce, tell the PTO about it, and pay an additional fee.

1. The Allegation of Use for Intent-to-Use Application

To actually get your mark registered, you will use a form called Allegation of Use for Intent-to-Use Application. This form may be filed at any time prior to the date the PTO authorizes the publication of your proposed mark, and any time after the PTO issues a Notice of Allowance. It may not be filed between those two dates, which has come to be known as the "blackout" period.

The Allegation of Use can be prepared and filed online using TEAS. To find the Allegation of Use form in TEAS, use the instructions provided for filling in the actual-use application contained in Section G above. (The primary difference between an actual-use and an intent-to-use application is that when answering the first question (What is Your Basis for Filing?), choose "Yes" under Intent to Use.

You do not need to supply specimens with an intent-to-use application, but you'll have to include one with your Allegation of Use. In addition to the information in this chapter, the PTO's help system should easily get you through this form.

⚠ Remember that your specimen, mark drawing, and description of goods and services must all be consistent. That is, if your specimen shows a different mark than what you put in your original application, you'll have some explaining to do. Similarly, if your specimen shows a different product or service than that described in your application, you'll have to submit another specimen or change your product/service description.

2. When to Divide Your Application

When using TEAS you will be asked whether you wish to divide your application. You would only want to divide your application if:

- your original application designated your mark to apply to more than one good or service
- you have used the mark in connection with one or some, but not all, of those goods or services, and
- you still intend to use the mark in connection with one or more additional good(s) and service(s).

In that event, you should consider dividing your application so that one application now claims usage for one or more of the goods or services while the other application remains on an intent-to-use status in respect to the other goods or services.

> **EXAMPLE:** Suppose Etta's intent-to-use application claimed she was going to use *Quick-Bytes* in connection with computer consulting services and computer programs. If she began offering services two months after her application was filed, she may want to amend her application to claim use of *Quick-Bytes* in connection with the services. When she divides the application, she will then have two applications: one, in which she alleges actual use of the mark for her services; and one in which she plans to use the mark for computer programs in the future.

The benefit of dividing an application, rather than waiting until the mark is in use for all goods or services originally contemplated, is that the mark in use can be placed on the Federal Register more quickly.

The downside of dividing the application is that additional paperwork is involved (another Allegation of Use), and you will have to pay an additional filing fee each time you claim usage under an additional classification. If money is scarce, or you soon expect to have the mark in use with all the goods or services you claimed, it's probably best not to divide your application. Just wait until you are using the mark in all the ways you intend and then file one Allegation of Use.

If you decide to divide your application, TEAS has a form for this purpose. However, we recommend that you not file it with the PTO until your work is reviewed by a trademark attorney.

⚠ Even if you are filing a Request to Divide, you must respond to any office actions on time, or risk giving up your application.

3. Getting a Six-Month Extension to File Your Statement of Use

As long as you still intend to use your mark on at least one of the goods or services mentioned in your application and are willing to pay $150 per class as a filing fee, you can request an extension and get an extra six months before you have to file your Statement of Use. As stated earlier, the request must be filed before your six months run out.

You can request six-month extensions up to five times, as long as each is filed before the last extension runs out. After the first

request (for which no reason need be given), you must convince the PTO that there is a good reason why your mark hasn't been used yet, as explained below. No extension of time will be granted beyond 36 months after the Notice of Allowance was issued. If it is your second, third, fourth, or fifth request, you will need to explain what you have done to get ready to use the mark in commerce. Your explanation need not be lengthy; a sentence or two will do. Some possible explanations include the following:

- the need for more research or development of your product or service
- the need for more research about your market, including where and how to sell the product or service
- a delay in efforts to arrange for product manufacturing
- the need for more time to develop advertising or promotional activities
- attempts to get government approval are still in progress
- attempts to set up marketing networks are still in progress
- any other reasonable explanation (for instance, a prolonged illness or destruction of vital records of your factory due to fire or other disaster).

Some may be tempted not to seek these extensions but to abandon the application and file a new application when the mark is finally put into use in commerce. Although this may save you money, it will lose you the date of first use (your original filing date) that you will be able to claim if you get your mark into actual use within the 36-month period.

If you are mailing these forms, see Section H regarding mailing information to the PTO. Your Allegation of Use and fees should be mailed to this address:

Commissioner for Trademarks
BOX AAU/SOU
P.O. Box 1451
Alexandria, VA 22313-1451

M. Follow-Up Activity Required After Registration

While you are entitled to hearty congratulations upon receiving your Certificate of Registration, your efforts will be for naught if you forget to file with the PTO some additional paperwork known as the Section 8 and Section 15 Declaration (which tells the PTO that you are still using the mark). (We cover this in Chapter 8.) Because this declaration must be filed between the fifth and sixth year after your original registration date (unless you purchase a six-month grace period), it's easy to let the deadline slip by, especially because the PTO doesn't remind you, and very few people have calendars that last beyond the current year.

You will also have to renew your registration prior to ten years after your registration date and submit both a renewal form and a Section 8 Declaration that again proves that your mark is still in use. (The combined filing is called a Section 8/9 Declaration and Renewal and is explained in Chapter 8.) ■

How to Use and Care for Your Trademark

*H*ere we assume that you are a trademark owner who wants to take all the right steps to keep your mark legally healthy. Trademark ownership of the mark can be lost if you don't use the mark correctly. And if you have registered the mark with the PTO (see Chapter 7, Federal Trademark Registration), your registration may lapse if you fail to take certain required follow-up steps. This chapter identifies the major pitfalls that owners of marks—registered or unregistered—can encounter, and suggests some easy steps for keeping your mark strong against all potential copiers.

A. Use of the Trademark Registration ® Symbol

If your mark is federally registered—on either the Principal or Supplemental Register—you have the right to use the symbol ® with your mark and should begin doing so immediately. If your mark is not on either of the federal trademark registers, you may not use the ® symbol.

The ® symbol, which lets others know that the mark is federally registered, is usually printed in a very tiny type—next to the mark. By placing the ® next to your mark, you place potential infringers on notice as to your federal registration and improve your chances of collecting damages or a defendant's profits if it is ever necessary to take an infringer to court. However, you won't lose ownership of the mark by omitting this notice.

EXAMPLE: While searching for a name for his new word-processing program, Phil Programmer sees an advertisement in a trade magazine for a new program called *Sorcerer's Apprentice* that allows the user to construct databases for hobby collections. No "notice of registration" is displayed in the advertisement, so Phil foolishly decides the mark is probably not registered and proceeds to use it as a trademark for his program. The work is in fact registered. Although the owners of the mark *Sorcerer's Apprentice* could sue Phil for infringement because the goods are so closely related (they're both software) and can probably force him to stop using the mark, they might have trouble collecting the damages allowed for willful infringement (triple damages, the defendant's profits, and possibly attorneys' fees) because they didn't use the ®.

It is enough that the symbol appears at least once on each label, tag, or advertisement. You don't need to use the symbol on every occurrence of your mark. Incidentally, instead of using the ® symbol, you may state that "[Your Mark] is a registered trademark of [Your Name]." This has the same legal effect as the ® symbol, but it takes up much more space.

Be sure to specify how you want the symbol used when hiring advertising services or printers, or when you allow others to use your mark—for example, on a website or in conjunction with another product or service. It is your responsibility to make sure the world knows your mark is registered. However, it isn't necessary to include the symbol when your mark is being referred to for reasons that have nothing to do with the underlying goods and services. For instance, this book refers to many marks, including McDonald's, without an accompanying registration symbol, because the reason we are referring to the marks is to discuss their characteristics as marks and not to sell the goods or services associated with them.

Use of ® If Your Federal Registration Is Canceled

The PTO will cancel your federal trademark registration if you fail to file certain required follow-up documents after your initial registration (see Section C below). However, you won't receive notice of this fact from the PTO. It is easy, therefore, to inadvertently continue using the ® on a mark that is no longer technically registered. Obviously, the easiest way to prevent this from happening is to meet the follow-up requirements. But if you slip up—and many do—use your best efforts to stop using the ® unless and until you reregister the mark.

B. Use of the TM or SM Symbol for Unregistered Trademarks

You may use TM (for trademarks) or SM (for service marks) alongside an unregistered mark to show that you claim ownership of the mark and intend to assert your rights against imita-

tors. These symbols are usually placed in smaller type to the right of the mark, for example The Purple World™. Use of the TM or SM symbol provides no statutory legal benefits, but it warns would-be copiers that the name or other device is already being claimed as a mark, and in most instances this will keep others away from the mark. As with the ® symbol, you don't need to place the TM or SM symbol next to every appearance of your trademark. Nothing can be more distracting than seeing the same word appear over and over again on a page with a little TM mark appearing next to it. The principle in using these symbols is to make sure you get the "lay off—this is a trademark" message across once, or if there are many pages, at most once on every page. There is no rule for how often the symbol should be used; common sense should do fine.

C. File Your Section 8 and 15 Declarations

Trademark owners who are not federally registering their marks should skip this section and Section D, but read Sections E, F, and G, as they contain general principles that apply to all mark owners.

Between the fifth and sixth year after federally registering your mark, you should complete and file two important forms with the PTO: the Section 8 Declaration and the Section 15 Declaration. You can file each declaration separately, or you can use one form that combines both the Section 8 and 15 Declarations and can be filled out online using the PTO's TEAS program. You can access the form at www.uspto.gov/teas/eTEASforms.htm.

By filing these declarations, you'll protect your mark in two extremely important ways. The Section 8 Declaration officially advises the PTO that your mark is still in use and that your registration should continue in force. The Section 15 Declaration advises the PTO that your mark has been in continuous use from the date of registration and therefore deserves extra protection against potential challengers. In PTO jargon, you're requesting "incontestability status" for your mark. You'll need to briefly evaluate the use of your mark to make sure you're eligible to file these declarations. Here's how.

1. Is Your Mark Still in Use?

To file the Section 8 and Section 15 Declarations, you must still be using your mark in the manner described in your registration certificate. This means that you must still be using it, at a minimum, on the same products or services and in the same way (on packaging or pamphlets, etc.) as you originally stated, and be able to come up with samples that demonstrate your continued use.

File in Name of Current Owner. The Section 8 and 15 Declarations must be filed by the current owner of the federal trademark registrations. (The current owner should calculate the filing period from the date of registration, not the date the mark was transferred or acquired.) If you have acquired the trademark registration by an assignment, or if your company has changed its business name or form, for

example, from a sole proprietorship to a corporation, you will also need to file a record of the transfer of ownership with the PTO. (See Section H, below.)

2. Has Your Mark Been in Continuous Use for Five Years?

As mentioned, you'll qualify for incontestable status (the Section 15 Declaration) if your mark is in continuous use for five years after being placed on the Principal Register. More specifically, your mark can become "incontestable" if all of the following apply:

- Your mark was placed on the Principal Register at least five years ago and you have used the mark continuously—without a lapse—since that registration date in the same manner and on the same goods or services for which it was originally registered. (If you are using the mark for some of those original goods or services but not for others, it may become incontestable for the goods and services you are still using it for.)
- No court has rendered a final decision that affects your ownership claim since the date of registration.
- There is no pending court or PTO challenge to your right to use the trademark.
- You file the Section 8 and 15 Declarations on time.
- The mark is not and has not become generic (that is, synonymous with the underlying product or service—see Section G).

Incontestability status makes it more difficult —but not impossible—for anyone to challenge the validity of your mark. The result is that it will be easier for you to protect your mark from infringement. Even though an incontestable mark can still be challenged on a number of grounds in an infringement lawsuit (see sidebar, "'Incontestable' Really Means 'Harder to Contest'"), it is safe from attack on the basis that it lacks distinctiveness. This is a key benefit—once a mark is considered distinctive beyond argument, it gets very strong protection.

> **EXAMPLE:** Park 'N Fly, Inc., sued Dollar Park and Fly, Inc., for trademark infringement. Dollar Park and Fly defended on the ground that the Park 'N Fly mark was too weak to deserve protection. But the U.S. Supreme Court ruled that the Park 'N Fly mark had obtained incontestability status and couldn't be challenged on that ground. (*Park 'N Fly, Inc. v. Dollar Park and Fly, Inc.,* 469 U.S. 189 (1985).)

Of course, even after the mark attains incontestability status, the mark can be deemed abandoned and dropped from the Federal Register if you stop using it for a sufficiently long time. (See Section E, below, on what constitutes abandoning your mark.)

> **EXAMPLE:** In 2003, Frank Brown invents an inexpensive but highly accurate blood pressure testing kit and starts distributing it under the trademark *F/B Stresstest*. The mark is registered on the Principal Register in 2004. In 2009, the mark is entitled to incontestable status if Frank has kept the mark in continuous use for this five-year period. But if he later stops using it

for three years or more, he will risk losing his incontestable status as well as his federal registration altogether.

"Incontestable" Really Means "Harder to Contest"

Paradoxically, you can contest an incontestable trademark in quite a few ways. The upshot is that "incontestable" really means "harder to contest."

If accused of infringing a particular mark that has achieved incontestability status, you can defend on any of the following grounds:

- the registration or its incontestability was obtained fraudulently
- the mark has been abandoned by the registrant
- the mark is being used to misrepresent the source of the goods or services with which it is being used (for instance, a mark is used to deceive consumers into believing they are buying another company's products or services)
- your mark is your own name being used in your own business or is descriptive of your goods or services or geographic locale
- your mark was used in interstate commerce before the incontestable mark was used and registered
- your mark was registered before the incontestable mark, or
- the incontestable mark is being used to violate the antitrust laws of the United States. (37 U.S.C. § 1115(b).)

3. Can You File on Time?

Both the Section 8 and Section 15 Declarations must be signed and filed with the PTO between the fifth and sixth years of registration. The fee for the combined filing is currently $300 per mark per class ($100 for the Section 8 Declaration, $200 for the Section 15 Declaration). Your timing is crucial, because if you miss the deadline you'll have to pay an extra $100 and file within the six-month grace period. For that reason, file these declarations well before the six-year deadline so that you'll have time to clear up questions or provide the PTO with more information, if needed.

> **EXAMPLE:** If your mark was registered on May 15, 2001, you must sign and file your Section 8 and 15 Declaration between May 15, 2006, and May 14, 2007. It would be best to file it in June or July of 2006 so there is plenty of time to make corrections.

Failure to file the Section 8 Declaration on time will result in your federal registration being canceled unless you pay the $100 fee and file within the six-month grace period. If the mark is canceled, you will have to reregister if you still want the benefit of federal registration. In addition, the failure to file the Section 8 Declaration means that you will not be able to obtain incontestable status for the mark until an additional five years has passed from your reregistration date. It is in your interest to make sure this document is filed on time.

4. Filing Section 8 and 15 Declarations Online

The Section 8 and 15 Declarations (whether filed separately or as one application) are available for filing online through the PTO's TEAS program. On the PTO home page, click "File" under Trademarks. Then choose "File a POST-registration form or Renew an Existing Registered Mark." Then choose either the combined 8 and 15 form or the Section 8 form, depending on your needs. After that, you must answer a series of questions similar to those asked of applicants under the TEAS new trademark application (see Chapter 7). Like other TEAS form, you can pay by credit card at the end of the procedure.

D. File Your Section 8 Declaration and Section 9 Application for Renewal

If your mark was registered on or after November 16, 1989, it must be renewed within ten years from the date of registration. If your mark was registered before November 16, 1989, it must be renewed 20 years from date of registration. In addition to filing a renewal application (Section 9) you also must file another Section 8 Declaration at the same time. These two documents have been combined into one document and can be filled out online using the PTO's eTEAS program. You can access the form at www.uspto.gov/teas/eTEASforms.htm.

The renewal application should be filed within the six-month period directly preceding the ten- (or 20-) year anniversary of your mark's registration. Currently the fee for the combined filing is $500 per mark per class ($100 for the Section 8 Declaration, $400 for the Section 9 renewal application). For an additional $100 per class fee, the renewal may be filed within a six-month grace period after the anniversary date. No renewal application will be accepted after that date. For instance, if your registration expires on May 15, 2006, your renewal application (1) must be dated after November 15, 2005, and (2) may be filed between November 16, 2005, and May 15, 2006 (or between May 16 and December 15, 2006, with the $100 grace period fee). We strongly recommend that you file your renewal application as soon as you are able, to allow the maximum time possible for curing glitches.

E. Use It or Risk Losing It

The adage "use it or lose it" applies to trademark protection. A mark must be in continuous use for the owner to keep others from using it. If the mark falls out of use for a long enough period of time, it may be considered abandoned. A mark that has been registered with the PTO, if not used for three years or more, will be presumed abandoned. A "presumption" is a legal standard that means it is "more likely than not" that something has happened. Every presumption can be rebutted by credible evidence to the contrary. For example, a company challenges the validity of a trademark arguing that it has not been used for three years. If the trademark owner can present a good explanation of why the nonuse does not constitute an "intent to abandon," the mark will not be abandoned.

Despite the "use it or lose it" rule, the law often permits nonuse for a considerable amount of time. Such contingencies as temporary financial difficulty, bankruptcy proceedings, and the need for a product revision may all qualify as satisfactory explanations for nonuse of a mark. There is no particular time period that the mark must be out of use to be considered abandoned (other than the three-year presumption mentioned above). Rather, abandonment will be decided on a case-by-case basis.

F. Maintain Tight Control of Your Mark

As we explain in other parts of the book, trademarks serve the primary function of identifying a particular product or service in the marketplace. If an owner allows others to use its trademark without restriction, the mark will no longer serve as a meaningful indicator of a particular product's or service's origin. If this occurs, the mark can be considered abandoned. For instance, if a fast food hamburger chain allows its franchise operators to have complete discretion as to the food, decor, and type of service they offer under the company logo, the logo quickly loses its ability to indicate a particular type of food service. In this situation, the logo can be abandoned—it no longer serves its original function of product or service identification—and anyone will be free to use it.

The way that McDonald's controls its marks exemplifies the type of vigilance over the product or service that is necessary to avoid the possibility of abandonment. This company uses its service mark not only to distinguish its service from its competitors generally but also to call to a consumer's mind such characteristics as a specific level of service, a specific type of meal at a specific price, and a specific level of cleanliness. It does this by requiring every owner of a McDonald's franchise to operate the franchise under tight rules and restrictions, designed to ensure that the characteristics associated with the McDonald's mark are always present. Without such restrictions, the McDonald's mark soon would stand for nothing; a McDonald's franchise operation would cease to provide the consumer with meaningful information about its products based on its usage of the McDonald's mark.

Another aspect of controlling your mark is to police its use by others. Even if you don't particularly care whether others use your mark, your failure to assert your exclusive ownership rights means that the mark may be considered abandoned. Policing your mark might mean annual checks of the trade literature applicable to your business, weekly scrutiny of the *Official Gazette* for new trademark applications, or even periodic full trademark searches.

You can also hire a third party to police your trademark. Most trademark search companies (See Chapter 4, Section G) offer trademark-watching services for a monthly or annual fee. In addition, companies such as TrademarkTracker (www.trademarktracker.com) will watch for use of your trademark in online databases, Web pages, and even online auction sites.

If you do discover other businesses using your mark, you can respond in the ways we suggest in Chapter 11, If Someone Infringes Your Mark. Or you could hire a lawyer to sue if necessary. To maintain your rights, you don't have to take an unauthorized user to court, but you should send a letter protesting the use of the mark and asserting your claim of ownership. If their use goes on for a long time—for example, several years—your delay may provide them a defense against your legal action, or you may lose your right to obtain an injunction (to order them to stop using the mark) once you finally do sue.

Beware Naked Licenses

If you grant others the right to use your trademark (known as a trademark license), you must always supervise the nature and quality of the goods or services being produced using that trademark. For example, if you are the owner of a trademark for clothing and license its use to a shoe company, you must supervise the quality of the shoe company's products using your trademark. Your failure to supervise is referred to as a "naked license," and the results can be disastrous. For example, in a 2002 case, a court cancelled the trademark rights of a licensor (the owner) of a wine trademark because the company failed to supervise a company that had licensed the trademark. (*Barcamerica International USA Trust v. Tyfield Importers Inc.*, 289 F.3d 589 (9th Cir. 2002).) Most trademark licenses are drafted to avoid this result by requiring that samples of all licensed trademark goods be periodically submitted to the trademark owner for approval and quality control.

Authorized Uses of Your Trademark

Not all uses of your trademark by others place it in jeopardy. For example, it is common for stores to use marks belonging to other companies to tell their customers that the goods or services identified by the marks can be purchased at that store. When using marks in this way, however, the stores must make it clear that the marks belong to their owners, not to the store. Usually this fact is clear from the context ("Levi's sold here," or, "An authorized distributor of Apple Computer products"). Often you will see—on labels of goods that incorporate others' products, like a sofa—a message like "Wear-Dated ® is a trademark of the Monsanto Company," indicating that the name of the sofa's fabric is a trademark of another company. Such uses become a problem only when it is not clear that the trademark belongs to the rightful trademark owner.

Generally, textual use of a trademark—simply typed—is not a problem. However, if used in a comparative advertisement, the mark must have the same typeface and logo as used by the original mark owner. If the trademark does not look like it normally does, the use of the mark may be confusing or diluting.

G. Use the Mark Properly—Avoid Genericide

A few businesses—mostly large ones—have the apparent good fortune of owning a mark that has become a household word. But, paradoxically, once the mark becomes so much of a household word that it becomes synonymous with any product or service of the sort it originally represented, it ceases to be a mark—it becomes generic. For example, some people refer to all facial paper tissues as Kleenex, and all acetaminophen analgesics as Tylenol. These marks would be in danger of becoming lost through "genericide" if the companies did not protest such improper uses of the marks.

The problem is this: The more well-known a particular mark becomes, the more the public is prone to equate the mark with the underlying product rather than view it as one brand name among many. This is just another way of saying that the mark loses its ability to identify a particular brand and becomes generic. Only a tiny number of companies will face this problem—it tends to arise with revolutionary new products that the public comes to associate with the name their first manufacturer gives them, like Rollerblades for in-line skates. But because genericide is avoidable, you ought to know how to prevent your mark from going generic if that seems to be even a remote possibility.

The best way to keep a mark from becoming generic is to:

- accompany every use of the mark with the generic product or service (for example, Kleenex tissues)
- never use the mark as a verb (for instance, you never go "roller blading," you skate on Rollerblade skates)
- always capitalize your mark (Tylenol)
- never use the mark as a general noun (for instance, don't call a photocopy a "Xerox").

If you become aware that your mark is being used improperly, you must remind the public that it is a mark and not a generic name. For instance, the Xerox Corporation has spent millions advising the public that *Xerox* is a registered mark that must always be capitalized and used as a proper adjective describing a noun (for instance, a *Xerox* brand photocopier). If later on someone challenges the Xerox Corporation's right to the exclusive use of the word "Xerox" on the ground it has become generic, Xerox will prevail if it can show that people understood these advertisements and that most use the term "Xerox" as a brand name—not a generic one.

H. Transferring Ownership of a Trademark

You should consider your registered mark as property with a title, the same as a house or car. The title document is your Certificate of Registration. (See Chapter 7, Federal Trademark Registration, Section I.) If for any reason you sell your business or the rights in products you manufacture or distribute, you will also need to sell the marks used to identify the business and products in the marketplace. The complete transfer of ownership in a mark to another person or entity is called an "assignment." An assignment of a registered mark must be in writing to be valid. It can—and should—be filed with the PTO. The new owner can obtain a new Certificate of Registration in its name. If you anticipate a sale (assignment) of your mark, see a trademark attorney. A sample assignment form is set forth below. When filing an assignment of trademark ownership with the PTO, use Form 1594, Recordation Form Cover Sheet (trademarks only), which can be downloaded from the PTO website (www.uspto.gov).

If you are selling a business, chances are you are also selling any trademarks associated with it. If so, it makes sense to assign your ownership of the marks in a document that is separate from the contract of sale. This enables the new mark owner to record only the transfer of mark ownership with the PTO, while keeping private the many details of the deal that do not affect the transfer of trademark rights.

Note that in the sample assignment form, below, the trademark owner transfers ownership of the business's "goodwill" as well as the mark itself. Goodwill is an intangible asset measured in large part by customer recognition of and loyalty to the mark in question. Any transfer of ownership in the mark must include a transfer of the goodwill associated with the mark.

Assignment

_____ *name of registrant* _____ (Assignor),

of _____ *mailing address* _____,

has adopted, used, and is using a mark that is registered in the United States Patent and

Trademark Office, Registration No. _____ *get number from registration certificate* _____,

dated __ *get date from registration certificate* ___.

_____ *name of person or company that will be the new owner of the mark* _____ (Assignee)

of _____ *mailing address* _____,

wants to acquire the mark and the registration thereof.

For good and valuable consideration, receipt of which is hereby acknowledged, Assignor hereby assigns to Assignee all right, title, and interest in and to the mark, together with the goodwill of the business symbolized by the mark, and the above-identified registration.

_____

Signature of Assignor

if assignor is a business, list official title of person signing

Title

State of _____)

)

County of _____)

On this _____ day of _____ *month* _____, *year*, before me appeared

_____ *assignor's name* _____, the person who signed this

instrument, who acknowledged that he/she signed it as a free act on his/her own behalf (or

on behalf of the identified entity with authority to do so).

_____

Signature of notary public

NOTE: This form is valid only when the assignee is a United States resident or company. ∎

Chapter 9

Evaluating Trademark Strength

7his chapter helps you evaluate a particular mark's legal strength—that is, the degree to which the courts will protect it or something similar against use or misuse by others. You will want to read this chapter if you feel the need for a deeper understanding of the material in Chapter 3, or if you have:

- been accused of violating someone else's mark, or
- think that someone else is treading on your mark.

Assuming you are involved in a conflict situation, once you digest this material you should read Chapter 10, which discusses who has priority in case two marks—or a mark and an Internet domain name—come into conflict. Then you should go to Chapter 11 (if your mark is being infringed) or Chapter 12 (if you are accused of infringement) for suggestions on how to deal with the dispute.

In Chapter 3, How to Choose a Good Name for Your Business, Product, or Service, we have already touched on the basics of what makes a mark legally strong—inherent distinctiveness or distinctiveness acquired through secondary meaning. This teaches you how to classify your mark by type (for instance, geographic names and personal names) and explains how far the courts are willing to go to protect that type of mark in case of a dispute.

A. A Brief Review of What Makes a Strong Mark

A legally strong trademark meets two basic tests:

- It successfully identifies your goods or services in the consumer's mind.
- Because of your prior usage (and maybe registration), competitors can't use it or anything like it in any context where customers might (1) be confused about the source of goods or services, or (2) might, because of the similarity of the marks, erroneously conclude your business is associated in some way with the goods or services being marketed under the conflicting mark.

How your mark measures up to these tests helps determine your mark's strength in relation to any other mark. Below we set out an approach that will help you apply these tests in the real world.

As you have heard repeatedly by now, the tools we give you to evaluate a trademark's strength are guidelines, not guarantees. These rules represent the best guesses that most lawyers would be likely to make based on the relevant court decisions. But we don't promise specific results for a specific mark because that depends on many factors, including use, timing, and how the facts strike the judge who decides the particular dispute.

B. The First Step: For Marks Consisting of Words, Identify the Distinctive Part of the Mark

To evaluate the strength of your product or service mark, first separate its distinctive component from the part of the mark that identifies the type of product or service it identifies. For example, the mark *Apple Computers* contains a distinctive element—Apple—and a product/service identifier, Computers. Another example: The distinctive aspect of the name *Guess?* jeans is the word "Guess" followed by a "?".

Sometimes all or most of the individual words of a mark are equally distinctive (or nondistinctive), and it is the combination of the words that is distinctive. Examples: *Trader Joe's* (food market) and *Music Now and Then* (a disk jockey service). Even when there is no specific distinctive part of a word mark, the mark will still have a tail that identifies the underlying product or service. So it's still important to understand where the words that give the mark at least some distinctiveness drop off and common identifiers of goods or services kick in. Because the nondistinctive aspect of a word mark can never be protected, we simply disregard it in evaluating the legal strength of the name as a mark.

After you have isolated the word or phrase that forms the distinctive aspect of your mark, match it with one or more of the categories listed in Section C below to understand why your mark does or doesn't have legal strength.

C. Assess the Legal Strength of the Trademark Aspect of Your Word Mark

Earlier we spoke of the distinctive part of your word mark. That distinctive part is in fact the trademark aspect of your mark. Here we place the different categories of trademarks on a spectrum. We start with the most distinctive

marks—the ones with the greatest legal strength. We then move to more ordinary marks, which may be easier to promote but harder to protect legally, and finally conclude with generic marks, which can't be protected at all because they utterly lack all distinctiveness. Along the way we provide lists of examples of each category and discuss why various names are classified as they are.

Remember to consider the whole effect of your mark—its sound, its look, and all the meanings of the individual elements of the mark—before drawing conclusions about its legal strength. This includes the style of the typeface, as well as its color, shape, size, and any other aspect of the overall impression the mark makes. In addition, how the mark is used and the timing of its first use are all relevant in determining relative trademark strengths.

Some of the distinctions that place a mark in one category or another may appear arbitrary and even, at times, hairsplitting. At first you may feel that it is impossible to tell the difference. If you take your time with this material, however, the better you know it, the more it will make sense.

Remember: We're All Human. Do keep in mind that live human beings—with their individual strengths and weaknesses—are the ultimate arbiters of whether a particular mark is to be considered strong or weak. Whether the person is a trademark examiner (employee of the U.S. Patent and Trademark Office), a judge, a juror, or the author of this book, his or her analysis of a particular mark is based on a subjective response to mostly visual stimuli, which makes for fuzzy decision making. So, if you find yourself disagreeing with the category a particular mark has been consigned to by the PTO, courts, or even the author of this book (in the many made-up examples provided), try to understand (if not accept) the rationale rather than dissent in the name of some absolute truth.

1. Varieties of Distinctive Marks

Distinctive marks fall into three basic categories—coined, arbitrary, and suggestive. All are strong, but coined and arbitrary marks are considered stronger than suggestive marks and therefore receive more protection.

a. Coined Trademarks

These are words that you won't find in any dictionary; they have been made up just to serve as trademarks, so they have no other meaning. Words such as *Blistex*, *Kodak*, *Exxon*, *Tylenol,* and *Actifed* are the marks lawyers like best. They are inarguably distinctive, and therefore legally strong. Such household words as *Kodak*, *Kleenex,* and *Reebok* were all coined specifically as marks. Whether it is registered or not, chances are that a coined mark will automatically entitle you to the strongest protection against copying that courts can provide.

In practice, coined marks can't be used by others in any commercial context. By contrast, most other types of marks can be used by more than one owner as long as:

- the goods and services they are used on are not related and don't compete with each other, and

- it is unlikely that customers will be confused by the multiple use of the mark.

The reason for the special treatment afforded a coined mark is its uniqueness. Because a coined mark's exclusive role is to identify a specific product or service (or product line) in the marketplace, most consumers would expect linkage between all businesses who use the mark, and would therefore be confused as to the origins of the products or services carrying it. So it is highly unwise to borrow a famous coined trademark even for a vastly different product or service.

Not all made-up marks fall into this strongest-of-all category. Marks that are coined wholly new, like *Maalox*, are treated differently and are given more protection than are marks that are composites of recognizable elements of words, like *Accuride*. *Maalox* is automatically strong because it is not like anything we have heard before. But *Accuride* is too close to "accurate ride" to be considered a purely coined term. Such a mark is therefore usually considered suggestive rather than coined. We discuss suggestive marks below.

b. Fanciful or Arbitrary Marks

Fanciful or arbitrary names, such as *Penguin* books, *Arrow* shirts, and *Camel* cigarettes, also make distinctive and legally strong marks. These marks use common words in an unexpected or arbitrary way, so that their normal meanings have nothing to do with the nature of the product or service they identify. They creatively juxtapose unexpected combinations of words and products or services. That's how a skating rink came up with the appealing name *Jellibeans*. Another wonderful example of a fanciful name is *We Be Bop* for a local children's store, and it's difficult to think of a more arbitrary name than *Diesel, A Bookstore*.

These arbitrary or fanciful marks have almost as broad a scope of exclusive use as do coined marks. Most of the time, using an arbitrary or fanciful mark for one type of product or service will prevent the use of the same mark on similar or related services or products. However, unlike a coined mark, arbitrary or fanciful marks may be used if the context of use is entirely different and the original mark is not too well known. If, on the other hand, the arbitrary or fanciful mark has become famous, then—under a principle known as trademark dilution—the mark may be protected against use by others, no matter what the context of use. (See Chapter 1, A Trademark Primer.)

c. Suggestive Marks

A close relative of the arbitrary mark is the suggestive mark. This type of mark uses ordinary words in a clever manner to create a desirable idea or feeling about a product or service but stays away from literally describing any aspect of the product or service. Examples of suggestive marks are *Verbatim* (for computer disks), *Banana Republic* (for a style of clothing), *Greyhound* (for bus service), *Thistle Dew Inn* (for a bed and breakfast service), and *Panache* (for a beauty salon).

Suggestive marks are considered distinctive and therefore legally strong because they indirectly associate favorable qualities with specific goods and services in a creative way. For example, a *Jaguar* car conveys the idea of aggressiveness, beauty, and speed, desirable attributes for a car; *Dove* soap conveys softness and gentleness; *Greyhound* implies speed and sleekness—not adjectives normally associated with bus lines but desirable ones nonetheless.

Sunkist is an interesting example of a suggestive mark. Although it is just a novel spelling of the adjective "sun-kissed," its creative use on fruit and juices evokes a wonderfully fresh and healthy image. It is the originality of the mark that makes it legally strong.

An excellent example of a suggestive mark is *Thistle Dew Inn*, used by a quaint bed and breakfast establishment just off the town square in Sonoma, California. The composite term *Thistle Dew* evokes both a ubiquitous local purple-flowered plant and a feeling of freshness and renewal that people in Northern California seek when they visit Sonoma, the heart of the wine country. (It also—perhaps unintentionally—echoes the sentiment, "This'll do.")

And finally, *Panache*, a French word that means spirited self-confidence, style, flamboyance, and daring elegance of manner, suggests the qualities that customers might hope to obtain from an upscale beauty shop located in Lakeport, California.

d. More Examples of Distinctive Marks by Category

The line between arbitrary, fanciful, and suggestive marks is often a fine one. A mark that might appear to be fanciful or arbitrary may in fact be derived from a little-known source and might, therefore, be suggestive to those in the know. For example, some marks employ mythical or fantasy allusions to suggest desirable connotations, like the *Janus* investment fund (Janus = Roman god of beginnings) or *Midas Muffler* (King Midas = the golden touch). A clever mark of this sort is *Prints Valiant* for a copy shop, which combines the name of a cartoon hero with a pun on the kind of shop it is, and implies heroic effort.

Below is a chart showing examples of the different categories of distinctive trademarks. Examine it carefully to see if these distinctions make sense to you.

Perplexed? Don't be. Many of these examples can go either way. For example, while some trademark authorities consider *Ivory* soap to be an arbitrary trademark, others argue that it describes the color of the soap, or that it suggests the desirable qualities of ivory—smooth, clean, white, valuable. *Nyquil*, a cold remedy, can be seen either as a coined term, or a composite suggestive mark, combining "night" and "tranquil" to evoke peaceful sleep. *Cachet*, for a women's clothing store, rides the border between suggestive and descriptive, because it means a mark of

Categories of Distinctive Trademarks		
Suggestive	**Fanciful/Arbitrary**	**Coined**
Accuride tires	*Ajax* cleanser	*Actifed*
Chicken of the Sea tuna	*Apple* computers	*Amtrak*
Coppertone tanning lotion	*Arrow* shirts	*Barbasol* shaving lotion
Esprit clothes	*Banana Republic* clothes	*Blistex* lip balm
Glacier ice	*Beefeater* gin	*Curel* hand lotion
Greyhound bus	*Camel* cigarettes	*Exxon*
Liquid Paper	*Domino* sugar	*Kodak*
Maternally Yours clothes	*Double Rainbow* Ice Cream	*Maalox*
Q-tips	*Hang Ten* clothes	*Nyquil*
Roach Motel insect trap	*Hard Rock Cafe*	*Reebok* shoes
7-Eleven stores	*Ivory* soap	*Tylenol*
Suave shampoo	*Jellibeans* skating rink	
Verbatim computer discs	*Nova* TV series	
Wearever cookware	*Penguin* books	

distinction or individuality, thus promising unique style to the customer. *Banana Republic* could be either arbitrary, because it has nothing to do with clothes, or it could be suggestive of adventure and travel.

As long as your mark is distinctive in the sense of it being unique, clever, or just plain memorable, the practical importance of what category it fits in is nil—until you find yourself in a conflict with another mark. Then, to the extent that your mark qualifies as a coined term, it will get the widest scope of protection. We explained more about what this means in Chapter 6, How to Evaluate the Results of Your Trademark Search. For now, it's enough to understand what category your mark falls in and why.

2. Varieties of Nondistinctive (Ordinary) Marks

In Chapter 3 we lumped all the marks that aren't distinctive into a category called ordinary marks. An ordinary mark is one that communicates in a descriptive or otherwise mundane way something about the product or service to which it is attached. It includes five sorts of terms:

- descriptive, describing the nature of the service or product (*Self-Help Divorce Center* for a consulting service helping people file their own divorce forms)
- geographic, describing the geographic area it's in (*Downtown Auto Service*, if it's really downtown)
- laudatory, praising the business or the customer (*Pretty Nails*, for a manicurist; *Fast Feet*, for athletic shoes)

- personal names, consisting primarily of first names, surnames, personal initials, or nicknames (*Maury's Deli, Gooden Chevrolet*)
- business name initials.

While these types of word marks ordinarily are considered to be legally weak, they can each become distinctive through long use and customer recognition, via the secondary meaning rule that we discussed in Chapter 3, Section C2. For example, *IBM*, the acronym for International Business Machines, originally was a legally weak mark until it became well known over time, thereby acquiring legal strength under the secondary meaning rule.

In the following four subsections we detail the pros and cons of each kind of ordinary mark and give you rules about when a term will be considered strong enough to qualify for protection in the courts.

 Generic Name Note. We discuss generic marks—names that have become synonymous with the product itself, such as aspirin and cellophane—in Section C3 below.

a. Descriptive Words and Words of Praise

We lump marks using these kinds of words together because there is little practical difference between them. As long as you know your mark is one or the other, you'd be wasting your time trying to decide which. So let's briefly recap what these marks are before we try distinguishing them from marks that are legally strong.

Descriptive marks are those that literally describe a feature or attribute of a product or service, such as *10-Minute Lube* (auto care),

Hi-Tech Computers, Char-broiler hamburgers, *FindUHome* (real estate broker), or *Nuts and Bolts* (hardware store).

Laudatory marks (words of praise) hype a product or service's quality or quantity, using common words like *Original Blend* (cat food), *America's Freshest Ice Cream* (ice cream), *Maple Rich* (syrup), *Blue Ribbon* (bakeries), or *Best Foods* (organic food distributors); or they describe the qualities of the product or service the business hopes to deliver, like *Joy* detergent or *Pride* furniture polish.

Descriptive marks make very weak trademarks for two reasons.

- Consumers are so used to commercial hype that descriptive terms don't make the kind of impact on them that would help them to effectively distinguish one product or service from another. For example, the name *Canine Clipping Centers* doesn't by itself clearly differentiate that pet care shop from any other.
- Descriptive terms need to remain freely available for everyone's commercial or everyday use. Trademark law will only protect terms that are unique to a particular product or service brand and that aren't, therefore, necessary for another business to use if it wishes to describe or hype its business in advertising or marketing copy.

You may think that changing the spelling or language—from English to French, for example—makes an otherwise weak mark strong. It usually doesn't work that way. So *La Bread Shoppe*, or *Tastee Kookie*, remain weak marks despite the spelling/language variations. But a relatively obscure foreign

term, or one that most consumers wouldn't recognize as a foreign language equivalent of a descriptive term, can create a strong mark. So, although "xerox" is the ancient Greek word for dry, and "dry" describes the photocopying process Xerox invented, *Xerox* was a strong mark from the beginning—because only a few Greek scholars knew its meaning. In addition, *La Posada Inns*, directed at English speakers, is considered a distinctive mark although the Spanish translation (The Inn) is descriptive.

How *Xerox* Almost Became a Generic Mark

Over a number of years *Xerox* became more and more synonymous with photocopy machines and the photocopying process ("I need a xerox," or "I'm going to xerox that"). This common usage put the *Xerox* mark in danger of becoming generic and therefore not protectible at all. To prevent this, Xerox undertook an aggressive and expensive advertising campaign to encourage people to use *Xerox* properly, as a proper adjective, and not as a generic term (a verb or a noun). (See also Section C3, below.)

As we have emphasized in earlier chapters, even descriptive names can become legally strong enough to get full trademark protection, through the secondary meaning rule. That's when a trademark becomes so closely identified with a specific product or service that the public no longer thinks first of the original ordinary meaning of the words. Then the mark is said to have taken on a new "secondary"—and distinctive—meaning, and rivals can no longer use it to identify their products or services.

But even after descriptive marks have acquired distinctiveness through the secondary meaning rule, others still can use the ordinary words that make up such marks in non-trademark ways—that is, to legitimately describe their product or service in advertising. This is known as "fair use" of a trademark, and it is a valid defense in court if a mark owner challenges the use of your words in their mark.

For example, once *Standard Brands* acquired secondary meaning and became protectible as a trademark, others could not use those words as a trademark on goods, but a store could advertise that they carry "all standard brands" of paint, or tools, or whatever they sell, without fear of infringing.

Continuous Use for Five Years. If the owner of a weak mark can prove that the mark has been in continuous use for a five-year period, it will be presumed to have acquired a secondary meaning and be eligible for placement on the federal principal trademark register. (See Chapter 7.)

One final point: Even without secondary meaning, ordinary trademarks can get limited protection—under unfair competition laws—from a rival with a confusingly similar name in the same area and the same line of business. (See Chapter 10, Sorting Out Trademark Disputes.)

Deceptive and Misleading Marks Get No Protection

Marks that describe a product or service misleadingly get no protection at all. So neither *Neo-Hide* nor *Softhide* can be protected as marks for imitation leather. Most state and federal trademark laws specifically bar these types of marks from registration both to protect consumers from being ripped off and to protect businesses that accurately describe their products from unfair competition by those who don't.

A second category of marks that are only slightly misleading—called "deceptively misdescriptive"—are viewed as less seriously deceptive. *American Beauty* as a mark for a Japanese sewing machine is one example of this type of mark. When first used, this type of mark does not receive legal protection either. But once it acquires secondary meaning, then it becomes distinctive, and protectible as a mark, on the theory that it is no longer considered misleading. That's because the public no longer thinks of the literal meaning of the words and instead only associates the words in the mark with the product or service.

b. Geographic Marks

These are marks with a geographic term in them, such as Eastern, Miami, Indiana, English, or any other place names, from streets to continents, or regions to rivers. There are several subspecies of marks containing geographic terms:

- **Literal Geographic Descriptors.** Like other ordinary marks, the general rule is that if you use a geographic term descriptively (for example, if the product or service is really connected to the place name), it can't be protected as a mark, absent a showing of secondary meaning. That's because everyone has a right to use accurate geographic words to describe the origin of their services or products. So marks like *Manhasset Drugs, Central Realty, North Moline Hardware,* or *Chestnut Street Pub* (if it's on Chestnut Street) are weak and can't be protected, unless, of course, they gain secondary meaning in connection with the particular product or service for which they're used. Examples of geographic marks that got protection by acquiring secondary meaning are *American Airlines, Continental Can Corp.,* and *The New Yorker* magazine.

⚠ Although not protectible as marks, these extremely common types of business names may be entitled to some relief in court if a competitor uses the same name in a manner that would be highly likely to confuse customers. For example, *Manhasset Drugs* could stop a competitor from using that exact name in Manhasset. (See Chapter 1, A Trademark Primer, Section F, for a discussion of unfair competition principles.)

- **Indirect Geographic Descriptors.** Even if your service or product is not factually associated with the place named in your mark, the mark may still be if the public is likely to assume that such a link exists. For example, Chicago is famous for a kind of pizza, so it's descriptive, not distinctive, to call a Dallas pizzeria *Chicago Pizza*. Likewise, *Thai Videos* is weak if it sells videos from Thailand, even though it does so in Los Angeles. So, too, *Phnom Penh* is weak for a Cambodian restaurant located in Trenton, New Jersey.

- **General Geographical Descriptors.** Some words like "World," "Globe," and places in outer space may be far too broad to suggest any specific place of origin, but they are still weak because they operate like laudatory or descriptive marks (see Section C2a above). Thus *American Engineer* on an engineering trade magazine is descriptive and weak because it's aimed at a readership made up of American engineers.

- **Ambiguous Geographical Descriptors.** Some geographic terms are ambiguous in meaning when used in a trademark. For instance, the term "Continental" can be interpreted as referring to a literal continental land mass or, more quaintly, to the European continent. "National" may indicate nationwide scope or patriotism, again depending on how it is used. Whether it's a weak or a strong mark would depend on which meaning applies.

c. Geographic Terms As Strong Marks

As with all marks consisting of ordinary terms, there are times when geographic marks are protectible, apart from acquiring secondary meaning. The best way to make a geographic term distinctive as a mark is to use it in an arbitrary or fanciful way. For example, *American Express* (for travel and

credit services) and *California Girl* (for clothes) don't really describe either the service or the product or imply their origins. Instead, these words project an image that is fanciful and distinctive for the items on which they are used. So they are protectible as marks.

Likewise, *English Leather* is a distinctive (suggestive) mark, as long as it does not describe a leather product. If it did, it would be either descriptive, if it comes from Britain, or deceptive, if it does not. (See below for more on why deceptive terms can't be marks.) And a fabric store called *Taos Fabrics* has a weak mark if it's in New Mexico but a strong one if it is in Chattanooga.

This makes sense. The sellers of products or services have a right to truthfully tell where an item came from without infringing another's mark. It would be unfair to all other New York businesses to give any one company in that city a monopoly on the name. But if an entrepreneur elsewhere wants to evoke the Big Apple in Fargo, North Dakota, for example, that's fair. (If the owner of the Fargo-based *Big Apple* decided later to market its products in New York City, it's possible that its rights would be greater than if the business had started there from the begin-

ning. This would depend on how well-known the *Big Apple* mark had become in the meantime, whether the mark had been placed on the Federal Register, and what competing uses of the mark already existed in New York City at the time of the desired expansion.)

d. Personal Names

Words in this category refer to a person, whether their first name, last name, whole name, nickname, or initials. Examples are *Juan's, Houlihan's, Larry Blake's, C.J.'s,* and *H&R Block.* As a general rule, anyone can use their personal name as a mark for their service or product, unless the same name is already in use on directly competing products or services.

This means that personal names (at least common ones) make weak marks. But as we discovered in an informal study of the Yellow Pages, more small businesses use a surname or first name as their mark than any other kind of name. Marks using personal initials are also popular. It's understandable why businesspeople are drawn to these types of names; they demonstrate pride of ownership. But using a personal name or initials has potentially serious drawbacks from a trademark point of view.

First, most personal names are legally weak because they are not particularly memorable, especially if they are used in one or more competing businesses. We saw this problem with *Ray's Pizza* in New York (see Chapter 3, How to Choose a Good Name for Your Business, Product, or Service). When someone there says "*Ray's Pizza*," no one can tell which of the 24 *Ray's* in the city is the right one. Nor does adding an initial make a personal name inherently distinctive enough to become a legally strong trademark. On the other hand, the odder your name, the less likely others will use it on a similar business and the more memorable it will be. Will the real *Orville Redenbacher* please stand up?

Second, as with other ordinary marks, a personal name trademark must usually acquire secondary meaning through being identified with your business to be protected as a strong trademark. However, many personal names have garnered such a large degree of public recognition that the courts permit only very limited other uses of them. *McDonald's* and *Levi's* are two good examples.

Despite the general principles governing personal name marks just described, a few personal name marks do manage to get strong trademark protection without secondary meaning. The general rule is that if the public would not view the mark primarily as a personal name, then it can be protected outright. Put another way, a personal name only works as a trademark if it is so unusual that no one recognizes it as a personal name, like *Garan*. Other personal names that can be distinctive trademarks are ones that have additional meanings, like *Bird, Kent,* or *Fairbanks*, which also have common descriptive or geographic significance. The distinctiveness of such marks would depend on how they are used.

Another exception to the general rule that personal names make weak trademarks is well-known historical names, like Da Vinci, Lincoln, Rameses, and Robin Hood, which are considered fanciful and distinctive. The use of such marks clearly does not imply that the person named is commercially connected to the product or service—so their trademark use is not primarily as a personal name. On the other hand, some historical names, like Webster and Longfellow, have been treated as weak marks. What's the difference? Perhaps because the latter names are less mythic— Daniel Webster and Henry Wadsworth Longfellow are less famous by far than Da Vinci or Abraham Lincoln—they carry more of a personal name meaning than do the former. This is another of those gray areas of the law, where the differences are slim.

The Right of Publicity

There is a related but separate right that protects people's names and personas from commercial use by others. It's called the right of publicity, and it allows celebrities to prevent others from making money by the unauthorized use of their names. Although the right of publicity is commonly associated with celebrities, every person, regardless of how famous, has a right to prevent unauthorized use of their name or image to sell products. The right of publicity extends beyond the commercial use of a person's name or image and includes the use of any personal element that implies an individual's endorsement of a product, provided that the public can identify the individual based upon the use. In many states, the right of publicity survives death and can be exercised by the person's estate.

Even using a famous name on unrelated services or products can be a problem. John Walker probably can't operate a motel under the name *Johnny Walker Inn*, but he might be able to use a name that sounds sufficiently different, like *John M. Walker Inn*. Often in order to resolve such potentially confusing uses, a disclaimer such as "not associated with …" is required. For example, *Hyatt Corp.* sued *Hyatt Legal Services* over the use of that surname. The suit was eventually resolved when the defendant agreed to use the statement: "Hyatt Legal Services is named after its founder, Joel Z. Hyatt."

Some names are so famous and applied to such a variety of products that any additional use of them would be confusing to the public, even on a completely unrelated product or service. *DuPont* or *Yves St. Laurent* are examples.

YVESSAINTLAURENT

Other names may be equally famous but are associated so exclusively with specific products or services that even though the public would recognize any use of a similar name, no actual confusion is likely to result where the mark is used on a totally different type of product or service. If such is the case, then you can use your name even if it's also a famous mark. That's why Bob Fanta won a suit by *Coca-Cola* over his use of "Keep Tab with Fanta" to advertise his tax return service: His business is so logically remote from soft drinks that actual confusion is unlikely.

In one famous case detailed by Calvin Trillin in the *The New Yorker* magazine (1988), a small bar opened up in Milwaukee under the name of *Mike Houlihan's* (the first name of one of the owners and the last name of the other owner). W.R. Grace, a conglomerate, already owned a chain of family restaurants called *Houlihan's Old Place*, one of which was in Milwaukee.

The two concerns coexisted peaceably in the same city for a couple of years. It was only when *Mike Houlihan's* opened a second pub in St. Louis, where there was another *Houlihan's Old Place*, that the conglomerate protested the bar's use of a similar mark and threatened to sue. The pub owners were furious and refused to back down: "What do you mean I can't use my surname?" fumed John Houlihan to his lawyer.

The lawyer knew that W.R. Grace appeared to have the law on its side—the Houlihan name was first used and first federally registered in connection with *Houlihan's Old Place*. (How first use and federal registration affects conflicts between marks is discussed in detail in Chapter 10, Sorting Out Trademark Disputes.) But then luck intervened.

It turned out that there really was a Mr. Houlihan, after which *Houlihan's Old Place* was named, and that his written consent for the use of his name had never been obtained— a prerequisite to registering a mark using the name of a living person. For this omission, the court canceled Grace's trademark registration of *Houlihan's Old Place*. And yet the restaurant eventually succeeded in barring the bar's use of the mark in Missouri based on unfair competition, common law trademark rights, and state dilution laws. Moral of the story: Using personal names in a mark can be tricky, so always get permission when using the name of a living person.

3. Generic Labels

In Chapter 3, How to Choose a Good Name for Your Business, Product, or Service, we introduced you to the concept of generic labels—words that are synonymous with the underlying product or service and that therefore can't distinguish it from others. Examples of generic terms are "aspirin," "linoleum," and "lite beer." Here we follow up on that discussion to help you distinguish generic labels from marks that are merely weak. It's an important distinction, because while weak marks can gain protection once they acquire secondary meaning, generic labels will never receive any protection at all.

You will see problems with generic words in three different trademark contexts:

1. When you try to protect your weak mark against an infringer, and they defend by saying your mark is generic and therefore freely copyable.

2. When you adopt a mark and seek to have it registered under the secondary meaning rule, but it is rejected because the term is generic rather than merely weak.

3. When a mark that was once distinctive (and perhaps even registered) loses all legal protection because it has become synonymous with the product and not just one brand of it. An example of a distinctive mark that is in danger of

becoming generic is *Rollerblades*, which many people use for the product itself (more accurately called in-line skates).

We are more concerned with the first circumstance than with the second or third, but most of our examples are drawn from court cases in which a mark was denied protection because it always was or had become synonymous with the product. For example, *Thermos* was once a trademark, but is now seen as a kind of insulated bottle. Although they emerge from a different context, such examples are useful because they illustrate the thinking of a judge or trademark examiner in determining if a mark is protectible at all or simply generic.

Distinguishing generic labels from weak marks may not always be easy to do. Courts ask what a buyer is likely to think of when he or she hears the term—a product or a specific source for that product? Another approach is to try to come up with a generic label for the underlying type of product or service that is different from the mark itself. As long as a generic label for a product or service can be articulated, a name that is different from the label will qualify for treatment as a mark, no matter how weak it is. Only if the name and the generic label merge over time will the mark suffer genericide.

It usually takes some market research to discover what a term's generally accepted meaning is and some legal advocacy to convince a court of this point of view.

Here's a list of generic labels. Examine them to see if they clarify the concept.

Generic Labels

Aspirin	Jujubes candy
Baby Oil	Lite beer
Bath Oil beads	Matchbox toys
Brassiere	Monopoly game
Cellophane	Montessori method
Cola	Shredded Wheat
copperclad	Softsoap
dry ice	Superglue
escalator	Thermos
Hoagie sandwich	Yo-Yo

Why, you may ask, is matchbox on this list but not *Tinkertoy?* Perhaps the public associates *Tinkertoy* more specifically with one company, whereas matchbox indicates a variety of small toy. Why is copperclad generic but not *Teflon?* Again, *Teflon* is a material that the public associates with a company, whereas copperclad is more of a process.

Let's take one example a little farther. Montessori has been ruled a generic term for a variety of child care centers that share a general philosophy of early childhood education based on the teachings of Maria Montessori. Even though the American Montessori Society certifies certain Montessori schools but not others, any school is free to use the Montessori name to describe the kind of education it provides.

But what makes the name Montessori generic instead of being descriptive of the philosophy of the school? The bottom line is, what does the public think when it hears such a term? It thinks, "Montessori—that's an educational method." Put simply, since the name describes the kind of thing involved, it's generic. By contrast, if the name tells you which thing is involved—even if it does so very descriptively—it has the potential for being a trademark.

Does this mean that no Montessori school can ever have a protectible trademark? Not at all. Many protectible marks have generic terms in them. As long as the trademark contains a nongeneric part that distinguishes the service or product from others, in addition to the generic part, then the whole is not generic and may be protected. So to have a protectible name, any Montessori school can simply add a distinguishing modifier to its name, such as *Big Trees Montessori School.* The modifier, *Big Trees,* becomes the mark.

4. Composite Terms and Slogans

In this section we discuss composite terms, slogans, designs, shapes, and containers. These types of marks also can be distinctive or ordinary, so we discuss them at some length to help you evaluate what makes them weak or strong.

a. Composite Terms

These marks can also be called cross-category marks. They are made up of one or more of the different sorts of words discussed above in Section C2. Examples are: *Shorty's Mean Motorcycles, Gino's New York Pizza, Stormy Weather Home Rehab Services,* and *Kmart.*

Composite marks are not easy to analyze. They usually consist of weak components but still may be considered strong marks. As a general rule, if all the components of a mark are descriptive, the trademark as a whole is also descriptive, and therefore weak. (See Section C2, above.) But this is by no means always true. In some circumstances, the kind of service or product a mark is attached to, the context of the mark's use, and even the public's reaction to the mark can result in weak words combining to form a strong mark.

b. Composites of Whole Words

This type of composite mark consists of individual words with different trademark strengths, like *Gino's Chicago Style Pizza*, which contains a personal name and a geographic term. The first rule about these types of marks is that the whole name is stronger than the sum of its parts. So, for example, *Such a Business* is a strong mark for a children's store. It consists of ordinary words, but they are not used descriptively: that is, "Such a Business" tells you nothing about what the business is or what it hopes to purvey. It's the combination of the phrase and the nature of the service that makes it funny, surprising, unique, and memorable. The same could be said of *Pea in a Pod* for a maternity store.

Another recent example is a line of books that uses "Don't Know Much About" as a prefix to the subject matter of the book, as in *Don't Know Much About the Civil War.* This prefix is a well-known line from an old Sam Cooke song. The line is sure to grab the attention of most prospective readers over the age of 50 and therefore serves admirably as a trademark, even though it consists entirely of ordinary words. Incidentally, book titles are

not, by themselves, entitled to trademark status, but a name that indicates a series of books (*Hardy Boys, Nancy Drew, Dummy*) is entitled to protection.

Other composites of weak elements can also make a stronger whole. For example, *Houlihan's Old Place* is an effective trademark for a restaurant. This composite of two sorts of names is much more suggestive than simply *Houlihan's* (which as a personal name can get no trademark protection without secondary meaning), or *The Old Place* (which, although not necessarily descriptive, is vague and not particularly memorable.) Again, taken together, the elements of this mark are more distinctive than either is alone.

On the other hand, *Bette's Oceanview Diner*, in the Oceanview section of Berkeley, California, is a moderately weak composite mark. That's because it combines two ordinary terms, a personal name and a geographic term, and uses them descriptively. As we have learned, this is not a recipe for a strong mark. Unless such a mark can show secondary meaning, the only protection Bette is likely to get is under state unfair competition laws, and then only if a rival restaurant uses a similar mark in the same local area, and if customers are likely to be confused by it. (Chapter 6, Section F, discusses this sort of protection in more detail.)

Now consider the composite mark, *I Can't Believe It's Not Butter!* For the uninitiated, this is a brand of margarine, not just a promotional slogan. It is descriptive because it conveys the information that the product is a close imitation of butter. Furthermore, it's exactly the kind of phrase that a rival margarine producer might want to use in advertising. But the fact that the brand name is a complete sentence with an exclamation point at the end makes it unusual, and even memorable, which means it's distinctive, which gives it legal strength.

Take another example. Colin Moriarity runs a chimney cleaning service called *The Irish Sweep*. The mark is a composite of descriptive terms, because he is in fact an Irish chimney sweeper. But we bet you'd remember the name. Why? Because it plays on a famous horse race, the Irish Sweepstakes. Also, one word, "sweep," is an archaic term for a chimney sweeper, and gives the whole trademark a more evocative feel. To some extent the strength of this trademark depends on whether many people recognize "sweep" as equivalent to chimney cleaner. If they do, it's descriptive. And yet, people can know what it means and still recognize it as archaic. On the other hand, if the mark's key feature, "sweep," is just a term in common use, then the trademark using it is just descriptive and too ordinary to be a protectible mark, without secondary meaning.

c. Composites of Elements of Words

These are one-word marks, such as *Ultraswim*, *Bushhawk,* and *Microsoft*, made up of recognizable separate words. These marks are different from those consisting of coined words discussed in Section C1, above. Coined terms are wholly new words that mean nothing. But because composite marks contain elements of words, they carry meaning, even if it is only to evoke an image. That makes them more akin to suggestive or descriptive marks than to coined terms. (If you are confused, see coined marks and suggestive marks in Section C,

above.) What makes this kind of composite mark strong or weak is not what its elements are, but how it is used. For example, *Ultraswim* as a trademark for a piece of swimming equipment would be descriptive, and therefore weak. But as used on a shampoo designed for swimmers, it is suggestive, and thus stronger. On the other hand, *Bufferin* is considered a descriptive mark, even though it's a composite that's not in the dictionary. That's because it's simply a contraction of "buffered aspirin," and the result is too close to the descriptive word "buffered" and the generic term "aspirin" to be distinctive.

Many businesses have latched on to the idea of creating a mark out of word fragments. Unfortunately, they often select terms, at least in computer and technological fields, that are so overused that they have become hackneyed and therefore descriptive. The result is that trademarks using elements like web-, laser-, super-, macro-, -tech, -soft, data- and compu-, even though they are made up, are not unusual, and so not very distinctive or memorable. This is really an instance where the early bird got the worm. Only the first ones to pick such marks, like *Microsoft*, who got in before the genre became so common, had a strong mark even before they built up extensive public recognition.

d. Slogans

Slogans such as "When it absolutely, positively has to be there overnight" (FedEx), "Because I'm worth it" (L'Oréal), and "the ultimate driving machine" (BMW) are valuable trademarks because they create indelible consumer impressions. Distinctive (or strong) slogans can be registered as trademarks with the PTO. Some slogans are inherently distinctive—that is, by their very nature they create a memorable association with a particular product or service. For example, "Reach Out and Touch Someone" is inherently distinctive because it does not describe phone services; rather, it cleverly suggests or promotes a quality of life enhanced by phone communication. The same is true of "Just Do It," a slogan that connotes the active life without describing any aspect of Nike or its products. An inherently distinctive slogan is usually a pithy, short phrase that does more than inform or describe—it promotes.

By contrast, a slogan such as "Extra Strength Pain Reliever," is merely informative and does not, by itself, distinguish *Excedrin* from other analgesics. However, even though this particular slogan is not inherently distinctive, it has become distinctive by acquiring a secondary meaning through sales and advertising. This was also the case with "Hair Color So Natural Only Your Hairdresser Knows For Sure" for *Miss Clairol* hair products.

As with other types of marks, slogans that are inherently descriptive or that have become distinctive under the secondary meaning rule may be federally registered and protected nationwide. (See Chapter 7, Federal Trademark Registration.)

Some slogans, like some generic terms, can never function as marks. For example, the phrases "Why Pay More!" and "Proudly Made in the U.S.A." were both rejected for registration because they were common commercial phrases and failed to distinguish the goods or services to which they were attached.

If your mark is a combination of a business or product name and a slogan, such as *Happy Clown —America's Favorite Ice Cream*, the slogan part must meet the same standards for distinctiveness as if the slogan stood alone. For example, if you attempted to federally register *Happy Clown—America's Favorite Ice Cream* as a mark, the trademark examiner would break the mark into two parts—*Happy Clown* and *America's Favorite Ice Cream*. Although "Happy Clown" would by itself probably qualify as a distinctive mark, "America's Favorite Ice Cream" would not be considered distinctive, primarily because it uses a common phrase to describe rather than promote the product. For that reason, the trademark examiner would require you to disclaim the slogan as a condition of having "Happy Clown" placed on the Principal Register.

See Chapter 7 for more on what it means to disclaim a word or phrase.

Tips for Selecting a Slogan

1. Avoid using common commercial phrases, especially if the phrase is part of the trade language ("Think Green" for recycled paper).
2. Avoid describing the product or service ("Finest Salsa That Money Can Buy").
3. Keep it short and pithy ("Just Do It").
4. Use the slogan vigorously on the product, in conjunction with the service and with all advertising.

Chapter 10

Sorting Out Trademark Disputes

*M*ost businesses first become aware of trademark principles when:

- the business learns—usually from a customer or trade journal—that a competitor is using a copycat name for a similar product or service in a situation where money may be lost as a result of customer confusion
- the business receives a stiff letter from another company's lawyer alleging that the business is improperly using a name or other type of trademark that belongs to the lawyer's client and demanding that the business stop using the mark or suffer the legal consequences, or
- the business's application to register a trademark or use its business name as its Internet domain name is denied because the name is already being used.

Few things disturb a business owner quite as much as a dispute over the exclusive right to use the business's chosen name to identify its goods or services. A business's mark is normally intimately linked with the recognition and goodwill the business enjoys in the marketplace. So a dispute over that mark sets off alarm bells. In this chapter, we provide information on sorting out these types of squabbles.

The world of trademark disputes can be boiled down to three main types of disagreements:

- Infringement
- Dilution
- Cybersquatting.

Infringement disputes arise when the simultaneous use of the same or similar marks by two different businesses is likely to confuse customers.

Two main issues underlie an infringement dispute:

- who first used the mark? and
- are customers of the first trademark user likely to be confused by the second user's use of a similar trademark on similar goods or services?

Dilution involves the wrongful use of a famous mark, either by weakening the famous mark or tarnishing its reputation. The primary inquiry in a dilution dispute is whether the mark is famous. If the mark is found to be famous, the owner of the mark has the power to stop certain uses of the mark that dilute the strength of the mark or that harm the mark's reputation for quality.

Traditionally, infringement and dilution were the only two types of trademark disputes. With the rise of the Internet, however, a third main type of dispute has arisen—cybersquatting. Cybersquatting involves holding domain names hostage. It is the registering and owning of a domain name that mirrors a valuable trademark for the sole purpose of selling the domain name to the owner of the mark. Cybersquatting was made illegal in the United States by the passage of the Anti-cybersquatting Consumer Protection Act by Congress in 1999, and cybersquatting also has been found to violate the rules of the Internet Corporation for Assigned Names and Numbers, the international committee that regulates the Internet.

Your particular trademark dispute could involve one or more of these main types of conflicts. For example, you could find that someone has registered your trademark as a domain name and, at the address, has set up a website selling goods that are similar to yours under the same name. You contact the scoundrel, and he says that if you want him to stop, you can just buy the domain name from him. This person is infringing your trademark by using the mark in a manner likely to confuse your customers. He also may be cybersquatting, because he is holding the domain name of your trademark hostage. Thus, it is important to keep in mind that your dispute could involve a number of types of wrongful activity. Sections A and B of this chapter deal with infringement, including the main issues underlying infringement and the common types of disputes. Section C covers dilution, and Section D describes cybersquatting and arbitration of cybersquatting disputes.

If you are not familiar with basic trademark principles, we recommend that you review Chapter 1, A Trademark Primer, in which we explain trademark basics and the sources of trademark law.

The rules in this chapter are based on the premise that the business complaining of infringement, dilution, or cybersquatting has a valid trademark. If a trademark is not distinctive, has been abandoned, or has become generic, the owner has no rights to enforce and will not prevail in a trademark dispute.

A. Trademark Infringement

As a general rule, the first user of a trademark in a marketing territory (known as the "senior user") will be able to stop a subsequent user (called the "junior user") from using the same or a similar mark on similar goods and services. Below, we discuss the most important elements used when a court sorts out an infringement dispute between a senior and junior user.

1. Customer Confusion

When courts attempt to sort out trademark disputes, the most important issue is often whether customers are likely to be confused. Will the purchaser of goods or services likely be confused as to the source of the goods or services? Or will the purchaser of goods or services likely be confused as to which product or service is being purchased?

> **EXAMPLE 1:** Sally Lee Humbold sells frozen pizzas under the name *Sally Lee's Italian*. Because customers might think that the pizzas are a *Sara Lee* product, chances are excellent a judge would prevent her from using the name, even though pizzas and baked goods don't directly compete with each other. In addition, because *Sara Lee* is used on such a wide variety of frozen foods that it's reasonable to foresee a *Sara Lee* frozen pizza in the future, Sally Lee's use will likely cause confusion.

EXAMPLE 2: Oliver LaRocque of Sedona, Arizona, markets a brand of garlic-stuffed olives to several Sedona markets under the name *Ollie's Stinking Olives*. Pollie Jones, an unfriendly neighbor, decides to compete with Oliver and names her product *Pollie's Garlic Olives*. Because Ollie and Pollie have competing products under marks that could easily be confused by customers (they might mistakenly buy Pollie's olives thinking they are Ollie's olives), the marks legally conflict.

Generally, it's fair to say that customer confusion will be a factor in your dispute if:

- you believe that customers might currently confuse your goods or services with a competitor's because of a physical or perceptive similarity between the two marks and an overlapping of marketing territories or channels; or
- you purposely selected your mark because of its similarity to another mark, and the owner of the other mark is now calling you on it.

The purposes of the customer-confusion rule are to ensure that businesses that invest in a mark benefit from the resulting goodwill that attaches to the mark and to protect consumers from marketplace confusion that would result from overlapping marks.

We briefly discuss here three of the main factors in a customer-confusion inquiry. These include the similarity of the goods or services, the marketing territories, and the intent of the junior user of the mark. (In Chapter 6, Section C, we provide all of the factors used to evaluate customer confusion.)

Answers Are Hard to Come By

No book can give you the definitive answer as to when customer confusion is likely in a given case. Even an attorney can only give you an educated guess. Many trademark cases involve attorneys on opposite sides who are seriously convinced that customers both would and would not be confused by a simultaneous use of the disputed marks. The bottom line is, it is very difficult to tell who is right in any given trademark dispute.

a. Similar Goods and Services

As a general rule, a junior user is permitted to use a similar mark on dissimilar goods. That's because customers are less likely to be confused when similar marks are used on different goods and services. Therefore, when courts are considering the likelihood of confusion in a given case, they ask whether the products or services are similar to each other. If the goods or services in question are not similar or even related, confusion is not likely to result, so no infringement will be found. For example, many similar names coexist legally as marks on different goods, like *Cascade*, which separately identifies a whiskey, a baking mix, and a dishwashing detergent— all of which are names owned by different companies. *Dunhill* cigarettes and *Dunhill* shoes, and *Sunkist* fruits and *Sunkist* baked goods, are other examples of identical names used to identify goods in product categories that are sufficiently different to avoid the likelihood that customers will be confused as to the products or their sources. One exception to the principle of similarity of goods is if the senior user is likely to expand into the junior user's product area (see "Bridging the Gap," below).

Similarity of goods is not a factor in dilution cases (see Section C).

Bridging the Gap

Even though the two parties in an infringement dispute have dissimilar products, a court may consider whether consumers would reasonably expect that the senior user would expand its product line into that of the junior user. This potential expansion of the product base is referred to as "bridging the gap." For example, a federal court determined that consumers would be likely to be confused by the *McDonald's* trademark for food establishments with *McSleep* for motel services because the "Mc" prefix has been used so extensively by the McDonald's Corporation that its expansion into non-food categories is expected by consumers. "Bridging the gap" is usually only an issue in disputes involving a popular mark, because the customers of a well-known company such as Microsoft, McDonald's, or Nike are more likely to expect an expansion of the company's product base.

b. Marketing Territories

Two marks come into legal conflict only if they are used in the same market or marketing territory. Trademark law as it exists today developed at a time when geography played an important role in resolving trademark conflicts. If the same trademark was used by different businesses in different parts of the country, there was no likelihood of customer confusion and therefore no need for intervention by a court unless and until one of the users expanded into the other user's territory.

In the age of modern communications and the Internet, the definition of what constitutes a marketing territory is rapidly changing. Because of cable TV superstations, the Internet, online computer services such as *America Online*, national newspapers and periodicals, and syndicated radio and TV programs, the producers of more and more goods and services are able to claim a national marketing territory.

Still, many businesses in the United States are local in nature, and unless they are doing business on the Internet and reaching out to a wider customer base, they may reasonably claim only a relatively small portion of a city or county as their marketing territory. For instance, two video rental businesses using the same name are likely to have completely different marketing territories if one of them is in Pasadena and the other is in Manhattan Beach, which are separate cities 30 miles apart yet still within the greater Los Angeles area. And even if both businesses have sites on the Internet, their customer bases will almost certainly remain local.

But what if you are operating a business online and offline that can deliver goods or services on a mail-order basis? As the use of the Internet increases, the chances are greater that you and any other user of the same mark in the country or the world will be offering goods and services that will compete in that new territory we call cyberspace. This competition will put your marks in conflict, a state of affairs that can only lead to trademark infringement issues.

Though a marketing territory is impossible to define with precision, it is relatively easy to recognize. It is the rough geographic area from which a business of your type can reasonably expect to attract its customers. If anyone anywhere can order products or services from you through your website, or your mail-order business is advertised in national periodicals, or your products are regularly reviewed in national trade magazines, your marketing territory is the entire country. If your only marketing is done in your local Yellow Pages, the phone company has, in effect, defined your marketing territory for you.

Rules for evaluating marketing territories are evolving with the development of the Internet and, in coming years, there may be clearer standards to judge the size and scope of any particular cybermarketing territory.

c. Intent of the Junior User: Good Faith/Bad Faith

The outcome of a likelihood-of-confusion analysis is often influenced by the junior user's intent. In an infringement dispute, courts will inquire as to whether the junior user initiated use of its mark in good faith. Good faith involves two issues:

- Did the junior user know of the existing mark at the time he or she began using the mark in commerce?
- Was the existing mark known in the junior user's marketing territory at that time?

If either question can be answered "yes," then good faith is not present, and the junior user must stop use of the mark upon a challenge by the senior user. Let's take a closer look at these questions.

How Most Disputes Are Resolved

If you can't tell for sure who is in the right, then how should you proceed if you are locked in a trademark dispute? The only way to force a resolution is to go to court and find out what a judge has to say. But courts are expensive. It may be possible—if both parties agree—to resolve the dispute through mediation or by submitting the issue to arbitration. However, most trademark disputes are resolved through negotiation and typically end up with the economically weaker party agreeing to back down, regardless of who was first to use the mark. If, however, the economically weaker party has a strong legal claim to ownership of the mark, the larger company usually will be willing to pay something in exchange for the weaker party's acquiescence. Please understand that the author isn't endorsing what appears to be a cynical view of how trademark disputes get resolved. It's just the way things are.

⚠️ **A Fine Legal Point.** Technically, the good faith issue only extends to whether the junior user knew of the existing mark. The issue of whether the existing mark was known in the junior user's marketing territory is usually discussed in terms of remoteness—that is, the junior user must qualify as a distant user, separated in distance from the marketing territory of the senior user, in order to preserve some rights. We have combined the good faith and remoteness factors under the good faith label for greater simplicity of presentation. It should cause no problem in understanding your rights as we discuss them in this chapter.

If the junior user knew of the first use before adopting the mark, the dispute will be resolved entirely in favor of the senior user. However, if the junior user didn't know of the first use, that user may have some rights— although limited—in case of a dispute, unless the mark was known to the customers in the junior user's marketing territory. If it was, it won't make any difference that the junior user didn't actually know of the mark. The senior user will be given priority on the ground that its marketing territory was already established when the junior use was initiated. If, on the other hand, neither the junior user's customer base nor the junior user had knowledge of the existing mark, the junior user may continue to use the mark in its current marketing territory, but nowhere else.

As we'll see in the rest of this chapter, the junior user will be presumed to know about any mark that is on the Principal Register. This, of course, means that a search of the federal trademark register is always wise before adopting and using a new business name or other device as a service mark or trademark. Although there is no similar presumption that a junior user ought to know of an unregistered mark just because it is well known, we are fast becoming a global village, and more and more marks can be said to have a nationwide exposure. And, as we explained above, if the senior user can establish this fact, the senior user will prevail over the junior user.

The Concept of Reverse Confusion

In traditional trademark infringement cases, the junior user of a trademark confuses consumers into believing that they are buying goods from the senior user. In the 1970s a federal court created a variation on this principle, known as "reverse confusion."

In early 1974, Big O Tires, a midsized regional tire distributor, began marketing a bias belted tire under the unregistered mark *BigFoot*. The tire giant Goodyear coincidentally decided to market a radial tire under the *BigFoot* mark in late 1974. The larger company pumped millions of dollars into its advertising effort, which overlapped Big O's advertising effort to some extent. As a result, the public began coming to Big O asking for Goodyear's tire. Angry and disappointed, consumers suspected Big O of stealing the idea from Goodyear.

But, in fact, Goodyear had become aware of Big O's prior use of the same mark midway into its marketing plans and had unsuccessfully negotiated to buy the mark from them. Nevertheless, Goodyear continued to use the mark. In this case, Goodyear spent so much money on advertising in such a short period of time (including expensive Super Bowl advertisements), that the public associated Goodyear with the trademark and believed that Big O was the junior user (and thus an infringer). This resulted in a judgment for Big O of $4.7 million dollars and the debut of a new type of infringement based on reverse confusion.

2. Priority of Use: Who Used the Mark First?

As a general rule, if a legal conflict erupts between two businesses using the same or a similar mark, the business that first used the mark is considered the owner of the mark and will prevail against the junior user. Therefore, it should not be surprising that most of the rules for resolving trademark disputes that we use in this chapter turn on the question of who used the mark first. "Use" is defined as either:

- actual use in commerce, or
- constructive use through an application to the PTO to register the mark on an intent-to-use basis.

a. Actual Use in Commerce

A mark is in actual use when it is attached to a product that is being sold in the marketplace or is used in a business's marketing materials for the purpose of selling the business's service. Actual use must be a commercial use, not simply a token use to obtain trademark priority. (See Chapter 7, Federal Trademark Registration, for more on what constitutes "actual use.")

b. Constructive Use

It is possible to apply to have a mark placed on the federal Principal Register on the basis of intended use—even though the mark is not yet in actual use. The date an "intent to use" application is filed with the PTO is considered the date the mark was first used, assuming the applicant goes on to actually use the mark at a later time and files the necessary documents to place the mark on the Principal Register. This type of use is termed a constructive use because it is created by the law rather than by real events.

> **EXAMPLE:** In March 2003, Paul begins distributing a line of distinctive jewelry (bracelets and earrings) called *Cleopatra Designs*. Unknown to him, Oscar had previously applied to register *Cleopatra Designs* on the Principal Register in connection with his intended use on a line of women's clothing. Even though Paul actually began using the mark first, and Oscar's application is still pending, Oscar will have priority on the basis of first use if his application is ultimately approved and a legal conflict develops between the two marks.

Priority of use is a crucial question in infringement disputes and often turns on the status of the mark (federally registered or unregistered) and the territory. We discuss various priority scenarios in Section B.

3. Domain Names and Trademark Infringement

If a domain name is used as a trademark— that is, it's being used to identify goods or services in the marketplace—it is subject to the same rules regarding infringement as any other trademark. If the domain name is not being used for a commercial purpose, then it would not be subject to a claim of infringement.

> **EXAMPLE:** Jonah Ishmael creates a personal website with the domain name Ahab.com. Jonah uses the site to post pictures of his family, some poems he writes from time to time, and a statement of his political philosophy. Because Jonah is not using the term "Ahab" as a means to identify goods or services or an entity doing business on the Web, the domain name isn't being used as a trademark. If *Ahab Tours*, a business that offers whale-sighting tours and a collection of historically famous whale art, decided to accuse Jonah of trademark infringement, Jonah would respond that because he isn't using the name as a trademark, there is no likelihood of customer confusion and therefore no infringement.

> **EXAMPLE:** Jonah becomes interested in whale art and decides to open a cyberart gallery featuring contributions by various contemporary artists who like to feature whales as part of their art. At this point, there is little question that Jonah is using ahab.com as a trademark, and *Ahab Tours* would have a basis to sue for trademark infringement.

As with any trademark owner, a domain name registrant uses its new domain name at its peril if it doesn't first conduct its own thorough trademark search. If someone else is already using the proposed domain name as a mark, and the context of the two uses— the other mark and the domain name—would likely lead to customer confusion, the business seeking to register a domain name should pick a different name at the outset.

Defensive Maneuvers

In addition to disproving priority and likelihood of confusion, a junior user accused of infringement has other potential defenses, most of which have been introduced in previous chapters. Below, we provide a brief summary of the available defenses, most of which will apply to infringement, dilution, and cyber-squatting. For more information on these legal defenses, review the related chapters or, in the case of more-obscure defenses, such as laches, estoppel, unclean hands, trademark misuse, and fair use, consult an attorney versed in trademark law. The possible defenses include:

- **The mark is descriptive.** A junior user can defend its use if a senior user's mark is weak and lacks secondary meaning (see Chapter 1, Section B).
- **Abandonment.** A junior user can defend its use if the senior user has abandoned its mark (see Chapter 8, Section E).
- **Genericness.** A junior user can defend its use if the senior user's mark has become the generic term for the goods or services (see Chapter 8, Section G).
- **Trademark misuse.** A senior user may be prohibited from recovering damages for infringement if it has violated antitrust laws or used fraud to obtain a registration.
- **Fair use.** Can you run an ad for your company selling dishwashing machines that refers to the "joy of dishwashing"

without infringing the trademark "Joy" as used for dishwashing soap? Yes. A company may defend its use of a trade-marked term (owned by someone else) when the term is used to describe products or services. In 2005, the U.S. Supreme Court ruled that the fair use defense can be made even when the use results in consumer confusion.

- **Free speech and parody.** In certain cases, a junior user can defend its use under First Amendment principles (see Section C of this chapter).
- **Unclean hands.** A junior user can defend its use by claiming that the senior user acted in bad faith.
- **Estoppel.** A junior user can defend its use if the junior user has justifiably relied on the senior user's behavior.
- **Laches.** A junior user can defend its use if the senior user waited too long to file the lawsuit.
- **Trade dress and product configuration defenses.** In cases of trade dress infringement, two defenses are particularly important: functionality and distinctiveness. If a senior user's trade dress or product shape is functional or lacks distinctiveness, it is not protectible and cannot be infringed. (See Chapter 1, Section E.)

B. Determining Priority in an Infringement Dispute

Now that you have some general information about trademark disputes under your belt, it's time to get specific. The rest of this guide will give you a pretty good idea of who has legal priority over the use of a mark in case a legal conflict develops between you and another business. But to apply the discussion to your particular situation, you will need to answer the following questions (except in dilution claims—see Section C):

- Is the other mark registered on the Federal Register?
- If the other mark is federally registered, what is the date of registration?
- Was the federal registration based on actual use, or intended use?
- When was the other mark first used, if the federal registration is based on actual use?

If you don't know the answers to these questions, they can be obtained through a trademark search. See Chapters 4 and 5 for more on trademark searching. Below are some of the common scenarios when determining priority.

1. Your Unregistered Mark Conflicts With a Federally Registered Mark

Here we discuss who has priority in case your mark is not registered on the Principal Register and the other mark is. If your mark is on the Principal Register, skip to Section B3 or B4, below. Note that the information in this section and Section B4, while written

from opposite points of view, is basically the same. For the best possible understanding of what happens in case one mark is registered and the other mark isn't, read both.

Assume you receive a letter from a lawyer informing you that your unregistered mark conflicts with another mark that is on the federal Principal Register and demanding that you cease and desist from any further use of your mark. The fact that the other mark is on the federal Principal Register while yours is not may be pretty scary. And in truth, the other mark's owner holds some high cards. But as you will see from the discussion and examples below, despite the other claimant's federal registration, you may still have some rights, depending on the timing of events.

a. If You Are the Senior User

If you used your mark before the other party used its mark and can prove it, you have a right to continue using your mark based on the following rules:

i. In your existing marketing territory

You may use your mark in the same part of the country where you were using it when the junior user applied for federal registration.

EXAMPLE 1: You opened the *Date Palm* restaurant in Kansas City in 2001. In 2003, a chain, *Date Palm Inn*, opens hotels in four Southeastern states. The *Date Palm Inn* mark was registered with the PTO that same year. In 2006, the *Date Palm Inn* chain discovers your *Date Palm* restaurant and a lawyer sends you a cease and desist letter, citing the *Date Palm Inn*'s

registration of the *Date Palm Inn* mark on the Principal Register. The lawyer demands that you immediately change the name of your restaurant. You may continue operating in Kansas City on an exclusive basis under your existing name because you were the senior user of the *Date Palm* mark in that territory.

ii. In all other areas

You may claim the exclusive right to use your mark in all other parts of the country if you can prove that the owner of the registered mark actually knew of your mark's use at the time of the registration application and failed to disclose this fact to the PTO. The deliberate failure of a junior user registration applicant to disclose the existence of a conflicting mark can lead to cancellation of the trademark registration.

If the owner of the registered mark didn't know of your unregistered mark's use, however, the registered owner will be given priority (that is, the right to exclusive use) in all other parts of the country where a later simultaneous use of the two marks would create the likelihood of customer confusion.

EXAMPLE 2: Continuing the *Date Palm* example, assume you can prove that the *Date Palm Inn* owners actually knew of your use of the *Date Palm* mark prior to 2003, the year it registered the mark with the PTO. This fact would allow you to continue using the *Date Palm* mark in Kansas City on an exclusive basis and to expand your right of exclusive use to the rest of the country, even to the four states in which the *Date Palm Inn* currently operates. That's right. If the owner of *Date Palm Inn* trademark knew of your mark's prior use on a restaurant when it registered its mark and failed to disclose the fact to the PTO, you would most likely be able to have the federal registration canceled, and the company would have to change its name if you decided to enter its marketing territory.

EXAMPLE 3: Continuing the *Date Palm* example, assume you can't show that the *Date Palm Inn* knew of your mark prior to the time it registered its mark. In this situation, you can remain in your current marketing territory, but the *Date Palm Inn* will have the exclusive right in the future to use the mark in any other part of the country it chooses to expand into, even if later you have expanded into that area ahead of the *Date Palm Inn*. This is because the *Date Palm Inn*'s registration was in good faith (neither it nor the PTO knew of your mark, and your mark wasn't known in the *Date Palm Inn*'s original marketing territory).

b. If the Registered Owner Is the Senior User

If the owner of the federally registered mark is the senior user (actual use or constructive use through the filing of an "intent to use" application), the following rules apply:

i. In your marketing territory—without knowledge of the senior user's mark

If neither you nor the customers in your marketing territory had knowledge of the senior user's mark when you first used your mark, and your first use was before the senior user's mark was placed on the federal trademark register, you can continue using the mark in your marketing territory on an exclusive basis.

> **EXAMPLE 1:** Modifying our *Date Palm* example, after the *Date Palm Inn* chain starts operating in 2003, and, without knowledge of that earlier use, you open the *Date Palm* Restaurant in Shreveport, Louisiana, in 2004, an area in which the *Date Palm Inn* is unknown. The *Date Palm Inn* then places its mark on the federal register in 2005. You may continue using the *Date Palm* mark in Shreveport on an exclusive basis in your marketing territory. This is probably only Shreveport, but could be argued to include nearby areas of Louisiana.

ii. In your marketing territory—with knowledge of the senior user's mark

If you knew that the senior user's mark was in use prior to yours, or if the senior user's

mark was known in your marketing territory even though you didn't know of it, the senior user may expand into your marketing area and force you to stop using your mark. If you first used your mark after the senior user's mark was registered, knowledge of the senior user's first use will be presumed. In either situation—actual or presumed knowledge—you may only continue using the mark in your area until the senior user decides to expand its market into your area. Then you will have to stop using the mark altogether. Otherwise, you may be liable for large damages as a willful infringer.

> **EXAMPLE 2:** Assume that you know of the *Date Palm Inn*'s registered mark when you open your restaurant in 2004, and the *Date Palm Inn* can prove it. (In this situation, all *Date Palm Inn* would have to do to prove your knowledge is to show that their federal registration occurred prior to your first use of the mark.) If and when the *Date Palm Inn* decides to expand into Shreveport, you can be forced to change your restaurant's name. Your name may also be at risk if

the *Date Palm Inn* expands into any area that draws its customers from Shreveport, because Shreveport would then be part of its marketing territory, and it would have a right to exclude your use of the name. If *Date Palm Inn* launches an advertising campaign designed to draw customers from all over the country—or creates and maintains a site on the Internet—its marketing territory will be national, even if it doesn't move into Shreveport.

What If You Are Asked to Change Your Mark?

In fact, many marks used by small and medium-sized businesses can be modified without significant damage, especially if there is time to plan the change. While some customers may be lost when a new mark is introduced, most will continue patronizing a business or using a product that has served them well. And a name change can even provide a convenient opportunity for a business to draw attention to its goods or services by announcing the change in the media and direct mail pieces. Also, if a big company is challenging a small company's mark, the small company can often get a lot of mileage in the media if it emphasizes how it has been bullied into making the change.

---

iii. In other marketing areas

If the other company is the senior user but did not federally register the mark until after you

started using your mark, the other company will have priority wherever the two marks come into conflict.

EXAMPLE 3: You start using the *Date Palm* mark before *Date Palm Inn*'s registration of the mark. You can use the mark as long as it doesn't come into conflict with the *Date Palm Inn*'s registered mark. In territories where conflicts do develop, you will have to withdraw, and *Date Palm Inn* will be able to use the mark.

If the registered mark is being used nationwide and you started using your mark after the date of registration, you may be subject to heavy damages as a willful infringer.

EXAMPLE 4: A San Francisco Bay Area comedy group puts together a satirical review called *Lawbonics*, a series of skits about lawyers and their bizarre professional speech patterns. The comedy group places *Lawbonics* on the federal register and seeks national bookings. A year later, without actual knowledge of the California group, you start a similar act in Vermont. Because the California *Lawbonics* group first used and federally registered it prior to your use of the mark, you have infringed the California group's service mark. And, because that group's registration gave you "constructive notice" of its prior ownership of the mark, you will be considered a deliberate infringer if the matter gets to court, even though you really were unaware of the prior use.

2. Your Unregistered Mark Conflicts With Another Unregistered Mark

Conflicts between unregistered marks are the most common types of business name disputes small businesses are likely to face. These types of disputes are usually between business names that are also being used as service marks. They are usually governed by state trademark and unfair competition principles, which are designed to combat customer confusion in the marketplace and protect the first user of a mark because of fairness considerations. However, you may also invoke the federal unfair competition provision of the Lanham Act if one of the unregistered marks is used in interstate, interterritorial, or international commerce.

As a general rule, the more distinctive the mark in issue, the more willing the courts are to find the likelihood of customer confusion and protect the senior user's right of exclusive use.

> **EXAMPLE:** You open a day care center for the elderly in St. Paul, Minnesota, named *The Seniors Club*. Several years later, in the same part of town, another day care center called *The Senior Citizen's Club* opens its doors. You will be able to get the second business to change its name if you can convince a court that customer confusion between the two names is likely—that is, the other center is likely to draw from your customer base and the court believes your name is distinctive enough to protect. In this example,

however, the court may find that your name is ordinary and weak rather than distinctive, and rule that *The Senior Citizen's Club* is different enough to not risk customer confusion (because customers attach little significance to weak marks). It is also possible that a court may invoke the state's unfair competition laws (see Chapter 1, Section F) to order the second user to alter its name in some respect to protect the first user.

> **EXAMPLE:** Since 2000, you have sold your ready-to-eat barbecued ribs to a number of Missoula, Montana, supermarkets under the mark *Clarence's Rockin' Ribs*. They are very popular throughout the Missoula area. In 2005, Steve starts selling *Steve's Rockin' Ribs* to markets in a three-state area, including Missoula. You can force Steve to adopt another mark for his ribs, since "Rockin'" as applied to ribs has become a distinctive mark over time and belongs exclusively to you, at least in the Missoula area.

If your mark and another unregistered mark have been used in different geographical areas without coming into conflict, but then simultaneously (more or less) come into conflict in a new marketplace, unfair competition principles may resolve the conflict in several ways: Dual use may be authorized with certain conditions attached:

- one of you may prevail on the grounds that the area in question was a natural part of your original marketing territory or

- one of you may be ordered to change your mark somewhat to distinguish it from the other.

EXAMPLE: You start a sign business in Newport, New Hampshire, that specializes in magnetic signs for trucks (they stick to the truck panel). You call your business *Sign Up* but don't register the name, even though you do a little business across state lines with Massachusetts and Vermont customers. Within the next several years, similar sign businesses are started by other entrepreneurs in San Francisco, Dallas, Chicago, and Miami, using the same name. They also don't register the name. Because the name is used in different marketing areas, there is no legal conflict.

What happens, however, if you and one of the other businesses simultaneously decide to operate a national mail-order sign business under *Sign Up* by creating a site on the Internet? Because both businesses would be in conflict everywhere in the country, and because both businesses would be in conflict with the other regional users of the name, even if those regional businesses weren't on the Web, clearly something would have to give.

Theoretically, of the two companies that were using the Web to market the sign service, the senior user would have priority and could stop the other Web-based company (the junior user) from using it. As for the other regional companies, it's possible that they also could be prevented from further use of the mark on the ground that when they adopted their names, they did so at the risk of being forced to stop using them if and when one of the senior users decided to go national.

Traditionally, these regional companies might have been able to continue using the mark in their regions on an exclusive basis, but the way the Internet works, regional markets are becoming less feasible.

The solution ultimately favored by the courts in this type of scenario is an adjustment of one of the marks so that both businesses can continue their operations with a minimum of disruption without creating customer confusion. But if it appears that the junior user is deliberately trying to piggyback on the senior user's goodwill, the junior user may be forced to choose a completely different name and even pay some damages as punishment.

3. Your Federally Registered Mark Conflicts With Another Federally Registered Mark

Here we explain what your rights are if your mark and the other mark are both registered on the federal trademark register.

It occasionally happens that two marks that both have been placed on the federal trademark register come into conflict with each other in the marketplace. This can occur for a variety of reasons. The PTO may approve two identical or very similar marks for registration because:

- the registration applications state that the marks will be used on goods and services in different classes, and it appears that the goods or services won't compete in the marketplace and aren't related enough to create the likelihood of customer confusion, or

- an examiner honestly but mistakenly believes the two marks are sufficiently different to eliminate the likelihood of customer confusion.

As stated earlier, once a trademark is placed on the Federal Register, its owner is presumed to be the rightful nationwide owner of the mark. When you have two presumed rightful nationwide owners claiming title to the same (or very similar mark), the conflict can be difficult to unravel. Sometimes this can be accomplished in proceedings brought in the PTO itself, while other times court action may be necessary. The result will depend on why and when the conflict developed.

EXAMPLE 1: You use the mark *TeeTotaler* on a brand of fruit juice, while Julie uses this same mark on her chain of vegetable juice bars. Although unlikely, it is possible that you and Julie will both get your respective marks onto the federal trademark register because one is a trademark being used on a juice product sold in supermarkets while the other is a service mark used on a health-drink service business. Though there is no direct competition between you and Julie, it's easy to see that consumers might think that your product is really being marketed by Julie's business or vice versa. In short, customer confusion is likely if the mark is used in a context where consumers might experience both uses. In this instance, you and Julie might be restricted by a court in the use of your marks to your respective and

distinct marketing territories, and whoever can prove first use might be given priority when expanding to areas where the mark is not in use.

EXAMPLE 2: Assume now that you originally applied to register the mark *TeeTotaler* for use on a brand of biodegradable golf tee but later changed your mind and used the mark on your fruit juice line. Because your use of the mark was vastly different than that described on your registration application, your registration would not count when resolving the conflict with Julie's mark. In other words, Julie would be treated as a registered owner of the mark, and you would be an unregistered owner for purposes of resolving the dispute.

4. Your Federally Registered Mark Conflicts With an Unregistered Mark

You're in a strong position if your mark is registered and the other mark is not. You are presumed to be the nationwide exclusive owner, and the other owner is definitely on the defensive. However, the fact of registration doesn't mean you'll win a trademark dispute. It depends, as with other disputes over your mark, on the following principles:

a. If You Were First to Use the Mark Anywhere and Registered the Mark Before the Second Use Began

If you used your mark and federally registered it before the other business used its mark, you have the exclusive nationwide right to use the mark and can stop the other owner from using the mark in any geographic market in which you decide to market your goods or services. If you maintain a site on the Internet or otherwise nationally market your goods or services, you can require the other business to stop using the mark immediately. However, if your use is local or regional and the other user's local or regional market is completely separate from yours, you will have to wait until you are on the verge of entering the other market to require your competition to adopt another mark.

> **EXAMPLE:** You are a Rhode Island publisher of travel guides that specialize in the Northeastern states and carry the mark *Yankee Visions*. You successfully obtain a federal registration for the mark. Two years later you learn that a travel guide publisher for the Northwestern states began using the same mark for its publications after the date of your registration but has not registered it. Because of your registration, the competitor will be deemed to have had knowledge of your mark's previous use, which means you can force the competitor to stop using the mark if and when you decide to market your guides in the Northwest. But if your marketing efforts remain restricted to one portion of the country—say the Northeast and Eastern Seaboard—and the competitor stays in the Northwest, you won't win a trademark infringement case unless you can show that you

want to enter the Northwestern market and are prepared to do so.

As we emphasize throughout this material, the Internet and other national marketing techniques make a collision between marketing territories more and more likely.

b. If You Were First to Use the Mark Anywhere but Registered the Mark After the Second Use Began

It is possible that the other user started to use the mark after your first use but before your mark was placed on the Federal Register. In this situation, the rights of the second (junior) user will turn on the answers to these two questions:

- Did the junior user have actual knowledge of your mark's use?
- Was your mark known in the junior user's marketing territory?

If the junior user had actual knowledge of your mark's previous use (and you can prove it), the junior user has no rights and must give way if and when your mark and its mark come into conflict in a marketing territory.

And regardless of the junior user's knowledge, if your mark was known within the marketing territory from which the junior user's customer base was being drawn, the junior user will have to give way if you decide to use your mark in that territory.

> **EXAMPLE:** Continuing our *Yankee Visions* example, assume you can show that the Northwest competitor knew of your mark before it started using its mark. If you

later decide to market your guides in that area, you can force the competitor to drop the name. Similarly, if your guides were being distributed in the Northwest prior to the junior use, you can force the competitor to stop using the mark if you now decide to market the guides in the Northwest.

If, however, neither the competitor nor its customer base knew of your *Yankee Visions* mark when the competitor's use of the mark began, and your product wasn't being sold in your competitor's marketing territory, the competitor can continue using the mark in the Northwest and freeze you out of that market. This result stems from the fact that the competitor would be deemed to be a good faith junior user (no actual knowledge of your mark) in a remote marketing territory (no marketing or other activity that would make the customers aware of your mark when the junior use began).

c. If the Other Owner Used the Mark Both Before You Used It and Before You Registered It

If the owner of the unregistered mark was the senior user, you may continue to use your registered mark in the marketing territory where you are currently using it if the following two statements are true:

- You didn't know of the senior use when your use began.
- The senior use was largely unknown in your marketing territory when your second use began.

EXAMPLE: You invent a digital device that attaches to a tennis racquet handle and keeps track of the score during the game. You attach the trademark *Total Recall* to your invention and register it with the PTO. Test marketing is initiated in California and Arizona. Unknown to you, Felix had earlier been using this same mark on a product designed to keep track of the score of ping pong games he is test marketing in Miami, Florida. Because you had no knowledge of Felix's earlier use when you registered the mark, and because knowledge of Felix's device had not penetrated into your test markets, you may continue using it in your test markets.

However, you cannot use the mark in any area of the country where the senior user was using it as of the date of your registration.

EXAMPLE: Because Felix was the senior user, he has the exclusive right to use the *Total Recall* mark in Miami, and you would be excluded from marketing your invention in that area.

If you didn't know of the other mark's previous use when you registered your mark, you will have priority over the senior user in all areas of the country that he or she has not yet entered. In other words, you will be rewarded for promptly registering your mark, and the senior user will stay frozen in his or her territory.

EXAMPLE: Assuming that you didn't know of Felix's use of the *Total Recall* mark when you registered, Felix's use will be limited to the Miami area, and you can market your product nationwide.

If any of the following statements is true, the senior user will be given priority in case conflict between the two marks develops:

- You knew of the senior use when you first used your mark.
- Your customer base knew of the previous mark when you first used your mark.
- You knew of the senior use when you registered your mark.

EXAMPLE: If you knew that Felix was using the *Total Recall* mark when you first used yours, or you knew of the use when you registered the mark, or if Felix's test marketing had been going on in the area where you first used your mark, Felix would be given priority in all parts of the country, including your test area.

C. Dilution

Famous trademarks acquire additional rights compared to their not-so-famous cousins. Famous marks that are tarnished or degraded, regardless of whether customers are confused, can halt another company's use of a similar mark. This rule, known as dilution, permits the owner of a famous trademark owner to sue because the famous trademark will lose its distinctive character and legal strength if degrading or diluting uses of the mark are permitted. Also, according to some courts, the public would be confused in any event by the use of a famous mark in that they would necessarily expect the business owning the famous mark to be associated in some way with the second user.

In 1996, Congress added a law to the Lanham Act prohibiting activity that leads to the dilution of famous marks (42 U.S.C. § 1125(a)(c)). About half the states also have antidilution laws.

1. The Federal Trademark Dilution Act

The Federal Trademark Dilution Act (FTDA) provides that the owner of a famous mark shall be entitled to protection against a junior user's commercial use of a mark if the use begins after the mark has become famous and causes dilution of the distinctive quality of the mark. The Act defines dilution as "the lessening of the capacity of a famous mark to identify and distinguish goods or services" regardless of whether the dual use would likely confuse customers or involve competing goods. So, to prevail under the FTDA, a senior user must prove all of the following:

- The senior mark is famous
- The senior mark is distinctive
- The junior use is commercial in nature
- The junior use began after the senior mark became famous, and
- The junior use lessens the senior mark's capacity to identify and distinguish goods and services.

However, the senior user need not prove the likelihood of customer confusion as to product, service, or the source of either.

a. What Makes a Mark Famous?

The FTDA lists a number of factors to use in deciding whether a mark is famous:

- the degree of inherent or acquired distinctiveness of the mark
- the duration and extent of use of the mark in connection with the goods or services with which the mark is used
- the geographical extent of the trading area in which the mark is used
- the channels of trade for the goods or services with which the mark is used
- the degree of recognition of the mark in the trading areas and channels of trade used by the mark's owner and the person against whom the injunction is sought
- the nature and extent of use of the same or similar marks by third parties, and
- whether the mark was registered on the Principal Register. (15 U.S.C. Section 1125(c) (1).)

None of these factors is weighted, and the list is not exclusive. As a practical matter, this means that courts have almost complete discretion in deciding whether a particular mark is famous for purposes of protection under the FTDA. All they have to do is base their decision on one or more of the listed factors. Put differently, deciding on the fame of a mark is a crapshoot. On the other hand, most people know a famous mark when they see one, and the fuzziness of the concept may not produce all that many disputes.

b. What Makes a Mark Distinctive?

We covered distinctiveness in Chapters 3 and 9. So far the courts have ruled that those same tests should be used to decide whether a mark is distinctive for purposes of the FTDA. However, some courts have ruled out marks that are only distinctive under the secondary meaning rule (acquired distinctiveness). This is because the FTDA, by its terms, only applies when there has been "dilution of the distinctive quality of the mark." Courts have reasoned that this phrase requires an inherent distinctiveness for dilution to occur. Thus, Sears Department Store (acquired distinctiveness and famous) might not be protected from dilution under the FTDA, but Exxon (inherent distinctiveness and famous) would be protected from dilution.

c. Dilution After Victoria's Secret

Victor's Secret, a New Jersey store, sold adult videos, adult novelties, hosiery, temporary tattoos, and lingerie. The company that owns Victoria's Secret—which distributes over 400 million catalogs annually—asked the New Jersey store to change its name, and the store complied, altering its name to "Victor's Little Secret." When the store refused to modify the name further, the owners of the Victoria's Se-cret trademark sued for dilution, arguing that Victor's Little Secret tarnished and blurred their famous mark. The Supreme Court ruled that the Victoria's Secret trademark was a valuable and famous mark and that consum-ers made a mental association when seeing the two trademarks—Victoria's Secret and Victor's Little Secret. But the mental associa-tion, by itself, was not enough to prove dilu-tion. To prove dilution, the trademark owner must demonstrate *actual* harm.

Although the ruling generally makes it harder to advance a dilution argument be-cause more proof is required, in the two years since the case, trademark owners using the federal dilution act have had success when seeking to stop the use of an identical mark. That's due to a suggestion by the Su-preme Court that no proof of actual harm is needed to stop a use of an identical mark. (*Moseley v. Secret Catalogue, Inc.,* 537 U.S. 418 (2003).

d. When Does a Junior Use Lessen the Senior Mark's Ability to Identify and Distinguish Goods and Services?

The final element of proof of dilution under the FTDA that we need to explain is when the use of a famous mark "lessens the capacity of the mark to identify and distinguish goods and services." There are two ways in which this can happen: blurring and tarnishment. These concepts are discussed below.

2. Tarnishment and Blurring

In 1996, Hasbro, the owner of the trademark *Candyland* (used on children's games) stopped a company providing adult sex services and products from using the name "Candyland" for its website. (*Hasbro Inc. v. Internet Enter-tainment Group, Ltd.,* 40 USPQ 2d 1479 (W.D. Wa. 1996).) In 1999, the National Bas-ketball Association stopped a rap music com-pany from using an altered version of its logo featuring a silhouette of a basketball player. (The rap company's silhouetted basketball player held a gun.) (*NBA Properties v. Untertainment Records LLC,* 1999 U.S. Dist. LEXIS 7780 (S.D. N.Y. 1999).) In both cases, it was unlikely that consumers would confuse the junior and senior user's goods, yet both Hasbro and the NBA prevailed because the junior use tarnished and blurred their famous marks. Below we distinguish the standards of:

- blurring—diluting the strength of the mark by taking away from its distinctive-ness, and
- tarnishment—damaging the mark's reputation for quality.

a. Blurring a Mark's Distinctiveness

How is the strength of a mark diluted through the use of the same or similar marks on completely unrelated goods or services? The more common a mark becomes by its use on a variety of products and services, the less ability it has to stand out in the minds of consumers for any one product or service.

For example, in one case brought under a state dilution statute, *Polaroid* was able to enjoin the use of *Polaraid* as a service mark for installing refrigeration systems, because it would blur the mental image and immediate identification that consumers have between the mark *Polaroid* and cameras. On a similar basis, *Bacardi Rum* stopped a jewelry store from using its mark, and *Tiffany & Co.*, the New York jewelers, prevented a Boston restaurant from using its mark. In each of these cases, the two marks were identical or very similar, the goods/services did not compete, and no likelihood of confusion existed. Rather, the question was whether the distinctive and famous mark in each of those cases was made less distinctive by the second use of the mark—a question decided in favor of the famous mark owners.

The tarnishment aspect of the dilution rule was also the reason that the owners of *Cabbage Patch Dolls* were able to stop the sale of *Garbage Pail Kids* under a state dilution statute. Likewise, Anheuser-Busch prevented an insecticide maker from using the phrase, "Where there's life, there's bugs."

Courts are especially likely to find tarnishment—and trademark owners are more likely to sue—when the offending marks are attached to products that are "unwholesome or unsavory." Examples of marks that have been enjoined under this prong of the dilution theory are the fake American Express card shown with a condom that said, "Never Leave Home Without It," the use of Dallas Cowboy cheerleader uniforms in a pornographic film, and the "Enjoy Cocaine" poster that used a script and coloring identical to *Coca-Cola*'s.

b. Tarnishment, or Injury to Reputation for Quality

Tarnishment of a mark occurs when the second use creates an unwanted association with the original mark, or detracts from its image for quality goods or services.

> **EXAMPLE:** Mike decides that his plumbing fixture business would gain visibility with the name *Gucci Plumbing Fixtures*. Because plumbing detracts from the fashionable image invoked by the well-known *Gucci* trademark, Mike would probably be prevented from using the *Gucci* name.

Parody and Satire Are Not Dilution

Satirical uses or parodies of marks might appear as obvious examples of tarnishment. Nevertheless, our Constitution's First Amendment protects satires and parodies that clearly aren't using a mark to market goods or services commercially. In addition, the Lanham Act excludes from its definition of dilution the use of a famous mark for noncommercial purposes, such as parodies, advertising (including comparative advertising), consumer product reviews, and news coverage. For example, in one case dealing with a website titled "Bally sucks," a U.S. District Court ruled that because the website was operated for a noncommercial purpose—to criticize Bally's (a health club)—the use of the *Bally* mark did not offend the Lanham Act's antidilution provisions. (*Bally Total Fitness Holding Corp. v. Faber,* 29 F. Supp. 2d 1161 (C.D. Cal. 1998).)

But what about parodies in the form of marks used on commercial products? Even commercial parodies may not be barred by the dilution doctrine unless all the criteria for dilution are met. For example, when Jordache sued Hogg Wyld, Ltd., under a state dilution statute for using the mark *Lardache* on wearing apparel, it was not considered dilution. That's because the mark was not identical, and the parody tended to increase, not dilute, the public's identification of Jordache's mark with Jordache's products.

Although the federal dilution law does not directly prohibit activity that would tarnish a mark's reputation for quality, it is clear that Congress intended it to do so. For example, in one U.S. District Court case, *America Online v. LCMG Inc.,* 1198 U.S. Dist. LEXIS 20243 (E.D. Va. 1998), the court ruled that the use of forged aol.com headers in 92 million email messages sent to AOL subscribers for the purpose of advertising porn websites constituted dilution under the Lanham Act because it tarnished AOL's good name.

3. Federal Dilution Defenses

The Federal Dilution Act at 15 U.S.C. §§ 1125 (c)(3)&(4) also provides certain defenses including:

- **comparative advertising.** It is not dilution to use a famous mark in comparative advertising. However, the mark should not be altered or modified.

   EXAMPLE: In a comparative advertisement, a tractor company modified and animated the John Deere "leaping deer" logo and gradually diminished its proportional size in a comparative advertisement. This was determined to be dilution and was not excused under the comparative advertising defense. (*Deere & Company v. MTD Prods. Inc.,* 34 USPQ 1706 (S.D. N.Y. 1995).)

- **noncommercial use of a mark.** There is no dilution unless the junior use is commercial. Because all uses usually have some commercial aspect, a "commercial use" is considered to be one that is primarily to help sell a product or service.

EXAMPLE: A pro-life minister used the Internet domain name *plannedparenthood .com* and included a misleading opening screen entitled "Welcome to the Planned Parenthood Home Page." The site provided anti-abortion information and services. A court determined that the use was commercial because it was primarily being used to identify the source of a product or service, not simply to criticize Planned Parenthood. (*Planned Parenthood v. Bucci,* 42 USPQ 2d 1430 (S.D. N.Y. 1997) *affirmed* 152 F.3d 920 (2d Cir. 1998*).)*

- **news reporting.** Use of a trademark in journalism or news commentary is exempt from dilution claims.
- **federal registration.** There can be no dilution if the junior user has a federally registered mark.

4. Relief for Dilution

Although the main relief the courts are authorized to provide under the new Lanham Act provision is injunctive relief against further diluting or tarnishing uses of the famous mark, the federal antidilution statute also authorizes money damages, including triple damages and attorneys' fees, if the infringer willfully intended to trade on the owner's reputation or to cause dilution of the famous mark. This factor alone provides the antidilution law

with considerable punch, because the use of indisputably famous marks such as *McDonald's* is usually intended in precisely this way, for example *McClaim* and *McSleep.* In summary, do not get caught trying to ride on the coattails of a famous mark belonging to someone else. It may end up costing you a bundle.

State Trademark Dilution Laws

Although in the future most dilution lawsuits will rely primarily on the federal dilution statute, because of its potential for awarding triple damages and attorneys' fees, suits filed in states that have state dilution statutes will also include claims under those state statutes. The states that have these dilution statutes are: Alabama, Arizona, Arkansas, California, Connecticut, Delaware, Florida, Georgia, Hawaii, Idaho, Illinois, Indiana, Iowa, Kansas, Louisiana, Maine, Massachusetts, Minnesota, Missouri, Montana, Nebraska, New Hampshire, New Mexico, New York, Oregon, Pennsylvania, Puerto Rico, Rhode Island, Tennessee, Texas, and Washington. An additional five states recognize the dilution doctrine under cases decided by their courts: Kentucky, Maryland, Michigan, New Jersey, and Ohio.

You can find the dilution statutes of most states by visiting the *All About Trademarks* website (www.ggmark.com) and clicking on "U.S. State Trademark Laws."

D. Cybersquatting

A cybersquatter is a person who registers a well-known trademark as a domain name hoping to later profit by selling the domain name to the trademark owner. The practice of cybersquatting originated at a time when most businesses were not savvy about the commercial opportunities on the Internet. Some entrepreneurial souls registered the names of well-known companies as domain names—the now familiar www.companyname.com—with the intent of selling the names back to the companies when they finally realized the economic potential of the Internet. Panasonic, Fry's Electronics, Hertz, and Avon were among the "victims" of cybersquatters. Opportunities for cybersquatters are rapidly diminishing, because most businesses now know that registering and protecting their domain names is essential.

Keep in mind that in some instances, a conflict over the use of a domain name is due to an honest mistake and may not involve the degree of bad faith to prove cybersquatting. When we talk about cybersquatters, we are referring to those who deliberately stake out a domain name with the intent of profiting from use of someone else's trademark.

 For more information about domain names, see Chapter 2.

1. Federal Anticybersquatting Protection Act

The new federal anticybersquatting law authorizes a trademark owner to sue an alleged cybersquatter in federal court and obtain a court order transferring the domain name back to the mark's owner. In some cases, the cybersquatter must pay money damages. To stop a cybersquatter, the mark's true owner must prove all of the following:

- the domain name registrant had a bad faith intent to profit from the mark
- the mark was distinctive at the time the domain name was first registered
- the domain name is identical to or confusingly similar to the mark, and
- the mark qualifies for protection under federal trademark laws—that is, the mark is distinctive and its owner was the first to use the mark in commerce.

If the person or company who registered the domain name had reasonable grounds to believe that the use of the domain name was fair and lawful, they would avoid a court decision that they acted in bad faith. In other words, if the accused cybersquatter can show a judge that he or she had reason to register the domain name other than to sell it back to you, the trademark owner, for a profit, then a court will probably allow the person to keep the domain name. That's because the name was not acquired in bad faith.

Congress has developed some guidelines for the courts to use in looking for bad faith. They include:

- Is the registrant using the domain name to divert users from the mark owner's site to another site, where customer confusion is likely to result or the mark's reputation for quality is harmed? In other words, is the domain name being used in a way that negatively affects the mark owner's website or the value of its trademark?
- Has the registrant offered to sell the domain name to the mark owner without ever legitimately using the domain name on a commercial website?
- Has the registrant provided false or misleading contact information to the domain name registrar or failed to keep this information up to date?
- Has the registrant registered multiple names that are the same or confusingly similar to distinctive marks? In other words, is there an apparent pattern of cybersquatting?
- Is the mark in question famous or highly distinctive? The more distinctive or famous the mark, the more the court is likely to conclude that the registrant acted in bad faith.

The Long Reach of the ACPA

One nice feature of the federal Anticybersquatting Consumer Protection Act (ACPA) is that a trademark owner does not need to obtain personal jurisdiction over the cybersquatter. Personal jurisdiction refers to the court's right to bind the cybersquatter. For example, it is often difficult to obtain personal jurisdiction over out-of-state or foreign cybersquatters. Instead, the trademark owner can proceed under a legal principle known as "in rem," in which the court has control over the property—in this case, the domain name—and the court can award the domain name to the winning party. In a 2002 case involving Harrods and 60 domain names filed by an Argentinean company, this right was further expanded when a federal court ruled that the in rem provisions could also be used for adding claims of infringement and dilution against cybersquatters. (*Harrods Ltd. v. Sixty Internet Domain Names*, 302 F.3d 214 (4th Cir. 2002).)

2. The Uniform Domain Name Dispute Resolution Policy

All domain name registrars require their registrants to agree that any dispute between a trademark owner and a domain name registrant over the right to use the domain name may be submitted to arbitration. The arbitration system was created and is run by the Internet Corporation for Assigned Names and Numbers

(ICANN), the same international organization that is now in general charge of domain name registrations. The arbitration system is referred to as the Uniform Domain Name Dispute Resolution Policy, or UDRP.

Under the UDRP, the arbitrator is authorized to order the domain name transferred to the trademark owner if the owner proves the following elements:

- The domain name at issue is identical or confusingly similar to the trademark in question
- The registrant has no rights or legitimate interests in the domain name, and
- The domain name was registered and/or is being used in bad faith.

Similar proof is required to prevail in a lawsuit based on the federal Anticybersquatting Consumer Protection Act, described in Section D1 above. The Anticybersquatting Act is only enforceable in the United States. The ICANN procedure, on the other hand, can be used against domain name registrants inside and outside the United States.

Here's a look at each of the three elements that must be established by a trademark owner if he or she is to prevail under the UDRP:

(1) The domain name is confusingly similar to the trademark. The trademark owner must prove ownership (the exclusive right to use the mark) and must also establish that the domain name is confusingly similar to the mark (see Chapter 6, Section B, for more on likelihood of customer confusion). If the domain name at issue is preventing the trademark owner from using its mark as its own domain name, the "identical or confusingly similar" test will probably be satisfied.

(2) The domain name registrant has no rights or legitimate interests in the domain name. To prove this element, the trademark owner must show three things:

- The registrant has never tried to use the domain name (or a similar one) in connection with legitimate commerce, on or off the Web
- The registrant was never generally known by the domain name, even if the name wasn't used in commerce as a trademark, and
- The registrant isn't using the domain name in any legitimate way.

A legitimate use would, for example, consist of use on a noncommercial website that engages in satire or criticism. But the use would not be legitimate if the registrant's actual intent is to divert consumers from the mark owner's website or business location, or to tarnish the mark by lessening its reputation for quality.

(3) The domain name registrant acted in bad faith when registering or using the domain name. This one is really the flip side of the second item. The registrant has acted in bad faith if any of the following is shown:

- The registrant acquired the domain name with the intent to sell it back to the mark's owner—or to a competitor of the mark's owner—for profit. This wouldn't apply to those who acquire domain names with the intent to auction them off to the highest bidder later, because the plan was not directed specifically at the mark's owner.

- The registrant has a pattern of acquiring domain names with the intent to block their use by legitimate trademark owners. That is, the registrant is a true cybersquatter. (See Section D1 above.)
- The registrant is a competitor who acquired the domain name primarily to disrupt the mark owner's business.
- The registrant is using the domain name to attract users to the registrant's website by creating customer confusion. (See Chapter 6.)

The procedure for initiating and prosecuting a complaint under the UDRP is for the trademark owner to choose a dispute resolution "provider," which is an organization approved by ICANN. So far, ICANN has approved four providers. Each provider has its own supplemental rules for dispute resolution, so in addition to ICANN's procedural rules (available on the ICANN website at www.icann.com), you must follow the provider's rules. You can check them out at each provider's website, which may be reached through the ICANN website. These sites offer detailed discussions about how to navigate the UDRP.

To begin a case, the mark owner sends a complaint to the provider, setting out specific facts that prove the three elements discussed above. As a general rule, the mark owner (the initiator of the process) will be responsible for payment of the provider's fees, although the fees will be shared if the domain name registrant asks for three arbitrators instead of allowing the case to be presented to a single arbitrator.

After reviewing the complaint for completeness, the provider will send the registrant a copy of the complaint, along with directions on how the registrant can respond and within how much time. The domain name registrant can continue to use the name until the dispute is resolved.

The provider will usually issue a decision based solely on the complaint and the response. Either party may go to court if the decision is not to their liking. However, if the decision is in the trademark owner's favor, the domain name will be transferred to the owner unless the registrant promptly files a lawsuit to prevent it.

The UDRP procedure is still relatively new, and there no doubt will be numerous changes to it. (The rules may have changed by the time you read this book.) Make sure you become familiar with the ICANN website if you want to remain up to speed.

The Odds of Success Under ICANN

As of 2004, over 14,000 proceedings involving domain names have been brought under the ICANN UDRP system. Of the cases in which a decision was reached by the arbitrator, over 85% of cases were decided in favor of the petitioner (which is almost always the trademark owner). The ICANN website offers a searchable database of all decisions rendered under the UDRP as well as a statistical summary. You can access this information at www.icann.org/udrp/udrp.htm.

Chapter 11

If Someone Infringes Your Mark

*Y*ou have encountered another business that is using a name for its product or service that is identical or very similar to yours, and you feel you are losing customers and profits as a result. How can you stop them?

Before you pick up the phone to call an attorney, let us take a minute to look at how and whether a lawsuit is likely to solve your problems. If at the end of this chapter you still feel you want to litigate, then grab that phone—after reading Chapter 14, Help Beyond This Book, for suggestions on finding a lawyer—and good luck!

A. What Litigation Costs

Start by reminding yourself that lawsuits usually cost a bundle—a big bundle. Typically, lawyers who handle trademark cases charge $200 per hour and up. It doesn't take a genius to understand that if you hire a lawyer for a month's worth of work (surely a low estimate for a full-blown trademark fight) it will cost you close to $40,000. From start to finish a trademark infringement lawsuit averages about $120,000 in attorneys' fees for each party.

Perhaps these figures will help you understand why we have great respect for the ancient Gypsy curse that says, "May you be

involved in a lawsuit in which you know you are right."

B. How Much Is Your Mark Really Worth to You?

Given the horrendous costs, it pays to carefully consider whether a particular dispute over a mark is worth litigating. Let's look at this issue a little closer.

1. Can You Recover Attorneys' Fees in State Court?

If your mark is being used in one state only, your infringement suit will most likely be brought in state court, and the laws of your state will determine how attorneys' fees will be paid. In most states the courts will not require the loser of a lawsuit to pay the winner's attorneys' fees. Or stated bluntly, even if you win, you'll have to pay your own lawyer and risk ending up in the poorhouse. However, in a few jurisdictions, such as Colorado, North Carolina, Wisconsin, and Puerto Rico, the prevailing party is awarded attorneys' fees as a matter of course, and in a few others (Alaska, Iowa, Maine, Minnesota, Missouri, Oklahoma, Texas, and Washington), the court has discretion to award attorneys' fees, usually in exceptional cases only.

2. Can You Recover Attorneys' Fees in Federal Court?

If your mark is used across state, territorial, or international boundaries, you will probably end up in federal court. Federal law permits an award of attorneys' fees to a victorious plaintiff, but only when the trademark infringement is exceptional—that is, obviously intentional. The bottom line is this: Unless you are dealing with a clear case of bad intentions, don't count on attorneys' fees in federal trademark litigation.

How Treble Damages Can Help Pay Attorneys' Fees

Although courts have discretion to award attorneys' fees in unusual cases, they are required to award treble (or triple) damages—and order the defendant to disgorge any profits caused by the infringement—in cases where willful infringement is proven. Willful infringement cases therefore have the potential to generate a considerable sum of money over and beyond what the true trademark owner actually suffered from the infringement. Since the goal in most cases is to stop the infringing use—which will happen if the court finds that infringement occurred—the trademark owner can use the damages to pay whatever legal fees are incurred. Trademark lawyers understand this and may therefore be willing to represent plaintiffs in willful infringement cases and defer payment of their fees until the case settles or a judgment is obtained. This is not a contingency fee, because the fee isn't based on the outcome of the case. It's only a method of deferring fees until the plaintiff is in a better position to pay them.

---

3. Litigation Short of Trial

A common strategy is to file an infringement lawsuit and ask the court to grant emergency relief until the case can be fully litigated and decided in a trial. This type of relief—termed a preliminary or temporary injunction—typically orders the alleged infringer to stop using the mark in question pending the outcome of the lawsuit. Because, as a practical matter, getting slapped with an order of this type puts the alleged infringer in an untenable position from the outset, the party bringing the suit usually reaches a settlement on very favorable terms.

To obtain a preliminary injunction, you must convince the court of two basic facts:

- If the emergency relief isn't granted, your business will suffer irreparable injury.
- Your case is strong enough on the face of things to make it probable that you'll win if and when a trial eventually takes place.

The first fact is very easy to show. The mere existence and use of an infringing mark daily robs the owner of the infringed mark of its customer base and the business goodwill that the mark represents. Because there is no real way to measure the loss of goodwill in monetary terms, this type of injury is usually considered irreparable as a matter of course.

The second fact—probable success—is another matter. Here the judge has to be convinced that the plaintiff's infringement claim is strong enough to warrant depriving the infringer of the right to use its mark without first holding a trial. Some judges are more willing to do this than others, and it is impossible to predict whether an attempt to get a preliminary injunction will be successful.

Once the court rules on a request for a preliminary injunction, the losing party has a powerful incentive to settle. If the defendant is enjoined from using the disputed mark pending trial, it means that the judge has found it probable that infringement has occurred. Furthermore, the injunction leaves the defendant little choice but to adopt a new mark to use during the pendency of the case. These facts usually drive the defendant to cave in unless the plaintiff is seeking treble damages and refuses to settle the case (which is unusual). Conversely, if the plaintiff loses, it means that the defendant will be able to continue using the disputed mark during the pendency of the trial, and that the judge has concluded that infringement probably hasn't

occurred. Most plaintiffs are willing to settle rather than pursue the case on such facts.

Because the outcome of the preliminary injunction request usually results in an early termination of the case, the legal fees associated with the normal trademark case often are much less than if the case were fully litigated. But they may still be high—routinely at least $10,000—because it takes a lot of preparation to successfully handle the preliminary injunction proceeding.

4. Beware of Being Right

Whether a preliminary injunction and settlement are obtained or the case goes to trial (tack on at least another $50,000), using the courts to resolve an infringement claim clearly can be, and usually is, very costly. But many otherwise reasonable people insist on it. Why? Probably for the same reason many otherwise reasonable people behave like pit bulls in divorce proceedings—emotional attachment to being right. And remember the Gypsy curse we discussed earlier—many lawyers get rich because clients try to vindicate their positions.

Sadly, the question of who has the right to use a mark often affects people in an emotional way that doesn't always serve their long-term economic interests. They get addicted to their mark, and as with any addiction, they may be willing to spend way beyond what common sense would dictate to keep it. And it may be hard to perceive if your litigation is motivated by ego, principle, or a sense of outrage when the name of your business (which may even get confused with the existence of the business itself) is threatened.

The Mental State of the Infringer Matters in Trademark Litigation

When a mark infringer knew about the infringed mark at the time the infringement began, he or she will be considered a willful infringer. This knowledge is either something that is proved in a trial (such as continued use by the infringer after having been notified of the infringement), or is presumed to have existed if the mark was on the federal Principal Register when the infringement began and the owner of the infringed mark properly used the registration notice with the mark (an ® or a statement to the effect that "This is a registered trademark belonging to Rackafrax Company"). Once the willful label attaches to an infringer, the infringer can be forced to pay treble damages and surrender its profits made from the goods or services carrying the infringing mark.

On the other hand, if the infringer is considered innocent—the business had no knowledge of the infringed mark—the plaintiff-owner usually cannot collect treble damages or the defendant's profits, and in some cases cannot even prevent the infringer from continuing to use the mark, at least in a limited geographical area.

C. Negotiate—Don't Litigate

Negotiation offers you lots of options that litigation doesn't. For one, it's cheaper; for two it's quicker; and for three, you help fashion the outcome. It gives you a chance to devise a solution both parties can live with rather than wasting time and money trying to allocate fault.

How do you get a purported infringer to the negotiating table? As mentioned, some would advocate a lawsuit to seek a preliminary injunction for that purpose. But that is obviously an expensive method of getting the defendant's attention. And, of course, whenever litigation is started, there is a risk that it will gain too much of its own momentum and escalate.

A better way to start is to send the infringing business a letter, stating the problem and proposing that you negotiate. The fact that both parties must bear the high cost of a lawsuit may even become part of the common ground on which you build a solution, instead of a threatening weapon. But no need to give up all your weapons at once. Even if you don't plan to litigate (or would only do so reluctantly), your opponent need not know that at the start.

On the other hand, negotiation does necessarily imply give and take. So you have to decide what you are willing to give, and what you need in exchange. For example, must the infringer change the mark completely, or can you live with it if modifications are made? Do you need the matter resolved right now, or are you able to provide the infringer with some time to make necessary changes? What's the maximum you feel it is worth spending on this dispute? How much would you pay to buy the right to use the name, even if you think you already own it?

Insurance for Trademark Litigation

If you are reading this chapter prospectively and have not yet suffered any harm by another's infringement, check into the option of trademark litigation insurance. This is a rider that can be purchased to augment the coverage of a Comprehensive General Liability policy that all businesses have. The rider offers "advertising injury coverage," which is the coverage that courts have interpreted to extend to trademark and unfair competition claims. This is not yet available in all states, but California, Illinois, and Minnesota permit it, among others. Even if you don't have such a rider, there's no harm in asking your agent whether the risk is covered by your regular policy. You may be pleasantly surprised.

You might even consider this: How many dollars would it take for you to change your mark?

Let us add our personal perspective: Changing your mark need not be a disaster. In fact, depending on who you are and how you do it, it may hardly cause a ripple.

For example, a very popular Berkeley restaurant had to change from *Fat Albert's* to *Fat Apple's* as a result of an ownership dispute. It never lost a beat in the local restaurant scene and still has 45-minute waits out the door for weekend breakfasts.

Even Nolo, the publisher of this book, has had to change its marks from time to time. Its computerized will-writing program, now called *WillMaker*, was originally called *WillWriter*. After Nolo had launched the product and established it in the market, it received a series of threatening letters from a New York law firm stating that *Will Writer* was a federally registered trademark belonging to a small company in New York City that registered wills and printed will forms.

Admittedly, Nolo should have done a more thorough check of the mark before using it, but even if it had, it might have gone ahead and used the mark, because the other company's use was different. It did not make wills or sell computer programs. In addition, the other company's trademark was weak, because it described what the product did—provide a form on which to write a will.

Nolo's first response was to write back to each of these letters, which arrived about six months apart, to say basically, "Don't bother us; you don't have a case." However, the letters kept coming, and the idea of having to defend a suit on the other coast—even one that it might win—loomed as a waste of time and money. So against the almost universal advice of friends and business associates ("You'll lose thousands of sales, confuse your customers, and make yourself a commercial laughingstock"), Nolo cast about for a new name, and came up with *WillMaker*, a mark that was similar to the old one but with a crisper edge to it.

Nolo notified everyone they could of the change, and placed ads that prominently featured the house mark *Nolo* to provide continuity. A few trade journals noted the change, but the upshot was that nobody cared one way or the other.

WillMaker flourished, despite the change, perhaps because of Nolo's reputation, perhaps because it was a distinctive product in a narrow field, and perhaps because Nolo's main competitors didn't yet have a comparable product on the market. Still another possibility is that there was nothing all that distinctive about the name *WillWriter* in the first place.

Whether a name change would be similarly trouble-free for another company depends on the business, the product or service, and the nature of competition in that field. It may be harder for a fledgling business than for an established one to weather a change in a trademark. A main concern would be how expensive and feasible it would be to notify all the customers, distributors, or suppliers who would need to know about the change. And for manufacturers of products, the expense of restamping the products or obtaining new containers may be prohibitive.

Certainly the Internet complicates this issue. If you are using the mark in dispute as your Internet domain name, the cost and hassle associated with changing a domain name (such as getting other websites and search engines to change their links to your site) may be so great that changing it may not be a viable option for you.

If you are a small business in a specific market, you can probably contact your client list either through mailings, in-store flyers, or targeted advertising. You will be surprised how much conversation the name change will generate.

If you are a larger business, perhaps you can make the name change into a news story that industry magazines or newsletters would mention, either as a story or in a column. You might make the name change the basis of a new and different ad campaign. While it does appear a little careless to have adopted someone else's mark, most customers can relate to the misfortune of inadvertently stepping on the toes of some unknown business in a distant city. So it need not ruin your reputation at all. In fact, it may be a shot in the arm. In the metaphor of the self-help therapy industry, you got lemons, so get busy selling lemonade.

D. How to Handle an Infringer

Regardless of how your dispute is finally resolved, you will want to take some or all of the following steps when dealing with infringement of your mark. Obviously, since no two infringement situations are exactly the same, you'll need to adopt and change these steps to fit your needs.

Step 1: Discover the Registration and Use Status of Your Opponent's Mark

Your first step is to discover:
- whether the mark is federally registered and/or registered in your state
- when the other mark was first used anywhere, and
- when the mark was first used in a manner that came into conflict with your mark.

You can find out the registration information by doing a trademark search in the manner described in Chapter 5. If the mark is federally registered, your trademark search can also tell you the date the owner claimed it was first used anywhere. To find out when the mark was first used in a manner that conflicts with your mark, you will need to do a little investigation.

Step 2: Read Chapter 10, Sorting Out Trademark Disputes, to Discover Who Is the Infringer

That chapter explains who has priority when two marks conflict in the marketplace. It will teach you which mark owner—you or your opponent—has the stronger legal case. This information is vital in the negotiation process, because your negotiating position is likely to be far different if you are clearly the top dog from a legal point of view than if you are just as clearly the infringer.

Step 3: Research as Much as You Can About the Business With Which You Will Be Negotiating

You need to know its size, financial health, ownership, market share, products or services and, most important, its litigation history. Obviously, this information will help greatly when you have to decide on a negotiating strategy. For example, if the company is on shaky financial ground, you can play harder ball than if they have a robust balance sheet. And if the other business has gone to court before on this or another mark, you should be very cautious in your dealings with it, unless you too are willing to invest a great deal in your favorite law firm. Also, you need to

know what kind of product the company makes and how and where it is marketed to properly evaluate their use of the mark in question. If their use is an obvious case of infringement (identical mark, closely related markets) and you have legal priority, you have a much stronger negotiation position than if it is a borderline case.

These pieces of information are not as hard to find as you may think. The computer databases that are available for your use (see Chapters 4 and 5) contain a great deal of information on businesses, in the form of business descriptions and revenue.

For either large or small businesses, litigation history is available in state or federal court files, which are public records and increasingly available on the Internet. (See Chapter 14 for more on Internet resources.) They are usually indexed by the names of the parties. In this way you can discover most cases that the business has initiated (assuming they filed in the county in which they operate), but not necessarily those in which they have been sued (which is also relevant to their financial health) because that could have happened anywhere.

You can do all this yourself or hire a lawyer, business investigator, or information broker to do it for you. Of course, you may not need all the pieces of information we've discussed, so just obtain the facts you think are relevant or you can afford.

Step 4. Write a Letter

The next step is to write a letter to the infringer. This is what attorneys do and, if you are more comfortable having an attorney write the letter, find one to do it. (See Chapter 14, Help Beyond This Book.) Write to the owner or president or whatever person is the highest level of management for which you can obtain a name, address, and phone number.

The letter should be businesslike and firm but not accusatory, and it should state the key facts in a clear and concise way. "It has come to our attention that your business is using x trademark or trade name in x manner" is an acceptable way to start. State your claim that your mark has legal priority—including the nature of your business, how you use the mark, when and where you began using it, when you registered it (if you registered it), and whatever else you think is relevant. Then state that you believe the use of the mark by the other business infringes on your rights, and firmly ask the business to cease and desist its use of the mark.

Let Sleeping Dogs Lie. If the material in Chapter 10, Sorting Out Trademark Disputes, indicates that you and not your opponent clearly are in the wrong, the worst thing you can do is bring the conflict to the opponent's attention. Here the old adage of "Let sleeping dogs lie" is very appropriate.

Make sure you provide the other business with enough information, including, for example, a copy of your registration certificate, so they can independently verify the basic facts that you allege and respond appropriately. But there is no need to exhaustively recount your business history or give extraneous information. Whatever you put in this

letter must be accurate because it can be used later in court as evidence of some sort of inconsistency or misdescription.

Don't Set Deadlines or Make Threats. Don't set deadlines or make threats of litigation in this first letter. If you do, you will feel compelled to take some action if the business doesn't comply with your demand, in order to show that you are serious. And it is likely that your action will be premature. Better to give yourself room and expect to write a second or even a third letter before giving your opponent an ultimatum.

There is another potential downside to threatening litigation. The infringing party may interpret your threat as a statement that litigation is inevitable and file an action for declaratory judgment in its local federal court. If that court is in a different part of the country than you are, you will be at a significant disadvantage and will no longer have a choice about whether to litigate or use some other, less costly, method of resolving the dispute.

Sample Letter

Dear [Name of Infringer},

It has recently come to our attention that your business is using x trademark or trade name on x [service or product]. We believe that this use infringes on our ownership rights in x trademark. We first became aware of your mark [state the circumstances—e.g., at the 2000 Weaving Trade Show in Albuquerque].

We have the exclusive right to use this trademark based on the following facts: [Now list the bases of your rights—federal or state registration numbers, date of first use, date of registration, on what products or services you use it, and in what geographical areas. Attach copies of your registration papers and samples of how you use the mark.]

We believe that your use of this mark is likely to confuse our customers [and suppliers] and will damage the good reputation that our [goods, services] have enjoyed until now. Therefore, we request that you cease any further use of this mark.

Please reply with an acknowledgment of the ownership right that we claim in this mark and a proposed timetable for halting its continued use.

Sincerely,

(Your name)
(Your title)

If There Is No Actual Conflict

Sometimes the use of a mark that—on its face—overlaps with another mark does not result in a conflict in the marketplace. For instance, if you own the national right to a mark but are only using it in the Southwest, an infringing use in the Northeast won't affect you. However, if you later decide to move into that region, the dual use of the marks would be very confusing. Also, as we indicated in Chapter 8, How to Use and Care for Your Trademark, it is important for you to police the use of your mark so it won't be weakened by overuse or considered abandoned.

If you discover an infringer whose use of the mark isn't in conflict with yours, consider writing a letter pointing out that you own the exclusive national right to the mark and intend to enforce your right when you start using your mark in that part of the country. You need not demand that their use cease immediately. If you never expand in that direction, no harm is done. But if you do want to start using your mark in that part of the country, you've at least preserved your right to force the other user to adopt a different mark at that time. The Internet makes these kinds of situations less likely because use on the Internet often immediately creates a national or international market.

Step 5: Negotiate

This process can be as flexible as you wish it to be. The outcome is only limited by the creativity of the negotiators. But once you reach an agreement, it makes sense to be aware of all its ramifications. For instance, if you agree to let the defendant continue using the mark in exchange for a license fee, your pocketbook may be in better shape, but you may lose control of the mark (it will be considered abandoned) if it no longer serves its function of uniquely identifying the source of goods or products in the marketplace. On the other hand, if the mark is being used on entirely different goods and services and no customer confusion is likely, it may not hurt to assign the defendant all rights to the mark for that other purpose in exchange for cash. The bottom line is, have a trademark attorney read over the agreement before you commit to it.

Here are five possible negotiation strategies.

1. You can bluff your opponent into thinking you are on the verge of filing a lawsuit. This strategy works best when your mark is federally registered and theirs is not, and it appears that they began to use their mark after your mark's registration date. The reason for this is that under these facts, your opponent is legally liable to you for treble (triple) damages, the profits they realized from the sale of the goods or services carrying the mark, and possibly your attorneys' fees. You might scare your opponent into stopping use of their mark entirely. Or you might just get them to agree to modify the

mark. Of course, you must be prepared to spend a fair amount of energy (and attorneys' fees if you use an attorney as part of your bluff) to convince them that you're not bluffing. And you ought to be prepared to go to court if the bluff fails.

Don't Put Your Bluff in Writing. If you send a written letter threatening litigation, you run the risk of finding that letter as an exhibit on a complaint for declaratory judgment filed by the other party in a federal court far from your place of business. If you decide to threaten litigation as part of your bluff, make sure you do it orally unless the infringing party is located in the same part of the country as you are and, as mentioned, you are prepared to litigate if the other party calls your bluff.

2. A good fallback position is to suggest an agreement on territory or manner of usage—such as, "You can have the name in Nebraska and Kansas, and I'll use it in Oklahoma and Texas," or "You use it only as a trade name for your crockery-manufacturing business, and I'll use it only as a mark on my line of stuffed animals."

3. Perhaps you and the other party can make a few modifications to the way your marks appear to distinguish each more clearly from the other. For instance, you change your mark from the *Homemade Cafe* to *Homemade Diner*, and the other party changes from *HomeMade Cafe* to the *Home Cooking Cafe*.

4. You may offer to buy your opponent's rights in the trademark. It may seem unfair to have to pay the other party to

change their name, but that might solve your problem in an economical way, considering that you are saving yourselves and them the cost of litigating over the trademark.

5. You might even sell your rights to the mark to the other party for a handsome sum in exchange for adopting a new mark. The money could serve as a much-needed capital infusion, as well as the means to afford an advertising campaign around your new name.

Step 6: Consider Other Dispute Resolution Options

Traditionally, trademark-related disputes have been settled by negotiation or ended up in court before a judge or jury. However, in recent years several alternative, informal, and private ways to handle these and other types of disputes have become popular. They are faster and cheaper than traditional court processes; they often produce superior solutions; and, because of their informality, they don't necessarily require representation by an attorney.

Unless a written contract provides that a particular approach to dispute resolution must be followed in case a dispute under the contract arises, these alternative approaches are usually voluntary, which means all parties have to agree to use them. However, some courts are beginning to require litigants to first attempt one of these alternative approaches before the case is allowed to proceed to a trial.

The two best-known alternative ways to resolve disputes are arbitration and mediation.

Although arbitration and mediation are often mentioned in the same breath and are frequently confused with each other, they are actually quite distinct in the way they approach disputes. The most striking difference between them is that in arbitration you still present your case to a third party—called an arbitrator—for a decision, while in mediation you enlist the aid of a third party to help you and the other parties reach your own solution, without any particular resolution being imposed on you. Think of it as structured negotiation. Let's take a closer look at how each approach works.

a. Arbitration

In arbitration, the parties agree to select and pay one arbitrator—or a panel of three arbitrators—to hear the dispute. If three arbitrators are desired, the usual selection method is for each party to select its own arbitrator and then leave it to these arbitrators to pick the third.

As a general rule, arbitrators are selected from panels put together by such large national organizations as the American Arbitration Association (www.adr.org) and JAMS-Endispute (Judicial Arbitration and Mediation Services) (www.jams-endispute.com). However, smaller, more specialized groups of arbitrators may also be available in your locality (see the Yellow Pages).

Although many of the arbitrators offered by the larger organizations are attorneys or retired judges, many are not. It is up to the parties to decide whether their particular dispute should be decided by someone with a legal background or someone who perhaps has a more appropriate expertise—such as a contractor in a construction dispute, or an insurance broker if the dispute involves the interpretation of an insurance contract. In the case of a trademark dispute, it is likely that you will in fact want at least one experienced trademark lawyer to arbitrate the dispute.

The rules used to choose the arbitrator(s) and conduct the arbitration are also usually provided by the organization to which the parties turn to provide the arbitrators. For instance, it is common to agree to have the arbitration conducted under the "rules of the American Arbitration Association."

Unlike court, arbitration can proceed very rapidly and be finished in a matter of weeks, although several months is more common. Obviously, the length of time a particular arbitration will take depends on the complexity of the dispute and the eagerness of the parties to push the matter. Even if one party to an arbitration is in a hurry, it is usually possible for the other party to slow things down.

As a general rule, the arbitrator's fees are paid equally by the parties, by agreement. These fees can be considerable. If the arbitration only takes an hour or two of the arbitrator's time, this can be reasonable. However, if the arbitration takes days, then the expense will mount accordingly. The arbitrator's fees are in addition to what each side is paying their attorney, if they decide to use one.

Probably the biggest issue in any arbitration is whether the decision of the arbitrator(s) is to be final or if the loser will be permitted to go to court for a regular trial.

This issue is typically addressed by the parties when they decide to arbitrate unless the matter has already been addressed in a contract. Because a decision to arbitrate usually is based on a wish to resolve the dispute quickly and cheaply, most parties opt to make the arbitrator's decision final, meaning that it can be entered in a court with competent jurisdiction as a final, non-appealable judgment, which makes it enforceable.

Beware of Binding Arbitration. The finality of an arbitration can be troublesome if the arbitrator strays far from established legal principles in arriving at the decision. Under most court rules dealing with binding arbitration, an arbitrator's departure from the law cannot be challenged in an appeal. For that reason, businesses that believe they are legally in the right are often reluctant to turn their fate over to a decision maker who is, in essence, unconstrained by the law. Better the costs of litigation, these businesses believe, than creating the risk of a runaway and crippling arbitration result.

If you are asserting your trademark rights against the owner of a domain name, you may invoke nonbinding arbitration under rules established by an international body known as ICANN. See Chapter 10, Sorting Out Trademark Disputes, for more on how this procedure works.

b. Mediation

The central idea underlying mediation is simple. Most disputes can be settled in a manner that is at least minimally satisfactory to each of the disputing parties—the colloquial win-win scenario. Mediators use a number of techniques designed to identify potential points of agreement and help the parties understand and move towards these points on a voluntary basis.

If the mediation does not produce a settlement, the parties are free to pursue other avenues, including litigation.

The same organizations that provide arbitrators usually also furnish mediators. Also, a number of individual business attorneys and law firms are beginning to offer mediation services to people engaged in business disputes—including disputes over trademarks. The best way to locate these services is to use the Yellow Pages and look for announcements that emphasize business mediation.

Another good way to find potential mediators is to visit the websites maintained by the Association of Intellectual Property Law Attorneys (AIPLA) (www.aipla.org) and the International Trademark Association (INTA) (www.inta.org).

A list of business mediators in your area may also be obtained from the Mediation Information and Resource Center (www.mediate.com).

Because mediation is about reaching agreement rather than trying to convince a decision maker—as is the case with arbitration—there is no need to involve an attorney. However, attorneys often can help you find an appropriate mediator. They also can be helpful as advisors during the course of the mediation, and, assuming an agreement is reached, can reduce a general oral agreement to a detailed written agreement that both you and the other party will feel comfortable signing.

Step 7: Consult an Attorney

If none of the above gets you anywhere, by all means call a trademark lawyer. The lawyer might have a better letter-writing technique, or might tell you to forget about the conflict. The lawyer probably will be able to help you find a mediator or arbitrator, if you want to pursue one of these options, or the lawyer might advise that your best shot is to go to court. If you've tried everything else first, the lawyer might be right. (See Chapter 14, Help Beyond This Book.) ∎

Chapter 12

If Someone Claims That You Infringed Their Trademark

ou have gotten an irate letter from Ms. Blowhard in North Noluk demanding not only that you immediately cease using your new mark for clothing designs, Nines, but also that you account for all your profits derived from the use of that name and pay them treble (triple) damages for the insult, or they will see you in court. What to do?

Stay calm.

First, you need to know that no matter how threatening the letter, the world won't fall on your head today, tomorrow, or even next week. However, legal steps may eventually follow. So first we'll tell you what those are. Next we will help you decide what your options are in response. Finally, before you actually adopt a strategy, you'll need to think about your version of the big name picture— how valuable is your name, and given the legal realities, how much energy and money are you willing to spend to protect it?

Much of this discussion is very similar to the information in Chapter 11, If Someone Infringes Your Mark. It's a good idea to read that whole chapter (it's short) to get an idea of the other guy's point of view.

Start by understanding the same key point we emphasize in Chapter 11, that trademark lawsuits are extremely expensive.

From the point of view of either the infringer or the infringee, negotiation is a more pragmatic, cost-effective, and often more fruitful way to resolve a trademark dispute. With that guiding principle, let us help you respond to someone's claim that you infringed on their mark.

A. What the Complaining Party Can Do to You

Right away you should know that your opponent can only stop your use of your mark with a court order (that is, a temporary injunction). To get this, they must leap two legal hurdles:

1. They must convince a judge that they have suffered, or will suffer, irreparable immediate damage without an immediate court order barring your continued use of the mark.

2. They must convince a judge that they are likely to eventually win in court (that is, they must show that they have superior rights to the mark and that you infringed on those rights).

In cases where the two names compete in the marketplace, the first hurdle will often be assumed, because trademark infringements siphon off goodwill in a way that cannot easily be measured and repaired in a later action for damages (which is why the injury is called irreparable).

The second hurdle is much more difficult to overcome, because the judge, without the benefit of a full trial, is being asked to make an important finding about the primary issue in the case: Has infringement really occurred? To develop and prove the facts that the judge will need to arrive at this conclusion normally involves quite a bit of (always expensive) legal time. So unless your opponent is both solvent and determined, he or she will not likely leap into court without first: (1) finding out as much about you and your use of the mark as they can, and (2) testing your reaction to their infringement claims. The upshot is, you probably have a little time to figure out what to do.

B. Steps You Should Take

We don't mean to imply that you should ignore the letter. On the contrary, you should get busy with the following steps, lest you end up with a process server at your door.

Step 1: Find Out What You Can About the Complaining Firm and Their Use and Registration of the Mark at Issue

Here we echo the discussion in Chapter 11, Section D, on the same issue from the opposite perspective. Please read that material. In essence, the more you know about the other party, the better you can evaluate how to respond to their allegations. In addition, it's essential to the development of your case that you know exactly how they use their mark, and where and how long they have used it.

Once you get all that information, you should reread Chapter 10, Sorting Out Trademark Disputes, to help you make up your mind if your opponent has a case against you.

Step 2: Get Advice

After you have gathered as much information as possible, consult a trademark attorney to confirm or correct your understanding of the situation as well as to get the point of view of a disinterested experienced party. Although you may understandably want to avoid attorneys and their attendant costs, paying several hundred dollars for a reasoned legal opinion about your situation is cheap given the probable cost of ending up on the losing side of a lawsuit or even retooling your stationery and marketing materials if your decision is to switch rather than fight. You may also want to get the advice of friends or business associates whom you trust. They may have had comparable experiences, or they may simply have reliable common sense and good tactical reactions.

Once you fully inform yourself of the legal and practical implications of the trademark dispute, trust your gut. It's almost always a mistake to follow a course of action you don't feel comfortable about. Fortunately, because the complaining business is likely to write you several letters before taking legal action, you probably have enough time to consider your next step carefully.

Step 3: Choose Your Tactical Responses

Here are some common responses, and at least some of the possible consequences of each.

1. **The Ostrich Technique.** You can ignore the infringement claim and hope it goes away. In fact, if you are convinced that the other business doesn't have a case and knows it, this may work. Otherwise, it's probably a mistake, as it risks your being sued just to get your attention.

2. **The German Shepherd Response.** You can send back a letter full of sound and fury, informing them that under no circumstances will you ever stop using your mark, and the mere suggestion that you are infringing is a shocking insult. Remember, however, that this is a typical lawyerly tactic, and lawyers often profit most when they fan the flames of small disputes into true conflagrations.

3. **The Elephantine Response.** You reply in a calm and polite letter, stating the facts as you see them, and explaining why you disagree with the infringement claim. Your tone makes it clear that you are reasonable and flexible, perfectly willing to engage in further discussion, and to hear more information on the subject. This sort of letter does not predispose you to any particular strategy, because you can always dig in your heels later, but in our view it's most likely to put you farther along the road to fruitful discussion than does either of the other two responses.

Step 4: Plan Your Negotiation Strategy

Now let's assume that negotiation by letter, fax, or phone has begun. What sort of strategies should you consider? These are identical to the ones discussed in Chapter 11, If Someone Infringes Your Mark, and we suggest you read (or reread) that material. Also, once again let us make the point that changing your name need not be a disaster and may even be a marketing opportunity.

Step 5: Seek Mediation

One approach that may help you reach agreement without being dragged into court is to seek arbitration or mediation. These alternative approaches to dispute resolution are described in more detail in Chapter 11, If Someone Infringes Your Mark, Section D, Step 6. ■

Chapter 13

International Trademark Protection

*I*t's possible as your mark becomes well known that you'll want to protect it in another country. If so, you should take some steps to do that, or at least look into the process.

Trademark laws are different abroad. Many countries follow the U.S. principle and require actual use in commerce before registration. These "use" countries include the United Kingdom, Canada, Australia, New Zealand, and other current and former British Commonwealth members.

But in the majority of nations, registration alone forms a basis for ownership rights. In these countries, anyone can get a registration on your mark without having used it there first. This presents a serious problem for marks that appear to be headed for international use after becoming well known in this country. Some businesses have made money by spotting these types of marks, preemptively registering them in key countries, and then demanding large fees to transfer (assign) the names back to their original U.S. owners. Also, in some countries you may not be able to import your goods without first registering your mark there.

In this chapter we discuss the two basic issues to resolve if you're considering seeking foreign trademark rights: (1) Where will you seek protection? and (2) What method will you use to register your trademark abroad?

⚠️ Our basic advice about international trademarks is that when in doubt about how to proceed, get an experienced trademark attorney who has done international registrations to help. It is possible, as explained below, for a layperson to accomplish international registrations under the Madrid Protocol, but you may have dificulty assessing your likelihood of success in foreign countries unless you consult with a trademark expert.

A. Where Will You Seek Protection?

Where you seek protection depends, obviously, on where you plan to market your services or products. All countries require that you use the mark within a period of time after registration or it will lapse, so only register in those countries where it is reasonable to foresee sales in the next several years.

Unfortunately, you may not yet know into which countries you will be expanding. If so, consider registering your trademark in Canada and Mexico, which are natural choices, following the signing of the North American Free Trade Agreement (NAFTA) in 1993.

💡 Canada and Mexico don't belong to the Madrid Protocol, a group of nations that uses a simplified system for international registrations, described below. To register in Canada and Mexico, you'll need to file applications in each nation.

Additional candidates for international registration will depend on the nature of your product and how it might fit into the international market. Because you can't foresee all contingencies, your basic business philosophy will dictate this decision: Either cover as many possibilities as you can by registering in many countries (the expensive choice), or restrict your international registrations to your one or two best choices and hope your decision pays off.

Once you're certain about foreign registration, you must arrange for or conduct an international trademark search. In those countries in which registration alone forms a basis for ownership rights, such searches are much simpler to do than in "use" countries, because all potential conflicts will be found on the national register of trademarks, without the need to search for unregistered trademarks.

What Does It Mean in Italian?

Check to see if your mark has an unintended meaning in the country in which you plan to register. For example, *Pschitt* was a French mark that could not be marketed as a soft drink in the United States. This suggestion also applies to English-speaking countries—in Australia, a "Whopper" (a U.S. trademark for a hamburger) is slang for male genitalia, and so not advisable as a trademark there. To get an opinion on this, consult a native speaker of that country.

Free and Fee-Based Resources for International Trademark Searching

You may search the trademark registries of many foreign countries for free. Visit the All About Trademarks website (www.ggmark.com) and click "International Trademark Laws, Rules, Databases, and Treaties." You may also use the fee-based services identified in Chapter 4, Section G, and have a search company perform these national searches.

COVER
THE
EARTH

Making Money (But Losing Your Name)

In 1971 a young, recently divorced mother and her friend started a unique low-profile company that:

- sold pure and simple cosmetics, lotions, and perfumes
- offered its products in small-size, recyclable bottles with no extraneous ingredients, and
- didn't test its products on animals.

The business was named *The Body Shop* (because its first place of business was in a former auto repair shop). The owners had the foresight to register the name with the PTO not long after business started to blossom. It was a timely enterprise, and a great success, eventually opening several outlets within its region. It was the kind of business that made people who moved out of the area beg friends traveling back there to bring them some *Body Shop* products. Soon it also had a booming catalog business.

Years passed. Meanwhile, in London, another entrepreneur had the same idea for similar products and the same name. The second *Body Shop* also took off, even faster and on a wider basis than the original had in the United States. Eventually, the *Body Shop* (U.K.) had over 500 flourishing franchises throughout Europe. It was confusing to travelers, but because the U.S. company had obtained only the exclusive rights to the name in the United States, they could not stop the British *Body Shop's* use.

Then came the day when the British store owners sought to enter the U.S. market. The U.S. corporation had the legal right to the name and therefore potent weapons at its disposal. But the British firm had many times the capital of its U.S. counterpart. Like reasonable businesspeople, the U.S.-based *Body Shop* heeded the bottom line, settling the dispute amicably. It sold the U.S. rights to its name to the British company, agreeing to change its name within 18 months, in exchange for an undisclosed (but sizable) sum of money. Everybody's happy, more or less.

The point of this story depends on your perspective. Some might say: Trademark your name everywhere you can at once! Others could reflect that the protagonists in our story, by federally registering their trademark, showed foresight that was unusual at the time for a small "New Age" concern. That act gave them the leverage they needed to extract a price from the English company for use of the trademark in the United States.

In the end, the U.S. company suffered the inconvenience of changing its name, but that's something that many companies do willingly when their circumstances change. Furthermore, they weren't, as a practical matter, deprived of expansion opportunities. They hadn't expanded much before the conflict arose, and even now they are still a relatively small—but profitable—concern with a few regional outlets and a catalog. And that's fine with the owners. They bargained for enough time to reach all their regular customers and notify them of the new name *Body Time*, and they received a handy infusion of capital from the sale of their trademark.

B. How Will You Register Abroad?

There are three ways for the owner of a U.S. trademark registration to acquire a foreign registration—under the Madrid Protocol (among 66 member nations), as a Community Trademark (among 25 European nations), or via separately filed registrations in each nation.

1. The Madrid Protocol

The Madrid Protocol is a system that allows an applicant to file simultaneous registration applications in any of the 66 nations that (as of July 2005) belong to the Madrid Protocol treaty. (A listing of member nations is pro-vided below, and you can find more compre-hensive details about each country's filing re-quirements at the International Trademark Association website, www.inta.org/madrid. Click on "List of Member Countries.")

The Madrid Protocol, adopted in the United States in November 2003, is adminis-tered by the World Intellectual Property Or-ganization (WIPO, www.wipo.org) and is considered a more efficient and less expen-sive route for simultaneous registration of several foreign marks.

For U.S. applicants, the first step under the Madrid Protocol is to federally register your mark with the PTO. (This procedure is explained in Chapter 7.) This application/

Madrid Protocol Members as of November 15, 2004

Albania	Democratic People's	Italy	Poland	Swaziland
Antigua and	Republic of Korea	Japan	Portugal	Sweden
Barbuda	Denmark	Kenya	Republic of	Switzerland
Armenia	Estonia	Kyrgyzstan	Korea	Syrian Arab
Australia	European	Latvia	Republic of	Republic
Austria	Community	Lesotho	Moldova	The former
Belarus	Finland	Liechtenstein	Romania	Yugoslav
Belgium	France	Lithuania	Russian	Republic of
Bhutan	Georgia	Luxembourg	Federation	Macedonia
Bulgaria	Germany	Monaco	Serbia and	Turkey
China	Greece	Mongolia	Montenegro	Turkmenistan
Croatia	Hungary	Morocco	Sierra Leone	Ukraine
Cuba	Iceland	Mozambique	Singapore	United
Cyprus	Iran (Islamic	Namibia	Slovakia	Kingdom
Czech	Republic of)	Netherlands	Slovenia	United States
Republic	Ireland	Norway	Spain	of America
				Zambia

registration is then referred to as either the basic application or basic registration. The nations in which you choose to register after the United States are referred to as nations for which "extension of protection" is sought.

Each of these nations will decide, using its national criteria, whether to register the mark. If registration is refused in one of these countries, it will not affect the main Madrid Protocol application. For example, if you apply to register in Denmark and Estonia but are rejected in Estonia, it will not affect the status of your application in Denmark. Only if the basic registration (the U.S. registration) is abandoned or declared invalid within the first five years of the international registration will the other registrations be terminated.

To file, start with the TEAS program at the PTO website. Click on "File" under Trademarks on the home page. Then click "Madrid Protocol Forms," and then click "Application for International Registration" and fill out the form. If you later wish to add other nations to your application, you may do so by filing a "Subsequent Designation," also provided in TEAS format.

2. The Community Trademark

The Community Trademark is a method of registering for a trademark that is good in the 25 European countries that belong to the European Union (Austria, Belgium, Cyprus, the Czech Republic, Denmark, Estonia, Finland, France, Germany, Greece, Hungary, Ireland, Italy, Latvia, Lithuania, Luxembourg, Malta,

Netherlands, Poland, Portugal, Slovenia, Slovak Republic, Spain, Sweden, and the United Kingdom). To qualify for Community Trademark status, the proposed mark must be acceptable in all countries. If your application is rejected by even one country, you must file separate national applications for trademark registration in each country.

Unlike a trademark issued under the Madrid Protocol, the CTM is good throughout the European Union nations and can be enforced throughout the EU. So, instead of having to file separate lawsuits in each member nation, you can file one lawsuit for infringement in many nations.

Generally, trademark lawyers advise that a CTM is worthwhile if registration would otherwise be sought in more than three of the EU nations. An application for a Community Trademark may be made to the Office for Harmonization of the Internal Market, in Alicante, Spain. For more information about how the community mark works and how to apply for one, visit http://oami.eu.int.

3. Registering On a Country-by-Country Basis

The good news if you are filing separate trademark applications in foreign countries is that most nations where you will file belong to the International Convention for the Protection of Industrial Property (known as the Paris Convention).

This law has standardized a few things. One of the most important is that a trademark owner from one Paris Convention country who registers their trademark in another Paris Convention country is entitled to the same rights as are native trademark owners of that country. Although each country's laws are different, the Convention at least puts all trademark owners in any one Paris Convention country on the same legal footing.

Another important benefit is that once a U.S. citizen applies to register a federal trademark in the United States, the date of that application serves as the effective date of application in all other Paris Convention countries in which you apply, if you do so within six months of the U.S. application. This is important because in most of those countries rights are based on registration, and the effective date of application (or priority date) is an important method of determining rights. Thus, it is imperative to file an international registration soon after filing one in the United States, if you plan to do so at all.

If you plan on handling the filing in a foreign country, you'll need to research the trademark laws of that nation. You can do this online—start at either the WIPO website (www.wipo.org) or the All About Trademarks Site (www.ggmark.com). These foreign laws are usually summarized at each nation's trademark office website and will inform you how soon you must begin to use your mark after registration and whether there are special licensing and tax rules that may apply to your service or product and its mark. Again, this is why you should consult an experienced international trademark attorney—to make sure you find out about and comply with all applicable laws. ■

Chapter 14

Help Beyond This Book

*W*e hope that this book provides all the information you will need to choose and protect your trademark, service mark, or trade name. But you may need additional help, either in the form of more advanced legal resources or a trademark attorney's assistance.

In Section A, we introduce you to some basic research resources found in most large law libraries. Written for law students and lawyers, these resources discuss recent legal trends and developments and provide citations to substantive trademark law, including statutes, court decisions, and trademark office rules and regulations. In Section B we point you towards some particularly helpful websites that contain both basic information and links to other trademark-related sites. Finally, in Section C we provide some tips for finding a good trademark lawyer.

Don't Be Afraid of Legal Research

Looking up the law for yourself needn't be scary. By reading this book you will have already learned the basic trademark vocabulary necessary to understand the more technical legal materials we discuss in Section A. In addition, Nolo publishes a basic legal research guide, *Legal Research: How to Find & Understand the Law,* by Stephen Elias and Susan Levinkind, which teaches you how to efficiently do basic legal research. You will also find most law librarians to be of great help.

A. Doing Your Own Research in a Law Library

When seeking answers in a law library, you will find useful the three-step approach that we describe below:

1. Read one or more discussions by experts in the field to get a background and overview of the topic being researched. In this case, you will already have a basic background from this book and will be looking for additional details on a particular topic.
2. Read the law itself (cases and statutes) upon which the experts base their opinions. Reading primary materials such as these can be confusing without first digesting an expert's analysis (Section 1).
3. Make sure the law you read is completely up to date.

1. Read One or More Discussions by Experts

The following are some recommended publications written by trademark law experts. You can find others via your law library's subject matter catalog.

Federal Trademark Law. The most authoritative book on trademark law is the two-volume set entitled *McCarthy on Trademarks and Unfair Competition,* by J. Thomas McCarthy, published by Clark Boardman Callaghan. McCarthy, a law professor at the University of San Francisco, is the most widely respected trademark law expert in the United States. His book is so comprehensive and well respected that judges often consult it and refer to it in their decisions. You can find this treatise, with its annual supplements, in most public and academic law libraries.

Trademarks and Unfair Competition includes discussions of virtually every issue that has arisen with respect to the trademark and unfair competition areas of law. Each point that McCarthy makes is supported by footnote references to court cases and statutes—the primary sources that you may want to consult next as part of your overall legal research plan.

You can find your topic of interest in *Trademarks and Unfair Competition* by consulting the detailed table of contents, the extensive index, or the headings that precede each chapter.

Don't overlook the handy appendices in Volume 2, which include the complete text of the Lanham Act (the federal trademark statute), other statutes related to trademark law, and the *Trademark Rules of Practice* of the U.S. Patent and Trademark Office (PTO).

Although very comprehensive, McCarthy's material may not give you enough detail on how to apply trademark law to real-life situations, such as rules on using the ® symbol, or filing and prosecuting a trademark action in the PTO. Probably the best resource for questions of this type is the *Trademark Manual of Examining Procedure* (TMEP), published by the PTO and available both in law libraries and on the Internet (see Section B). Also, there are two respected resources that provide how-to information. They are:

- *Trademark Law—A Practitioner's Guide*, by Siegrun D. Kane, published by the Practicing Law Institute
- *Trademark Registration Practice*, by James E. Hawes, published by Clark Boardman Callaghan.

The first of these resources provides practical advice for lawyers about the practice and litigation of trademark cases, which may prove helpful if you end up in court or if you want a better idea of what lies ahead should a lawsuit loom.

The second resource provides detailed advice and forms about dealing with the PTO. Although Chapters 7 and 8 of this book should suffice for most transactions with the PTO, you will need to consult *Trademark Registration Practice* if:

- your federal trademark registration is opposed
- you wish to oppose someone else's federal trademark registration, or
- someone files an action in the PTO to cancel your mark.

State Trademark Law. A good source of information on state trademark law is *State Trademark and Unfair Competition Law*, a publication of the International Trademark Association (see "Trademark Associations and Legal Publishers," below). It has chapters discussing trademark and unfair competition laws of every state. At the end, it has a chart listing the registration requirements for each state. Clark Boardman Callaghan publishes it for the INTA, with updates, one or more times a year. You can find this resource in most major law libraries.

Law Review Articles. If you have a very unusual trademark problem that is not covered by the resources already mentioned (for example, how to register a distinctive sound as a trademark), or a problem in an area in which the law has changed very recently (perhaps because of a new Supreme Court case), the best sources of available information may be articles appearing in scholarly journals called law reviews. You can find citations (references) to all the law review articles on a particular topic by looking under "trademark" or "unfair competition" in the *Index to Legal Periodicals*, the *Current Law Index*, or one of the cumulative electronic indexes that are (with increasing frequency) found in law libraries. A key to the abbreviations used in these indexes is located at the front of each index volume. Substantial collections of law reviews are usually located in large public law libraries or university libraries.

Trademark Associations and Legal Publishers

Two associations of trademark lawyers offer other materials that you might find helpful. You can get a list of their publications by writing or calling them.

International Trademark Association (INTA)
1133 Avenue of the Americas
New York, NY 10036
212-768-9887
www.inta.org

Among other materials, the INTA publishes an annual paperback, *Trademark Law Handbook*, which analyzes current trademark issues, and *The Trademark Reporter*, a bimonthly law review that discusses recent trademark cases and issues. Only members can subscribe to it, but law libraries carry it for the public's use.

American Intellectual Property Law
    Association (AIPLA)
Suite 203, 2001 Jefferson Davis Highway
Arlington, VA 22202
703-415-0780
www.aipla.org

The AIPLA is an association of lawyers that conducts scholarly studies and publishes articles by its members. Materials by AIPLA are available only in libraries or through members of the association.

2. Read the Law Itself (Cases and Statutes)

Statutes. The main law governing trademarks in the United States is the Lanham Act, also known as the Federal Trademark Act of 1946 (as amended in 1988). It is codified at Title 15, Chapters 1051 through 1127, of the *United States Code*. You can find it in either of two series of books, *United States Code Annotated* (U.S.C.A.) or *United States Code Service*, Lawyers Edition (U.S.C.S.). All law libraries carry at least one of these series. To find a specific section of the Lanham Act, consult either the index at the end of Title 15, or the index at the end of the entire code.

Regulations. The regulations implementing the Lanham Act consist of the specific rules that govern registration of a trademark. They are found in Title 37, Chapter 1, of the *Code of Federal Regulations* (C.F.R.). It comes in a paperback form, which you can purchase from the Superintendent of Documents, U.S. Government Printing Office, Washington, DC 20402, and is available in most law libraries.

Court Decisions. There are several ways to find the pertinent court decisions on a particular trademark issue. As we discussed, an excellent way to get started is to consult *Trademarks and Unfair Competition*, by J. Thomas McCarthy, a law review, or one of the other secondary sources we mentioned above. These will list ("cite" in legal parlance) and usually discuss all the significant pertinent cases. In addition, the *U.S. Code Annotated* and *U.S. Code Service* both refer to and briefly summarize all the decisions relevant to each

section of the Lanham Act. These "case notes" are located just after each section of the act.

You can also get cites to cases from a series of books by West Publishing Company called the *Federal Practice Digest*. If you look under the term "trademark," in the detailed table of contents, or under a more specific topic in the very detailed subject matter index, you will find short summaries of trademark law decisions.

3. Make Sure the Law You Read Is Completely Up to Date

Once you have found a statute or case that seems to address your research question, you will need to check that it is still good law. For statutes, this usually means checking the back of the volume you are using for an insert called a "pocket part." Pocket parts are published annually and include any recent changes in the statute. Updating the status of rules announced in cases means using a tool that is known throughout the legal research world as *Shepard's Case Citations*.

Explaining how to use this valuable tool is beyond the scope of this book. We recommend *Legal Research: How to Find & Understand the Law*, by Stephen Elias and Susan Levinkind (Nolo), for a crash course on the subject.

⚠️ If you intend to do legal research yourself, be aware that interpreting statutes and cases can be difficult, even for those with legal training and a specific background in the area you are researching. Before you act in reliance

Case Citations

Throughout the secondary sources we have described you will find citations to trademark cases of four sorts:

1. Citations to cases decided by federal district courts. Each state is divided into different regions over which individual federal district courts have jurisdiction.

2. Citations to decisions by federal appellate courts, which review decisions of the federal district courts. The nation is geographically divided into 12 federal courts of appeals plus the Court of Appeals for the Federal Circuit.

3. Citations to the U.S. Supreme Court, which is the last level of review possible for any federal or state case.

4. Citations to decisions by state appellate courts. These are more rare because most trademark cases occur in federal court.

Opinions by federal district court judges are cited this way: *Pedi-Care v. Pedi-A-Care Nursing, Inc.*, 656 F.Supp. 449 (D.C. N.J. 1987). This identifies a particular court decision and tells you where to find it. Any case decided by a federal district court is published in a series of books called the *Federal Supplement.* The cite above tells us that the *Pedi-Care* case is located in the *Federal Supplement* (F.Supp.) in volume 656 at page 449. The cite also tells us that the *Pedi-Care* case was decided by a district court for the central district of New Jersey (D.C. N.J.) in 1987.

Federal court of appeals citations look like this: *Accuride International, Inc. v. Accuride Corp.*, 871 F.2d 1531 (9th Cir. 1989). This tells you to look in the second series of the *Federal Reporter* (F.2d.) in volume 871 at page 1531. It also tells you that the court was the Ninth Circuit Court of Appeals and that the decision was issued in 1989.

Trademark cases from both the district and appeals courts are also often published in the first and second series of the *U.S. Patent Quarterly* (U.S.P.Q.), which you will find cited in this way: 10 U.S.P.Q.2d 1589. For example, *Accuride* can also be found in the second series of the U.S.P.Q., volume 10, at page 1589. Most major law libraries carry the *Federal Reporter,* the *Federal Supplement,* and the *U.S. Patent Quarterly.*

Cases decided by the U.S. Supreme Court are located in three publications, any of which is fine to use: *United States Reports* (identified as U.S.); the *Supreme Court Reporter* (identified as S.Ct.); and the *Supreme Court Reports,* Lawyers Edition (identified as L.Ed.). Supreme Court case cites may refer to all three or to only one, for example, *Park 'N Fly, Inc. v. Dollar Park & Fly, Inc.*, 469 U.S. 189, 83 L.Ed.2d. 582, 105 S.Ct. 658, 224 U.S.P.Q. 327 (1985).

State cases are reported in such a wide variety of ways that we can't describe them all here. Instead, we suggest that if you find a cite that does not look like the above, and that has a state abbreviation in it, you may assume it is a state appellate court decision. Ask the librarian for help in finding those cites.

on anything you find in the law library, it usually makes sense to double check with a knowledgeable attorney. (Section C below.)

B. Finding Trademark Laws and Information on the Internet

The Internet offers convenient access to an enormous amount of trademark materials, including:

- the federal trademark database
- the federal trademark statutes and regulations
- informative articles by trademark experts
- the PTO's *Trademark Manual of Examining Procedure*
- the *Design Search Code Manual*
- the *Acceptable Identification of Goods and Services Manual*
- guides to various aspect of trademark practice
- recent changes in PTO rules and procedures, and
- much much more.

Here is a brief list of sites that will either have the information you are looking for or will provide you with links to other sites that do.

www.uspto.gov The U.S. Patent and Trademark Office is the place to go for recent policy and statutory changes and transcripts of hearings on various trademark law issues. This site also lets you do your own trademark search for free, search the *Trademark Manual of Examining Procedure* (the guide the PTO examiners use when processing trademark

applications and handling other proceedings), complete your trademark registration application online, and check the status of any trademark. This site also links to other useful trademark-related sites.

www.findlaw.com This search engine offers an excellent collection of trademark-related materials on the Web, including trademark statutes, regulations, classification manuals, and articles of general interest. Click the intellectual property link in the topics section on the Findlaw home page, and then click "trademark" in the subcategory section on the intellectual property page.

www.ggmark.com This site, maintained by a trademark lawyer, provides basic national and international trademark information and a fine collection of links to other trademark resources.

http://trademark.blog.us The Trademark Blog, written by Martin Schwimmer, has become the leading site on the Web for current news about trademark law.

C. Finding a Lawyer

If you become involved in a trademark dispute, are having trouble getting your mark registered, or simply want some advice from a professional about a trademark issue, you will want to consult a trademark lawyer—but not just any trademark lawyer. Start by understanding that if you have read substantial portions of this book, you already know more about trademarks than most lawyers. This puts you in the difficult position of finding someone who knows more than you do and yet is willing to acknowledge the considerable competence that you've now gained in this area. You want a trademark lawyer who:

- knows the trademark field well
- is willing to acknowledge your competence gained from using this book, and
- is honest and conscientious.

Fortunately, by arming yourself with the information in this book, you have a good shot at finding a lawyer with all of these characteristics.

1. Find a Lawyer Who Knows the Trademark Field Well

Trademark lawyers usually advertise in the Yellow Pages and legal journals as intellectual property specialists, able to handle patent, trademark, copyright, and trade-secret cases. Because each of these fields is increasingly becoming a complicated legal world all to itself, in fact the ads lie—most intellectual property law specialists tend to be very knowledgeable in one or two of these areas, and only passingly familiar with the others.

For instance, it is common for patent lawyers to be far more knowledgeable in that area than in trademark law, even though both patents and trademarks involve practice before the PTO. Similarly, some lawyers specialize in trademarks and do little or no patent work.

The point of knowing this, of course, is that you want a trademark lawyer who really knows trademarks, not someone willing to brush up on trademarks at your expense.

When you call on the intellectual property specialist, ask these questions:

- What percentage of your practice involves trademark work?
- Are you a member of the International Trademark Association or the American Intellectual Property Law Association?

The first inquiry will help you find a true specialist in this area, while the second will help you find a lawyer who is curious enough about the subject of trademarks to join these associations of trademark specialists.

2. Find a Lawyer Who Is Willing to Acknowledge Your Competence

In addition to satisfying yourself that a lawyer is competent, you want to find someone who is reasonably congenial to work with. You don't need us to tell you that lawyers tend to look down on laypersons when it comes to the lawyer's area of expertise. Which means that many of the lawyers you initially encounter are likely to be turned off by your expertise. Fortunately, however, some lawyers are willing to respect their clients' knowledge and know how to work with it rather than against it. It is this type of lawyer you should be looking for.

You can find a lawyer who isn't intimidated by a competent client if you:

- explain over the phone that you have been using this book
- articulate exactly what you want the lawyer to do, and
- carefully monitor the lawyer's reaction.

If the lawyer scoffs at the idea of a self-help law book or you get a whiff of, "Don't tell me what you need, I'm the lawyer," go on to the next name on the list. If the response appears to respect your self-help efforts and admits the possibility that you are a competent human being, make an appointment.

3. Find a Lawyer Who Is Honest and Conscientious

If you are just seeking advice, then you needn't worry much about the lawyer's character. But if you are looking for someone to represent you, the human being you are dealing with becomes paramount. The best analytical trademark lawyer in the world can bring you to financial and emotional ruin, if he or she lacks the ability to understand your needs and to represent you with your best interests in mind.

a. Honesty
While some would argue that there's no such thing as an honest lawyer, we maintain that it is possible to have honest dealings with your lawyer. Start by clearly understanding that the lawyer's financial interest—to run up lots of billable hours over a period of time—is the opposite of yours—which is to arrive at a fast, cost-efficient, and reasonably livable resolution of the problem.

Once you understand this you'll also understand that it is essential that you and your lawyer agree up front about what the lawyer is to do and the amount of control you are to have over the lawyer's activities. Rule one is that the lawyer is working for you, not vice versa; and rule two is that you have a right to understand the reason for every minute of the lawyer's time that will be billed to you.

b. Conscientiousness
Your lawyer must be willing to agree to have you regularly consulted on all phases of the case and to promptly return your phone calls. Although nothing leads to a ruinous relationship faster than bad communication, too few lawyers keep their clients well posted. Lawyers faced with complaints about their lousy client-contact habits often reply that many clients call or expect too much. But because the client is paying for the lawyer's time, this seems like a pretty weak excuse. Our experience tells us that the usual reason lawyers don't return phone calls is that they have neglected some facet of the case and simply don't want to face the client.

Your lawyer must also be willing to follow through on your case to its completion. This one is tricky to monitor, because it involves predicting the future. However, as long as good communication is established at the outset, there's an improved chance that your lawyer will give you good service.

4. Find a Lawyer Who Is Open to Dispute Resolution Alternatives

In recent years many lawyers have discovered that there often are better ways to resolve disputes than the old "haul 'em into court" technique. The two most common of these alternative approaches are arbitration and mediation. When you search for an attorney, make sure that the attorney is fully up to speed on these private, fast, inexpensive, and often successful techniques and is willing to help you explore them as a potential way to solve your problem. Arbitration and mediation are discussed in Chapter 11, If Someone Infringes Your Mark, Section D, Step 6.

5. Internet Resources

A number of websites offer listings for domestic and international trademark lawyers, including:

- the International Trademark Association (www.inta.org)
- the American Association of Intellectual Property Attorneys (www.aipla.org), and
- *Marksonline* (www.marksonline.com). ■

Appendix A

Class Descriptions

International Schedule of Classes of Goods and Services

Goods

1. Chemical products used in industry, science, photography, agriculture, horticulture, forestry; artificial and synthetic resins; plastics in the form of powders, liquids or pastes, for industrial use; manures (natural and artificial); fire extinguishing compositions; tempering substances and chemical preparations for soldering; chemical substances for preserving foodstuffs; tanning substances; adhesive substances used in industry.

2. Paints, varnishes, lacquers; preservatives against rust and against deterioration of wood; colouring matters, dyestuffs; mordants; natural resins; metals in foil and powder form for painters and decorators.

3. Bleaching preparations and other substances for laundry use; cleaning, polishing, scouring and abrasive preparations; soaps; perfumery, essential oils, cosmetics, hair lotions; dentifrices.

4. Industrial oils and greases (other than oils and fats and essential oils); lubricants; dust laying and absorbing compositions; fuels (including motor spirit) and illuminants; candles, tapers, night lights and wicks.

5. Pharmaceutical, veterinary, and sanitary substances; infants' and invalids' foods; plasters, material for bandaging; material for stopping teeth, dental wax, disinfectants; preparations for killing weeds and destroying vermin.

6. Unwrought and partly wrought common metals and their alloys; anchors, anvils, bells, rolled and cast building materials; rails and other metallic materials for railway tracks; chains (except driving chains for vehicles); cables and wires (nonelectric); locksmiths' work; metallic pipes and tubes; safes and cash boxes; steel balls; horseshoes; nails and screws; other goods in nonprecious metal not included in other classes; ores.

7. Machines and machine tools; motors (except for land vehicles); machine couplings and belting (except for land vehicles); large size agricultural implements; incubators.

8. Hand tools and instruments; cutlery, forks and spoons; side arms.

9. Scientific, nautical, surveying and electrical apparatus and instruments (including wireless), photographic, cinematographic, optical, weighing, measuring, signalling, checking (supervision), life-saving and teaching apparatus and instruments; coin or counterfreed apparatus; talking machines; cash registers; calculating machines; fire extinguishing apparatus.

10. Surgical, medical, dental, and veterinary instruments and apparatus (including artificial limbs, eyes and teeth).

11. Installations for lighting, heating, steam generating, cooking, refrigerating, drying, ventilating, water supply, and sanitary purposes.

12. Vehicles; apparatus for locomotion by land, air or water.

13. Firearms; ammunition and projectiles; explosive substances; fireworks.

14. Precious metals and their alloys and goods in precious metals or coated therewith (except cutlery forks and spoons); jewelry, precious stones, horological and other chronometric instruments.

15. Musical instruments (other than talking machines and wireless apparatus).

16. Paper and paper articles, cardboard and cardboard articles; printed matter, newspaper and periodicals, books; bookbinding material; photographs; stationery, adhesive materials (stationery): artists' materials; paint brushes; typewriters and office requisites (other than furniture); instructional and teaching material (other than apparatus); playing cards; printers' type and cliches (stereotype).

17. Gutta percha, india rubber, balata and substitutes, articles made from these substances and not included in other classes; plastics in the form of sheets, blocks and rods, being for use in manufacture; materials for packing, stopping or insulating; asbestos, mica and their products; hose pipes (nonmetallic).

18. Leather and imitations of leather, and articles made from these materials and not included in other classes; skins, hides; trunks and travelling bags; umbrellas, parasols and walking sticks; whips, harness and saddlery.

19. Building materials, natural and artificial stone, cement, lime, mortar, plaster and gravel; pipes or earthenware or cement; roadmaking materials; asphalt, pitch and bitumen; portable buildings; stone monuments; chimney pots.

20. Furniture, mirrors, picture frames; articles (not included in other classes) of wood, cork, reeds, cane, wicker, horn, bone, ivory, whalebone, shell, amber, mother-of-pearl, meerschaum, celluloid, substitutes for all these materials, or of plastics.

21. Small domestic utensils and containers (not of precious metals, or coated therewith); combs and sponges; brushes (other than paint brushes); brushmaking materials; instruments and material for cleaning purposes, steel wool; unworked or semi-worked glass (excluding glass used in building); glassware, porcelain and earthenware, not included in other classes.

22. Ropes, string, nets, tents, awnings, tarpaulins, sails, sacks; padding and stuffing materials (hair, kapok, feathers, seaweed, etc.); raw fibrous textile materials.

23. Yarns, threads.

24. Tissues (piece goods); bed and table covers; textile articles not included in other classes.

25. Clothing, including boots, shoes and slippers.

26. Lace and embroidery, ribbons and braid; buttons, press buttons, hooks and eyes, pins and needles; artificial flowers.

27. Carpets, rugs, mats and matting; linoleums and other materials for covering existing floors; wall hangings (nontextile).

28. Games and playthings; gymnastic and sporting articles (except clothing); ornaments and decorations for Christmas trees.

29. Meats, fish, poultry and game; meat extracts; preserved, dried and cooked fruits and vegetables; jellies, jams; eggs, milk and other dairy products; edible oils and fats; preserves, pickles.

30. Coffee, tea, cocoa, sugar, rice, tapioca, sago, coffee substitutes; flour, and preparations made from cereals; bread, biscuits, cakes, pastry and confectionery, ices; honey, treacle; yeast, baking powder; salt, mustard, pepper, vinegar, sauces, spices; ice.

31. Agricultural, horticultural and forestry products and grains not included in other classes; living animals; fresh fruits and vegetables; seeds; live plants and flowers; foodstuffs for animals, malt.

32. Beer, ale and porter; mineral and aerated waters and other nonalcoholic drinks; syrups and other preparations for making beverages.

33. Wines, spirits and liqueurs.

34. Tobacco, raw or manufactured; smokers' articles; machines.

Services

35. Advertising and business.

36. Insurance and financial.

37. Construction and repair.

38. Communication.

39. Transportation and storage.

40. Material treatment.

41. Education and entertainment.

42. Miscellaneous.

Descriptions of Goods and Services (From USTA—International Classes)

Goods

Class 1: Chemicals

Chemicals used in industry, science and photography, as well as in agriculture, horticulture and forestry; unprocessed artificial resins, unprocessed plastics; manures; fire extinguishing compositions; tempering and soldering preparations; chemical substances for preserving foodstuffs; tanning substances; adhesives used in industry.

This class includes mainly chemical products used in industry, science and agriculture, including those which go to the making of products belonging to other classes.

Includes, in particular: compost; salt for preserving other than for foodstuffs.

Does not include, in particular: raw natural resins (Cl. 2); chemical products for use in medical science (Cl. 5); fungicides, herbicides and preparations for destroying vermin (Cl. 5); adhesives for stationery or household purposes (Cl. 16); salt for preserving foodstuffs (Cl. 30); straw mulch (Cl. 31).

Class 2: Paints

Paints, varnishes, lacquers; preservatives against rust and against deterioration of wood; colourants; mordants; raw natural resins;

metals in foil and powder form for painters, decorators, printers and artists.

This class includes mainly paints, colourants and preparations used for the protection against corrosion.

Includes, in particular: paints, varnishes and lacquers for industry, handicrafts and arts; dyestuffs for clothing; colourants for foodstuffs and beverages.

Does not include, in particular: unprocessed artificial resins (Cl. 1); laundry blueing (Cl. 3); cosmetic dyes (Cl. 3); mordants for seed (Cl. 5); paint boxes (articles for use in school) (Cl. 16); insulating paints and varnishes (Cl. 17).

Class 3: Cosmetics and cleaning preparations

Bleaching preparations and other substances for laundry use; cleaning, polishing, scouring and abrasive preparations; soaps; perfumery, essential oils, cosmetics, hair lotions; dentifrices.

This class includes mainly cleaning preparations and toilet preparations.

Includes, in particular: deodorants for personal use; sanitary preparations being toiletries.

Does not include, in particular: chemical chimney cleaners (Cl. 1); degreasing preparations for use in manufacturing processes (Cl. 1); deodorants other than for personal use (Cl. 5); sharpening stones and grindstones (handtools) (Cl. 8).

Class 4: Lubricants and fuels

Industrial oils and greases; lubricants; dust absorbing, wetting and binding compositions; fuels (including motor spirit) and illuminants; candles, wicks.

This class includes mainly industrial oils and greases, fuels and illuminants.

Does not include, in particular: certain special industrial oils and greases (consult the Alphabetical List of Goods).

Class 5: Pharmaceuticals

Pharmaceutical, veterinary and sanitary preparations; dietetic substances adapted for medical use, food for babies; plasters, materials for dressings; material for stopping teeth, dental wax; disinfectants; preparations for destroying vermin; fungicides, herbicides.

This class includes mainly pharmaceuticals and other preparations for medical purposes.

Includes, in particular: sanitary preparations for medical purposes and for personal hygiene; deodorants other than for personal use; cigarettes without tobacco, for medical purposes.

Does not include, in particular: sanitary preparations being toiletries (Cl. 3); deodorants for personal use (Cl. 3); supportive bandages (Cl. 10).

Class 6: Metal goods

Common metals and their alloys; metal building materials; transportable buildings of metal; materials of metal for railway tracks; nonelectric cables and wires of common metal; ironmongery, small items of metal hardware; pipes and tubes of metal; safes; goods of common metal not included in other classes; ores.

This class includes mainly unwrought and partly wrought common metals as well as simple products made of them.

Does not include, in particular: bauxite (Cl. 1); mercury, antimony, alkaline and alkaline-earth metals (Cl. 1); metals in foil and powder form for painters, decorators, printers and artists (Cl. 2).

Class 7: Machinery

Machines and machine tools; motors and engines (except for land vehicles); machine coupling and transmission components (except for land vehicles); agricultural implements other than hand-operated; incubators for eggs.

This class includes mainly machines, machine tools, motors and engines.

Includes, in particular: parts of motors and engines (of all kinds); electric cleaning machines and apparatus.

Does not include, in particular: certain special machines and machine tools (consult the Alphabetical List of Goods); hand tools and implements, hand operated (Cl. 8); motors and engines for land vehicles (Cl. 12).

Class 8: Hand tools

Hand tools and implements (hand operated); cutlery; side arms; razors.

This class includes mainly hand operated implements used as tools in the respective professions.

Includes, in particular: cutlery of precious metals; electric razors and clippers (hand instruments).

Does not include, in particular: certain special instruments (consult the Alphabetical List of Goods); machine tools and implements driven by a motor (Cl. 7); surgical cutlery (Cl. 10); paperknives (Cl. 16); fencing weapons (Cl. 28).

Class 9: Electrical and scientific apparatus

Scientific, nautical, surveying, electric, photographic, cinematographic, optical, weighing, measuring, signalling, checking (supervision), lifesaving and teaching apparatus and instruments; apparatus for recording, transmission or reproduction of sound or images; magnetic data carriers, recording discs; automatic vending machines and mechanisms for coin operated apparatus; cash registers, calculating machines, data processing equipment and computers; fire extinguishing apparatus.

Includes, in particular: apparatus and instruments for scientific research in laboratories; apparatus and instruments for controlling ships, such as apparatus and instruments for measuring and for transmitting orders; the following electrical apparatus and instruments: certain electrothermic tools and apparatus, such as electric soldering irons, electric flat irons which, if they were not electric, would belong to Class 8; apparatus and devices which, if not electrical, would be listed in various classes, i.e., electrically heated clothing, cigar-lighters for automobiles; protractors; punched card office machines; amusement apparatus adapted for use with television receivers only.

Does not include, in particular: the following electrical apparatus and instruments: electromechanical apparatus for the kitchen (grinders and mixers for foodstuffs, fruit-presses, electrical coffee mills, etc.), and certain other apparatus and instruments driven by an electrical motor, all coming under Class 7; electric razors and clippers (hand instruments) (Cl. 8); electric toothbrushes and combs (Cl. 21); electrical apparatus for space heating or for the heating of liquids, for cooking, ventilating, etc. (Cl. 11); clocks and watches and other chronometric instruments (Cl. 14); control clocks (Cl. 14).

Class 10: Medical apparatus

Surgical, medical, dental and veterinary apparatus and instruments, artificial limbs, eyes and teeth; orthopedic articles; suture materials.

This class includes mainly medical apparatus, instruments and articles.

Includes, in particular: special furniture for medical use; hygienic rubber articles (consult the Alphabetical List of Goods); supportive bandages.

Class 11: Environmental control apparatus

Apparatus for lighting, heating, steam generating, cooking, refrigerating, drying, ventilating, water supply and sanitary purposes.

Includes, in particular: air conditioning apparatus; bedwarmers, hot water bottles, warming pans, electric or nonelectric; electrically heated cushions (pads) and blankets, not for medical purposes; electric kettles; electric cooking utensils.

Does not include, in particular: steam producing apparatus (parts of machines) (Cl. 7); electrically heated clothing (Cl. 9).

Class 12: Vehicles

Vehicles; apparatus for locomotion by land, air or water.

Includes, in particular: motors and engines for land vehicles; couplings and transmission components for land vehicles; air cushion vehicles.

Does not include, in particular: certain parts of vehicles (consult the Alphabetical List of Goods); railway material of metal (Cl. 6); motors, engines, couplings and transmission components other than for land vehicles (Cl. 7); parts of motors and engines (of all kinds) (Cl. 7).

Class 13: Firearms

Firearms; ammunition and projectiles; explosives; fireworks.

This class includes mainly firearms and pyrotechnical products.

Does not include, in particular: matches (Cl. 34).

Class 14: Jewelry

Precious metals and their alloys and goods in precious metals or coated therewith, not included in other classes; jewelry, precious stones; horological and chronometric instruments.

This class includes mainly precious metals, goods in precious metals and, in general, jewelry, clocks and watches.

Includes, in particular: jewelry (i.e. imitation jewelry and jewelry of precious metal and stones); cuff links, tie pins.

Does not include, in particular: certain goods in precious metals (classified according to their function or purpose), for example: metals in foil and powder form for painters, decorators, printers and artists (Cl. 2); amalgam of gold for dentists (Cl. 5); cutlery (Cl. 8); electric contacts (Cl. 9); pen nibs of gold (Cl. 16); objects of art not in precious metals (classified according to the material of which they consist).

Class 15: Musical instruments

Musical instruments.

Includes, in particular: mechanical pianos and their accessories; musical boxes; electrical and electronical musical instruments.

Does not include, in particular: apparatus for the recording, transmission, amplification and reproduction of sound (Cl. 9).

Class 16: Paper goods and printed matter

Paper, cardboard and goods made from these materials, not included in other classes; printed matter; bookbinding material; photographs; stationery; adhesives for stationery or household purposes; artists' materials; paint brushes; typewriters and office requisites (except furniture); instructional and teaching material (except apparatus); plastic materials for packaging (not included in other classes); playing cards; printers' type; printing blocks.

This class includes mainly paper, goods made from that material and office requisites.

Includes, in particular: paper knives; duplicators; plastic sheets, sacks and bags for wrapping and packaging.

Does not include, in particular: certain goods made of paper and cardboard (consult the Alphabetical List of Goods); colours (Cl. 2); hand tools for artists (for example: spatulas, sculptors' chisels) (Cl. 8).

Class 17: Rubber goods

Rubber, gutta-percha, gum, asbestos, mica and goods made from these materials and not included in other classes; plastics in extruded form for use in manufacture; packing, stopping and insulating materials; flexible pipes, not of metal.

This class includes mainly electrical, thermal and acoustic insulating materials and plastics, being for use in manufacture in the form of sheets, blocks and rods.

Includes, in particular: rubber material for recapping tyres; padding and stuffing materials of rubber or plastics; floating anti-pollution barriers.

Class 18: Leather goods

Leather and imitations of leather, and goods made of these materials and not included in other classes; animal skins, hides; trunks and travelling bags; umbrellas, parasols and walking sticks; whips, harness and saddlery.

This class includes mainly leather, leather imitations, travel goods not included in other classes and saddlery.

Does not include, in particular: clothing, footwear, headgear (consult the Alphabetical List of Goods).

Class 19: Nonmetallic building materials

Building materials (nonmetallic); nonmetallic rigid pipes for building; asphalt, pitch and bitumen; nonmetallic transportable buildings; monuments, not of metal.

This class includes mainly nonmetallic building materials.

Includes, in particular: semi-worked woods (for example: beams, planks, panels); veneers; building glass (for example: floor slabs, glass tiles); glass granules for marking out roads; letter boxes of masonry.

Does not include, in particular: cement preservatives and cement-waterproofing preparations (Cl. 1); fireproofing preparations (Cl. 1).

Class 20: Furniture and articles not otherwise classified

Furniture, mirrors, picture frames; goods (not included in other classes) of wood, cork, reed, cane, wicker, horn, bone, ivory, whalebone, shell, amber, mother-of-pearl, meerschaum and substitutes for all these materials, or of plastics.

This class includes mainly furniture and its parts and plastic goods, not included in other classes.

Includes, in particular: metal furniture and furniture for camping; bedding (for example: mattresses, spring mattresses, pillows); looking glasses and furnishing or toilet mirrors; registration number plates not of metal; letter boxes not of metal or masonry.

Does not include, in particular: certain special types of mirrors, classified according to their function or purpose (consult the Alphabetical List of Goods); special furniture for laboratories (Cl. 9); special furniture for medical use (Cl. 10); bedding linen (Cl. 24); eiderdowns (Cl. 24).

Class 21: Housewares and glass

Household or kitchen utensils and containers (not of precious metal or coated therewith); combs and sponges; brushes (except paint brushes); brush-making materials; articles for cleaning purposes; steelwool; unworked or semi-worked glass (except glass used in building); glassware, porcelain and earthenware not included in other classes.

This class includes mainly small, hand-operated, utensils and apparatus for household and kitchen use as well as toilet utensils, glassware and articles in porcelain.

Includes, in particular: utensils and containers for household and kitchen use, for example: kitchen utensils, pails, and pans of iron, aluminum, plastics and other materials, small hand-operated apparatus for mincing, grinding, pressing, etc.; candle extinguishers not of precious metal; electric combs; electric toothbrushes; dish stands and decanter stands.

Does not include, in particular: certain goods made of glass, porcelain and earthenware (consult the Alphabetical List of Goods); cleaning preparations, soaps, etc. (Cl. 3); small apparatus for mincing, grinding, pressing, etc., driven by electricity (Cl. 7); razors and shaving apparatus, clippers (hand instruments), metal implements and utensils for manicure and pedicure (Cl. 8); cooking utensils, electric (Cl. 11); toilet mirrors (Cl. 20).

Class 22: Cordage and fibers

Ropes, string, nets, tents, awnings, tarpaulins, sails, sacks and bags (not included in other classes); padding and stuffing materials (except of rubber or plastics); raw fibrous textile materials.

This class includes mainly rope and sail manufacture products, padding and stuffing materials and raw fibrous textile materials.

Includes, in particular: cords and twines in natural or artificial textile fibres, paper or plastics.

Does not include, in particular: certain nets, sacs and bags (consult the Alphabetical List of Goods); strings for musical instruments (Cl. 15).

Class 23: Yarns and threads

Yarns and threads, for textile use.

Class 24: Fabrics

Textiles and textile goods, not included in other classes; bed and table covers.

This class includes mainly textiles (piece goods) and textile covers for household use.

Includes, in particular: bedding linen of paper.

Does not include, in particular: certain special textiles (consult the Alphabetical List of Goods); electrically heated blankets (Cl. 10); table linen of paper (Cl. 16); horse blankets (Cl. 18).

Class 25: Clothing

Clothing, footwear, headgear.

Does not include, in particular: certain clothing and footwear for special use (consult the Alphabetical List of Goods).

Class 26: Fancy goods

Lace and embroidery, ribbons and braid; buttons, hooks and eyes, pins and needles; artificial flowers.

This class includes mainly dressmakers' articles.

Includes, in particular: slide fasteners.

Does not include, in particular: certain special types of hooks (consult the Alphabetical List of Goods); certain special types of needles (consult the Alphabetical List of Goods); yarns and threads for textile use (Cl. 23).

Class 27: Floor coverings

Carpets, rugs, mats and matting, linoleum and other materials for covering existing floors; wall hangings (nontextile).

This class includes mainly products intended to be added as furnishings to previously constructed floors and walls.

Class 28: Toys and sporting goods

Games and playthings; gymnastic and sporting articles not included in other classes; decorations for Christmas trees.

Includes, in particular: fishing tackle; equipment for various sports and games.

Does not include, in particular: Christmas tree candles (Cl. 4); diving equipment (Cl. 9); amusement apparatus adapted for use with television receivers only (Cl. 9); electrical lamps (garlands) for Christmas trees (Cl. 11); playing cards (Cl. 16); fishing nets (Cl. 22); clothing for gymnastics and sports (Cl. 25); confectionery and chocolate decorations for Christmas trees (Cl. 30).

Class 29: Meats and processed foods

Meat, fish, poultry and game; meat extracts; preserved, dried and cooked fruits and vegetables; jellies, jams, fruit sauces; eggs, milk and milk products; edible oils and fats.

This class includes mainly foodstuffs of animal origin as well as vegetables and other horticultural comestible products which are prepared for consumption or conservation.

Includes, in particular: milk beverages (milk predominating).

Does not include, in particular: certain foodstuffs of plant origin (consult the Alphabetical List of Goods); baby food (Cl. 5); dietetic substances adapted for medical use (Cl. 5); salad dressings (Cl. 30); fertilised eggs for hatching (Cl. 31); foodstuffs for animals (Cl. 31); living animals (Cl. 31).

Class 30: Staple foods

Coffee, tea, cocoa, sugar, rice, tapioca, sago, artificial coffee; flour and preparations made from cereals, bread, pastry and confectionery, ices; honey, treacle; yeast, baking-powder; salt, mustard; vinegar, sauces (condiments); spices; ice.

This class includes mainly foodstuffs of plant origin prepared for consumption or conservation as well as auxiliaries intended for the improvement of the flavour of food.

Includes, in particular: beverages with coffee, cocoa or chocolate base; cereals prepared for human consumption (for example: oat flakes and those made of other cereals).

Does not include, in particular: certain foodstuffs of plant origin (consult the Alphabetical List of Goods); salt for preserving other than for foodstuffs (Cl. 1); medicinal teas and dietetic substances adapted for medical use (Cl. 5); baby food (Cl. 5); raw cereals (Cl. 31); foodstuffs for animals (Cl. 31).

Class 31: Natural agricultural products

Agricultural, horticultural and forestry products and grains not included in other classes; living animals; fresh fruits and vegetables; seeds, natural plants and flowers; foodstuffs for animals, malt.

This class includes mainly land products not having been subjected to any form of preparation for consumption, living animals and plants as well as foodstuffs for animals.

Includes, in particular: raw woods; raw cereals; fertilized eggs for hatching; mollusca and crustacea (live).

Does not include, in particular: cultures of micro-organisms and leeches for medical purposes (Cl. 5); semi-worked woods (Cl. 19); artificial fishing bait (Cl. 28); rice (Cl. 30); tobacco (Cl. 34).

Class 32: Light beverages

Beers; mineral and aerated waters and other nonalcoholic drinks; fruit drinks and fruit juices; syrups and other preparations for making beverages.

This class includes mainly nonalcoholic beverages, as well as beer.

Includes, in particular: de-alcoholised drinks.

Does not include, in particular: beverages for medical purposes (Cl. 5); milk beverages (milk predominating) (Cl. 29); beverages with coffee, cocoa or chocolate base (Cl. 30).

Class 33: Wine and spirits

Alcoholic beverages (except beers).

Does not include, in particular: medicinal drinks (Cl. 5); de-alcoholised drinks (Cl. 32).

Class 34: Smokers' articles

Tobacco; smokers' articles; matches.

Includes, in particular: tobacco substitutes (not for medical purposes).

Does not include, in particular: cigarettes without tobacco, for medical purposes (Cl. 5); certain smokers' articles in precious metal (Cl. 14) (consult the Alphabetical List of Goods).

Services

Class 35: Advertising and business

Advertising; business management; business administration; office functions.

This class includes mainly services rendered by persons or organizations principally with the object of: help in the working or management of a commercial undertaking, or help in the management of the business affairs or commercial functions of an industrial or commercial enterprise, as well as services rendered by advertising establishments primarily undertaking communications to the public, declarations or announcements by all means of diffusion and concerning all kinds of goods or services.

Includes, in particular: services consisting of the registration, transcription, composition, compilation, or systematization of written communications and registrations, and also the exploitation or compilation of mathematical or statistical data; services of advertising agencies and services such as the distribution of prospectuses, directly or through the post, or the distribution of samples. This class may refer to advertising in connection with other services, such as those concerning bank loans or advertising by radio; the bringing together, for the benefit of others, of a variety of goods (excluding the transport thereof), enabling customers to conveniently view and purchase those goods.

Does not include, in particular: activity of an enterprise the primary function of which is the sale of goods, i.e., of a so-called commercial enterprise; services such as evaluations and reports of engineers which do not directly refer to the working or management of affairs in a commercial or industrial enterprise (consult the Alphabetical List of Services); professional consultations and the drawing up of plans not connected with the conduct of business (Cl. 42).

Class 36: Insurance and financial

Insurance; financial affairs; monetary affairs; real estate affairs.

This class includes mainly services rendered in financial and monetary affairs and services rendered in relation to insurance contracts of all kinds.

Includes, in particular: services relating to financial or monetary affairs comprise the following: services of all the banking establishments, or institutions connected with them such as exchange brokers or clearing services; services of credit institutions other than banks such as cooperative credit associations, individual financial companies, lenders, etc.; services of "investment trusts," of holding companies; services of brokers dealing in shares and property; services connected with monetary affairs vouched for by trustees; services rendered in connection with the issue of travellers' cheques and letters of credit; services of realty administrators of buildings, i.e., services of letting or valuation, or financing; services dealing with insurance such as services rendered by agents or brokers engaged in insurance, services rendered to insured, and insurance underwriting services.

Class 37: Building construction and repair

Building construction; repair; installation services.

This class includes mainly services rendered by contractors or subcontractors in the construction or making of permanent buildings, as well as services rendered by persons or organizations engaged in the restoration of objects to their original condition or in their preservation without altering their physical or chemical properties.

Includes, in particular: services relating to the construction of buildings, roads, bridges, dams or transmission lines and services or undertakings specializing in the field of construction such as those of painters, plumbers, heating installers or roofers; services auxiliary to construction services like inspections of construction plans; services of shipbuilding; services consisting of hiring of tools or building materials; repair services, i.e., services which undertake to put any object into good condition after wear, damage, deterioration or partial destruction (restoration of an existing building or another object that has become imperfect and is to be restored to its original condition); various repair services such as those in the fields of electricity, furniture, instruments, tools, etc.; services of maintenance for preserving an object in its original condition without changing any of its properties (for the difference between this class and Class 40 see the explanatory note of Class 40).

Does not include, in particular: services consisting of storage of goods such as clothes or vehicles (Cl. 39); services connected with dyeing of cloth or clothes (Cl. 40).

Class 38: Telecommunications

This class includes mainly services allowing at least one person to communicate with another by a sensory means. Such services include those which: allow a person to talk to another, transmit messages from one person to another, and place a person in oral or visual communication with another (radio and television).

Includes, in particular: services which consist essentially of the diffusion of radio or television programmes.

Does not include, in particular: radio advertising services (Cl. 35).

Class 39: Transportation and storage

Transport; packaging and storage of goods; travel arrangement.

This class includes mainly services rendered in transporting people or goods from one place to another (by rail, road, water, air or pipeline) and services necessarily connected with such transport, as well as services relating to the storing of goods in a warehouse or other building for their preservation or guarding.

Includes, in particular: services rendered by companies exploiting stations, bridges, railroad ferries, etc., used by the transporter; services connected with the hiring of transport vehicles; services connected with maritime tugs, unloading, the functioning of ports and docks and the salvaging of wrecked ships and their cargoes; services connected with the functioning of airports; services connected with the packaging and parcelling of goods before dispatch; services consisting of information about journeys or the transport of goods by brokers and tourist agencies, information relating to tariffs, timetables and methods of transport; services relating to the inspection of vehicles or goods before transport.

Does not include, in particular: services relating to advertising transport undertakings such as the distribution of prospectuses or advertising on the radio (Cl. 35); services relating to the issuing of travellers' cheques or letters of credit by brokers or travel agents (Cl. 36); services relating to insurances (commercial, fire or life) during the transport of persons or goods (Cl. 36); services rendered by the maintenance and repair of vehicles, nor the maintenance or repair of objects connected with the transport of persons or goods (Cl. 37); services relating to reservation of rooms in a hotel by travel agents or brokers (Cl. 42).

Class 40: Treatment of materials

Treatment of materials.

This class includes mainly services not included in other classes, rendered by the mechanical or chemical processing or transformation of objects or inorganic or organic substances.

For the purposes of classification, the mark is considered a service mark only in cases where processing or transformation is effected for the account of another person. A mark is considered a trademark in all cases where the substance or object is marketed by the person who processed or transformed it.

Includes, in particular: services relating to transformation of an object or substance and any process involving a change in its essential properties (for example, dyeing a garment); consequently, a maintenance service, although usually in Class 37, is included in Class 40 if it entails such a change (for example, the chroming of motor vehicle bumpers); services

of material treatment which may be present during the production of any substance or object other than a building; for example, services which involve cutting, shaping, polishing by abrasion or metal coating.

Does not include, in particular: repair services (Cl. 37).

Class 41: Education and entertainment

Education; providing of training; entertainment; sporting and cultural activities.

This class contains mainly services rendered by persons or institutions in the development of the mental faculties of persons or animals, as well as services intended to entertain or to engage the attention.

Includes, in particular: services consisting of all forms of education of persons or training of animals; services having the basic aim of the entertainment, amusement or recreation of people.

Class 42: Miscellaneous

Providing of food and drink; temporary accommodation; medical, hygienic and beauty care; veterinary and agricultural services; legal services; scientific and industrial research; computer programming; services that cannot be placed in other classes.

This class contains all services which could not be placed in other classes.

Includes, in particular: services rendered in procuring lodgings, rooms and meals, by hotels, boarding houses, tourist camps, tourist houses, dude ranches, sanatoria, rest homes and convalescence homes; services rendered by establishments essentially engaged in procuring food or drink prepared for consumption; such services can be rendered by restaurants, self-service restaurants, canteens, etc.; personal services rendered by establishments to meet individual needs; such services may include social escorts, beauty salons, hairdressing salons, funeral establishments or crematoria; services rendered by persons, individually or collectively, as a member of an organization, requiring a high degree of mental activity and relating to theoretical or practical aspects of complex branches of human effort; the services rendered by these persons demand of them a deep and extensive university education or equivalent experience; such services rendered by representatives of professions such as engineers, chemists, physicists, etc., are included in this class; services of travel agents or brokers ensuring hotel accommodation for travellers; services of engineers engaged in valuing, estimates, research and reports; services (not included in other classes) rendered by associations to their own members.

Does not include, in particular: professional services giving direct aid in the operations or functions of a commercial undertaking (Cl. 35); services for travellers rendered by travel agencies (Cl. 39); performances of singers or dancers in orchestras or operas (Cl. 41).

1401.02(b) Short Titles for International Trademark Classes [R-1]

The United States Patent and Trademark Office associates the following word titles with the respective international trademark class numbers:

Goods

1. Chemicals
2. Paints
3. Cosmetics and cleaning preparations
4. Lubricants and fuels
5. Pharmaceuticals
6. Metal goods
7. Machinery
8. Hand tools
9. Electrical and scientific apparatus
10. Medical apparatus
11. Environmental control apparatus
12. Vehicles
13. Firearms
14. Jewelry
15. Musical instruments
16. Paper goods and printed matter
17. Rubber goods
18. Leather goods
19. Nonmetallic building materials
20. Furniture and articles not otherwise classified
21. Housewares and glass
22. Cordage and fibers
23. Yarns and threads
24. Fabrics
25. Clothing
26. Fancy goods
27. Floor coverings
28. Toys and sporting goods
29. Meats and processed foods
30. Staple foods
31. Natural agricultural products
32. Light beverages
33. Wines and spirits
34. Smokers' articles

Services

35. Advertising and business
36. Insurance and financial
37. Building construction and repair
38. Telecommunications
39. Transportation and storage
40. Treatment of materials
41. Education and entertainment
42. Miscellaneous

These short titles are not an official part of the international classification. Their purpose is to provide a means by which the general content of numbered international classes can be quickly identified. Therefore, the titles selected consist of short terms which generally correspond to the major content of each class but which are not intended to be more than merely suggestive of the content. Because of their nature, these titles will not necessarily disclose the classification of specific items. The titles are not designed to be used for classification but only as information to assist in the identification of numbered classes. For determining classification of particular goods and services and for full disclosure of the contents of international classes, it is necessary to refer to the Alphabetical List of Goods and Services and to the class headings of international classes and in the volume entitled *International Classification of Goods and Services for the Purposes of the Registration of Marks* (7th ed. 1997), published by the World Intellectual Property Organization (WIPO). The full names of international classes appear in § 6.1 of the Trademark Rules of Practice, 37 C.F.R. § 6.1.

The short titles are printed in the *Official Gazette* in association with the international class numbers under MARKS PUBLISHED FOR OPPOSITION, Sections 1 and 2; under TRADEMARK REGISTRATIONS ISSUED, PRINCIPAL REGISTER, Section 1; under TRADEMARK REGISTRATIONS ISSUED UNDER SECTION 1(d), Sections 1 and 2; and under SUPPLEMENTAL REGISTER, Sections 1 and 2.

The international trademark classification was adopted by the United States as its system of classification as of September 1, 1973. See TMEP § 1401.02 and 911 TMOG 210 (June 26, 1973).

The use of short titles was announced in a notice at 924 TMOG 155 (July 16, 1974).

1401.03 Classification Marked on Copies in Trademark Search Library

As of September 1, 1973, all published marks, registrations and renewals are assigned not only an international class number but also a class number according to prior United States classification.

While the international classification is the official classification system of the United States as of September 1, 1973, placing a prior United States class number, as well as an international class number, on copies of registrations which are placed in the Trademark Search Library allows searching to continue to be conducted on the basis of the prior United States classification. Registration copies placed in the Search Library prior to September 1, 1973, bear prior United States class numbers, so that placing prior United States class numbers on registration copies on and after September 1, 1973, provides continuity in the identification of classes on copies of registrations. ■

Glossary of Terms

abandonment loss of trademark rights resulting from nonuse of mark and demonstrated by sufficient evidence that the owner intends to discontinue use of the mark; may also occur when mark has lost its distinctiveness, through owner's misuse of trademark rights or as a result of naked license.

Allegation of Use a PTO form that combines the Statement of Use and Amendment to Allege Use.

Amendment to Allege Use an amendment to an intent-to-use application indicating use of a mark in commerce; it can only be filed before the PTO approves the mark for publication (or if there is a rejection, within six months of the response period). An applicant would complete the Allegation of Use form when filing an Amendment to Allege Use.

answer a written response to a court complaint in which the defendant admits or denies the allegations and provides a list of defenses.

arbitrary mark a word or group of words that has a dictionary meaning that does not pertain to the goods or services with which it is associated.

assignment a permanent transfer of trademark rights and goodwill.

blurring a form of dilution in which a famous mark loses some of its distinctiveness due to the use of a similar mark.

cancellation proceeding an action brought before the Trademark Trial and Appeal Board to cancel a federal registration of a mark; must be based upon one of the statutory grounds provided in the Lanham Act, and the party bringing the action must prove that it would be damaged.

certification mark a mark that indicates that third-party goods and services meet certain standards such as regional origin, material, mode of manufacture, quality, accuracy, or that the work or labor was performed by a member of a certain organization.

civil cover sheet a form required at the time of filing of the complaint for use by the court in maintaining certain statistical records.

collateral estoppel a defense to infringement; a senior user is required to abide by factual or legal determinations made in a previous lawsuit.

collective mark used by members of a cooperative, an association, or other collective group or organization to indicate membership or to indicate the source of the organization's products or services.

commerce for purposes of protection of U.S. trademarks, any trade or business lawfully regulated by the United States.

common law a system of legal rules derived from the precedents and principles established by court decisions.

concurrent use a legal determination that more than one person is entitled to use a similar mark.

confidentiality agreement (also known as non-disclosure agreement or disclosure agreement) a contract that restricts or prohibits the disclosure of confidential information.

counterfeiting the act of making or selling look-alike goods or services bearing fake trademarks

cybersquatter a person who registers a well-known trademark as a domain name hoping to later profit by selling the domain name to the trademark owner.

declaratory relief request that the court sort out the rights and legal obligations of the parties in the midst of an actual controversy.

defamation of business false statements that injure a business's reputation. Defamation affects the manner in which the public perceives the company's trademarked products.

descriptive mark A name or term that merely describes a product or service (or its nature, quality, characteristics, ingredients, or origin) and is considered "weak."

design patent legal protection granted for a new, original, and ornamental design for an article of manufacture; it protects only the aesthetic appearance of an article, not its structure or utilitarian features.

dilution a form of trademark injury that occurs when a famous mark's reputation is blurred or tarnished by the commercial use of a similar mark. Unlike traditional trademark infringement, there is no requirement of consumer confusion, and the parties do not have to be competitors selling similar goods or services.

disclaimer a statement that a trademark owner asserts no exclusive right in a specific portion of a mark, apart from its use within the mark.

disparagement false statements that interfere with a company's business relations and negatively affect a company's ability to do business.

distinctive mark a mark that is either immediately distinguishable, such as an arbitrary, fanciful, suggestive mark, or a descriptive mark that has acquired secondary meaning.

diversity the right to file a lawsuit based upon non-federal claims in federal court; parties must be from different states and the matter in controversy over $50,000.

domain name an identifier of a website location consisting of two parts; a generic top-level domain (such as .com, or .org) and a second level that is the name of the business or organization, (such as amazon or eBay).

drawing a substantially exact representation of the mark as used or (in the case of intent-to-use applications) as intended to be used. A drawing is required for all federal trademark applications and for many state trademark applications.

estoppel a defense to infringement in which the junior user prevents the senior user from contradicting behavior upon which the junior user has justifiably relied. To assert an estoppel defense successfully the senior user must know the facts of the junior user's conduct, and the junior user must have a justifiable belief that the infringing conduct is permitted.

fair use a company may defend its use of a trademarked term (owned by someone else) when the term is used to describe products or services. For example, an ad for a dishwashing machine may refer to the "joy of dishwashing" without infringing the trademark "Joy" as used for dishwashing soap. In 2005, the U.S. Supreme Court ruled that the fair use defense can be made even when the use results in consumer confusion.

fanciful marks an invented word that is created solely to be used as a trademark or service mark, for example, *Exxon* or *Kodak*. These fanciful coined marks are immediately distinctive and are considered to be the strongest of all marks.

franchise agreement a contract in which a trademark owner (the "franchiser") permits another business (the "franchisee") to operate under the trademark and offer trademarked (or "branded") products and services, for example a *Ford* dealership, a *Baskin & Robbins* ice cream store, or an *H&R Block* tax preparation business.

functionality the usability of a product feature or design; functional features or design will not be protected under trademark law.

generic term a term that describes an entire group or class of goods.

genericide the process by which trademark rights are abandoned because consumers have begun to think of the trademark as the descriptive name for the goods; results from a judicial determination or inter partes proceeding at the Patent and Trademark Office.

geographically descriptive (weak) a geographic term describes the origin, location, or source of the product or service, for example, *First National Bank of Bloomington* for a bank located in Bloomington, Indiana.

geographically misdescriptive (unprotectible) a geographic term that misleads consumers into believing that the product originates from a region when it does not. For example, *Danish Maid Cultured Products* is geographically misdescriptive of products that were not from Denmark.

goodwill the tendency or likelihood of a consumer to repurchase goods or services based upon the name or source of the goods or services.

gray market goods when goods are manufactured abroad with the authorization of the trademark owner but are imported into the United States without authorization of the trademark owner.

house mark a word or group of words that functions as the source for various products or services from one company; it is often used in conjunction with other trademarks.

incontestable a trademark that is immune from challenge except for certain grounds specified in Section 33(b) of the Lanham Act; conclusive evidence of the registrant's exclusive right to use the registered mark in commerce in connection with the specified goods or services.

infringement occurs when the junior user's goods or services create a likelihood of confusion with the senior user's goods or services.

inherently distinctive a mark that is immediately distinguishable, such as an arbitrary, fanciful, suggestive mark. Marks that are not immediately distinguishable but describe some quality or aspect of the goods or services may acquire distinctiveness through sales and advertising (see *secondary meaning*).

injunction a court order directing the defendant to stop certain activities.

intellectual property any product of the human mind that is protectible under law.

intent to use an application for federal trademark registration based upon the trademark owner's bona fide intention to use the mark in commerce.

inter partes a formal administrative hearing governed by federal rules of civil procedure and evidence.

interference proceeding a mini-trial before the Trademark Trial and Appeal Board brought when two trademark applications that are pending conflict, or when a pending application conflicts with a registered mark that is not incontestable; only permitted under extraordinary circumstances.

interference with business relations a defendant intentionally interferes with the plaintiff's business relationship with a third party.

interference with prospective economic advantage a defendant intentionally interferes with a probable business relationship between the plaintiff and a third party.

international schedule of classes of goods and services a system for classification of goods and services applicable to federal trademark applications filed on or after September 1, 1973.

junior user a party who adopts and uses a trademark similar to a mark previously adopted and used by a senior user.

jurisdiction the right of a court to hear a type of case or to bind the participants.

laches a defense to infringement in which the junior user argues that the senior user's delay in bringing the lawsuit is so unreasonable that the senior user should be barred from proceeding.

likelihood of confusion the probability of whether consumers will be confused as to the sponsorship, affiliation, or connection between the products or services of companies with similar marks; a standard for infringement, registration, and inter partes proceedings.

merchandise license a contract between the trademark owner and licensee permitting the licensee to apply the trademark to certain consumer goods, for example, coffee mugs featuring images of *Bugs Bunny* or the logo of a university.

merely descriptive see *descriptive mark*.

motion for preliminary injunction a request that the court order the defendant to halt the infringing activity until the outcome of the trial.

motion for summary judgment a request that the court grant a judgment without having a trial because there is no dispute as to the facts.

naked license a trademark license in which a trademark owner fails to supervise the nature and quality of the goods or services being produced under the license. A naked license can result in loss of all trademark rights.

opposition proceeding an action brought before the Trademark Trial and Appeal Board to prevent the federal registration of a mark; must be based upon one of the statutory grounds provided in the Lanham Act, and the party bringing the action must prove that it would be damaged.

parody a defense used by a junior user who seeks to justify its imitation on the premise of humor or satirical social commentary. As a general rule, the same likelihood of confusion standards are applied in a case involving parody as in any other type of infringement. The difference is that the junior user attempts to argue that consumers could not be confused because the use is obviously a joke.

permanent injunction a court order issued after a final judgment on the merits of the case; it permanently restrains the defendant from engaging in the infringing activity.

preliminary injunction a court order granted after a noticed hearing when the parties have an opportunity to present evidence as to the likelihood of plaintiff's success on the merits and irreparability of the harm to be suffered if the injunction is not granted; it lasts until a final judgment has been rendered.

priority a senior user's right to prevent a junior user from using a mark.

related goods or services goods or services that the consuming public is likely to believe come from a certain company.

remedies forms of judicial relief available in a lawsuit, for example, damages, injunctions or attorneys' fees.

request to divide out a statement included in an **Allegation of Use** asking to separate from the application certain goods for which the trademark has not been used.

reverse confusion when a junior user, usually a larger, more powerful company, attempts to usurp the power of the senior user's mark and create the impression that the senior user is the infringer.

right of publicity the legal right to control the commercial exploitation of a person's name, image, or persona.

secondary meaning demonstration that the consuming public associates a mark with a single source; it's usually proved by advertising, promotion and sales. A weak (descriptive) mark is said to acquire distinctiveness when it takes on a secondary meaning.

Section 8 declaration (also known as a Declaration of Continued Use) a declaration by a trademark owner that the mark is still in use. Filed between the fifth and sixth year following registration and at the time of each trademark renewal. Failure to file in this time period or within the six-month grace period may result in loss of trademark rights.

Section 9 application for renewal an application seeking renewal of a federal trademark registration; it must be filed within six months of the expiration of the initial term of trademark registration.

Section 15 declaration (also known as a Declaration of Incontestability) a declaration that a trademark has been in continuous use for five years since registration. Filed between the fifth and sixth year following registration. If filed and accepted by the Patent and Trademark Office the mark becomes incontestable.

Section 44 application an application for federal trademark registration by the owner of a mark registered in a foreign country, provided that country is a party to an international convention or treaty of which the United States is a member.

senior user the first party to adopt and use a particular mark in connection with its goods or services.

service mark a mark used in the sale or advertising of services to identify and distinguish services.

Statement of Use a declaration indicating use of a mark in commerce; it can only be filed after a Notice of Allowance has been issued. An applicant would complete the Allegation of Use form when filing a Statement of Use.

strong mark achieved by an inherently distinctive mark or by a nondistinctive mark that has achieved secondary meaning.

suggestive mark a mark that alludes to or hints at (without describing) the nature or quality of the goods.

summons a document served with the complaint that explains that the defendant has been sued and has a certain time limit in which to respond.

sweetheart sales shipments or transactions within a company and performed solely to qualify for registration or for a claim of priority.

tarnishment a form of dilution that occurs when a famous mark is damaged by an unpleasant or unwholesome use of a similar mark.

TARR (Trademark Application and Registration Retrieval) a PTO database available to the public (www.uspto.gov) that allows the user to retrieve information about the status of applications or federally registered marks.

TDR (Trademark Document Retrieval) debuting in 2005, TDR offers the public an advanced electronic portal to PDF viewing, downloading, and printing of an array of trademark information and documents.

TEAS (Trademark Electronic Application System) a PTO database available to the public (www.uspto.gov) that allows the user to apply for a trademark, a collective mark, or certification mark or file a Statement of Use/Amendment to Allege Use or other application and post-registration forms.

temporary restraining order (TRO) an injunction, often granted *ex parte*, that is short in duration and only remains in effect until the court has an opportunity to schedule a hearing for the preliminary injunction.

TESS (Trademark Electronic Search System) a PTO database available to the public (www.uspto.gov) that allows the user to search through federal trademark registrations and prior-filed applications.

trade dress a distinctive combination of elements, many of which may not be protectible by themselves under trademark law.

trade secret any business information that is kept in confidence and that gives the business an advantage over competitors who do not know it.

trademark any word, symbol, design, device, logo, or slogan that identifies and distinguishes one product or service from another.

trademark license an agreement granting limited trademark rights.

unclean hands a defense asserted when the senior user has committed a serious act of wrongdoing in regard to the lawsuit or the activity precipitating the lawsuit.

unfair competition a collection of common law principles and precedents, many of which are adopted as state laws, that protect against unethical business practices.

URL (Uniform Resource Locator) a system for locating a website; it generally begins with http://www. followed by a domain name.

use in commerce actual use of a mark in the ordinary course of trade (or if otherwise impracticable on documents associated with the goods). For federal registration, **commerce** is any commerce lawfully regulated by the federal government. For state registration, it is generally any commerce occurring within the state of registration. A service mark is deemed to be in **use in commerce** when it is used or displayed in the sale or advertising of services and the services are rendered in commerce.

weak nondistinctive name or term that cannot be registered or protected as a trademark unless the owner proves a consumer awareness or "secondary meaning." ■

Appendix C

Trademark Search Report

Trademark Search
Report

Sc[i]³ Patents and Trademarks
Sunnyvale Public Library
665 W. Olive
Sunnyvale, CA 94086
(408)-730-7300

email: patents@sci3.com

www.sci3.com

TABLE OF CONTENTS

FEDERAL REGISTRATION SEARCH ON X-SEARCH

This section shows results from X-SEARCH, the database used by the United States trademark examiners themselves. It covers applied for (pending), and registered marks in both the Principal and Supplemental Registers. A detailed description of the database and the search codes used is found at the beginning of this section.

FEDERAL REGISTRATION SEARCH ON TRADEMARKSCAN®

This section also shows federally applied for or registered marks, but is done in a commercial database as a crosscheck against the X-SEARCH file. A detailed description of the database and the search codes used is found at the beginning of this section.

STATE REGISTRATION SEARCH

This section shows the results of a search of the trademark records of all 50 states. A detailed description of the database and the search codes used is found at the beginning of this section.

REPORT ON COMPANY and PRODUCT NAMES

This section shows the results of a search of over 250 Dialog® supplied databases which contain over 10 million names comprised of domestic and international company names, trade names and brand names. A detailed description of the database and the search codes used is found at the beginning of this section.

INVOICE (LAST PAGE)

X-Search Codes

bi	basic index search
ti	translation index search
fm	full mark (exact search)
ic	international class number
gs	goods and services description
on	owner name search
dc	design code search
sd	single design code
	truncation symbol which tells the computer to search a word "stem" and any words that contain it. For example, a search for *comput** would find *compute, computing, computers* etc.
$	truncation symbol as above
d	dead indicator
v	viewed by searcher

```
Display of Hit List

 #      Hits      Live      Dead     Tagged  Printed  Pl. Search term
                  Viewed    Marks
 01      151       11        55                  4      *corpor*[bi,ti] and
                                                        legal$[gs]


 #    Serial Filed   Status Mark
  1  78088103 20011012  t   ACUMEN LEGAL CONSULTING, INC.
  2  78074120 20010716  ®   ROBERT F. DANELEN, A LAW CORPORATION
  3  78006221 20000501      THE PEOPLE BUSINESS INC.
  4  78128686 20020514      THE CORPORATE LAW GROUP
  5  78036010 20001120  ®   LEGAL DOCUMENTS FOR LE$$, INC.
  6  78123479 20020423      STRATEGIC CORPORATE LEGAL SERVICES
  7  78042909 20010112  ®   THE CORPORATE LAW GROUP
  8  78111222 20020226      OUTSIDE LEGAL, INC.
  9  78103806 20020121      THE INTERNATIONAL SERVICES CORPORATION
 10  76318495 20010927  D   CORPRASOFT LEGAL DESKTOP
 11  76433519 20020722      VISION LAW CORPORATION
 12  76433517 20020722      VISION LAW CORPORATION
 13  76357649 20020111      SOURCECORP HEALTHSERVE
 14  76345909 20011205  V   SOURCECORP
 15  76333796 20011102      SOURCECORP
 16  76318494 20010927  t   CORPRASOFT LEGAL DESKTOP
 17  76433067 20020722  t   CDI CORPORATION
 18  76346011 20011207      MEDNICK LAW CORPORATION STRATEGIC IN-HOUSE COUNSEL
 19  76187105 20011229  t   CORPORATE EDGE
 20  76392351 20020405      MAGNUS RESEARCH CONSULTANTS, INC.
 21  76201601 20010130      CORPORATION SERVICE COMPANY
 22  76422033 20020617      123EZCORP
 23  76269151 20010608      GLOBAL CORPORATE COUNSEL ASSOCIATION
 24  76284720 20010703      MCCA
 25  76301695 20010817      DOTS OFFICE PRODUCTS, INC.
 26  76309727 20010906  t®  REALCORPORATELAWYER.COM
 27  76215588 20010226      ACCESSKANSAS A SERVICE OF THE INFORMATION NETWORK
                            OF KANSAS, INC.
 28  76213876 20010220      ACCA AMERICAN CORPORATE COUNSEL ASSOCIATION
 29  76281468 20010706  D   CORPORATE LEGAL TIMES SUPERCONFERENCE
 30  76088200 20000717  ®   SOLUTIONS BUTZEL LONG A PROFESSIONAL CORPORATION
 31  76401315 20020429  t   ATTORNEYS CORPORATION SERVICE
 32  76201602 20010130      INCSPOT
 33  76208141 20010212  D   SHORT-TERM SOLUTIONS SERVICING THE CORPORATE ,
                            LEGAL AND CONVENTION MARKETPLACES
 34  76284468 20010703      MINORITY CORPORATE COUNSEL ASSOCIATION
 35  76190723 20010105      INSTITUTE FOR CORPORATE COUNSEL
 36  76394077 20020411      ASCEND ONE CORPORATION
 37  76272084 20010613  D   HOLLYWOOD SOFTWARE, INC.
 38  76233383 20010330      KOWALSKI & ASSOCIATES, INC.
 39  76271956 20010615  D   HOLLYWOOD SOFTWARE, INC.
 40  76270836 20010614  D   LAWYERS INCORPORATED, P.C.
 41  76284719 20010703  ®   MCCA
 42  76237471 20010406  ®   JENNER & BLOCK, LLC
 43  76117786 20000828  D   CORPORATE COUNSEL DIRECT
 44  76193941 20010112      DELCORP
 45  76182502 20001215  D   LONG ISLAND'S CORPORATE AND SECURITIES LAW FIRM
 46  76166754 20001116  ®   EMPLOYER SERVICES ASSURANCE CORPORATION
 47  76351497 20011220      GOODWILL INDUSTRIES INTERNATIONAL, INC.
 48  76351496 20011220      GOODWILL INDUSTRIES INTERNATIONAL, INC.
```

```
 49 76198391 20010123    THE CORPORATE PLACE, INC.
 50 76154311 20001026 D  CORPORATE DECISION ALERT
 51 76126094 20000911 D  CHELL CORPORATION
 52 76028962 20000419 ®  NATIONWIDE GUARANTEE AND TRUST CORPORATION
 53 76174012 20001201    NORDEA CORPORATE BANKING
 54 76166755 20001116 ®  ESAC BUILDING TRUST PROVIDING ASSURANCE
 55 76146982 20001016 ®  ACCIDENT LAW CENTER, DI MARCO AND ARAUJO, A
                         PROFESSIONAL LAW CORPORATION
 56 76075147 20000619 ®  REES, BROOME & DIAZ, P.C.
 57 76031655 20000421 ®  OMNILEX OMNILEX CORPORATION
 58 76023650 20000412 ®  ADAMS MEDIA CORPORATION
 59 76007378 20000323 ®  CORPORATEBUREAU.COM
 60 75882116 19991228    F.N.B. CORPORATION
 61 75940941 20000310 D  LSI
 62 75075806 19960320 ®  SIROTE & PERMUTT A PROFESSIONAL CORPORATION
 63 75483701 19980512    BARBARA RAE-VENTER, PH.D. ATTORYNEY AT LAW
                         RAE-VENTER LAW GROUP A PROFESSIONAL LAW
                         CORPORATION
 64 75933616 20000301    PERFECTLY LEGAL, INC.
 65 75915927 20000129 ®  XOC CORPORATION
 66 75905750 20000128 ®  XOC CORPORATION
 67 75858740 19991129 t® THE INC. LINK
 68 75978908 19980804 ®  DELAWARE CORPORATE LAW REPORTER
 69 75951160 20000306 ®  L & J LAWYERS & JUDGES PUBLISHING COMPANY, INC.
 70 75943429 20000311 ®  INFOSPI.COM SOURCE PROVIDERS INC.
 71 75852670 19991118 D  CORPORATEONLINE
 72 75846890 19991112    METLIFE, INC.
 73 75846094 19991110 D  WISE-UP, INC.
 74 75824410 19991018 D  SUPPORT SERVICES ALLIANCES, INC.
 75 75798328 19990913    YOUDECIDECORPORATE.COM
 76 75749358 19990713 ®  GFG GIBRALTAR FINANCIAL GROUP, INC.
 77 75744478 19990707 ®  FIRST NATIONAL CORPORATION
 78 75716761 19990528 D  F.Y.I. INCORPORATED SOLUTIONS FOR YOUR INFORMATION
 79 75715285 19990621 D  MYZEBRA CORPORATION
 80 75710020 19990610 D  INCORPORATE USA
 81 75698971 19990506 ®  CORPORATE LAW WEEKLY
 82 75693985 19990430 D  CORPORATE LAWYERING
 83 75675105 19990421 D  INCORPME
 84 75594489 19981124 D  THE LEGAL-EZE GRAPHICS COMPANY, INC
 85 75589206 19981116 D  X-RAY COPY SERVICE, INC.
 86 75580205 19981030 ®  CORPORATE COUNSEL
 87 75552322 19980914 ®  CORPORATE BRIEF
 88 75552320 19980914 ®  THE CORPORATE COUNSELOR
 89 75547813 19980903 ®  HANSON LAW CORPORATION
 90 75543823 19980827 ®  CORPORATE SCORECARD
 91 75530606 19980804 D  DELAWARE CORPORATE LAW REPORTER
 92 75508698 19980625    SWISS BANK CORPORATION
 93 75491533 19980526 ®  ESQUIRE CORPORATE SERVICES
 94 75404152 19971211 ®  INTERNET INCORPORATORS
 95 75364952 19970929 D  AMERICAN GUARANTEE AND TRUST CORPORATION
 96 75360088 19970919 ®  WINSTON & CASHATT, LAWYERS, A PROFESSIONAL SERVICE
                         CORPORATION
 97 75324517 19970715 ®  CSR INCORPORATED
 98 75310717 19970617 ®  1 STOP REALTY CYBER MALL CREDIT TITLE INSURANCE
                         CORPORATE SERVICES INFORMATION SERVICES INSURANCE
                         BANK FOR RENT REAL ESTATE LEGAL SERVICES
 99 75261929 19970324 D  THE ANYWHERE CORPORATION
100 75258091 19970317 ®  BIODYNAMIC RESEARCH CORPORATION
101 75244617 19970220 D  THE CORPORATE MULTIMEDIA MBA
```

```
102 75211279 19961210  ®  BALLANTINE & STERLING CALIFORNIA CORPORATION LAW
103 75144640 19960805 D   EARTHLING INC.
104 75128694 19960610 t®  INCORPORATE
105 75124946 19960625 D   YOUR ON-LINE CORPORATE SERVICES PROVIDER
106 75124945 19960625     INTERNET INCORPORATORS
107 75115698 19960607 D   SEVERSON & WERSON A PROFESSIONAL CORPORATION
108 75109463 19960524  ®  RECORDS DEPOSITION SERVICE INCORPORATED
109 75033067 19951215  ®  WORLD ACCESS SERVICE CORPORATION
110 74435774 19930915 D®  INCORPORATION EXPRESS
111 74611800 19941216 D®  F.Y.I. INCORPORATED
112 74471900 19931217 D®  CBB&B LITIGATION CORPORATE BANKRUPTCY CONSTRUCTION
113 74612139 19941219  ®  SSS STARK&STARK A PROFESSIONAL CORPORATION FOR ALL
                          WE REPRESENT.
114 74612140 19941219  ®  SSS STARK&STARK A PROFESSIONAL CORPORATION
115 74696131 19950703 D   CORPORATE COUNSEL ON-CALL
116 74682592 19950531  ®  IMSI
117 74653476 19950329  ®  AHAB PRESS INCORPORATED
118 74601284 19941121 t®  CORPORATEASSIST
119 74584610 19941012  ®  QUICKSOURCEINC
120 74549240 19940714 D   AMERICAN LEGAL DOCUMENT CENTERS INCORPORATED
121 74375937 19930406  ®  CORPORATE SERVICE BUREAU
122 74368108 19930315 D   CORPORATE
123 74365682 19930308 D®  AMERICAN CORPORATE LEGAL ASSISTANTS ASSOCIATION
124 74324254 19921021 D®  CBE CORPORACION BANCARIA DE ESPANA
125 74205127 19910919 D   MMC MMC INCORPORATED CONTRACT MANAGEMENT SOFTWARE
126 74195702 19910819 D®  THE CORPORATE PRINTING COMPANY, INC.
127 74148625 19910318 D   THE CORPORATION SPECIALISTS
128 74148573 19910318 D   INCORPORATE TODAY
129 74122669 19901212 D   CORPORATE INTEGRITY SERVICES
130 74105717 19901015 D   PEOPLES FINANCIAL CENTERS CORPORATION
131 74094005 19900904 D®  LA LEGAL ASSETS CORPORATION LEGAL SUPPORT SERVICE
132 74037234 19900312 D   CORPORATE INTEGRITY
133 74019566 19900116  ®  CHARLES RIVER ASSOCIATES INCORPORATED
134 74019565 19900116  ®  CHARLES RIVER ASSOCIATES INCORPORATED
135 73735404 19880620  ®  CORPORATECARE
136 73720648 19880404 D   MISSOURI CORPORATE FORMS
137 73682476 19870902 D   CITICORP TRAVEL ASSIST
138 73659199 19870506 D®  RESEARCH BOSTON CORPORATION
139 73636905 19861222  ®  AMERICAN CORPORATE COUNSEL ASSOCIATION
140 73615538 19860819 D®  RECORDS DEPOSITION SERVICE INCORPORATED
141 73604063 19860613 t®  CORPLAW
142 73583121 19860214 D   FORENSIC TECHNOLOGIES INTERNATIONAL CORPORATION
143 73556190 19850830  ®  REPRODUCTION SYSTEMS INCORPORATED
144 73505231 19841023 D®  CORPORATE PRACTICE SERIES
145 73469757 19840312 D   LEGAL SECRETARIES, INCORPORATED
146 73446216 19831003 D®  ACME CORPORATE BOOK & SEAL DIVISION
147 73444020 19830916  ®  AMERICAN CORPORATE COUNSEL ASSOCIATION ACCA
148 73429385 19830609  ®  XL CORPORATE SERVICES
149 73371435 19820624 D   GREAT WESTERN CORPORATION
150 73360106 19820416 D   DON CALDWELL CORPORATION
151 73304845 19810408 D   INTERCO INCORPORATED INTERCO
                          INCORPORATED
```

```
***   User: suns1   ***   Serial Number: 75128694   ***   9/13/02 4:22:26 PM   ***
                              [Typed Drawing]
Mark
      INCORPORATE

Goods and Services
      IC  009.  US 021 023 026 036 038.  G & S: software for creating the
      legal documents to form a corporation and installation and instruction
      manuals sold as a unit therewith.  FIRST USE: 19950323.  FIRST USE IN
      COMMERCE: 19950413

Mark Drawing Code
      (1) TYPED DRAWING

Serial Number
      75128694

Filing Date
      June 10, 1996

Supplemental Register Date
      February 17, 1997

Registration Number
      2085108

Registration Date
      July 29, 1997

Owner Name and Address
      (REGISTRANT) UNABRIDGED SOFTWARE, INC. CORPORATION TEXAS 5959 West Loop
      South, Suite 300 Bellaire TEXAS 77401

Type of Mark
      TRADEMARK

Register
      SUPPLEMENTAL

Live Dead Indicator
      LIVE

Attorney of Record
      Rita M. Irani




*** Search: 1 *** Document Number: 104 ***
```

```
*** User: suns1  *** Serial Number: 76187105 *** 9/13/02 4:25:16 PM ***
                          [Typed Drawing]
Mark
     CORPORATE EDGE

Goods and Services
     IC 035. US 100 101 102. G & S: Advertising and marketing consultation
     services, namely providing consultation relating to advertising of newly
     branded products and corporate identities; the conducting of marketing
     studies prior to the launching of newly branded products and corporate
     identities; business and market research and market analysis in the field
     of branding and corporate identity; marketing and research services for
     others in the nature of name and brand evaluation; business consultancy
     in the field of branding and corporate identity; corporate consultancy
     services in the field of branding and corporate identity

     IC 042. US 100 101. G & S: Brand, corporation and name creation;
     design and development services in the nature of new product design and
     testing and new brand name and corporate identity design; legal
     services; design services for others in the field of corporate identity
     design, office layout design, shop layout design, retail outlet design;
     printing and graphic art design services, namely letterhead design,
     design of marketing and publicity materials, design of stationery, design
     of printed matter, design of packaging, annual and company report design,
     product literature design and structural packaging design for others;
     computer site design for others, multi-media design services and website
     design services; animation and special effects design services for
     others, namely animation design, design of film and design of television
     commercials; print design

Mark Drawing Code
     (1) TYPED DRAWING

Serial Number
     76187105

Filing Date
     December 29, 2000

Owner Name and Address
     (APPLICANT) CORPRATE EDGE GROUP LTD LIMITED LIABILITY COMPANY ORGANIZED
     UNDER THE LAWS OF ENGLAND AND WALES BY CHANGE OF NAME ENGLAND 149
     HAMMERSMITH ROAD LYRIC HOUSE LONDON ENGLAND W14OQL

Assignment Recorded
     ASSIGNMENT RECORDED

Section 44 Indicator
     SECT44

Priority Date
     June 4, 1998

Disclaimer Statement
     NO CLAIM IS MADE TO THE EXCLUSIVE RIGHT TO USE "CORPORATE" APART FROM THE
     MARK AS SHOWN

*** Search: 1 *** Document Number: 19 ***                    (cont)
```

```
***   User: suns1   ***  Serial Number: 76318494  ***  9/13/02 4:25:26 PM   ***
                              [Typed Drawing]
Mark
      CORPRASOFT LEGAL DESKTOP

Goods and Services
      IC  009.  US 021 023 026 036 038.  G & S: Computer software that is
      user-modifiable for use in database management by the legal community.
      FIRST USE: 19980100.  FIRST USE IN COMMERCE: 19980629

Mark Drawing Code
      (1) TYPED DRAWING

Serial Number
      76318494

Filing Date
      September 27, 2001

Owner Name and Address
      (APPLICANT) Corprasoft, Inc. CORPORATION TEXAS 9400 N Central Expressway
      Suite 300 Dallas TEXAS 75231

Disclaimer Statement
      NO CLAIM IS MADE TO THE EXCLUSIVE RIGHT TO USE "LEGAL DESKTOP" APART FROM
      THE MARK AS SHOWN

Type of Mark
      TRADEMARK

Register
      PRINCIPAL

Live Dead Indicator
      LIVE

Attorney of Record
      Wendy Buskop
```

```
*** User: suns1  *** Serial Number: 76318495 ***  9/13/02 4:26:08 PM  ***
                            [Typed Drawing]
Mark
     CORPRASOFT LEGAL DESKTOP

Goods and Services
     (ABANDONED) IC 042. US 100 101.  G & S: User-modifiable software,
     namely a database to track information related to (a) legal matters;
     (b) costs related to those matters; (c) docketing, (d) calendaring
     information related to a matter; (e) contact information related to a
     matter; and (f) detailed ad-hoc and built-in reporting capability to
     track and analyze costs (both internal and external) associated with a
     matter

Mark Drawing Code
     (1) TYPED DRAWING

Serial Number
     76318495

Filing Date
     September 27, 2001

Filed ITU
     FILED AS ITU

Owner Name and Address
     (APPLICANT) CORPRASOFT, INC. CORPORATION TEXAS 9400 N Central Expressway,
     Suite 300 Dallas TEXAS 75231

Type of Mark
     SERVICE MARK

Register
     PRINCIPAL

Live Dead Indicator
     DEAD

Abandonment Date
     July 2, 2002

Attorney of Record
     Wendy K. Buskop
```

```
Display of Hit List

 #      Hits      Live      Dead      Tagged  Printed  Pl.  Search term
                  Viewed    Marks
02       50         2         23         1       1          *corpor*[bi,ti] and
                                                            incorp$[gs] not 1


 #    Serial Filed  Status Mark
  1 78104629 20020124 t   CORPORATEPHONES
  2 78068934 20010613 ®   AMERICAN INCORPORATORS
  3 78003641 20000411 D   NAMESTYLES INCORPORATED
  4 76440309 20020812     TRANSTAR MANAGEMENT SERVICES, INC.
  5 76440308 20020812     TRANSTAR MANAGEMENT SERVICES, INC.
  6 76418800 20020530     FOUNTAINHEAD ASSOCIATES, INC.
  7 76013853 20000330     BUSINESS FILINGS INCORPORATED
  8 76345329 20011206  N  NANO TITAN INCORPORATED
  9 76310565 20010910 D   PEDIATRIC HEALTHCARE, INC. CUSTOMIZING CARE FOR
                          KIDS
 10 76129243 20000918 D   EXECUTIVE CORPORATION
 11 76390648 20020402     UNITED STATES CRYSTAL CORP.
 12 76188786 20010102     BFI BUSINESS FILINGS INCORPORATED
 13 75545981 19980901     CHROMA CORPORATION
 14 75607305 19981224 D   $TART-A-BUSINESS.COM INC.   YOUR ONE STOP ON THE
                          INTERNET FOR NATIONWIDE AND OFFSHORE INCORPORATION
                          SERVICES, DOMAIN NAME REGISTRATION AND MUCH MORE!
 15 75257732 19970314 ®   CORPORATE ANSWERMAN
 16 75257677 19970314 ®   WE INCORPORATE EVERYBODY.
 17 75559902 19980928 D   SCC INDUSTRIES
 18 75619807 19990112 ®   DEL TORO
 19 75905050 20000121 D   CORPORATE TELEVISION CORP TV.
 20 75905049 20000121 D   MYWEBCORP.COM INCORPORATION MANAGEMENT SOLUTIONS
 21 75799643 19990915 D   INCORPERATE.COM
 22 75761988 19990426 ®   INCORPORATE AND GROW RICH
 23 75715876 19990527 D   REPACKAGING AMERICA INC. ASS-IT PROTECTION
                          WWW:REPACKAGINGAMERICA.COM
 24 75715444 19990622 ®   QUIK'N EASY INCORPORATING SERVICES, LTD.
 25 75715110 19990618 ®   THE QUICKEST WAY TO INCORPORATE!
 26 75653949 19990304 ®   NEVADA CORPORATE CENTER
 27 75642000 19990217 ®   TARAN INCORPORATED
 28 75570111 19981009 ®   WORLDWIDE INCORPORATORS LTD.
 29 75527447 19980724 D   MENU MARKETING INCORPORATED
 30 75525721 19980727 ®   AMERICAN INCORPORATORS
 31 75446034 19980306 D   NEVADA CORPORATE CENTER
 32 75390226 19971114 ®   SEG SIMULATION ENTERTAINMENT GROUP INCORPORATED
 33 75361561 19970923 D   CBR INCORPORATED
 34 75124925 19960625 D   CORPORATION MAKER
 35 75005707 19951016 ®   CORPORATE COMEDY
 36 74631551 19950208 t®  CORPCO
 37 74663089 19950418 ®   UNITED STATES CRYSTAL CORPORATION
 38 74631801 19950208 D   ACCUCORP
 39 74452930 19931101 D   NEVADA CORPORATE CENTER
 40 74446251 19931012 D   HOW TO FORM YOUR OWN CORPORATION
 41 74377745 19930412 ®   CORPORATE CREATIONS
 42 74029977 19900220 D®  USINC.
 43 73641725 19870128 D   OMNIA BONA, INCORPORATED "FOR ALL GOOD"
 44 73528039 19850321 D®  THE GREAT AMERICAN ORNAMENT CORPORATION
 45 73033105 19740926 D®  WHEN YOU INCORPORATE
 46 73033102 19740926 D®  INCORPORATION PRIMER
```

```
***  User: suns1   ***  Serial Number: 78026451  ***  9/13/02 5:21:07 PM  ***
```

```
Mark
    E-INCORP

Goods and Services
    IC  035.  US 100 101 102.  G & S: Business consulting services, namely,
    providing assistance in the preparation and filing of documents for the
    formation of corporations and limited liability companies. FIRST USE:
    19990207.  FIRST USE IN COMMERCE: 20000301

Mark Drawing Code
    (5) WORDS, LETTERS, AND/OR NUMBERS IN STYLIZED FORM

Serial Number
    78026451

Filing Date
    September 18, 2000

Supplemental Register Date
    August 22, 2002

Owner Name and Address
    (APPLICANT) Montero, Lilliana M. INDIVIDUAL UNITED STATES 1241 Knollwood
    Drive #B102 Cambria CALIFORNIA 93428

Type of Mark
    SERVICE MARK

Register
    SUPPLEMENTAL

Live Dead Indicator
    LIVE
```

```
*** Search: 1 *** Document Number: 1 ***
```

```
*** User: suns1   *** Serial Number: 73033102  *** 9/13/02 4:28:00 PM  ***
                              [Typed Drawing]
Mark
      INCORPORATION PRIMER

Goods and Services
      (CANCELLED) IC 016.  US 038.  G & S: BOOKLETS PUBLISHED FROM TIME TO
      TIME, RELATING TO THE INCORPORATION, QUALIFICATION, AND STATUTORY
      REPRESENTATION OF CORPORATIONS.  FIRST USE: 19560000.  FIRST USE IN
      COMMERCE: 19560000

Mark Drawing Code
      (1) TYPED DRAWING

Serial Number
      73033102

Filing Date
      September 26, 1974

Registration Number
      1065261

Registration Date
      May 10, 1977

Owner Name and Address
      (REGISTRANT) CT Corporation System UNKNOWN New York NEW YORK

      (LAST LISTED OWNER) CT CORPORATION SYSTEM CORPORATION DELAWARE 277 PARK
      AVE. NEW YORK, N.Y. 10017 NEW YORK NEW YORK 10017

Assignment Recorded
      ASSIGNMENT RECORDED

Type of Mark
      TRADEMARK

Register
      PRINCIPAL

Live Dead Indicator
      DEAD

Cancellation Date
      October 4, 1983




*** Search: 2 *** Document Number: 46 ***
```

```
***  User: suns1  ***  Serial Number: 73565723  ***  9/13/02 5:21:08 PM  ***
```

[Missing Image]

Mark
      INCORP

Goods and Services
      IC 042. US 100 101. G & S: COMPUTER ASSISTED LEGAL RESEARCH SERVICES
      INCLUDING CORPORATION INFORMATION. FIRST USE: 19850400. FIRST USE IN
      COMMERCE: 19850500

Mark Drawing Code
      (1) TYPED DRAWING

Serial Number
      73565723

Filing Date
      October 28, 1985

Publication for Opposition Date
      June 17, 1986

Registration Number
      1409012

Registration Date
      September 9, 1986

Owner Name and Address
      (REGISTRANT) MEAD DATA CENTRAL, INC. CORPORATION DELAWARE P.O. BOX 933
      DAYTON OHIO 45401

Assignment Recorded
      ASSIGNMENT RECORDED

Type of Mark
      SERVICE MARK

Register
      PRINCIPAL

Affidavit Text
      SECT 15. SECT 8 (6-YR).

Live Dead Indicator
      LIVE

```
***  Search: 1  ***  Document Number: 2  ***
```

```
***   User: suns1   ***   Serial Number: 73780541   ***   9/13/02 2:16:09 PM   ***
                              [Typed Drawing]
Mark
     PRO CORP

Goods and Services
     (CANCELLED) IC 009.  US 026.  G & S: COMPUTER ACCESSORIES, NAMELY,
     MODEMS AND MOUSE.  FIRST USE: 19880909.  FIRST USE IN COMMERCE: 19880914

Mark Drawing Code
     (1) TYPED DRAWING

Serial Number
     73780541

Filing Date
     February 13, 1989

Publication for Opposition Date
     January 23, 1990

Registration Number
     1591769

Registration Date
     April 17, 1990

Owner Name and Address
     (REGISTRANT) LIUSKI INTERNATIONAL, INC. CORPORATION NEW YORK 6585
     CRESCENT DRIVE NORCROSS GEORGIA 30071

Type of Mark
     TRADEMARK

Register
     PRINCIPAL

Affidavit Text
     SECT 15.  SECT 8 (6-YR).

Live Dead Indicator
     DEAD

Cancellation Date
     April 28, 2001

Attorney of Record
     LIDA RAFIZADEH, ESQ.




*** Search: 5 *** Document Number: 5 ***
```

```
*** User: suns1  *** Serial Number: 73492585 *** 9/13/02 2:16:17 PM ***
```

CORPORATION ®

Mark
    DIGITAL PRO CORPORATION

Goods and Services
    (ABANDONED) IC 009. US 038. G & S: COMPUTER SOFTWARE. FIRST USE:
    19840720. FIRST USE IN COMMERCE: 19840720

Mark Drawing Code
    (3) DESIGN PLUS WORDS, LETTERS, AND/OR NUMBERS

Serial Number
    73492585

Filing Date
    July 30, 1984

Owner Name and Address
    (APPLICANT) DIGITAL-PRO, CORP. CORPORATION TEXAS SUITE 106 4300 ALPHA RD.
    DALLAS TEXAS 75234

Type of Mark
    TRADEMARK

Register
    PRINCIPAL

Live Dead Indicator
    DEAD

Abandonment Date
    July 17, 1985

```
*** Search: 5 *** Document Number: 6 ***
```

*** User: suns1   *** Serial Number: 78090464   *** 9/13/02 2:39:52 PM   ***

The Incorporation Professionals

Mark
    NATIONWIDE INCORPORATORS, THE INCORPORATION PROFESSIONALS

Goods and Services
    IC 042. US 100 101. G & S: Preparation and filings to state agencies
    on behalf of business owners to form corporations and limited liability
    companies

Mark Drawing Code
    (3) DESIGN PLUS WORDS, LETTERS, AND/OR NUMBERS

Design Code
    260721 261103 261713

Serial Number
    78090464

Filing Date
    October 26, 2001

Filed ITU
    FILED AS ITU

Owner Name and Address
    (APPLICANT) California Incorporators CORPORATION CALIFORNIA 15928 Ventura
    Blvd., Suite 224 Encino CALIFORNIA 91436

Disclaimer Statement
    NO CLAIM IS MADE TO THE EXCLUSIVE RIGHT TO USE "NATIONWIDE INCORPORATORS"
    and " THE INCORPORATION PROFESSIONALS" APART FROM THE MARK AS SHOWN

Type of Mark
    SERVICE MARK

Register
    PRINCIPAL

Live Dead Indicator
    LIVE

*** Search: 8 *** Document Number: 1 ***

```
***  User: suns1  ***  Serial Number: 78068934  ***  9/13/02 2:39:53 PM  ***
                           [Typed Drawing]
Mark
      AMERICAN INCORPORATORS

Goods and Services
      IC  035.  US 100 101 102.  G & S: business consultation services, namely,
      providing incorporation and registered agent services to attorneys,
      accountants and individuals.  FIRST USE: 19910910.  FIRST USE IN
      COMMERCE: 19910910

Mark Drawing Code
      (1) TYPED DRAWING

Serial Number
      78068934

Filing Date
      June 13, 2001

Publication for Opposition Date
      November 13, 2001

Registration Number
      2536840

Registration Date
      February 5, 2002

Owner Name and Address
      (REGISTRANT) American Incorporators Ltd. CORPORATION DELAWARE 1220 Market
      Street Wilmington DELAWARE 19801

Prior Registration(s)
      2246863

Disclaimer Statement
      NO CLAIM IS MADE TO THE EXCLUSIVE RIGHT TO USE "INCORPORATORS" APART FROM
      THE MARK AS SHOWN

Type of Mark
      SERVICE MARK

Register
      PRINCIPAL-2(F)

Live Dead Indicator
      LIVE

Attorney of Record
      Stanley C. Macel, III, Esq.




***  Search: 8 *** Document Number: 2 ***
```

```
***   User: suns1   ***   Serial Number: 75570111   ***   9/13/02 2:39:55 PM   ***
                              [Typed Drawing]
Mark
      WORLDWIDE INCORPORATORS LTD.

Goods and Services
      IC  035.  US 100 101 102.  G & S: Business services, namely, providing
      incorporation and registered agent services to attorneys, accountants and
      individuals.  FIRST USE: 19980522.  FIRST USE IN COMMERCE: 19980522

Mark Drawing Code
      (1) TYPED DRAWING

Serial Number
      75570111

Filing Date
      October 9, 1998

Supplemental Register Date
      October 4, 1999

Registration Number
      2299102

Registration Date
      December 7, 1999

Owner Name and Address
      (REGISTRANT) Worldwide Incorporators Ltd. CORPORATION DELAWARE 2530
      Channin Drive Wilmington DELAWARE 19810

Disclaimer Statement
      NO CLAIM IS MADE TO THE EXCLUSIVE RIGHT TO USE "INCORPORATORS LTD." APART
      FROM THE MARK AS SHOWN

Type of Mark
      SERVICE MARK

Register
      SUPPLEMENTAL

Live Dead Indicator
      LIVE




*** Search: 8 *** Document Number: 3 ***
```

```
***  User: suns1  ***  Serial Number: 75525721  ***  9/13/02 2:39:56 PM  ***
                              [Typed Drawing]
Mark
     AMERICAN INCORPORATORS

Goods and Services
     IC 035.  US 100 101 102.  G & S: Business consultation services, namely,
     providing incorporation and registered agent services to attorneys,
     accountants, and individuals.  FIRST USE: 19910910.  FIRST USE IN
     COMMERCE: 19910910

Mark Drawing Code
     (1) TYPED DRAWING

Serial Number
     75525721

Filing Date
     July 27, 1998

Registration Number
     2246863

Registration Date
     May 18, 1999

Owner Name and Address
     (REGISTRANT) AMERICAN INCORPORATORS LTD. CORPORATION DELAWARE 1220 N.
     Market Street Suite 606 Wilmington DELAWARE 19801

Disclaimer Statement
     NO CLAIM IS MADE TO THE EXCLUSIVE RIGHT TO USE "INCORPORATORS" APART FROM
     THE MARK AS SHOWN

Type of Mark
     SERVICE MARK

Register
     SUPPLEMENTAL

Live Dead Indicator
     LIVE
```

```
***  Search: 8  ***  Document Number: 4  ***
```

```
***  User: suns1   ***  Serial Number: 75404152  ***  9/13/02 2:39:57 PM  ***
```

Mark
    INTERNET INCORPORATORS

Goods and Services
    IC 042. US 100 101. G & S: Legal services, namely, formation of
    corporations, resident agent services and office headquarters services
    for others. FIRST USE: 19980411. FIRST USE IN COMMERCE: 19980411

Mark Drawing Code
    (5) WORDS, LETTERS, AND/OR NUMBERS IN STYLIZED FORM

Serial Number
    75404152

Filing Date
    December 11, 1997

Filed ITU
    FILED AS ITU

Supplemental Register Date
    September 13, 1999

Registration Number
    2458702

Registration Date
    June 5, 2001

Owner Name and Address
    (REGISTRANT) Sierra Holdings Limited CORPORATION NEVADA PO BOX 1490 VERDI
    NEVADA 89438

Assignment Recorded
    ASSIGNMENT RECORDED

Disclaimer Statement
    NO CLAIM IS MADE TO THE EXCLUSIVE RIGHT TO USE "INTERNET INCORPORATORS"
    APART FROM THE MARK AS SHOWN

```
*** Search: 8 *** Document Number: 5 ***                    (cont)
```

```
***  User: suns1  ***  Serial Number: 75124945  ***  9/13/02 2:39:58 PM  ***
                            [Typed Drawing]
Mark
     INTERNET INCORPORATORS

Goods and Services
     IC  042.  US 100 101.  G & S: legal services, namely, formation of
     corporation, establishment of resident agents and office and headquarters
     for corporations.  FIRST USE: 19980411.  FIRST USE IN COMMERCE: 19980411

Mark Drawing Code
     (1) TYPED DRAWING

Serial Number
     75124945

Filing Date
     June 25, 1996

Filed ITU
     FILED AS ITU

Supplemental Register Date
     June 25, 1996

Owner Name and Address
     (APPLICANT) Sierra Holdings Limited CORPORATION ANGUILLA P.O. Box 801 The
     Valley ANGUILLA

Assignment Recorded
     ASSIGNMENT RECORDED

Disclaimer Statement
     NO CLAIM IS MADE TO THE EXCLUSIVE RIGHT TO USE "INCORPORATORS" APART FROM
     THE MARK AS SHOWN

Description of Mark
     The mark consists of a stylized fanciful character which is used in a
     variety of poses.  The stippling is for shading purposes.

Type of Mark
     SERVICE MARK

Register
     PRINCIPAL

Live Dead Indicator
     LIVE

Attorney of Record
     GARRETT SUTTON




***  Search: 8  ***  Document Number: 6  ***
```

```
*** User: suns1  *** Serial Number: 73305242 *** 9/13/02 2:19:42 PM ***
                        [Typed Drawing]
Mark
     INCORPORATOR

Goods and Services
     (CANCELLED) IC 007. US 023. G & S: Ground-Working Equipment-Namely,
     Seed-Bed Finishing Machines. FIRST USE: 19810217. FIRST USE IN COMMERCE:
     19810217

Mark Drawing Code
     (1) TYPED DRAWING

Serial Number
     73305242

Filing Date
     April 10, 1981

Publication for Opposition Date
     December 6, 1983

Supplemental Register Date
     October 18, 1982

Registration Number
     1260365

Registration Date
     December 6, 1983

Owner Name and Address
     (REGISTRANT) Dynamics Corporation of America a.k.a. Portable Elevator
     Division CORPORATION NEW YORK 475 Steamboat Rd. Greenwich CONNECTICUT
     06830

Type of Mark
     TRADEMARK

Register
     SUPPLEMENTAL

Live Dead Indicator
     DEAD

Cancellation Date
     April 9, 1990

Attorney of Record
     Everett J. Schroeder




*** Search: 8 *** Document Number: 8 ***
```

```
***  User: suns1   ***  Serial Number: 73303513  ***  9/13/02 2:19:51 PM  ***
```

[Typed Drawing]

Mark
    THE INCORPORATOR

Goods and Services
    (CANCELLED) IC 007. US 023. G & S: Ground-Working Equipment-Namely,
    Seed-Bed Finishing Machines. FIRST USE: 19810217. FIRST USE IN COMMERCE:
    19810217

Mark Drawing Code
    (1) TYPED DRAWING

Serial Number
    73303513

Filing Date
    March 30, 1981

Publication for Opposition Date
    June 5, 1984

Supplemental Register Date
    October 18, 1982

Registration Number
    1281053

Registration Date
    June 5, 1984

Owner Name and Address
    (REGISTRANT) Dynamics Corporation of America d.b.a. Portable Elevator
    Division CORPORATION NEW YORK 475 Steamboat Rd. Greenwich CONNECTICUT
    06830

Prior Registration(s)
    1260365

Type of Mark
    TRADEMARK

Register
    SUPPLEMENTAL

Live Dead Indicator
    DEAD

Cancellation Date
    November 23, 1990

Attorney of Record
    Schroeder Siegfried Ryan Vidas Steffey &

```
***  Search: 8 *** Document Number: 9 ***
```

```
***  User: suns1  ***  Serial Number: 74176021  ***  9/13/02 2:23:22 PM  ***
                         [Typed Drawing]
Mark
     PROCORP, INC.

Goods and Services
     (ABANDONED) IC 035. US 101. G & S: advertising and distributing all
     merchandise and products in Procorp, Inc. line. FIRST USE: 19910101.
     FIRST USE IN COMMERCE: 19910102

Mark Drawing Code
     (1) TYPED DRAWING

Serial Number
     74176021

Filing Date
     June 14, 1991

Owner Name and Address
     (APPLICANT) PROCORP, INC. CORPORATION FLORIDA P.O. Box 5218 Englewood
     FLORIDA 34224

Type of Mark
     SERVICE MARK

Register
     PRINCIPAL

Live Dead Indicator
     DEAD

Abandonment Date
     April 13, 1992
```

```
***  User: suns1  ***  Serial Number: 73588242  ***  9/13/02 2:34:35 PM  ***
                          [Typed Drawing]
Mark
     CORPRO

Goods and Services
     IC 009.  US 038.  G & S: COMPUTER PROGRAMS RECORDED ON MAGNETIC MEDIA.
     FIRST USE: 19851009.  FIRST USE IN COMMERCE: 19851009

Mark Drawing Code
     (1) TYPED DRAWING

Serial Number
     73588242

Filing Date
     March 17, 1986

Publication for Opposition Date
     July 1, 1986

Registration Number
     1450424

Registration Date
     August 4, 1987

Owner Name and Address
     (REGISTRANT) CORSTAR BUSINESS COMPUTING CO., INC. CORPORATION NEW YORK 1
     AQUEDUCT ROAD WHITE PLAINS NEW YORK 10606

Type of Mark
     TRADEMARK

Register
     PRINCIPAL

Affidavit Text
     SECT 15.  SECT 8 (6-YR).

Live Dead Indicator
     LIVE

Attorney of Record
     MARILYN MATTHES BROGAN




***  Search: 20 *** Document Number: 58 ***
```

```
*** User: suns1   *** Serial Number: 73407856   *** 9/13/02 2:34:52 PM   ***
                            [Typed Drawing]
Mark
     CAPRO INCORPORATED

Goods and Services
     (CANCELLED) IC 009. US 026. G & S: Computers and Peripheral Equipment
     for Computers-Namely, Printers and Video Display Terminals. FIRST USE:
     19820601. FIRST USE IN COMMERCE: 19820730

     (CANCELLED) IC 016. US 038. G & S: Instruction Manuals for Computer
     Hardware and Software. FIRST USE: 19820601. FIRST USE IN COMMERCE:
     19820730

Mark Drawing Code
     (1) TYPED DRAWING

Serial Number
     73407856

Filing Date
     January 3, 1983

Publication for Opposition Date
     December 13, 1983

Registration Number
     1268994

Registration Date
     March 6, 1984

Owner Name and Address
     (REGISTRANT) Capro Incorporated CORPORATION CALIFORNIA 12781 Pala Dr.
     Garden Grove CALIFORNIA 92641

Disclaimer Statement
     No claim is made to the exclusive right to use "Incorporated", apart from
     the mark as shown.

Type of Mark
     TRADEMARK

Register
     PRINCIPAL

Live Dead Indicator
     DEAD

Cancellation Date
     July 12, 1990

Attorney of Record
     Howard J. Klein


*** Search: 20 *** Document Number: 62 ***
```

FEDERAL REGISTRATION SEARCH ON TRADEMARKSCAN®

This section of your report includes a list of trademarks/servicemarks, registered and pending, with the U.S. Patent and Trademark Office. Pending applications include both marks that are actually being used, and those filed as intent-to-use. Both the Principal and the Supplemental Registers are searched. The database is updated weekly, and contains approximately 2.544 million records as of January, 2000. Some, but not all, records contain historical information, such as change of ownership or actions brought before the Trademark Appeal board. All active and inactive marks are covered through the dates specified in the body of the attached search report. You may need to research inactive marks with diligence as they may still be "in use" in the marketplace and simply have lost their "live" status temporarily. Consult your attorney for more information.

About Trademarkscan® Federal:
Your search covers **complete** trademark records through the following dates: Active **marks**: 1884-present date listed. **Inactive marks**: January 1, 1984-present date listed. Exact dates of coverage are provided at the beginning of attached search.

Classes Searched and Search Strategy
All trademarks are registered in one or more of the international classes which categorize goods and services by type. All classes are routinely searched. Specific international class numbers and/or goods or services may be used to narrow a search.

The search strategy used to search your mark appears at the beginning of each section of the search report, starting on the following page. The search strategy itself may be complex, and a list of "character codes" are provided on the back of this sheet to help you understand the search process.

Only records that have not been fully printed in the X-SEARCH section (section 1), are printed in this section.

```
File 226:TRADEMARKSCAN(R)-US FED  OG=020910/AP=020812
        (c) 2002 Thomson & Thomson
*File 226: *File 226: Preliminary Records through 8/23/02. * See HELP NEWS
for info. on UD=19991026 and changes to AP=9999.


Set    Items   Description
S1      76    INCORP? AND GS=(LEGAL? OR INCORP? OR CORP?)
S2      77    TR=INCORP? AND GS=(LEGAL? OR INCORP? OR CORP?)
? report s2/tx,sn,st/1-77
              DIALOG(R)File 226 :TRADEMARKSCAN(R)-US FED
            (c) 2002 Thomson & Thomson All rts. reserv.
```

TRADEMARK	APP NUMBER	STATUS
FOCUS GROUP, INCORPORATED	78-124,668	Abandoned - Express
CORPORATE OCCASIONS INCORPORAT	78-100,495	Pending_Published fo
NATIONWIDE INCORPORATORS THE I	78-090,464	Pending
AMERICAN INCORPORATORS	78-068,934	Registered
COMPANIES INCORPORATED	78-027,239	Misassigned Serial N
E-INCORP	78-026,451	Pending
COMPANIES INCORPORATED	78-025,099	Registered
1-STOP INCORPORATION SERVICES	78-004,887	Abandoned - No State
NAMESTYLES INCORPORATED	78-003,641	Abandoned - Failure
A WHOLE NEW WAY TO THINK ABOUT	76-379,033	Pending_Published fo
LEADING VISIONS INCORPORATED	76-349,968	Pending
N NANO TITAN INCORPORATED	76-345,329	Pending
LAWYERS INCORPORATED, P.C.	76-270,836	Abandoned - Failure
BFI BUSINESS FILINGS INCORPORA	76-188,786	Pending
LEADERSHIP DYNAMICS INCORPORAT	76-177,617	Registered
CREATE-A-CORP.COM INCORPORATIN	76-100,614	Abandoned - Failure
BUSINESS FILINGS INCORPORATED	76-013,853	Pending
MONTURA INCORPORATED	75-940,512	Registered
REVEAL ENTERTAINMENT, INCORPOR	75-937,604	Abandoned - Failure
MYWEBCORP.COM INCORPORATION MA	75-905,049	Abandoned - Failure
E-INCORPORATE.COM	75-869,826	Abandoned - Failure
TRIGEO INCORPORATED	75-837,657	Misassigned Serial N
INCORPERATE.COM	75-799,643	Abandoned - Failure
IWIDGETS.COM, INCORPORATED	75-788,701	Abandoned - Failure
INCORPORATE AND GROW RICH	75-761,988	Registered
F.Y.I. INCORPORATED SOLUTIONS	75-716,761	Abandoned - Failure
QUIK'N EASY INCORPORATING SERV	75-715,444	Registered
QUIK'N EASY INCORPORATING SERV	75-715,443	Misassigned Serial N
THE QUICKEST WAY TO INCORPORAT	75-715,110	Registered
INCORPORATE USA	75-710,020	Abandoned - Failure
INCORPME	75-675,105	Abandoned - Failure
TARAN INCORPORATED	75-642,000	Registered
$TART-A-BUSINESS.COM INC. YOUR	75-607,305	Abandoned - Failure
WORLDWIDE INCORPORATORS LTD.	75-570,111	Registered
PIU INC. PROFESSIONAL INSURANC	75-567,320	Abandoned - Failure
MENU MARKETING INCORPORATED	75-527,447	Abandoned - Failure
AMERICAN INCORPORATORS	75-525,721	Registered
AUTOMATAX INCORPORATED	75-422,487	Abandoned - No State
INTERNET INCORPORATORS	75-404,152	Registered

```
BEAU DIETL AND ASSOCIATES, INC    75-397,204   Abandoned - Failure
SEG SIMULATION ENTERTAINMENT G    75-390,226   Registered
CBR INCORPORATED                  75-361,561   Abandoned - Failure
CSR INCORPORATED                  75-324,517   Registered
WE INCORPORATE EVERYBODY.         75-257,677   Registered
BOSTONIA INCORPORATED             75-183,883   Registered
IPH POWERWORLD IPH INTERNET IN    75-182,175   Misassigned Serial N
INCORPORATE                       75-128,694   Registered
INTERNET INCORPORATORS            75-124,945   Pending
RECORDS DEPOSITION SERVICE INC    75-109,463   Registered
AHAB PRESS INCORPORATED           74-653,476   Registered
INCORP AMERICA, INC.              74-639,771   Registered
F.Y.I. INCORPORATED               74-611,800   Cancelled - Section
AMERICAN LEGAL DOCUMENT CENTER    74-549,240   Abandoned - Failure
TRAINCORP                         74-507,609   Registered
INCORPORATION EXPRESS             74-435,774   Cancelled - Section
CASCADIA INCORPORATED             74-348,987   Misassigned Serial N
SCHOOL PROPERTIES INCORPORATED    74-277,298   Registered
MMC MMC INCORPORATED CONTRACT     74-205,127   Abandoned - No State
SEI INCENTIVES INCORPORATED TH    74-198,320   Abandoned - Failure
MORGAN STANLEY & CO. INCORPORA    74-178,760   Registered
NOROMED INCORPORATED              74-174,344   Misassigned Serial N
INCORPORATE TODAY                 74-148,573   Abandoned - Failure
CHARLES RIVER ASSOCIATES INCOR    74-019,566   Registered
CHARLES RIVER ASSOCIATES INCOR    74-019,565   Registered
DESCO SUPREMA INCORPORATED        73-742,625   Abandoned - Failure
DOCUSEARCH, INCORPORATED          73-674,591   Abandoned - Failure
OMNIA BONA, INCORPORATED "FOR     73-641,725   Abandoned - Failure
LUCAS TRAVEL INCORPORATED         73-622,936   Cancelled - Section
RECORDS DEPOSITION SERVICE INC    73-615,538   Cancelled - Section
GUARANTEED INCORPORATING SERVI    73-607,064   Abandoned - Failure
INCORP                            73-565,723   Registered
REPRODUCTION SYSTEMS INCORPORA    73-556,190   Registered
LEGAL SECRETARIES, INCORPORATE    73-469,757   Abandoned - Failure
KW KEVIN WRIGHT, INCORPORATED     73-414,978   Abandoned - Failure
AXEM RESOURCES INCORPORATED       73-308,433   Abandoned File - Bac
INTERCO INCORPORATED INTERCO I    73-304,845   Abandoned - Failure
HORN BLOWER, WEEKS, NOYES & TR    73-129,822   Cancelled - Section
```

STATE REGISTRATION SEARCH

This section of your report includes a list of trademarks/servicemarks registered with the Secretary of State's offices in each of the 50 states as well as Puerto Rico and American Samoa. Note that corporate names are not searched in these records. Such things as trade names, fictitious names, and assumed names are not commonly included (or searched), although they may be shown in some individual records. Approximately 1.5 million marks are searched in the file. Marks each have a status, active or inactive. All active and inactive marks are covered through the dates specified in the body of the attached report. You may need to research inactive marks with diligence as they may still be "in use" and simply have lost their "active" status temporarily. Please consult your attorney for more information.

Period of coverage:
This search covers state registered marks as far back as each individual state has provided records. Dates of coverage are listed on the provided chart (see following page).

Search Strategy and Classes Searched
The U.S. Patent and Trademark Office uses a classification system (class numbers 1-42) which categorizes goods and services by type. All classes were routinely searched. Classification numbers or goods and services descriptions may be used to narrow a search.

The search strategy used to search your mark appears at the beginning of each section of the search report starting on the following page. The search strategy itself may appear complicated, and the list of "character codes" on the back of this sheet may help you understand the search process.

```
File 246:TRADEMARKSCAN(R)-U.S. State  2002/Sep 09
       (c) 2002 Thomson & Thomson

Set     Items   Description
S1        1     TR=(INCORPORATOR? AND PRO?)
S3        0     OW=(INCORPORATOR?()PRO?)
S4        0     OW=INCORPORATORPRO?
? t 1/9


 1/9/1
DIALOG(R)File 246:TRADEMARKSCAN(R)-U.S. State
(c) 2002 Thomson & Thomson. All rts. reserv.

        01238256    * TRADEMARK IMAGE AVAILABLE *
CALIFORNIA INCORPORATORS THE PROFESSIONAL SOLUTION    and Design
        T&T INTL CLASS:  42 (Miscellaneous Service Marks)
        T&T U.S. CLASS: 100 (Miscellaneous Service Marks)
        STATE: California
        STATUS: Registered
        GOODS/SERVICES: NEW BUSINESS IN CALIFORNIA
        REG. NO.: 47,569
        REGISTERED: March 20, 1997
        FIRST USE IN STATE: February 1996
        FIRST USE ANYWHERE: February 1996
        REGISTRANT(S): CALIFORNIA INCORPORATORS, (A California
          Corporation), 15928 VENTURA BOULEVARD, SUITE 108, ENCINO, CA
          (California), 91436
        MANNER OF DISPLAY: USED ON ADVERTISING BROCHURES, ON ADVERTISING
          LEAFLETS, ON BUSINESS CARDS, ON LETTERHEADS.
        DESIGN PHRASE: THE WORDS "CALIFORNIA INCORPORATORS" WITH THE
          FIRST LETTERS OF EACH NAME IN A DROP CAP STYLE, THE NAME IS
          ACCOMPANIED WITH A LOGO IN THE STYLE OF TWO CRESCENTS FACING
          EACH OTHER (LOCATED ABOVE THE NAME) AND THE WORDS "THE
          PROFESSIONAL SOLUTION" (LOCATED BELOW THE NAME)




? e et=incorporator pro

Ref    Items   Index-term
E1        1     ET=INCORPORATION WITHIN HOURS
E2        4     ET=INCORPORATOR
E3        0    *ET=INCORPORATOR PRO
E4        1     ET=INCOS INDEPENDENT CONSULTING SERVICES, INC.
E5        1     ET=INCOUNTRY
E6        1     ET=INCOURIER
E7        1     ET=INCREASE THE PEACE, LET THE VIOLENCE CEASE
E8        2     ET=INCREASE YOUR COMFORT LEVEL
E9        1     ET=INCREASE YOUR VALUE
E10       1     ET=INCREASE YOUR VALUE: HOW TO GET THE JOB, PROMO
E11       1     ET=INCREASE YOUR WELCOME MAT BY A FEW HUNDRED SQU
E12       1     ET=INCREASED PROFITS THROUGH KNOWLEDGE ACT

? s e2
       S5       4   ET='INCORPORATOR'
```

```
? e et=incorporatorpro

Ref    Items  Index-term
E1         1  ET=INCORPORATION WITHIN HOURS
E2         4  ET=INCORPORATOR
E3         0 *ET=INCORPORATORPRO
E4         1  ET=INCOS INDEPENDENT CONSULTING SERVICES, INC.
E5         1  ET=INCOUNTRY
E6         1  ET=INCOURIER
E7         1  ET=INCREASE THE PEACE, LET THE VIOLENCE CEASE
E8         2  ET=INCREASE YOUR COMFORT LEVEL
E9         1  ET=INCREASE YOUR VALUE
E10        1  ET=INCREASE YOUR VALUE: HOW TO GET THE JOB, PROMO
E11        1  ET=INCREASE YOUR WELCOME MAT BY A FEW HUNDRED SQU
E12        1  ET=INCREASED PROFITS THROUGH KNOWLEDGE ACT
? s e2
        S6      4  ET='INCORPORATOR'

? e et=incorporator-pro

Ref    Items  Index-term
E1         1  ET=INCORPORATION WITHIN HOURS
E2         4  ET=INCORPORATOR
E3         0 *ET=INCORPORATOR-PRO
E4         1  ET=INCOS INDEPENDENT CONSULTING SERVICES, INC.
E5         1  ET=INCOUNTRY
E6         1  ET=INCOURIER
E7         1  ET=INCREASE THE PEACE, LET THE VIOLENCE CEASE
E8         2  ET=INCREASE YOUR COMFORT LEVEL
E9         1  ET=INCREASE YOUR VALUE
E10        1  ET=INCREASE YOUR VALUE: HOW TO GET THE JOB, PROMO
E11        1  ET=INCREASE YOUR WELCOME MAT BY A FEW HUNDRED SQU
E12        1  ET=INCREASED PROFITS THROUGH KNOWLEDGE ACT
? s e2
        S7      4  ET='INCORPORATOR'


Set    Items   Description
S1         1   TR=(INCORPORATOR? AND PRO?)
S3         0   OW=(INCORPORATOR? () PRO?)
S4         0   OW=INCORPORATORPRO?
S5         4   ET='INCORPORATOR'
S6         4   ET='INCORPORATOR'
S7         4   ET='INCORPORATOR'
S8         3   (S5 OR S6 OR S7) AND IC=9
? t 8/49,k/all

 8/49,K/1
00769814
 INCORPORATOR

 INCORPORATOR
         T&T INTL CLASS: 7 (Machinery)
                         8 (Hand Tools)
                          9 (Electrical & Scientific Apparatus)
```

8/49,K/2
00610395
 INCORPORATOR

 INCORPORATOR
        T&T INTL CLASS: 7 (Machinery)
                        8 (Hand Tools)
                         9 (Electrical & Scientific Apparatus)

 8/49,K/3
00287125
 INCORPORATOR

 INCORPORATOR
        T&T INTL CLASS: 7 (Machinery)
                        8 (Hand Tools)
                         9 (Electrical & Scientific Apparatus)
? t 8/7/all
 8/7/1
DIALOG(R)File 246:TRADEMARKSCAN(R)-U.S. State
(c) 2002 Thomson & Thomson. All rts. reserv.

        00769814
 INCORPORATOR
        STATE: Tennessee
        STATUS: Not Renewed
        GOODS/SERVICES: GROUND WORKING EQUIPMENT IN THE FORM OF SEED-BED
            ETC
        REGISTRANT(S): DYNAMICS CORP OF AMERICA GREENWICH, CT
            (Connecticut)

 8/7/2
DIALOG(R)File 246:TRADEMARKSCAN(R)-U.S. State
(c) 2002 Thomson & Thomson. All rts. reserv.

        00610395
 INCORPORATOR
        STATE: Ohio
        STATUS: Registered
        GOODS/SERVICES: CUTLERY,MACHINERY,TOOLS & PARTS THEREOF
        REGISTRANT(S): DYNAMICS CORP OF AMERICA GREENWICH, CT
            (Connecticut)

 8/7/3
DIALOG(R)File 246:TRADEMARKSCAN(R)-U.S. State
(c) 2002 Thomson & Thomson. All rts. reserv.

        00287125
 INCORPORATOR
        STATE: Illinois
        STATUS: Not Renewed
        GOODS/SERVICES: CUTLERY,MACHINERY,TOOLS & PARTS THEREOF
        REGISTRANT(S): PORTABLE ELEVATOR DIVISION GREENWICH, CT
            (Connecticut)

REPORT ON COMPANY and PRODUCT NAMES

This section of your report includes a list of company names, trade names, or brand names which may be in conflict with your mark. This list was compiled from over 250 databases, some of which include over 30 million company names. Many of these company names are not registered as trademarks. However, because company names are often used as trademarks, and because trademark rights in the United States may be conferred by usage alone (known as common-law marks), any match in this section may indicate potential areas of conflict. Files consulted may vary according to the nature of your product or service.

We have provided a list of company names which may be in conflict with your mark. We can provide additional information on any of these companies at your request.

A.   **Dates Covered through:**
        Current

B.   **Databases Covered:**

   - **American Business Directory** - Offers information on over 10 million companies, large and small, public and private, government agencies or individual professionals. The American Business Directory is compiled by American Business Information, from nationwide yellow pages, annual reports, news releases, and other public records. The file is updated monthly

   - **DIALOG® Company Name Finder** - a search aid database designed to locate company information in other DIALOG® databases. Some 251 files on Dialog have a co=, or company name field. Each of these files is checked for company names that might potentially conflict with your mark. These files cover companies both domestic, and abroad. Thus you might find that a company registered in Great Britain, or Japan, or Brazil, is similar or an exact match for your name. While that will not be an impediment to your registering in the United States, you will at least be aware of what is being used worldwide. This file is updated quarterly.

   - **Thomas Register Online®** - Corresponds to the Thomas Register of American Manufacturers, a premier source of product information for North American manufacturing companies. This file is updated quarterly, and covers over 180,000 U.S. and Canadian public and private companies and over 115,000 brand names.

   - **Brands and Their Companies** - A worldwide directory of over 282,000 consumer brand names, approximately 400,000 trade names, and their owners or distributors. This file is updated semiannually, and corresponds to the Gale Publications print versions of: Brands And Their Companies, and: International Brands And Their Companies.

   - **New Product Announcements/Plus®** - This file contains approximately a million full-text records of product-related press releases from all industries; particularly product and service industries such as apparel, communications, financial services, paper, and many other categories. This file is updated daily, and covers the period from 1985 to present.

   - **Other databases searched as needed.**

C.   **Search Strategy**
        The exact search strategy used to search your mark appears at the beginning of the Company Names section on the following sheet. The search strategy itself may appear complicated, and the list of "character codes" on the back of this page may help you understand the search process.

```
File 416:DIALOG COMPANY NAME FINDER(TM)   2001/Aug
       (c) 2000 Dialog Info.Svcs.

Set    Items   Description
S2      62     INCORPORATOR?
? report s2/company
      S3       62   Sort 2/ALL/CO,TY,RC,D
              DIALOG(R)File 416 :DIALOG COMPANY NAME FINDER(TM)
                 (c) 2000 Dialog Info.Svcs. All rts. reserv.

              62 Companies Available
```

	Company	File Number	Type	Record Count
1	ACCUCORP INCORPORATORS, LTD.	226	Trademark	1
2	AMERICAN INCORPORATORS LTD.	18	Bibliographic	1
3	AMERICAN INCORPORATORS LTD	531	Directory	1
4	AMERICAN INCORPORATORS LTD	519	Financial	1
5	AMERICAN INCORPORATORS LTD	604	Fulltext	2
6	AMERICAN INCORPORATORS LTD.	16	FullText	1
7	AMERICAN INCORPORATORS LTD.	226	Trademark	2
8	AMERICAN INCORPORATORS LTD	226	Trademark	2
9	AMERICAN INCORPORATORS LTD (INC)	516	Directory	1
10	AMERICAN INCORPORATORS LTD (INC)	515	Directory	1
11	ATLANTIC INCORPORATORS, INC	516	Directory	1
12	ATLANTIC INCORPORATORS INC	531	Directory	1
13	ATLANTIC INCORPORATORS, INC	515	Directory	1
14	BOARD OF INCORPORATORS AFRICAN	519	Financial	1
15	BOARD OF INCORPORATORS AFRICAN METHODIST EPI	522	Directory	52
16	BOARD OF INCORPORATORS AFRICAN METHODIST EPI	516	Directory	40
17	BOARD OF INCORPORATORS AFRICAN METHODIST EPI	515	Directory	39
18	BUSINESS INCORPORATORS	516	Directory	1
19	BUSINESS INCORPORATORS	515	Directory	1
20	BUSINESS INCORPORATORS INC	516	Directory	1
21	BUSINESS INCORPORATORS INC	531	Directory	1
22	BUSINESS INCORPORATORS INC	515	Directory	1
23	CALIFORNIA INCORPORATORS	547	Credit	1
24	CALIFORNIA INCORPORATORS	246	Trademark	1
25	CHRISTIANA INCORPORATORS INC	547	Credit	1
26	DELAWARE BUSINESS INCORPORATORS, INC.	246	Trademark	1
27	FLORIDA INCORPORATORS INC	547	Credit	1
28	HAMMOCK, LON C., INCORPORATOR OF HAMMOCK-MAN	654	Patent	1
29	ILLINOIS INCORPORATORS	515	Directory	1
30	ILLINOIS INCORPORATORS	519	Financial	1
31	INCORPORATOR LIMITED	561	Directory	1
32	INCORPORATOR LTD	523	Financial	1
33	INCORPORATORS	533	Directory	1
34	INCORPORATORS	348	Patent	1
35	INCORPORATORS LTD	547	Credit	1
36	INCORPORATORS LTD (INC), THE	516	Directory	1
37	INCORPORATORS LTD (INC), THE	515	Directory	1
38	INCORPORATORS LTD (INC), THE	519	Financial	1
39	INCORPORATORS OF LIBERIA LIMITED(THE)	561	Directory	1
40	INCORPORATORS PLUS, INC.	246	Trademark	1
41	INCORPORATORS UNLIMITED INC.,	127	Trademark	1
42	K C METRO BUSINESS INCORPORATORS LLC	516	Directory	1
43	MARIE DIXNEUF, MULTI NATIONAL INCORPORATORS	126	Trademark	1

44	MULTI-NATIONAL INCORPORATORS LIMITED	561	Directory	1
45	MULTI-NATIONAL INCORPORATORS T/A TRADENETWOR	126	Trademark	1
46	NATIONAL BUSINESS INCORPORATORS, INC	515	Directory	1
47	ONTARIO INCORPORATORS INC	520	Directory	1
48	ONTARIO INCORPORATORS INC	533	Directory	1
49	OVERSEAS EXPRESS INCORPORATOR	547	Credit	1
50	ROLL SCREENS INC C O THE INCORPORATORS LTD	348	Patent	1
51	ROLL-SCREENS, INC., THE INCORPORATORS LTD.,	653	Patent	1
52	SOUND & CINEMA INCORPORATORS	547	Credit	4
53	THE INCORPORATOR, INC.	246	Trademark	1
54	VORTEX ARTESIAN INCORPORATOR AND CONSERVATOR	654	Patent	2
55	WILLIAM DALIN INCORPORATOR OF BUG BUSTERS, I	246	Trademark	1
56	WORLDWIDE INCORPORATORS	547	Credit	1
57	WORLDWIDE INCORPORATORS (LONDON) LIMITED	561	Directory	1
58	WORLDWIDE INCORPORATORS, INC	516	Directory	1
59	WORLDWIDE INCORPORATORS, INC	515	Directory	1
60	WORLDWIDE INCORPORATORS LIMITED	561	Directory	1
61	WORLDWIDE INCORPORATORS LTD.	226	Trademark	2
62	WORLDWIDE INCORPORATORS LTD	226	Trademark	1

Index

A

Abandoned (dead) marks, in search results, 5/19, 6/22–23

Abandonment of mark, 7/41, 8/5, 8/7, 8/8, 10/10

Abandonment of registration application, 7/35, 7/40–41, 7/43

ACPA (Anticybersquatting Consumer Protection Act), 10/2, 10/26–27, 10/28

Acquired distinctiveness. *See* Secondary meaning

Acronyms, 3/14

Actual use, 1/9, 1/13, 10/8
  continuous use, 8/7, 9/9
  defined, 7/4–5
  international registration and, 13/2
  proof of (specimens), 7/9–13, 7/29–30, 7/42

Advertising
  as trademark specimen, 7/9, 7/11, 7/12
  use of trademarks in, 8/9, 10/24

Advertising injury insurance coverage, 11/6

AIPLA (American Intellectual Property Law Association), 14/4

Allegation of Use, 7/35, 7/42–43

American Intellectual Property Law Association (AIPLA), 14/4

Analytical trademark searches, 4/5–6, 4/8–9, 4/12

Anticybersquatting Consumer Protection Act (ACPA), 10/2, 10/26–27, 10/28

Antitrust violations, 10/10

Arbitrary marks, 3/11, 9/4–5, 9/6, 9/10–11

Arbitration, 14/9–10
  domain name disputes, 10/27–29
  infringement disputes, 11/12–13, 12/4

Assignment of marks, 6/26, 8/11–12

Assumed names. *See* Fictitious business names

Attorneys, 6/4, 14/7–10
  for federal registration applications, 7/23, 7/38, 7/40
  fees, dilution actions, 10/25
  fees, infringement actions, 11/2–3
  for infringement cases, 11/14
  for international registrations, 13/2
  trademark search services, 4/11, 4/12, 4/15

Audio files or tapes, as trademark specimens, 7/12–13

Australian registration, 13/2, 13/5–6

CATALOG

...more from nolo

	PRICE	CODE
BUSINESS		
Becoming a Mediator: Your Guide to Career Opportunities	$29.99	BECM
Business Buyout Agreements (Book w/CD-ROM)	$49.99	BSAG
The CA Nonprofit Corporation Kit (Binder w/CD-ROM)	$69.99	CNP
California Workers' Comp: How to Take Charge		
When You're Injured on the Job	$34.99	WORK
The Complete Guide to Buying a Business	$24.99	BUYBU
The Complete Guide to Selling Your Business	$24.99	SELBU
Consultant & Independent Contractor Agreements (Book w/CD-ROM)	$29.99	CICA
The Corporate Records Handbook (Book w/CD-ROM)	$69.99	CORMI
Create Your Own Employee Handbook (Book w/CD-ROM)	$49.99	EMHA
Dealing With Problem Employees	$44.99	PROBM
Deduct It! Lower Your Small Business Taxes	$34.99	DEDU
Effective Fundraising for Nonprofits	$24.99	EFFN
The Employer's Legal Handbook	$39.99	EMPL
Federal Employment Laws	$49.99	FELW
Form Your Own Limited Liability Company (Book w/CD-ROM)	$44.99	LIAB
Home Business Deductions: Keep What You Earn	$34.99	DEHB
How to Run a Thriving Business: Strategies for Success & Satisfaction	$19.99	THRV
How to Create a Noncompete Agreement (Book w/CD-ROM)	$44.95	NOCMP
How to Form a California Professional Corporation (Book w/CD-ROM)	$59.99	PROF
How to Form a Nonprofit Corporation (Book w/CD-ROM)—National Edition	$49.99	NNP
How to Form a Nonprofit Corporation in California (Book w/CD-ROM)	$49.99	NON
How to Form Your Own California Corporation (Binder w/CD-ROM)	$59.99	CACI
How to Form Your Own California Corporation (Book w/CD-ROM)	$34.99	CCOR
How to Get Your Business on the Web	$29.99	WEBS

Prices subject to change.

	PRICE	CODE
How to Write a Business Plan	$34.99	SBS
Incorporate Your Business	$49.99	NIBS
The Independent Paralegal's Handbook	$34.99	PARA
Legal Forms for Starting & Running a Small Business (Book w/CD-ROM)	$29.99	RUNSF
Legal Guide for Starting & Running a Small Business	$34.99	RUNS
LLC or Corporation?	$24.99	CHENT
The Manager's Legal Handbook	$39.99	ELBA
Marketing Without Advertising	$20.00	MWAD
Mediate, Don't Litigate	$24.99	MEDL
Music Law (Book w/CD-ROM)	$39.99	ML
Negotiate the Best Lease for Your Small Business	$34.95	LESP
Nolo's Guide to Social Security Disability	$29.99	QSS
Nolo's Quick LLC	$29.99	LLCQ
Nondisclosure Agreements (Book w/CD-ROM)	$39.95	NAG
The Partnership Book: How to Write a Partnership Agreement (Book w/CD-ROM)	$39.99	PART
The Performance Appraisal Handbook	$29.99	PERF
The Small Business Start-up Kit (Book w/CD-ROM)	$24.99	SMBU
The Small Business Start-up Kit for California (Book w/CD-ROM)	$24.99	OPEN
Starting & Running a Successful Newsletter or Magazine	$29.99	MAG
Tax Savvy for Small Business	$36.99	SAVVY
Workplace Investigations: A Step by Step Legal Guide	$39.99	CMPLN
Working for Yourself: Law & Taxes for Independent Contractors, Freelancers & Consultants	$39.99	WAGE
Working With Independent Contractors (Book w/CD-ROM)	$29.99	HICI
Your Crafts Business: A Legal Guide (Book w/CD-ROM)	$26.99	VART
Your Limited Liability Company: An Operating Manual (Book w/CD-ROM)	$49.99	LOP
Your Rights in the Workplace	$29.99	YRW

	PRICE	CODE

CONSUMER

	PRICE	CODE
How to Win Your Personal Injury Claim	$29.99	PICL
Nolo's Encyclopedia of Everyday Law	$29.99	EVL
Nolo's Guide to California Law	$24.99	CLAW

ESTATE PLANNING & PROBATE

	PRICE	CODE
8 Ways to Avoid Probate	$19.99	PRAV
Estate Planning Basics	$21.99	ESPN
The Executor's Guide: Settling a Loved One's Estate or Trust	$34.99	EXEC
How to Probate an Estate in California	$49.99	PAE
Make Your Own Living Trust (Book w/CD-ROM)	$39.99	LITR
Nolo's Simple Will Book (Book w/CD-ROM)	$36.99	SWIL
Plan Your Estate	$44.99	NEST
Quick & Legal Will Book	$16.99	QUIC
Quicken Willmaker: Estate Planning Essentials	$49.99	QWMB
Special Needs Trust: Protect Your Child's Financial Future	$34.99	SPNT

FAMILY MATTERS

	PRICE	CODE
Building a Parenting Agreement That Works	$24.99	CUST
The Complete IEP Guide	$34.99	IEP
Divorce & Money: How to Make the Best Financial Decisions During Divorce	$34.99	DIMO
Do Your Own California Adoption: Nolo's Guide for Stepparents and Domestic Partners (Book w/CD-ROM)	$34.99	ADOP
Every Dog's Legal Guide: A Must-Have book for Your Owner	$19.99	DOG
Get a Life: You Don't Need a Million to Retire Well	$24.99	LIFE
The Guardianship Book for California	$34.99	GB
A Legal Guide for Lesbian and Gay Couples	$34.99	LG
Living Together: A Legal Guide (Book w/CD-ROM)	$34.99	LTK
Medical Directives and Powers of Attorney in California (Book w/CD-ROM)	$21.99	CPOA
Nolo's IEP Guide: Learning Disabilities	$29.99	IELD

	PRICE	CODE

Prenuptial Agreements: How to Write a
Fair & Lasting Contract (Book w/CD-ROM) .... $34.99   PNUP

Using Divorce Mediation: Save Your Money & Your Sanity .... $29.99   UDMD

GOING TO COURT

Beat Your Ticket: Go To Court & Win! (National Edition) .... $21.99   BEYT

The Criminal Law Handbook: Know Your Rights, Survive the System .... $34.99   KYR

Everybody's Guide to Small Claims Court (National Edition) .... $26.99   NSCC

Everybody's Guide to Small Claims Court in California .... $29.99   CSCC

Fight Your Ticket & Win in California .... $29.99   FYT

How to Change Your Name in California .... $34.99   NAME

How to Collect When You Win a Lawsuit (California Edition) .... $29.99   JUDG

The Lawsuit Survival Guide .... $29.99   UNCL

Nolo's Deposition Handbook .... $29.99   DEP

Represent Yourself in Court: How to Prepare & Try a Winning Case .... $34.99   RYC

Win Your Lawsuit: A Judge's Guide to Representing Yourself
in CA Superior Court .... $29.99   SLWY

HOMEOWNERS, LANDLORDS & TENANTS

California Tenants' Rights .... $27.99   CTEN

Deeds for California Real Estate .... $24.99   DEED

Every Landlord's Legal Guide (National Edition, Book w/CD-ROM) .... $34.99   ELLI

Every Landlord's Tax Deduction Guide .... $44.99   DELL

Every Tenant's Legal Guide .... $29.99   EVTEN

For Sale by Owner in California .... $29.99   FSBO

How to Buy a House in California .... $34.99   BHCA

The California Landlord's Law Book: Rights & Responsibilities
(Book w/CD-ROM) .... $44.99   LBRT

The California Landlord's Law Book: Evictions (Book w/CD-ROM) .... $44.99   LBEV

	PRICE	CODE
Leases & Rental Agreements	$29.99	LEAR
Neighbor Law: Fences, Trees, Boundaries & Noise	$26.99	NEI
The New York Landlord's Law Book (Book w/CD-ROM)	$39.99	NYLL
New York Tenants' Rights	$27.99	NYTEN
Renters' Rights (National Edition)	$24.99	RENT

IMMIGRATION

	PRICE	CODE
Becoming a U.S. Citizen: A Guide to the Law, Exam and Interview	$24.99	USCIT
Fiancé & Marriage Visas (Book w/CD-ROM)	$44.95	IMAR
How to Get a Green Card	$29.99	GRN
Student & Tourist Visas	$29.95	ISTU
U.S. Immigration Made Easy	$29.99	IMEZ

MONEY MATTERS

	PRICE	CODE
101 Law Forms for Personal Use (Book w/CD-ROM)	$29.99	SPOT
Bankruptcy: Is It the Right Solution to Your Debt Problems?	$21.99	BRS
Chapter 13 Bankruptcy: Repay Your Debts	$36.99	CHB
Credit Repair (Book w/CD-ROM)	$24.99	CREP
Getting Paid: How to Collect from Bankrupt Debtors	$29.99	CRBNK
How to File for Chapter 7 Bankruptcy	$29.99	HFB
IRAs, 401(k)s & Other Retirement Plans: Taking Your Money Out	$34.99	RET
Solve Your Money Troubles	$29.99	MT
Stand Up to the IRS	$29.99	SIRS
Surviving an IRS Tax Audit	$24.95	SAUD
Take Control of Your Student Loan Debt	$26.95	SLOAN

PATENTS AND COPYRIGHTS

	PRICE	CODE
All I need is Money: How To Finance Your Invention	$19.99	FINA
The Copyright Handbook: How to Protect and Use Written Works (Book w/CD-ROM)	$39.99	COHA

	PRICE	CODE
Copyright Your Software (Book w/CD-ROM)	$34.95	CYS
Domain Names	$26.95	DOM
Getting Permission: How to License and Clear Copyrighted Materials		
Online and Off (Book w/CD-ROM)	$34.99	RIPER
How to Make Patent Drawings	$29.99	DRAW
What Every Inventor Needs to Know About		
Business and Taxes (Book w/CD-ROM)	$21.99	ILAX
The Inventor's Notebook	$24.99	INOT
License Your Invention (Book w/CD-ROM)	$39.99	LICE
Nolo's Patents for Beginners	$29.99	QPAT
Patenting Art & Entertainment: New Strategies for Protecting Creative Ideas	$39.99	PATAE
Patent, Copyright & Trademark	$39.99	PCTM
Patent It Yourself	$49.99	PAT
Patent Pending in 24 Hours	$29.99	PEND
The Public Domain	$34.95	PUBL
Trademark: Legal Care for Your Business and Product Name	$39.99	TRD
Web and Software Development: A Legal Guide (Book w/ CD-ROM)	$44.99	SFT

RESEARCH & REFERENCE

Legal Research: How to Find & Understand the Law	$39.99	LRES

SENIORS

Long-Term Care: How to Plan & Pay for It	$19.99	ELD
Social Security, Medicare & Government Pensions	$29.99	SOA

Order Form

Name

Address

City

State, Zip

Daytime Phone

E-mail

Item Code	Quantity	Item	Unit Price	Total Price

Method of payment

☐ Check   ☐ VISA   ☐ MasterCard
☐ Discover Card   ☐ American Express

Subtotal	
Add your local sales tax (California only)	
Shipping: RUSH $9, Basic $5 (See below)	
"I bought 3, ship it to me FREE!"(Ground shipping only)	
TOTAL	

Account Number

Expiration Date

Signature

Shipping and Handling

Rush Delivery—Only $9

We'll ship any order to any street address in the U.S. by UPS 2nd Day Air* for only $9!

* Order by noon Pacific Time and get your order in 2 business days. Orders placed after noon Pacific Time will arrive in 3 business days. P.O. boxes and S.F. Bay Area use basic shipping. Alaska and Hawaii use 2nd Day Air or Priority Mail.

Basic Shipping—$5

Use for P.O. Boxes, Northern California and Ground Service.

Allow 1-2 weeks for delivery. U.S. addresses only.

For faster service, use your credit card and our toll-free numbers

**Call our customer service group
Monday thru Friday 7am to 7pm PST**

Phone	1-800-728-3555
Fax	1-800-645-0895
Mail	Nolo
950 Parker St.
Berkeley, CA 94710

**Order 24 hours a day @
www.nolo.com**

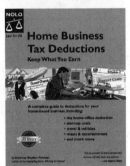
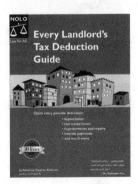